WILLIAM WETMORE STORY

AND HIS FRIENDS

WILLIAM WETMORE STORY

AND

HIS FRIENDS

FROM LETTERS, DIARIES, AND RECOLLECTIONS

BY

HENRY JAMES

IN TWO VOLUMES (COMBINED)

VOL. I

GROVE PRESS   NEW YORK

Originally published in 1903.

Library of Congress Catalog Card No. 57-5157

Grove Press Books and Evergreen Books
are published by Barney Rosset
795 Broadway   New York, N. Y.

MANUFACTURED IN THE UNITED STATES OF AMERICA

CONTENTS OF THE FIRST VOLUME.

CONTENTS OF THE SECOND VOLUME.

MIDDLE ROMAN YEARS—CONTINUED.

LAST ROMAN YEARS.

EARLY YEARS AND EARLY WORK

WILLIAM WETMORE STORY
AND HIS FRIENDS.

———

THE PRECURSORS.

IT may appear a new application of the truth
that honour, where honour, as to any frank
advance, attaches, is especially due to the light
skirmishers, the *éclaireurs*, who have gone before ; yet there are occasions on which it comes
home to us that, so far as we are contentedly
cosmopolite to-day and move about in a world
that has been made for us both larger and more
amusing, we owe much of our extension and
diversion to those comparatively few who, amid
difficulties and dangers, set the example and
made out the road. This is the lesson offered
us, on occasion, as we turn over old records,

spared by time and mischance, old letters, notes, diaries, faded pages often, even when patched with pages of print scarcely less faded, but testifying in their manner to the element of adventure once at play in relations and situations that we late-comers take all placidly for granted. I allude in this connection, I need hardly say, not to the great explorers and discoverers who have taken us to the Equator or the Poles, those who have bequeathed us the round globe to hang up in our drawing-rooms for ornament — as merely the largest of the silvered orbs in which we see, wherever the eye rests, the reflection of our own movement. I am conscious rather of the suggestions of a particular case, the case so common at this end of time, but common precisely because certain patient persons long ago were so good as to bear a certain brunt. Europe, for Americans, has, in a word, been *made* easy; it was anything but easy, however much it was inspiring, during that period of touching experiment, experiment often awkward almost to drollery too, in which the imagination of the present introducer must thus betray at the outset an inclination to lose itself. When we make such reflections as I here venture to throw out, it is as Americans, obviously, that we read most meaning into them—meaning of many sorts, the pursuit of which I confess myself perhaps almost extravagantly disposed, for reasons of my own, to cultivate. Great may the disposition thus become to remember the precursors; though doubtless it would take me far to make my own case clear and to set forth all the grounds of my tenderness. I should need more time than I am at liberty to ask for, and I must leave my general claim—this claim for tenderness—to bear fruit where it can. Many memories abide in it—with the shyest glance at which I must content myself. What is definite is the upshot of the matter, which may almost be described as a pious habit, the habit of friendly, kindly, often decidedly envious evocation. It becomes inveterate as the years add to the distance; it attaches itself to the vision, to the conception of the old order (into which we too are now so rapidly falling) as entertained by earlier pilgrims and more candid victims—attaches itself the more, no doubt, because of the sorrowful sense that the picture of our primitive phase has really never been painted.

The old relation, social, personal, æsthetic, of the American world to the European—a relation expressed practically, at the time, of course, in such active experiments as might be — is as charming a subject as the student of manners,

morals, personal adventures, the history of taste,
the development of a society, need wish to take
up, with the one drawback, in truth, of being
treatable but in too many lights. The poet,
the dramatist, the critic, would alike, on consideration, find it to bristle with appeals and
admonitions. It has, in short, never been
"done," to call done, from any point of view—
I am moved, at all events, to risk the assertion.
The pure and precious time — the time of the
early flowering — was the matter of a moment
and lasted but while it could; in consequence
of which who can say when it began or ended?
The further back we place the beginning of it the
better, assuredly, in the interest of our romantic
vision, though indeed we may meet thus, it must
be added, the principal lion in our path. The
dawn of the American consciousness of the complicated world it was so persistently to annex is
the more touching the more primitive we make
that consciousness; but we must recognise that
the latter can scarcely be interesting to us in
proportion as we make it purely primitive. The
interest is in its becoming perceptive and responsive, and the charming, the amusing, the
pathetic, the romantic drama is exactly that
process. The process, in our view, must have
begun, in order to determine the psychological

moment, but there is a fine bewilderment it must have kept in order not to anticipate the age of satiety. The reader of old records — I speak of the private sort—the reader surrounded by satiety has to decide for himself, on the evidence and so far as it may be his humour to piece the past together, just when and where extreme freshness, looking out on life, ceases to repeat itself. How soon *could* it begin, perceptibly, to taste ; how long could it, on the other hand, continue to taste with intensity ? Such are the questions that the " case," as I call it, fondly considered, disposes us to ask—quite as if we were to make some beautiful use of them. I see for them at present, however, a use of necessity limited and conditioned. Not that I think it perforce the less happy for that. A boxful of old papers, personal records and relics all, has been placed in my hands, and in default of projecting more or less poetically such an experience as I have glanced at—the American initiation in a comparative historic twilight—I avail myself of an existing instance and gladly make the most of it.

Its most general effect for me has been, I repeat, to renew my loyalty to the company of those—some of them here buried—without whose initiation we settled partakers of the greater extension should still be waiting for our own. We must of course not overdo it, but as they got theirs, often, in ways that were hard, I like to miss, in order to do them justice, not a step in the general story; all the more, naturally, too, that our contention is precisely that their satisfactions—could they only have known it—were to have been the finer and the more numerous. They came from a world that was changing, but they came to one likewise not immutable, not quite fixed, for their amusement, as under a glass case; and it would have quickened their thrill to be a little more aware than they seem generally to have been that some possible sensations were slipping away for ever, that they were no more than just in time for the best parts of the feast, and that a later and less lucky generation might have as many regrets as surprises. The hungrier among them thought perhaps sometimes of what even they might make out that they had missed; but this latter amount, for the first sixty years of the century, remained the extremely minor quantity. What we ourselves see is both what they still found and what they paid for it. And true at large of the American pilgrim of that unadministered age, these things are especially true of those who crossed the Atlantic to follow one or the other of those mysteries, arts, sciences, of

which at present—so far as the teaching of them
and the dealing in them has become a prosperous
traffic — we are perhaps, as a nation, the main
supporters. I think of them all, the artless
seekers of knowledge, would-be haunters of the
fountainhead; but I think of the artist - fra-
ternity in especial, the young Americans aspir-
ing to paint, to build and to carve, and gasp-
ing at home for vital air, whose fortunes it is
mostly impossible to follow, in particular cases,
without the disposition to handle them gently.
It is to them and the price *they* paid that we
pillars of *ateliers*, winners of medals, favourites
of "juries," ornaments of Salons, are above all
indebted. We have left the formal discipline
of Dusseldorf and Antwerp and Munich, we
have left even that of Venice and Florence and
Rome, far behind; but it is all because they
showed us the way, through having had first
to find it, with much more or less comic and
tragic going and coming, for themselves. As we
turn over the stray, pale testimonies out of
which we pick up their history, their simplicities
become sacred to us and their very mistakes
acquire a charm. These mistakes are sometimes, verily, great enough to make us wonder
what sensibility—the quality we assume in them
—could flicker in such darkness; then again we

see that their good faith was what supported
them through the tribulations from which we are
exempt, and their good faith thus becomes for us
the constant key to their pleasure, or at least to
their endurance. We admire and enjoy things
they admired and enjoyed, but they did this
with things for which it is now impossible to us.
Robert Browning and his illustrious wife burnt
incense, for instance, to Domenichino. Our
happy—much more happy, after all, than unhappy—predecessors almost to a man did this;
and the essence of my case is that I like them for
it, and that the case itself, as I put it, is that of
the period, of the conditions, in which such
"quaintness" was inevitable.

There came a moment when the spell in
question began to weaken, and in that subtle
revolution our subject, could we fully give ourselves to it, would find its dramatic climax. Its
limit is marked, in our own direction, its modern
side, by two or three such pregnant transitions.
They accord with many other things that represent the inevitable quickening of the pace. I
think of the American who started on his *Wanderjahre* after the Civil War quite as one of the
moderns divided by a chasm from his progenitors
and elder brothers, carried on the wave as they
were not, and all supplied with introductions,

photographs, travellers' tales and other aids to knowingness. He has been, this child of enlightenment, very well in his way; but his way has not, on many sides, been equally well, save as we think of it all as the way of railroads and hotels. Yet even from this point of view also the advantage was half with the precursor. The celestial cheapness of the early times made up for many a *train de luxe* and many an electric-bell. The old letters are full of it—it made even *them*, the old wanderers, marvel; it was in particular the last cloying sweet in the rich feast of Italy; it could add a grace even to the grace of Florence, and a thrill even to the thrill of Rome. America then, certainly, had her cheapness too, but Florence and Rome were a refinement even on that refinement. No wonder, in short, the Brownings admired Domenichino when they had to pay so little for it. We find some of the figures in Mrs Browning's beautiful Letters, and they are doubtless, in general, for much in the charm of our evocation. It is partly in the light of them, so to speak, that we repeople the States of the Church—how I remember the crooked, coloured spots so stamped in my school-atlas!—the Tuscany of the old paternal Grand Duke, and even the dreadful Naples of the Bourbons, with the blessed generation that crawled

by *vettura*, taking oxen for a spurt, that had its
letter-postage (when it got its letters) charged
twice and its newspapers mostly confiscated, but
that, enjoying the "margin" we have lost forever, enjoyed thereby the time to make its discoveries and to know what it felt. All the
discoveries now are made, and, with this, most
of the feelings, the sweetest and strangest, have
dropped. We know everything in relation to
the objects that used to excite them—everything
but that we do feel. We are in doubt of that—
everything has been so felt *for* us.

If the interesting boxful that I speak of as in
my hands forms practically a record of the many
Italian years of William Wetmore Story, sculptor
and man of letters, so let me yet immediately
make the point that, though I have been moved
to the foregoing remarks by the consideration of
the rather markedly typical case associated with
his name, I am at the same time well aware that
it is typical with many qualifications. He lived
on, worked on into what we may call the new
day, and he had doubtless not originally been,
as an American pilgrim, superlatively primitive.
There is a charming, touching anecdote of his
distinguished father, Mr Justice Story, which
tells us that, though he had never crossed the
sea, he excited the surprise of an English trav-

eller, one evening at Cambridge, Massachusetts,
by being able promptly to "place" some small
street in London, of which the name had come up
in talk, but of which the traveller was ignorant.
Judge Story, in other words, knew his London
because, even at that then prodigious distance
from it, he had a feeling for it.   His son was to
start from a home in which such things had been
possible, but he started, nevertheless, in time not
to miss the old order.   He died in 1895, but his
Italian span happily had been long.   It is part of
the interest of his career for us—or, as I cannot
help again putting it, of his case—that he saw
the change, felt it and, in a manner, both helped
it and suffered for it, that his pleasant, eminent,
happy, yet not *all* happy, history remarkably
testified to it.   Story had above all, among his
many gifts, the right sensibility, given his New
England origin ; the latter had left him plenty to
learn, to taste, to feel and assimilate, but it had
not formed him, fortunately, without a universal
curiosity, a large appetite for life or a talent that
yearned for exercise.   Nothing, indeed, seems to
me to have been more marked for envy than the
particular shade of preparation — about which
there will be presently more to say — involved
in his natural conditions.   I lose myself, once
more, as I turn them over, in the view of so

happy, so ideal an opportunity for freshness. The best elements of the New England race, of its old life and its old attitude, had produced and nourished him, and it is quite, for our imagination, as if he had thus been engendered and constituted to the particular end of happily reacting from them. There are reactions that are charming, adequate, finely expressive; there are others that are excessive, extravagant, treacherous. Story's was not of the violent sort, of the sort that makes a lurid picture for biography or drama; but it was conscious and intelligent, arriving at the pleasure and escaping the pain, a revolution without a betrayal.

So it is that generally, at all events, he fits into our category, and that he represents there, moreover, the appeal, the ghostly claim as we may almost call it, of a dislodged, a vanished society. Figures innumerable, if we like to recall them, and if, alas! we *can*, pass before us in the vividness of his company and meet us in the turns and twists—or perhaps I should say in the rather remarkably straight avenue—of his fortune. Boxfuls of old letters and relics are, in fine, boxfuls of ghosts and echoes, a swarm of apparitions and reverberations as dense as any set free by the lifted lid of Pandora. The interest is exquisite— when it is not intolerable—though doubtless an

interest always, and even at the best, more easy
to feel than to communicate. It is a matter of
our own memory, our own fancy, to say nothing
of our own heredity; I take it indeed for an
entertainment particularly subjective. It is everything for those who have known, but not much,
save in special cases, for those who have not, or
whose knowledge is obstinately *other*—is even
perhaps slightly invidious. It sometimes befalls,
however, that the very consciousness of this
limitation acts as a challenge to our piety.
We consent reluctantly to the mere re-burial
of our dead; we know at least that we must not
simply have waked them up and left them. The
meanings we have read into the hundred names
are meanings we feel ashamed not to have read
with some intensity that will speak for them to
others. We desire for them some profit of the
brush we have given them to make them a little
less dim. These remain at the end, I daresay,
but small ineffectual rites of our own; the
images we project may fall across the common
path as fairly shapeless shadows. This indeed
will depend on their intrinsic value—though of
that also there is no hard-and-fast measure. Let
us give them then, at the worst, the value of the
pleasure derived from the act itself, the act of remembrance lively almost to indiscretion. Every-

thing in a picture, it must be added, depends on the composition; if it be the subject that makes the interest, it is the composition that makes, or that at any rate expresses, the subject. By that law, accordingly, our boxful of ghosts "compose," hang together, consent to a mutual relation, confess, in fact, to a mutual dependence. If it is a question of living again, they can live but by each other's help, so that they close in, join hands, press together for warmth and contact. The picture, before it can be denied, is therefore so made; the sitters are all in their places, and the group fills the frame. We see thereby what has operated, we both recognise, so to speak, the principle of composition and are enabled to name the subject. The subject is the *period*—it is the period that holds the elements together, rounds them off, makes them right. They partake of it, they preserve it, in return; they justify it, and it justifies the fond chronicler. Periods really need no excuses. Which, again, is how I find my way round to a certain confidence.

Even if this argument be weak, I am moved further to observe, I should still not have been able to resist the charm working in the words by which I come nearest to the character of my boxful. "A vanished society" is a label before

which, wherever it be applied, the man of imagination must inevitably pause and muse. It
is, for any bundle of documents, the most touching title in the world, and has only to be fairly
legible to shed by itself a grace. What lurks
behind it is *necessarily* the stuff of pictures, and,
whether memory may assist or no, fancy, under
the appeal, never refuses her hand. However
generalised the effect must remain, there is something in it of the sweetness of old music faintly
heard, something of the mellowness of candlelight
in old saloons. Do we know why it is we all
ruefully, but quite instinctively, think of the
persons grouped in such an air as having had,
though they were not to know it, a better
" time " than we? For we are surely conscious
of that conviction, the source of which we perceive to be excess of our modern bliss. We have
more things than they, but we have less and less
room for them, either in our lives or in our
minds; so that even if our taste is superior we
have less the use of it, and thereby, to our loss,
less enjoyment of our relations. The quality of
these suffers more and more from the quantity,
and it is in the quantity alone that we to-day
make anything of a show. The theory would
perfectly be workable that we have not time for
friendships—any more, doubtless, than for en-

mities; luxuries, both, as to which time is essential. Friendships live on the possibility of contact, that contact which requires in some degree
margin and space. We are planted at present so
close that selection is smothered; contact we
have indeed, but only in the general form which
is cruel to the particular. That is logically the
ground of our envy of other generations. The
particular contact, under whatever delusion, could
flourish with them and give what it had; they
were not always on the way to some other,
snatching a mouthful between trains. Therefore
it is that under the candlelight and the music of
the old saloons we see our friends seated and
lingering, able to see and hear and communicate.
That perhaps is the great difference, but it is
everything. In our own world we are all on our
feet, with our elbows in each other's ribs, peering
as we can through small interstices and pushing
our way through the mass. We have abjured
the retentive sofa, which we view as the refuge
of simplicity, and, save the *buffet* at which we
scramble, the only piece of furniture that matters
for us is the clock that, so far from detaining,
urgently dismisses us. We think of the old
clocks, do what we will—and it is our moral—as
incorrigibly slow.

II.

CAMBRIDGE AND BOSTON.

WILLIAM STORY was served by fortune in this way as in various others, that he chose his career just at the right moment, was not moved to emigrate, or was not able to, before he could feel that he had faced his alternatives. The earliest impatiences of his youth were spent; he had imbibed what New England could give him in the way of preparation. He had left college and embraced a profession; he had married and become a father and written books—law-books, of accomplished merit, the value of which subsists: a substantial "Story on Contracts," that was to know five editions; a "Story on Sales," that was to be, down to our own day, variously re-edited, to be approved by the best judges; to say nothing of three volumes of Reports of the United States Circuit Court, First Circuit, 1837-1845. He was upwards of thirty when he left America for his long residence in Rome, a

residence which, though briefly interrupted during the first years, was the result of an act
particularly pondered and designed, and which
continued to the day of his death. The act was
a choice, if ever a choice was, with the sense of
what he renounced fully mature in him, and with
a lively intelligence, though doubtless with some
admirably confused ideas—and this is a part of
the interest of his record—in respect to what he
preferred. He preferred, with all the candour
with which people were at that time, all over the
world, preferring it, to become an "artist," and
he had to look his traditions well in the face to
enunciate the preference. He could indeed do
this the more easily as they were numerous and
positive, as rich as such matters admitted of
being; and, if the forces that make these situations dramatic need to be well confronted, they
fully met the requirement.

He published in the year 1851 a copious and
highly interesting Life of his distinguished
father, one of the Associate Justices of the
Supreme Court of the United States and author
of the celebrated Commentaries ; and the book
is practically itself, for the perceptive mind,
a statement of what may in this connection
especially be called the case of his future. These
volumes, which are excellently put together, are

still more a precious New England document,
giving, as they do, a picture of the local conditions that was the more luminous for being, as
we feel, but half designed.   It was impossible
that those conditions could have been better
expressed, altogether, than in the character and
the career of Judge Story ; because they were so
expressed in their highest beauty and amenity.
That, as we see his embarrassed son, is precisely
what illuminates and distinguishes the episode :
that William Story had not, like so many young
votaries of chisel and brush, young languishers
for Italy and " art," to react against the ugly,
the narrow or the cruel, but against an influence
that had everything in its favour save its being
the right one for *him*.   All the *light*, surely, that
the Puritan tradition undefiled had to give, it
gave, with free hands, in Judge Story—culture,
courtesy, liberality, humanity, at their best, the
last finish of the type and its full flower.   His
son's biography is an ample record of this, the
picture of a man in whom, as one reads, one encounters no element and no act that is not genial
and fine, not gentle in a high sense and not
positively marked—rarest in general of all impressions—with distinction.   The note is the old
and obvious note, for the observer of the race
from which Joseph Story sprang, the note of

active virtue, virtue cultivated and practised, as the aim and the meaning of life; only his is one of the cases in which it appears to us to shine without a shadow. If his morality was far enough from being, in the common sense, "easy," his temper, admirably so, evidently kept the air of intercourse with him free from the pedantry of morals and presented him in the happy aspect of a thorough New-Englander of his time who was yet also, to his great gain, a man of the world.

Nothing, moreover, in the connection, is more interesting than to see him wear this character on the very basis of *his* world, as it stood, without borrowing a ray, directly, from any other. He at least never crossed the sea nor attempted to force the hand of experience, which opened, to his open mind, freely enough. His biographer has indeed occasion to tell the story of his having, toward the end of his life, come sufficiently near the visit to Europe to have missed it by the turn of a hair—an episode touching, quite thrilling, to the interested reader, and as to which I shall say another word; all the more that our second thought is almost to rejoice at his hindrance. He was complete, to a particular shade, as we see him; and my point is, at any rate, that he had made up his high civility of the material immediately surrounding him. In the memorial

chapel of the cemetery of Mount Auburn, near
Boston, sits, among those of other good citizens
from other hands, the delightful figure of his
father produced early in William Story's career
as a sculptor and not afterwards, as a portrait-
statue, surpassed by him—he having been at his
happiest, in this way, when inspired by the
closest of his personal ties : witness as well the
admirably expressive symbolic image wrought by
him, in the fulness of time, as the last work of
his hand, for the tomb of his wife. I depend for
my impression of the monument in the Cambridge
chapel upon a remembrance from long ago, that
of an autumn walk, in funereal alleys, terminat-
ing in the lift given my depressing recreation by
a sudden turn, through open doors with which I
was unacquainted, into the company of those
eminent few whom native art had, in its degree,
effectively rescued from death — effectively, at
least, as then appeared to me, with Judge Story's
presentment (seated and gowned, with uplifted
emphatic hand, and benevolent head slightly
inclined), the most effective of all. One might
take him there either as delivering a judgment in
court or explaining a principle from his Harvard
chair—the thing, finely generalised, meets both
appearances ; but, whatever the moment selected,
it expressed the character that made one exclaim

"What a *lovable* great man!" The author of
these remarks is reminded by his type, and above
all by what we have called his amenity, of something once said to himself by an accomplished
French critic, the son of a famous father, who,
much versed in the writings of Englishmen and
Americans, had been dilating with emphasis and
with surprise upon the fine manner of Hawthorne,
whose distinction was so great, whose taste, without anything to account for it, was so *juste*. "Il
sortait de Boston, de Salem, *de je ne sais quel
trou*"— and yet there he was, full - blown and
finished. So it was, my friend surely would have
said, with the elder Story. He came, practically,
out of the same "hole" as Hawthorne, and might
to the alien mind have been as great a surprise.

Thus it is then, at all events, that we take
licence to think of him as very much so seated,
slightly smiling, discreetly insisting, but imper-
turbable, in the scale that his son's adoption of
the æsthetic answer to the problem of existence
had by its simple weight to bear down. We can
without impugning his discretion easily imagine
his asking if such a heritage as he himself, for
instance, represented had been duly weighed—
when the question, that is, was of the quantity
of stepping from under it that might be held
to be involved in the European art-life. It was

William Story's advantage that he was, by the
turn of his mind, sure—as he was afterwards also
sure, almost always sure, of many things, with
plenty of the love of discussion that makes our
certainties sociable ; for he could scarce have
afforded (with what may be called moral comfort)
to be materially less so.   He was launched, under
the highest auspices in the country, in the profession of the Law, to which a side of his mind
had shown itself as distinctly adapted ; his
activity in this direction had already excited a
just confidence, and those favouring circumstances for which many men long wait in vain
already showed him their fair face.   His great
awkwardness was in the fact that, for a rupture
with his particular conditions, he should have
greatly, not vulgarly, to justify himself—since
there would be otherwise in his case an element
of the ridiculous.   The justification, distinctly,
came with the years, as a man is always justified,
save for cruelty, when he has succeeded in living
the real life of his mind.   But it took, first and
last, a good deal of demonstration—the sense of
which, doubtless, for that matter, may well have
been, in part, the secret of Story's multifarious
æsthetic activities, his variety of experiment and
expression.   There was always a voice in the air
for him—" You would have made an excellent

lawyer." He would not perhaps, though, with some of his parts, he perhaps ought to have ; but that is one of the ways in which the conscience enriches existence. He had, at the last resort, before he took his step, the good fortune of a simple *want*. This was, dimly seen, for what he succeeded in enjoying—the air itself of the world of art, with which the air he found himself breathing had so little in common. He had, as the phrase is, nothing to show, could point, with confidence and effect, to no work of design stamped even with the appeal of having been achieved under difficulties. He could take his stand not on his strength, but only—it is not too much to say—on his weakness, that of having wants for which the world about him made no provision.

This it is again that has the interest of taking us back to the time. It was a time at which the appetite he professed was really not, in the absence of any light, any material, for recognising it, susceptible of recognition. And he on his side had to sail away with it into the void, which he gallantly did, with every presumption in his favour still to be established. His departure for Europe took place, as a matter of fact, after his father's death, but that he had in the latter's lifetime practically betrayed his peril is suggested

by his quoting somewhere the voice of home on
his mother's lips : " Well, William, I've known
in my life many a fool, but I've never known
so great a one." The character so conferred
was of application, naturally, but to the particular crisis ; what is touching, however, is
that it had, for the hour, to be quite consciously accepted and worn. The fool was
clever enough to see that he must be good-
humoured about that appearance — to which
precursors in general have, in fact, more or
less to resign themselves. It was unmistakable
that he could be accused of making light of
a heritage singularly precious ; which, on the
other hand, was an opportunity for discrimination *not*, in America in those days, the most
frequent. That in turn brings me again to my
claim for the special appeal made, to the retrospective mind, by this small passage of history.
There was half a century ago, in the American
world in general, much less to give up, for
" Europe," than there is to-day, but, such as it
was, Story gave it up all. To-day there is
vastly more, but, at the same time, people are
now not called upon for these detachments—by
which I mean that they are scarcely possible.
It has really ceased to be feasible, in other words,
to get away from America. The west is in the

east, the east, by the same token, more and more in the west, and every one and everything everywhere and anywhere but where they, in the vernacular, belong. Where any one or anything does belong is no longer a determinable, is scarce even a discussable, matter. In the simpler age I speak of these congruities might still be measured. And I may add that when I speak of the ingenuous precursor as giving up, I so describe in him but the personal act of absence. That was often compatible in him, after all, with the absolutely undiminished possession of the American consciousness. This property he carried about with him as the Mohammedan pilgrim carries his carpet for prayer, and the carpet, as I may say, was spread wherever the camp was pitched. The carpets of other pilgrims were certain, almost anywhere, to place themselves beside it—on which, in all good faith, amid the very depths they had sought to fathom, the little company could huddle. That good faith, among the perils, those that were perhaps even most of all perils of perception, forms half the quaintness of the old-time picture. It was impossible, at any rate, for a native to have been more absent, for long years, than William Story, but even on these terms, in the long-run his nativity was justified of him. Exactly that, however, is what I shall have better occasion to show.

To an Italian acquaintance who sought information of him for an article, of which he was to be the subject, in a Review, he made toward the end of his life such an enumeration of primary facts as I cannot do better, in respect at least to the earlier, than repeat in his own words.

" Born in Salem, Massachusetts, February 12th, 1819.   My father was the Hon. Mr Justice Story, of the national Supreme Court, and my mother the daughter of Judge Wetmore and granddaughter of General Waldo, a distinguished officer in the English army employed in the American colonies in the middle of the last century.   He commanded at the siege of Louisburg and at its capture and at the capture of the place from the French, and received from the Crown the grant of a whole county in Maine as a reward for his services.   My father was a man of extraordinary capacity, intellect and goodness. He was made Speaker of the House, in Massachusetts, at twenty - five years of age; then Representative to Congress, and then, at the age of thirty-two, Judge of the Supreme Court—the youngest man who ever received that dignity, which, in the U.S., outranks all but that of

President.   He wrote many and celebrated works
on jurisprudence, which are known throughout
Europe.   His decisions are quoted in England as
of highest authority.   He founded the college of
the Law at Harvard, and there lectured for many
years as professor.   Under his training many of
the most distinguished men of America were
brought up.   A noble man, a brilliant, and as
good as he was great.

"He left Salem when I was ten years of age,
and went to Cambridge, near Boston.   My life
was   thenceforward   chiefly   spent   there.   I
entered Harvard University at fifteen and gradu-
ated at nineteen, delivering a public poem on my
graduation.   I then studied the Law for three
years under my father, entered the profession,
and practised in all the courts on leaving him,
and was engaged in several most important cases.
I married when I was twenty-three, was appointed
commissioner in Bankruptcy and commissioner of
the U.S. Courts for Massachusetts, Maine and
Pennsylvania; also reporter for the U.S. Circuit
Courts.   I practised my profession for six years;
and during this time wrote a 'Treatise on the
Law of Contracts,' 2 vols. octavo, of about 1000
pages each (now in its 6th or 7th edition); a
'Treatise on Sales of Personal Property,' 1 vol.,
now in its 6th edition.   Both were adopted as

text-books in the Law school, and I also published 3 vols. of reports of Law Cases, all in their 3rd edition now. Further I published, at twenty-two, a first volume of poems. During the six years of my legal career I produced, sometimes under a feigned name, sometimes under my own, a good deal of poetry and criticism.

"On the death of my father in 1846 a public monument and statue were decreed to him, and to my great surprise I was requested to make them. I had hitherto amused myself, in hours of leisure, with modelling, but more with painting, and I used to get up early in the morning to work at these before going to my office. I had begun to model and paint while in college. On receiving the commission I have mentioned I declined it, from a sense of my incapacity—I didn't think I could carry it out. But I was so strongly urged to try that I finally consented on condition that I should come abroad first and see what had been done in these ways. I accordingly, in October 1847, sailed for Italy, and thence travelled over the Continent and England ; afterwards, on my return, making my sketch, which was accepted. I remained at home for eight months, working very hard all day at the Law, and wrote an additional volume to 'Contracts,' and a biography, in two volumes, of my father. I was haunted, however, by dreams of art and Italy, and every night fancied I was again in Rome and at work in my studio. At last I found my heart had gone over from the Law to Art, and I determined to go back to Rome. I came, and here modelled and executed the statue of my father, now in Cambridge, and another. I then once more returned to America and the Law, but at last, after another year of them, I definitely decided to give up everything for Art. My mother thought me mad and urged me to pursue my legal career, in which everything was open to me, rather than take such a leap in the dark. But I had chosen, and I came back to Italy, where I have lived nearly ever since."

He relates further that—somewhat to anticipate—recognition and success had been far from prompt in justifying him. He worked in Rome for several years with assiduity, producing, among various things, a figure of Hero holding up her torch to Leander, and those known as his Cleopatra and his Libyan Sibyl.

" These I executed in marble, but no one would buy them; so that, disappointed, I determined on a new rupture, a break with art and Rome,

and a return to my old profession. This was in
1862. But it so happened that the London universal exhibition was to take place and that I
was requested to allow these two statues to go
into the Roman Court, the Roman Government
taking charge of them and paying all expenses.
I gave them; I never wrote a word to any one
about them; but shortly after they arrived,
before the exhibition was open, I received a copy
of the 'Times' with a most flattering notice of
them, declaring them the most remarkable and
original works there, and, at the same time, by
letter, an offer of £3000 for them, by which I
was quite astounded. I had offered them only
two months before for their mere cost, and yet
had failed to sell them. This gave me confidence; I continued to work; and since then my
life has been dedicated to art. This was long
ago, but, as there is no end to art, I am as hard
at work as ever."

He enumerates, further, the volumes of prose
and verse that he has published, the papers, col-
lected and uncollected, that he has contributed
to periodicals; but these things are but the particulars, and I have thus promptly quoted the
greater part of the statement because it expresses
compactly the essence of Story's life. The life

itself, governed, in its singularly happy personal conditions, by the idea of free plastic production, was of the smoothest, brightest and simplest, as the lives of men of distinction go ; simplest, I say, because, though it was far from empty, was in fact quite enviably comprehensive, it unfolded itself altogether from within, and was at no moment at the mercy of interventions or shocks. He knew, in the course of his days, no interference of the fates—none, that is, with his personal plan ; he had no adventure beyond *the* adventure, which we take for granted, of having given way to his inspiration ; and this, I gather, is the great sign of good fortune. Ill fortune, for the man conscious of gifts, is *not* to have been able to unfold from within ; there is no other that in comparison with it matters. Of such ill fortune William Story, breathing from early manhood to the end the air he loved, which was the air, all round, of romantic beauty, never in any degree tasted ; so that his course—certainly in outward seeming—was almost the monotony of the great extremes of ease. Nothing really happened to him but to be his remarkably animated and various, his exuberant, sympathetic, intensely natural self : which had the effect of filling out quite sufficiently, and very richly, the frame of life for him, as well as contributing to its content for many other persons. We *have* his career, in short, if we read into the lines I have just cited from his note to the Italian critic, Signor Nencioni, all the play of imagination and taste, of eager feeling and eager energy, of passion, conviction, friendship, humour and curiosity, that they would take. The interest, therefore, is in the detail, and largely in the circumstances themselves (almost always, as we eternally say, picturesque) that kept producing the quantity of lively response. And the circumstances, precisely, are what we are still able more or less to recover. The circumstances are the personal names, the personal presences, the personal interests, beliefs, so queer and charming and touching, often, the general mass of current history and current sensibility, that, as a generation, we have moved away from. They are in short the vanished society that I began by speaking of.

I should like to begin again, much further back, under the impression of the earlier time that the record of Judge Story's life irresistibly produces. One hovers about it, this earlier time, as with a shy tenderness for people whom one wishes not to patronise, but who were so all unknowing of the greater interest their country, their society, their possibilities were likely to acquire. There is in particular in the first volume of the biography a chapter consisting of letters descriptive of a journey to Catskill, Trenton Falls and Niagara, made, in 1825, in company with Daniel Webster and his wife, which affects us somehow—for we cannot altogether say why —as a subtly suggestive document. The beauty of the land, the forests, rivers and lakes, then comparatively unblemished and as full as one wished of a sort of after - sense of Fenimore Cooper; the homeliness of the ways and conveniences, the decency and deliberation of the travellers, their cheerful austerity and the combination of their undeveloped standards and their enlightened interest—are all things that evoke for us the whole tone of a community and that refresh us in truth by their betrayal of what was absent from it. What was absent, we seem to feel, was our own precious element of the ready-made, whether in appreciation, in description, or in " effect" itself, as we are so fond of saying—so that effect itself has at last learnt to hand out to us automatically the counters with which we play at having perceived it. I lack space to quote from this record, but it would quite suggest a subject to a student of the history of manners. These, as we see them here, at Judge Story's level, are so good as to be admirable; with existence giving us, in the light of them, the sense of a large, square, high-windowed room, all clean and cool and thoroughly swept, of sparse, excellent furniture, of a delicious absence of rubbish. The only quarter in which this last element appears to have been more or less tolerated was that of literature; it was not tolerated in the moral quarter, or in that of conduct. Literature, on the other hand, was small and, like the old-fashioned room of my simile, cool. It was not the hothouse for rank growths that it has since become. One of the notes that most holds us—as to the vision of social intercourse, of personal ties—is the universal "Mr" of the male address. It was apparently in use with Judge Story for all his friends, for his colleagues, however familiar—a fact that we think of as throwing a light on *relations*, as they existed in that more straitened world, as showing how little provision, so to speak, was made for them. We see that the normal relation of intimacy, the only one at all conceived, was, rigidly, that of a man's fireside —his intimacy with his wife, his children and his Creator. The others, the outside ones, remained formal, civil, dutiful, but never could have become easy, we judge, without appearing to become frivolous. And if this was the case for men's relations with other men, it must have been still more marked for their relations with women. They had none, obviously, but with their proper wives, and with a wife every man was duly provided. The age of Sunday afternoon calls at tea-time, when all the men go out and all the women, in the odd phrase of to-day, " sit in," was still far in the future.

This light glance is directed, however, as we pass, but at the generation then about to disappear, not to Story's own, whose freedom of friendship, beginning early and lasting late, forms not the least interesting element of his life. We have seen that he went to college—as they must go in the Arcadia of our dreams, if they go at all— at fifteen, and in this connection the view, for us, immediately alters, shifts to a picture of young affections and alliances dancing, ever so mirthfully, of warm summer evenings, among the slim, vague Corot trees of the old Harvard " yard," to the sound of the oaten pipe. That note indeed — the murmur of Arcady itself, that of innocent versified homage, precocious and profuse, mingled with the rustle of feathery elms— pervades the crepuscular scene and makes us think of it wistfully. The young, by the usual American law, formed and cultivated more ties than their elders, besides naturally forming, with much promptness, the particular one that was to supersede all others. Marriage was early, in spite of an exception or two, and the frolic pipe was as brief as it was pure. William Story had the happiness of taking to wife at twenty-three, as we have seen, Miss Emelyn Eldredge, of Boston, and of entering thereby into a relation of which the security, the felicity, the general vivifying virtue, remained to the end of his days ideal. This union, in its unsurpassable closeness, was one of those things, in its kind, that still suffice to confer success in life, as Pater has it, even if everything else have failed. James Russell Lowell, of the same age as himself, his lifelong friend and his closest, ran his course at college during the same years, just after Charles Sumner, with whom he was to remain scarce less nearly allied ; and Lowell also married, for the first time, at twenty-five. Sumner was one of the few exceptions, and Sumner was in many ways—above all as to the supreme amplitude of the career reserved for him—exceptional. But the rest of the young company of the time were friends too of each other's friends, admirers, visitors, guileless invokers, of each other's brides that were to be ; and we see the whole little society, in the light of the decent manners of the time, as carrying out, with studies, emotions, enthusiasms, with confidences in short, all shared, the dim Arcadian appearance with which they beset us. If they were pleased with themselves and with each other they were pleased, for the most part, with every one else, from Goethe to Lydia Maria Child. Lowell was, among them, the most critical spirit, but even Lowell conceived that this lady, "of all American women who have yet put their minds into print, has shown the most of what can be truly called genius." Which might indeed, in those blessed years, very pleasantly be : the question had still the advantage of not becoming urgent.

It was, however, over the New England Cambridge of that and of later periods that Lowell's irony played most gently, and his admirable prose strain was to soften nowhere to such tenderness, or to flower in such brave paradox, as in musing, whether orally or in print, over that spacious village community of his youth which was at the same time a collegiate society ; the spot dedicated to all high pieties from the first, on which the most strenuous band of independents we know were to seat, from the first, in all impatience, their voluntary tribute to culture. He was ever ready to defend the thesis that it had been, from the day Washington took command of the Continental army under its historic

elm, the most virtuous and luminous, the most
distinguished and delightful, of human societies.
In this happy valley of the Charles, at any rate,
as described in " Fireside Travels," the finer spirits
of new boyhood and youth dreamed, adventured,
rejoiced together, inheriting those fruits of neighbourhood which their elders had more soberly
gathered; fruits that were to ripen afterwards
under other suns, in maturity, in Italy, in England, as more than one of the other papers in
" Fireside Travels," for instance, betrays. There
were of course other spirits than those I have
mentioned, more or less of the same original
participation, notably Richard Henry Dana of
the classic " Two Years before the Mast " and of
graver, and still higher, distinctions; but I am
limited to such reference, simply, as my bundle
of letters may illustrate; which, if it contains a
considerable number of Lowell's, and a still
greater number of Charles Sumner's, has no other
series beginning so far back. Only a few of
Story's own letters to Lowell appear to have
been kept by the latter, nor, evidently, do we
possess all of Lowell's to Story. Of these, however, those that remain are, as we shall see, full
of interest and character. None, nevertheless,
are so peculiarly full of character as Sumner's,
which, to my sense, quite excellently possess

that merit. If the value of a letter, for posterity, depends on the intensity with which this personal colour attaches—and save in the case of disclosures of unsuspected fact it can scarce attach to anything else so much—Sumner easily remains individual and inimitable. The four volumes of his copious Life by Mr Edward Pearce will doubtless already have appeared to testify sufficiently to this truth. I cannot, at all events, help seeing it shine out in the very earliest of his written communications that comes to my own hand; which I reproduce, without hesitation, and in spite of its somewhat invidious bearing, for the sake of its personal accent. Also, even, let me add, just *for* the invidious bearing—so little invidious at this time of day, and so conceivably to be taken with an easy allowance, all round; the appearance being that, like many young men of natural parts, Story, while at college, was inclined to let himself go in almost any direction but that of effort. And it is a question of the delinquencies of a boy of seventeen or eighteen, while his monitor sits within sound of Niagara; as to the impression of which wonder of nature it is characteristic that the latter, pointing his moral, will not frivolously relax into a remark.

Charles Sumner to W. W. Story.

"CLIFTON HOUSE, NIAGARA FALLS,
CANADA, *Aug.* 30*th*, 1836.

"MY DEAR WILLIAM,—I cannot be unmindful
of you even at this distant land in the imposing
noise of waters which fills my ears. I think of
your studies and of your employment of your
time often when you perhaps heed them quite
indifferently ; and I think of them now, especially as you are about commencing another
academic year. You told me to write you ; and
I know the goodness of your nature too well to
fear that you will take exception to what I
shall write under the shelter of that invitation.
There are few persons in the world in whom I
take so lively an interest as in yourself; whose
course I watch so anxiously and whose success
would give me such delight. Let me, then,
take the liberty of a friend and address one
word to you, from the fulness of my heart, in
regard to your future conduct. I shall speak
with plainness, and must allude to what you
have done, or rather (must I so phrase it?) to
what you have *not* done. Shortly before I left
home Dr Beck and Professor Felton were at
my office, and I inquired of them both what
were your standing, prospects of a part, and
general character. I was grieved and astonished

to hear from them that you were now so low as to be out of the range of a part, so that unless you rose you would never appear on the stage. All the faculty, they said, had the fullest confidence in your talents and capacity, but thought you remiss and gay and easily persuaded by others from your duties. Both spoke of you in the strongest terms of personal interest. What I had observed of your conduct had, in a degree, prepared me for this sad declaration.

"Now, shall this state continue? Will you refuse to repay the anxious care which your instructors exercise towards you by a respectful attention to your college duties? Do you decline to gratify my ardent hopes of you and my long attachment? Are you prepared to fill with grief, as I fear you have already with anxiety, the bosoms of your affectionate parents and sister? Let me ask you to forsake (in college phrase *cut*) all your idle acquaintance, begin the new year with new resolutions and follow them with performance, study all your lessons faithfully, never let an exercise go by without thoroughly understanding it, and devote that time which is not necessary to your college studies to some profitable reading. When I return talk with me about this and let me assist you in contriving how again to resume your old habits of study. I remember how pleasantly we used to talk over Virgil and the Latin metres, and the interest which you then expressed in study, and your ambition, laudable and generous, of distinction as a scholar. You know that I am no anchorite who would deny the young those pleasures which are innocent and agreeable, and that I would not advise to anything which I did not think for your good. The pleasures which you are now reaching after, and for which you are sacrificing the precious fruits of knowledge, are like the apples which floated on the Dead Sea, fair and golden to the sight, but dust and cinders to the touch. Unless you are willing to lay up stores for future repentance, I most affectionately ask you to return to your studies with new ardour, to forsake all idle acquaintances and bad habits which you may have contracted, and to give joy to your parents. From conversations which I have had with your mother I seriously believe that her health has been affected by her anxiety with regard to you. Remove, I pray you, that source of anxiety, and change it into one of honourable pride. Just imagine the power you possess—you can fill the hearts of your parents with rejoicing, or dash them with grief and melancholy. Do your duty, my dear boy, and you cannot fail to crown them with joy—to say nothing of your own happiness, which will be thereby secured, and that of your affectionate friend, CHARLES SUMNER."

Sumner, who had taken his degree in 1834, had had time to settle to his profession—he was launched, in Boston, in the practice of the law; but the portent of the great political career in which these preliminaries were promptly to lose themselves must surely, for his friends, already have hung about him. His allocution, admirable for weight and sincerity, is already almost Senatorial. These indeed are but stray lights. I catch, however, what I can, and, could I find anything of Lowell's prior to 1842, would make haste to give it for the love of any old-time touch, any faint light of adolescence groping in that medium, that it might contain. Of a date corresponding with the writer's twenty-third year there is one, addressed to the young lady to whom his friend was then engaged, which is happily producible, and in which, though concerned with trifles that have turned to dust, every lover of Lowell, among those who still remain, will pleasantly taste the promise of his quality. These, in fact, *are* the lights of adolescence, in the case of the eminent who have still

been juvenile at twenty-three, as Lowell himself
was, for that matter, to the last year of his life.
Adolescence even then, he would delightfully
have pleaded, was not complete in him.   There
appears here, moreover, for the first time, that
strange dim shade of William Page, painter of
portraits, who peeps unseizably, almost torment-
ingly, out of other letters, who looms so large to
Story's and to Lowell's earlier view, who offers
the rare case of an artist of real distinction, an
earnest producer, almost untraceable less than
half a century after his death, and about whom,
in fine, so far as is scantly possible, there will be
more to say.

J. R. Lowell to Miss Emelyn Eldredge.

"BOSTON, *April* 12*th*, 1842.

. . . "I am glad Jane 'Shore' is so charming a person. She will be quite an addition to
the 'band' when you bring her on hither with
you. She will be introduced, I imagine, to a
quite new and strange, and, I trust, pleasant,
state of society—I mean in our little circle. You
are very gay, I hear, in New York, balls, &c.,
being the standard amusements provided for
every evening. . . . Ah! we poor puritanical
Boston people will seem quite tame and flat, I
am afraid, to young ladies who have been in the

everyday society of Moustaches, and who have met foreign ambassadors face to face. One thing I beseech. Do not bring home a New York dress which with the extravagant tastes and propensities of the skirt will preclude the possibility of a friend's walking with you on one of our narrow side-walks. And so you have seen a 'New York trancendentalist'? Truly it is hard to imagine such a personage. However, by steadily bracing the mind to thinking of angels in tournures or in French boots and moustaches, one can gradually recall the natural state of the mind and prepare it for receiving the idea of the strange species above-named.

"But, my dear child, I will leave nonsense, and say half a dozen serious words. I have an excuse in the fact that I yesterday returned from Salem, where we had spent 'Fast' week. You were all that we missed. We had a very good time indeed, doing of course just what we pleased. We waltzed, or acted charades, or enjoyed *tête-à-têtes* on the stairs or in the library, or joked, or did *something* all the time. An ingenious friend who was patient enough to count the number of puns made in the space of twenty minutes, found them to be 75, or a little more than three in a minute. The recoil from such a state of mind is either into stupidity or a greater degree of nonsense. In my case, I experience an agreeable mixture of both.

"I am glad you have been to see Page. I think he is, in many respects, the most remarkable painter we have, and I freely confess that I had rather have his portrait of Mrs Loring than *the* Vandyke. If you see him again do give him my very best remembrance and love. I wish Jane Shaw were going to be painted by him. Has he finished his picture of Jephthah's daughter yet? That will, I hope, establish his fame. The fault of Page has been a propensity to try experiments, a propensity ruinous to present and often to lasting success—as Leonardo da Vinci proves. He has hardly ever profited by what experience he had already gained, so desirous has he been of acquiring more. In short, he has seldom painted as well as he could.

"I should advise you also to visit Mrs Child. Of all American women who have put their minds in print, she has shown the most of what can be truly called genius.

"Visiting persons like Page and her will keep your heart balanced when it is in danger from the fashion and frivolity of which you must necessarily see so much. This is the glory of Art. It is She who has nursed the soul and kept it alive so long. It is She who keeps fresh in us some touches of our higher nature, some memories of a more divine and blessed life. I have not any fear for a heart so pure and true as yours is, my dear Emelyn, but if I were exposed to similar influences I should take the same remedies myself. I should read more poetry, the more fashion and hollowness I saw. For it is impossible for any one otherwise to save themselves from infection."

Story's own earliest letters are few; but in those before me, of that period, all addressed to his father, the tone of the time, the somewhat pale panorama, is pleasantly and (if one must come back to that) even quaintly reflected. Youth, moreover, is seldom itself pale—when it is verily youth; visibly, at any rate, Story's was not; it flushed responsive to such colour, whatever that was, as the world about it could show. The *Lexington* was a steamboat, plying on Long Island Sound, in which Judge Story had just made part of his annual journey to Washington, and which, on its return voyage, had been horribly burned, with the all but total loss of its passengers and crew.

W. W. Story to Judge Story.

"CAMBRIDGE, MASS., *Jan. 25th,* 1840.

"DEAR FATHER,—I have a half hour before church to write to you, with nothing, however, to say. But a letter is a letter any way, and, inasmuch as its very being supposes all alive and well, is to that extent satisfactory. This therefore is my screen. We were all particularly glad to hear of your safe arrival at Washington, on account of the anxiety we felt concerning the *Lexington;* the news of its destruction having reached us several days before your first letter announcing your safe quarters at Washington. Your passage must have been of all passages the most disagreeable and dangerous. Indeed it seems now universally admitted that the boat was entirely unfit for its employment and has been considered as only a touch and go for some time. She was the same boat that I went to New York in, a year ago, and you may recollect, even then, my stating that she was almost unmanageable owing to a thunderstorm in the Sound. We were obliged to stop repeatedly, and she was so crank as to render every precaution in shifting the ballast necessary to enable her to proceed. This all have known, and the public therefore are, I think, in great measure to blame for this accident. The proprietors will, I hope, not be suffered to go unscathed, for such recklessness in the exposure of life I never heard of. One may well say that life is the cheapest commodity a-going in America! But you have probably thought this all over. Here it is a central point of discussion yet, and the loss of Dr Follen has thrown a great gloom over much of the society in which I am.

"Vacation of course has begun, and many of the students have gone or are on their way to Washington. Some are prevented by the stoppage on the Sound. I have seen and been introduced to a Mr Wilcox, who has come from Alabama to join the school, as I understood him. He is the only new arrival of which I know, though several strange bipeds are to be seen perambulating the deserts of Cambridge. He has the air of a Louisianian, gentlemanly in his manner, but not refined in his appearance—as most of the Southwesterners are. I have heard no prospectus of the school any further.

"The rage of Boston has turned from parties to lectures. What with Waldo Emerson and Useful Knowledge, and Lowell Institute and Grammar and Temperance, the whole world is squeezed through the pipe of science. All go to be filled, as the students of old went with their bowl for milk. Yesterday the tickets for

Dr Palfrey's lectures on Revealed Religion were given out gratis (being Lowell Institute), and the crowd was so immense that they were obliged to shut the doors and arrange the people in lines to receive them. Silliman's are just finished, and it has been usual to go at 6—the lectures beginning at 7.30 and ending at 10 !—in order to get seats. Besides this the lectures are repeated in the next afternoon for those who cannot be accommodated, and with this all who wish cannot hear. Even Whitfield had scarcely greater audiences. He will be obliged to take the Common to satisfy the Commons ! With all this there is no gaiety and no party-going ; all the world of fashion is closed.

"I am just reading Plutarch, with great pleasure and benefit, I think. His narrative is very amusing and captivating ; but it astonishes me to see how full of superstition and how easy a dupe he is. As soon as I forget that I am reading an old Greek writer, some absurd remark or story sends me back, over the waste of time, to the period in which he wrote. One of the least satisfactory lives is that of Cæsar. Why have all the world's greatest conquerors had the worst historians ? Napoleon, Cromwell, Alexander and Cæsar. The opposing parties seem to have had much more interest to pull down the reputation of each than the friends have to raise it up. Vengeance outlasts friendship, and sorrow cuts deeper than joy! The Indians are the only nation who remember *kindness* on principle. The principle of others seems to be ‘Cheat your best friends when their backs are turned!’ I'm at the end of my sheet; are you of your patience?”

The next has the interest of giving reality to that earlier professional character in the writer which, for many of those who knew him after his revolutions had taken place, might have seemed to belong to the realm of fable. But life was ever abundant in him; whatever he turned to was the reality, for him, of the hour; and, as he was nothing if not animated, it will be seen that he was as much so here as ever again in Roman studios and drawing - rooms, Roman excursions and discussions. The affair of the Ursuline Nuns, which strikes an odd note in the place and at the date, had been that of the destruction of their house at Somerville, near Boston, by an anti-Catholic mob.

W. W. Story to Judge Story.

“Boston, *Jan.* 21*st*, 1842.

“Dear Father,—I take the first moment which has been given me of leisure this week to send a word to you. We have been full of business in the Common Pleas, and have finished all but one of our cases. Judge Warren behaved very well; and upon the whole I found him a better judge than I had preconceived him to be. His worst fault is that he jumps too soon to a conclusion, and is obliged to retract. Such a contrast to Judge Sprague I have never seen; it was quite odd to go from one side of the court to the other—the cautious, fearful egg-treading of the one, and the slap-dash rapidity of the other. Our Long-wharf case broke down on the ruling of Warren; that no amount of usage could establish a prescriptive right, when in injury of a valuable easement or privilege, because the use is and must be construed as being permissive. I hope this is so. He took a verdict *pro forma* for 75 dolls. and the law goes up to Supreme Court. It seems to me that a public prescription can only be made out by proof of *universal* as well as adverse enjoyment. Our corn case, after a trial of two days and a half, turned up in our favour—though Judge Warren was inclined to think that the usage of trade could not modify a positive contract. But he gave that up.

"The restless spirit of the Bostonians has set them again by the ears. A man called Elder

Knapp has been preaching fire and fury against the Unitarians, with a spirit of rancorous hostility ; and the good people saw fit to mob and threaten, but the Mayor resorted to the universal American specific for all things, and speechified them all away. But there was some little excitement the next night because the Lancers had been ordered out with ball-cartridges. However, we are more like the English than the rest of the country in this respect, and have a great notion of order and obedience. This was only a sputter of fire out of iron ; and nobody doubts that we shall not hear any more of it.

"Our bankrupt law has set itself upon an overhanging cliff, and I fear that it will fall over. If Mr Clay will stand by his principles there is some hope, is there not ? that it will not pass the Senate. The House is always such a seething turbulent mass that no law has any foothold in it ; but this legislation is too fickle and outrageous. The people here are not disposed to sit down very quietly under it — but what can they do ? Is there any hope that Tyler will veto it ? if for nothing else than to show that he has the power so to do. In the House of R.'s here there is a petition offered to-day for a pecuniary remuneration of the Ursuline Convent Nuns. Curtis presents it."

He writes shortly afterwards with the advantage of referring to a contemporary matter that has still, comparatively, its vividness ; and I leave the last paragraph, too, in memory of his alertness.

W. W. Story to Judge Story.

"Boston, *Feb. 3rd,* 1842.

"DEAR FATHER,—I have been intending to write to you for several days, but my time has been very much occupied and this must be my excuse. I have not seen any letters from you since you went away, but suppose that you are as well and comfortable as the circumstances of the case admit. Yes, I did hear one letter from you, read by Mr Quincy, at the Dickens dinner ; but it was not peculiarly intimate in its character. The dinner, by the way, was the most successful that I ever knew in wit, eloquence and good feeling. The whole arrangements of the table were good, and no speech was out of taste except perhaps Bancroft's, who played to ' the people ' till the words tired me out. But the whole company was dead to him, and his words fell lifeless around him. It was a piece of declamation ! Hillard's was beautiful. I send you a report of the whole which will give you some idea of it—better, at least, than I can in

a short page. Dickens himself is frank and
hearty, and with a considerable touch of rowdy-
ism in his manner. ˙ But his eyes are fine, and
the whole muscular action of the mouth and
lower part of the face beautifully free and vibra-
tory. People *eat* him here ! never was there
such a revolution ; Lafayette was nothing to it.
But he is too strong and healthy a mind to be
spoiled even by the excessive adulation and
flattery that he receives. Mrs D. is said to be
a pleasant person, but I have not talked with
her. D., I hope, you will see at Washington ;
he leaves Boston on Saturday for N. Y. Sumner
has been tied to him ever since his arrival. Any
one might have found him all last week in his
room, with Alexander, on one side, taking his
portrait, and Dexter, on the other, modelling
his bust, with about 50 persons crowding up to
talk to him. He is now rather unwell, from excitement, I suppose, and disappointed Mrs Paige,
who gave a dinner to him yesterday."

Mr George Ticknor Curtis, already then eminent
at the Boston bar, and in whose office Story was
pursuing his initiation, adds a "My dear Sir"
to this letter. "William," he says, "has kindly
left me a corner. . . . He is getting on very
well, and if he has as much comfort in our con-

nection as I have, it is a very 'profitable' one in *one* sense. We have dined the Dickens, and a good and great soul he is. There will be no danger, I think, of spoiling him. As he himself told us, I am afraid you will miss him in the shifting of his and your scenes of action." And of the lion of the hour William again writes to his father : " Dickens let off so much of the gas of enthusiasm that people have been quiet since his departure. By the way, I gave him a letter of introduction to you, thinking perhaps he might reach Washington before you return. He is well worth seeing. The English authors have a sort of impersonality with us, and are as if they had died years ago ; so that this country is a sort of posterity to their works." Story adds in the same letter :—

" I am going on with the Reports, but shall defer any arrangement with regard to publication until I see you. I should prefer that you should look over the proofs, so that no material blunder should pass to the world, and in order that I may have the benefit of your suggestions. I should think now that there were from 20 to 25 cases ready for the press : some of them occupy quite a large space, so that at any time we shall be ready to go to printing. Several arguments have been sent in which will swell in measure its bulk, and we need not fear for *one* volume.

"William White has returned quite delighted with his journey to the South and as firmly fixed in abolition as ever. He has seen nothing to change his views with regard to slavery, and hates it quite as much as before. Adams's speech he heard, and thought it was a hailstone shower of wrath upon the South which they well deserved. I like the bull-headed sternness and defiance in the old man, and only wish he had had full swing."

Adams was of course ex-President John Quincy. All Story's letters to his father, meanwhile, show him as leading without reserve the life the time then imposed on him; and they make us, in view of the complete detachment he was afterwards so easily to practise, exclaim to ourselves afresh upon the facility of youth. It gives itself with a freedom that is apt to allow to the seasons that follow it a good deal of the gift to take back. We feel, moreover, to-day, or like to think we do, the pulse of the history of the time in many a mere private accident or unconscious sign: with the Civil War still to arrive, that is, though yet undreamt of, no breath of Northern *malaise* on the Slavery question but becomes, and quite dramatically—at least for the mind addicted to finding more in things than meets the eye—a straw in the dark current setting to great events.

W. W. Story to Judge Story.

"BOSTON, *Jan. 26th,* 1844.

"DEAR FATHER,—I should have written to you before now, but that my engagements have left me not a moment of time. I pinched out what I could however on Wednesday, and went to Cambridge, where I found Mother sitting in M.'s room, improving and in good spirits, having discussed thoroughly the 1st vol. of Princess Dashkow's 'Memoirs of the Court of Catherine II.,' and waiting quietly for the second. M. had then just gone to Boston to see us, taking advantage of as fine a day as ever flattered a winter month. She arrived soon, however, and we found her also getting well and strong. Nurse Wilson was as fat and important and un-intelligible as ever. I found at Cambridge your letter informing us of your safe arrival and of your winter quarters.

"I have signed my contract with Little & Brown, on the most advantageous terms. They give me a dollar per volume, and *twenty-five* presentation copies. This is even more than I hoped. We shall begin to print to-morrow I suppose : at all events as early as next week. You will find much added in the proof-sheets to what you have already seen, and I think will find it improved. I have written a few pages in the first chapter on the subject of Entire Contracts and Severable Contracts : the distinction between which, as it seemed to me, needed some explanation. I think that a sale of the *whole* of an indefinite quantity of anything, *warranted*, at so much per *measure,* is a severable contract, and that the sole criterion is whether the consideration be entire or divisible by the terms of the contract.

" There is the great Anti-slavery Convention in full blast here at present, threatening destruction to the Constitution and everything else which does not jump with their wishes. Garrison has been emitting serpents from his mouth, like the girl in the fairy story. Red Wendell Phillips is coming down to-day upon all creation. Abby Folsom and Father Lamson have, however, worried the souls of the Abolitionists almost out by insisting upon speaking all the time in reproof of the abolition measures. This is nuts for the audience, who are not devoted to *the cause.*

" I left you just as Sumner had requested you to write a letter concerning the Convention Debate about the Salaries of the Judiciary. He has

received it, as he told me yesterday, but I fear
that it will fail of much effect unless it be made
public; and I see the difficulty of making it
public. That one word *Retrenchment* can rouse
more spirits than can be put down in a century.
The proposal is, at present, with the acquiescence
of the Whig party, that the salaries as to the
present incumbents must be put back again, but
are to be diminished as to all future judges.
Ashmun of Springfield has given out among his
country-people that there is not such a terrible
breach of the Constitution, and has by his manner
persuaded them that there is none. This is from
jealousy of Boston members."

The *malaise* on the Slavery question to which
I refer took, as may be seen, with the Storys,
the form it was still long to keep throughout the
conservative north—that of soreness under the
great blot on the American scutcheon, cultivating
as a counter-irritant a soreness under crude reform. It is thus impossible, in looking back on
the "quiet" people of that time, not to see them
as rather pitifully ground between the two mill-
stones of the crudity of the "peculiar institution"
on the one side and the crudity of impatient
agitation against it on the other. *They* truly
were the comfortless class—all the more that

their sacrifices, when the war at last came, were but a continuance of their discipline and were not the price of any previous joy. These things, both for the South and for the party of agitation in the North, came at least as the consequences of blissful passion and action.

W. W. Story to Judge Story.

"BOSTON, *Feb. 6th*, 1844.

"DEAR FATHER,—I have just about three minutes to write to you in! I send you the first proof. Will you enclose it to me, instead of Little & Brown, and get an M. O. upon it? I seem to feel as if I wish to recast every sentence when I see it in print. It is like a prison to me.

"Webster's letter I have seen : it seems to be wrung out of him most reluctantly and, as it were, at the last gasp. Its egoism is offensive, and its hint that a strong man should be at the head of affairs indicates himself as the strong man.

"The Abolitionists are doing their best to ruin *this* State. They have organised a corps of lecturers who will nightly ply the abolition oar in the towns in the country. They have great hopes—and we great fears!

"The Legislature is stupid as ever, and is now talking over the constitutionality of the reduction of the Judges' salaries."

The question of the reduction of the Judges' salaries might well appear "stupid" in conditions in which public functionaries without exception were already expected, while the possession of private means to any considerable extent was infrequent, to be faithful, exemplary and happy on stipends that strike us at present as hardly larger than those of clerks in counting-houses or salesmen in shops. It was not, doubtless, that underpaid members of the high Judiciary could not maintain a character ; the question was whether, on a sordid material footing, they could maintain a dignity ; so that legislative movements for reduction may well have been depressing at an hour when any enlightened movement must have been for a rise. Nothing is more interesting, always, on the American scene, than the reflections induced by the constant disparity between the larger view of the measure of pecuniary need on the part of those carrying on the affairs of great States and a great country, and the comparatively uninspired imagination of the huge scattered democracy that votes the supplies and estimates the wants. No other population with personal wants so few has probably ever had so intimate a voice in the control of an administrative machine of which it was the inevitable effect positively to create wants; so that if I speak of the spectacle as interesting, this is precisely from our being able to trace in it, step by step, what may be called the de-barbarisation of the conception of life. Wants created on one side have, by patient arts, to create on the other the imagination, not easily elastic, by which they can be met ; so that what is the growth of such a faculty as that but a national, a social, a personal, an intellectual, an economic drama in itself? Such, truly, is the fascination of history! Story writes his father in this general connection a letter vivifying the matter, which I quote, in part, in this place, though it belongs to a date later in the year. The "other duties" alluded to were those of his professorship at the Harvard Law School, to which he was to give himself during the part of the year not spent at Washington, or while the Supreme Court was not sitting. He was to bring to that modestly remunerated chair all the lustre of his high judicial character; and we duly take it as a note of the time that if one of the positions was to be relinquished for the other, the natural sacrifice was held to be the seat on the Bench rather than the University lectureship.

. . . "It is rather on your account than on my mother's that I hope you will now [December

1844] renounce your judicial duties. They wear
upon your constitution more than all your others,
and your recompense is sour looks from one side
of every case and an inadequate salary. It
might be pleasant to spend one's life in the
service of a country which recognised the value
of the sacrifice, but in the shifting politics and
declining morality of a republic nothing is long
remembered, and the best are the most in the
way. . . . I lately met President Quincy
[Josiah Quincy, of Harvard College] in Little &
Brown's bookshop, and he earnestly desired me
to state to you that, in his opinion, you ought to
quit your office and devote yourself to those
occupations which bring you the best delight.
He reiterated, concerning the salary from the
Law School, that they would willingly raise the
sum to three thousand dollars. I hope, however,
that you will not accept of such an offer, which
seems to me a mean one. Out of your name and
reputation the Law School makes at least ten of
its sixteen thousand dollars of income, and it can
well afford, in consideration of its own wellbeing,
to grant you a larger sum. Do, pray, claim a
salary equivalent to your services. If you are
to give anything more to the College, let it be
tangible—a fund that may be credited to you.
What you have given so generously heretofore is

what the Persians call ' bosh,' nothing for them, and it might as well have been aboard Captain Kyd's vessel.   Resign, however, at all events, and spend a less laborious and more agreeable life."

There was no question, naturally, of a retiring life-pension ; which was the greater pity—one scarce abstains from cynically remarking — as Judge Story was at this time but sixty-five years old.   His span, however, was to stretch but another year ; he died in his sixty-sixth, in spite of the wealth of vital endowment which it is another quaint " note " of what was then in the air that we find a passage in his son's Biography comparing, with the charming French quotation in support, to the temperament of Consuelo, George Sand's great heroine, as vividly described by that writer.   Up to the time at which, shortly before his death, his emoluments at Harvard were augumented, they had not exceeded, annually, a thousand dollars.   He had planned in 1843 a visit to England, which was at once to afford him the opportunity of seeing face to face some of the eminent men of that period, with whom he was in correspondence, and to give him the first considerable rest—so far as so great a recreation could be rest — that his

laborious career had known. We follow, in his
son's volumes, the preparations, the *pourparlers*,
for this happy consummation, and, finding ourselves, as a result of the perusal of the book, in
intimate relation both with his beautiful spirit
and his final fatigue, we become conscious, fairly,
of a personal appetite for the experience that
appears to await him, as well as of the particular
impression we feel him destined to produce : so
that when the project begins, for various reasons,
suddenly to tremble in the balance, we almost
tremble, on our own side, with suspense—we
quite take it as one of the quiet tragedies of the
past that so much virtue and so much honour
should be doomed to fail of the just reward. The
crisis barely misses a dramatic interest — the
justice of the reward striking us as exquisite and
our vision making for itself a picture, on the one
side, of the richer London "forms," the graver
London courtesies, of that time, and, on the other,
of the deeper differences, the scene in proportion
more furnished than peopled, that the charmed
American celebrity—aware perhaps for the first
time, too, of the stately face that appreciation
may show in old societies—will have to recognise.
All this for the moment beguiles us ; we accept
for him Lord Denman's and Lord Brougham's
invitations to dinner, launched in advance—and

not by cable ; we assist at the preparations, in Portland Place, or wherever, of the then American Minister, Mr Edward Everett, feel, even across the slower seas, the cool breath of *his* perfect propriety, and then, on the turn of the page, drop to flat disappointment. The *Britannia* sails, but Judge Story does not ; the question of health, at the last moment, pricks the fond bubble, and we have to console ourselves with the thought that, given the image he presents, he is perhaps smoother and rounder just as the nature of his experience made him and just as that of his privation left him. All the same we close his record with a pang. He might have dined with Lord Brougham, " on the 26th," to meet the Lord Chancellor, Lords Denman, Campbell, Spencer, Lansdowne, Auckland and Clarendon, together with Lord Chief-Justice Tindal, Dr Lushington, Sir Frederick Pollock and Mr Austin ; and with Lord Denman, on the 27th, to meet the Lord Chancellor, Lords Abinger and Brougham, Barons Parke and Alderson, Mr Justice Wightman and Sir Frederick Pollock again : he might have enjoyed these chances, and many more, of the same pleasant old heavily served sort, as heavily washed down—so that we of a later, of a cabling and rushing age, should not patronise him with our pity. Is it indeed his curiosity that we feel

unassuaged, or is it only our own? We must
not at all events miss what he missed more than
he missed it himself. He measures it, to Mr
Everett, in thanking him for his enumeration of
the guests invited to meet him, but he is brief.
" I seem to myself, even at this distance, to have
partaken and enjoyed their conversation and con-
viviality as one invited to the pleasures of the
fabled feasts of the gods." And the son—which
is to our point—was to make up, in the future,
for much more absence than the father could, at
the best, or rather at the worst, be conscious of.
It was thus from a home in which the spell had
been unbroken that William Story set sail.

He had meanwhile begun early, as I have said,
to sacrifice, in the old phrase, to the Muses, and
I find an early letter in which this is modestly
signified, and which I give both on that account
and as pleasantly documentary in respect to his
lifelong friendship, already mentioned, with the
correspondent to whom it was addressed. He
had lately married and was in the flush of young
happiness. The Phi Beta Kappa association of
Harvard alumni hold, each year, at Commencement, a banquet to which one of their number
is immemorially appointed poet, and Story, in
1844, filled this office and declaimed his poem at
the close of the dinner. Worrick's was a house

of familiar entertainment at Nantasket Beach on the Massachusetts shore—then, like all shores, less conscious of such excrescences—where, during this summer, Lowell and his friend had stayed together, and some discussion and revision of the verses had taken place. These last are doubtless less to our purpose than the letter itself.

W. W. Story to J. R. Lowell.

"BOSTON, *Sept. 2nd*, 1844.

"DEAR JAMES,—I thank you most truly for your very hearty words about my Phi Beta poem. They were the most grateful that I have heard, coming as they did from one who could be so thoroughly depended upon both for sincerity and true judgment. You are the person who of all others I should wish to like it. I had many doubts concerning it, and was at one time perfectly disgusted with the whole affair. I found myself writing under the eye of the public, and I was cramped and coffined. I was writing didactically and impersonally, and felt as if I dragged a lengthening chain behind me. This was when I was at Worrick's. Then I intended to show it to you and ask your advice about it; but I thought this would be only a bore, and that if you did not like it you might thereby be thrust

into an unpleasant position.   However, despite
all this, I wanted sympathy and criticism, and
I meant to ask it of you as soon as I completed
the poem ; but your departure from W.'s before
its completion prevented me from so doing.

"I was well enough satisfied with my *success*,
but not with my poem.   Neither am I now.
The subject knocked me down as often as I
strove to measure myself with it.   I couldn't
say anything that I wanted to say.   I felt
everything slipping from my grasp just as I
thought I had it.   I had hoped before pen
went to paper that I should be able to condense in some measure my feelings, but the form
and circumstances continually baffled that hope,
and at the end I found myself encumbered with
the dead bones of my subject.

"I have been repeatedly requested to publish
the thing, but I cannot make up my mind to do
so—I really do not think it worth printing.   I
do hope, however, some of it will sink into the
hearts and minds of those who heard it, for if
it be stupid it is true.

"But if it is worthless, one other poem which
I have is not.   My child—how strange that
phrase seems to me !—is a recompense for everything, a fountain of joy, ever-increasing, perennial.
He is the best thing I have in life except E.   He

winds himself round my heart and teaches me a new life. He is a pure satisfaction, and when you taste it for yourself, which you will, you will know its value—and also know how foolish all words are about it."

He has meanwhile (earlier in the same year) written to his father that he is modelling by night a group of Hagar and Ishmael, and has just finished a " full-sized head " of his father-in-law. And he has in the same letter written other things that glance, characteristically, at the life about him and his own life, and that express the frankness and tenderness in him of the filial attitude.

. . . " Boston has been flooded with parties this winter, and I am heartily sick of them. My book goes on very well now that it is started, but it seems as if I should never have done altering. Sumner also desired to look over the proofs, and I have most gladly consented. His hints are very valuable at times. I have omitted to write to you about Bacon's eulogium upon you ; but I fear lest you are not satisfied fully that it is not fit for publication here. It is so fulsome, so inelegant and bald and undiscriminating, that I should be ashamed to see it reprinted. Here

and nowhere is it at all needed, and without in-
juring or benefiting you would be a mere football
of criticism and banter. Foolish praise is worse
than foolish blame at any time, for it involves
the subject often in the ridicule due justly to the
flatterer. This would not be your case, but it
had, I think, most decidedly better be hushed
up. Gilding refined gold and painting lilies is a
useless occupation, and I wish Mr Bacon knew
it; but it is well meant, and that is the best one
can say of it—his style is that of a drunken
Dr Johnson. And I should think that even one
' born amid the granite rocks of his native
Marblehead ' — where *can* one be born but in
one's native place ?—' and reared upon the arid
sides of its declivities' could scarcely regard it
with an auspicious eye."

If I am tempted to quote from one of his
letters to his father during the winter of the
following year, it is, I fear, mainly for the sake
of the shadowy name of the person mentioned,
and because this name has for me, even if in no
very definite or important connection, a certain
power of dim evocation. Dealing with ghosts,
we must let no ghost pass who turns to us the
least hint of a queer face, and cultivating, as I
have said, a vanished society, we must, if only

for whimsical pity, for proper tenderness of
memory, allow even the more vague of the
wandering shades as much of the poor freedom of
it as the more vivid. Of what "society" in particular, however, I ask myself, can have been Mr
Rufus Griswold, who peeps at me out of old New
York years, years of earliest boyhood, far away
and as of another planet, and shows a general
presence rather the reverse of prepossessing, yet
strangely distinct ?   I seem to see him pass in
and out of the house of childhood with a lurid
complexion, long, dark, damp-looking hair and
the tone of conciliation—unless I do him wrong.
Remembrance, I find, clutches at him with an
eagerness not explained by the patent facts, so
that I wonder at the obsession till there suddenly
breaks a light which I shall presently mention.
It was one of the patent facts that, with his
inflamed colour, the sharp apparition, whom I
also recall as with a couple of books, from which
papers protruded, always under his arm, should
have been, most unfortunately, further excoriated
by an explosion of gas on an occasion that I
perfectly recollect hearing described ; though I
remain without warrant, I am well aware, for
here obtruding it.   I should remain without
warrant indeed for any portion of my reference
had I not by this time caught, for a clue, as I

have just mentioned, the thread on which these pearls are strung. Rufus Griswold, a journalist, literary critic, discoverer and monitor of poets and poetesses in the New York of that time, had been, in fine, nothing less than the friend and protector of Edgar Allan Poe—which fact, glimmering in upon my childish, yet already disquieted, consciousness, was doubtless the cause of the impression he made : an impression in which there float other images, those, even, of the "Female Poets of America," or whatever, whom Mr Griswold edited, and notably, traceably, elusively, inexplicably, that of a certain Mrs Osgood, momentarily brightest of the band, who was the friend of Griswold and also the friend of Poe, and in connection with whom there supremely swims toward me one of those queer reminiscences that take form when we sometimes succeed in looking back hard enough. I should take time—that is if it mattered—to try to remember at what festive hour of infancy, in a strange house, amid other children, amid lights and Christmas fiddles, dances, games, grab-bags and sugar-plums, I lost myself in the intenser bliss of a picture, above a sofa, on a wall, which represented a lady, in Turkish trousers, with long tresses, seated on the ground and holding a lute, whom I knew to be Mrs

Osgood and whom I was bewildered to think of as Turkish, though I recognised her as beautiful. I seem to see that she was the wife of an artist as well as the friend of poets—though these are visions that nothing would induce me to verify—and that the portrait in question may therefore have been from the husband's hand. The great thing, at any rate, was the implication, through the Christmas party, through the Turkish lady, through the literary Griswold, of the terrible, the haunting Poe, since he, in his turn, was the supreme implication, that of " The Gold-Bug," " The Black Cat," and " The Pit and the Pendulum "—sensations too early absorbed, doubtless, and too inwardly active. But I approach my simple extract by too many steps.

" Mr Rufus Griswold stopped me the other day and carried me to the Tremont House and palavered for a long time about you. The amount of his palaver was a request for me to obtain from you, or to make myself, a selection of passages from your works to be inserted in a book, which he intends to publish, called the ' Prose Writers of America '; and in which he gives extracts from all the prominent writers in the country. Somebody is to write a sketch of your life, and he wants the dates of the different publications of your works. Besides all these things, he wishes, at some leisure time, that you would sit to some portrait - painter, either Page or Inman, in order to furnish himself with your likeness to adorn a picture-gallery of all the distinguished authors in England and America, which he has been collecting for some time past. If you will consent thereto, he (as I understood him) will have an engraving made from the portrait, which may do you some justice and may furnish the Law students with a copy if they shall desire it. Griswold has already made a collection of the Poets of America in one large volume, and another of the English Poets; and he is a professed dabbler in this sort of work, and does it well. What I want is that you would point out any particular passages which you should like to have printed, and also furnish me with the dates of your various publications. If you have anything in manuscript it will be especially desirable. To save you the trouble of dates I would suggest that Bacon (the judge of Utica), in his oration about you, has made a list which if it be correct will answer every purpose. Are the facts which he states concerning your life correct, so that I may send a copy of the said discourse to Griswold? Let me know soon and I will communicate the same to Griswold."

I give his next letter for its personal side.

W. W. Story to Judge Story.

"BOSTON, *Feb. 3rd,* 1845.

" DEAR FATHER,—I write to inform you that Uncle Tom and I intend to leave Boston for Washington on this day (Monday) week, and shall be much obliged to you if you will procure for us two rooms at Colman's (I think Colman keeps Gadsby's, does he not?) so that we may have them upon our arrival, which I suppose will be on Wednesday. We shall set out at 8 o'clock on Monday morning, and without delay (unless the weather be unfavourable) proceed to Washington. Uncle Tom has made me the generous offer to pay me through, and I have thought best to accept; for it is well to see Washington once in our life at least, though it be an Augean stable of politics.

" I do not know that there is anything happening here of much interest at present. I am in my old traces pulling away as usual, hearing music whenever I can hear good, eating oysters whenever I can afford it, playing whist when

I can get a chance, and thereby shaking off my
evenings and driving all day at my reports and
the office business.   If one can call it business
—for there seems to be nothing doing in this
office, except the Digest of the American Reports,
which is Curtis's business and scarcely mine.   I
might hesitate to go to Washington if there were
anything to do here in the way of law ; but you
can imagine how much work is done when I
tell you that my receipt for office profits during
the last six months has been 158 dolls.—which
is about enough to buy coal with.   I think my
chance of a *fortune* from my profession looks
promising !   316 dolls. per annum is a large sum,
and of course engenders a mighty enthusiasm."

Story's first visit to Italy—he sailed for Genoa
—was paid in the autumn of 1847, when he had
betaken himself to Europe, with his wife and
child, to acquire that knowledge of the art of
sculpture which was to qualify him for producing, according to the commission accepted from
his fellow-citizens, a monument to his father.
It strikes us certainly as characteristic enough
of all the conditions that this invitation had
preceded rather than followed any serious practice, on his part, of the sculptor's art : he was,
obligingly, to learn the trade in order to make

the statue for which the occasion had, not less
obligingly, been given him; he was not to make
the statue because he had learned the trade.
This latter position would not have provided
for the obliging in any quarter, and we seem to
feel it as in the thin local air, through which
confidence and kindness so freely could circulate,
that half the interest of the matter would have
failed had it not been thus an affair of the
general good-nature. The interest for ourselves,
moreover, is the greater that the good-nature
was, in the event, to be, all round, markedly
justified—since the ultimate work proved quite
as interesting as if the fairies who appeared so
absent from its birth had been present in force.
The one present fairy was the native cleverness
of the young man, then disguised even from
himself as an unknown quantity; the latent
plastic sense, the feeling for the picturesque in
attitude, for the expressive in line, for emphasised, romanticised character, in short, which was
to befriend him through his after-time and make
up to him in some degree for his loss of the early
discipline. "Art," in the easy view of the age,
was to be picked up in the favouring air—an
impression that, when we come to think of it,
touches us as having been natural, founded quite
in apparent reason, not less than as having been

innocent. If the influence invoked was clearly, in their own air, invoked in vain, so, inevitably, the good people of the time thought of it as resident in the air that in all the world differed most from their own. There, presumably, it hung in clusters and could be eaten from the tree, so that to be free of the mystery one had but to set sail and partake. The idea was the handsomest tribute, after all, to the supposed intensity of the presence of the boon where it was present at all; and what happier state of mind could there have been than that of those pilgrims to whom the prospect so beckoned ? They started surely as none others had ever done for the golden isles, and it may be doubted if in most cases they even on the spot discovered that they had simplified perhaps to excess. It was a discovery that their patrons at home were at any rate slow to make—very completely indeed as it may appear to have been made to-day. It is pleasant therefore to think of the spirit of youth, freshness, hope, with which William Story set forth ; pleasant to think, that is, of all the pleasantness that, with his law - books pushed away and his charming young wife, who was ever, from that moment, to abound in the sense of his own dispositions, on his arm, he took for granted. He appears then to have taken for granted, with the rest, that he could come back when he liked and open the law-books again; which was in fact exactly the feat that he after some months put to the test — with the still pleasanter consequences that were to have been foreseen.

Postponing, however, for a moment, our acquaintance with the series of his years in Italy, which may more conveniently be treated, even from his first interrupted connection, as one period, I embrace whatever may be to our profit in the brief remainder of his American time. Lively were his impressions on his first return, and uttered, to those to whom he *could* utter, with his habitual spontaneity; but the voice of Boston had meanwhile, in absence also, been much with him, and the voice of Boston, by the testimony of our documents, rings nowhere clearer and richer, as I have already hinted, than in those letters from Charles Sumner that my little collection happens to include. This, it should be added, without prejudice to Sumner's individual voice, always so personal, often so almost comical, essentially so natural, in spite of that note of the orator which is perceptible from the first, and precisely, in this connection, delightful, in emphasis, in abundance, for a forensic roundness and fulness. This correspondent of our friend's is decidedly one of his best; and I may even justify the plea by citing another letter of the early time. The letter, however, I must premise, is addressed not to the younger (who was nineteen years old) but to the elder Story. Sumner, then in his twenty - seventh year, was, for the first time, in Europe.

Charles Sumner to Judge Story.

"PARIS, *May* 14*th*, 1838.

" ' Let's talk of graves and worms and epitaphs,' says the fallen King Richard when his star of sovereignty has paled before the rising power of Bolingbroke. And I feel disposed to echo the language—I have just come in from that immense city of the dead, Père-la-Chaise. I have wandered round among its countless monuments, have read its characteristic inscriptions, and gazed on the memorials raised to genius and virtue and merit. The guide who conducted me assured me that there were more than *fifty thousand* monuments. They are as thick and close as corn that grows in the field; tomb touches tomb and monument adjoins upon monument. The eye is wearied by the constant succession; it solicits in vain the relief of a little green grass. . . . You may ask, then, how Père-la-Chaise compares with Mount Auburn. I can answer easily. There is an interest which Père-la-Chaise possesses, which Mount Auburn has not yet acquired, and I hope long years will pass away before it can assume this melancholy crown. Everywhere in the former you see the memorial which marks the resting-place of some man whose very name causes the blood to course quickly through the veins; your eyes rest on the modest tomb of Talma, and then on the more attractive monument of Laplace, and finally on the cluster of proud erections under which repose in peace the Marshals of Napoleon. Look in any direction and you will meet some name already consecrated on the page of history. Here indeed is a source of thrilling interest; to think of treading the ground which is sown with the dust of these children of fame is enough to fill the mind; and then the eye is occupied by the various shapes which are contrived for marble. And yet as a place of mourning, to be visited by the pious steps of friends and kindred, give me our Mount Auburn, clad in the russet dress of nature, with its simple memorials scattered here and there, its beautiful paths and its overshadowing grove. Nature has done as much for Mount Auburn as man has for Père - la - Chaise, and I need not tell you how superior is the workmanship of nature. . . .

"I leave Paris with the liveliest regret, and feeling very much as when I left Boston; leaving a thousand things undone, unlearned, and unstudied which I wished to do, to learn and to study. I start for England, and how my soul leaps at the thought! Lord of my studies, my thoughts, and my dreams! There, indeed, I shall 'pluck the life of life.' Much have I enjoyed and learned at Paris; but my course has been constantly impeded by the necessity of unremitted study. The language is foreign, as were the manners, institutions, and laws. . . . I shall at once leap to the full enjoyment of all the mighty interests which England affords; I shall be able to mingle at once with its society, catch its tone and join in its conversation, attend its courts and follow all their proceedings as those at home. Here then is a pleasure which is great almost beyond comparison—greater to my mind than anything else on earth except the consciousness of doing good."

The postscript too has the full tone.

"I shall go by the way of Calais, Dover and Canterbury, see the old fortresses of Calais which have withstood so many sieges, cross the famous Straits, at Canterbury, gaze on the altar of

Thomas à Becket, and then enter that mighty babel, London."

This next from the same hand is the first of many addressed to William Story during his many years in Europe.

Charles Sumner to W. W. Story.

"Boston, *Jan.* 14*th*, 1848.

"I have long intended a letter to you, and was glad to hear of your pleasant voyage and happy arrival at superb Genoa. I doubt if there is any port in Europe so entirely calculated to charm and subdue a voyager fresh from the commercial newness of America. I cannot forget my delight and awe at Havre. But Genoa is more than a continent of Havres. They tell me also that you seem to enjoy what you see. That is right. Cultivate the habit. You remember Smelfungus in Sterne's 'Sentimental Journey,' who quarrelled with all he saw, and finally fell foul of the Venus in the Tribune as a very drab? But you will not be Smelfungus. . . . I think that you and E. must return soon to keep E. E. right. He is stiffening and hardening into a staunch 'Old Whig,' and talks of 'regular nominations' and voting the 'regular ticket.' He seems to be inspired with an exalted idea of a combination to which I am entirely indifferent, the 'united Whig party.' Like Mr Webster, he sees no star in the heavens but Whiggery. What a dark place this would be if there were no other lights. . . . Tidings come constantly of Emerson's successes in England. An article in 'Blackwood' and a very elaborate criticism in the 'Revue des Deux Mondes' place him with Montaigne."

EARLY ROMAN YEARS

III.

THE SIEGE OF ROME.

STORY and his wife were meanwhile launched in the old Rome of the old order, the Rome of which the rough hand of history has so grievously deprived the merely modern pilgrim, but which to those still able to cherish, from years now distant, some memory of the comparatively inviolate scene, shows, in the light of their youth, a face inexpressibly romantic. I can remember but the last winter before the deluge, and only a portion of that; but it was at this time that, as if foreknowing the great assault to be suffered and the great change to be wrought, the sorceress of the seven hills gathered herself up, for her last appearance, her last performance, as it were, in her far-spreading, far-shining mantle. The Œcumenical Council of 1869, whatever other high matters it settled or failed to settle, was the making at least of a perpetual many-coloured picture—the vast, rich canvas in which Italian unity was, as we may say, to punch a hole that has never been repaired. The hole to-day in Rome is bigger than almost anything else we see, and the main good fortune of our predecessors in general was just in their unconsciousness of any blank space. The canvas then was crowded, the old-world presence intact. The French siege of 1849, indeed, was the first public event at which our special friends were to assist, but that was an episode followed by a reaction only too markedly in the sense of colour; besides which, as the Papacy was then not, as at present, ostensibly patient, but frankly militant, the drama filled the stage instead of going on, as we see it, behind the scenes. Our only gain, for the senses—putting aside the question of the gain, in each case, for the mind—is that the Pagan world has begun to bristle in proportion as the Christian has given ground. If there are fewer feasts of the Church—practically, that is, through curtailment and effacement; if the most ceremonial institution in the world has muffled itself in grey, there is, on the other hand, more of the recovered treasure of antiquity, a greater energy of excavation, a larger exploitation of that vast profane reliquary the packed and accumulated soil. The saints, the processions, the cardinals, all the Catholic pomp, have retired from the foreground, but the gods of Greece and of Rome, the statues of the heroes, the fragments of the temples, the rutted slabs of the old pavements, do what they can to occupy it, sharing it indeed with the polyglot people of the hotels, who, from year to year, are the steadily rising tide. The day is at hand, to all appearance, when it will be idle to talk of any foreground not constituted primarily by the Americans, the English, the Germans, made scarcely less alien by an admixture of Italian militarism; a menace the sharper, moreover, as any contingent is always free to ask when in the world Rome has *not* been a winter watering-place. Half the charm of the time we reach back to is in the fact that our friends of that time likewise, in their innocence, so viewed it; and we are doubtless rather arbitrary in preferring their innocence to ours. Since the question, however, is not so much of their merit as of their luck, we feel our discrimination not invidious.

I find much of the romance even in the scrappiest jottings in ink and pencil, the abbreviated memoranda, the snatches of small heartbreaking arithmetic, the suggested signs and sketches, of little old note-books, pocket *carnets* bought on the road but still lighting a little the old path, the old curiosities and felicities. They

were in Florence, the young Bostonians, between
their arrival at Genoa and their advance upon
Rome early in 1848, and it was during these few
weeks that, making the acquaintance of Robert
Browning and his wife, domiciled by the Arno
(first at Pisa) from the previous autumn, but not
for some months yet to be established at Casa
Guidi, they laid the foundation of the most interesting friendship of their lives. Story, in the
first flush of those perceptions and initiations
that regularly, for each of us, as we feel Italian
soil beneath our feet, promise to be infinite and,
for our individual development, epoch-making—
Story abounds in descriptions of pictures, statues,
museums, churches, and in enthusiasms, opinions,
disappointments, all the earnest discriminations
and ingenuous conclusions with which, inevitably
and blissfully, often funnily enough, his sense of
the general revelation was to be worked off. We
like, in faded records, the very mistakes of taste,
for they are what seems to bring us nearest to
manners, and manners are, changing or unchang-
ing, always most the peopled *scene*, the document
to be consulted, the presented image and beguiling subject. He goes to the Pitti Palace every
day, and responds, in his eagerness, to every
work on its walls. I like to look over his
shoulder, not because his judgments are rare—

for that, in him, for himself at least, would waste
time — but because they are delightedly usual.
"Allori's Judith.   This is the true original; a
fine sleepy-eyed, dark Jewish face, rich in colour;
yellow figured robes with white sleeves and white
mantle tied round the waist.   A fine handsome
face, but no Judith."   He was himself, later on,
to give the Judith he thought true; in prospect
of which, and of his monument to his father, he
indites a long note on Serravezza marble, through
which, as with a sense of something pleasantly
pathetic, we feel the state of eager amateurishness
to glimmer.   It is the first witnessed breath of his
long marmorean adventure.   "You must examine
with all your eyes every inch of all the surfaces
for flaws, holding your hand so as to regulate the
light, for sometimes, especially in sunlight, the
glare is such that unless moderated it may
deceive you."   And he puts down "178 frances-
coni, the price of a block of Maremma marble for
my statue."   He puts down prices, of other
matters, deliciously low; which is what I just
meant by his heart-breaking arithmetic.   It is
above all the terms on which the Italy of the old
order was so amply enjoyable that make us feel
to-day shut out from a paradise.   Out of one of
the books falls a little pale exotic card of 1847
—"F. Antonio Sasso.   Pittore al Olio e all'

Acquerelle, Negoziante di Quadri e di Mobilia Antica"—which evokes visions of bargains never to be recovered. Oh, for an hour, in the old Florentine street, of F. Antonio Sasso! *Sasso*, as we know, means a rock, but we feel the rock soften under pressure. We seem to see the good man arrive at the inn with a cinque-cento *cassone* on his back. When they travel they pay in pauls, and in admirably few; it reaches its climax at the hotel at Pisa, where Story notes *one* as bestowed upon "the man who ran somewhere." These charms are mixed, on the little pencilled page, with the verses that always flowed from him clearly and freely — verses mainly elegiac, with droll *charges* of Medici busts in Florence (say the portentous nose's end and underhung lip, like the semicircular basin beneath a water-tap, of Cosmo II.)

Mrs Story found in Rome, this and the following winter, the friend of Boston days, Margaret Fuller, whose incongruous marriage, at first, as would seem, rather awkwardly occult, had not yet offered her to the world, perhaps more awkwardly still, as Madame Ossoli; who, further, had secured and prepared apartments, and who, by this time, as a comparatively expert Roman, had, in addition to everything else, the value of a guide and introducer. At "everything

else," in this lady, it would also be interesting
to glance ; so that, space permitting, we must
not fail of the occasion.   Among the ghosts,
as I have called them, of the little related,
vanished world, none looks out at us more
directly and wistfully.   It was particularly
during the second winter, in presence of the
lamentable events of 1849, that she lived with
most zest her short hour ; as indeed it is with
these later months that the light notes before
me are most concerned.   It appears to have
been but by degrees that the Storys accepted
the inevitability of Rome rather than Florence,
for though they remained there through their
first spring, their return, on the next occasion,
was delayed to the end of the following February, after an autumn spent again in the little
Tuscan treasure-city.   The fullest compendium of
primary impressions is in a single spring-time
letter, which naturally reflects, more than anything else, the *obvious* of the traveller's view,
but reflects it with all the writer's talkative
emphasis.

W. W. Story to J. R. Lowell.

"Rome, *April 28th*, 1848.

"Dear James,—To-night, when the Girandola
should be, and is not, on account of rain, despite

utter fatigue of various kinds and a general
stupidity, I cannot help answering your letter.
. . . If I could sit down with you for an evening
and talk freely there are a many things, which I
could tell you, of some interest; but on paper
I can do nothing. There is here as much
humbug as anywhere in the world, and if you
come here you will enjoy laughing at your fellow-
creatures to your heart's content. All this week,
for instance, has been a series of the most consummate humbugs that it has been my fortune
to witness. Holy Week it has been, and all
sorts of ceremonies have been going on, most of
them senseless and superstitious, with a penny-
worth of religion to a ton of form. I have heroically done up the week, after crowding, pushing,
sweating and toiling day by day, and save some
one or two things the result has been 'bosh.'
I have seen the Pope wash the feet of twelve
fellows in white foolscaps, and at peril of my
life have obtained over the heads of a garlic-
smelling, fetid crowd a sight of the same august
person serving at the apostles' table twelve
fat fellows who eat away like mad and were
the only people in the room who at all enjoyed
the affair. It was with difficulty that the Pope
himself could keep his countenance while he was
performing this solemn farce, and every now and

then a grim smile would wrinkle up his features
despite his best endeavours.   Then again I have
seen the washing of the pilgrims' feet at the
Trinita dei Pellegrini, the pilgrims being without
exception the rummest set of customers I ever
saw, stupid, dirty and bestial in their appearance. . . . A crowd is always bad enough, but
an Italian crowd is of all the very worst.   Such
smells as are not to be imagined; asafœtida is
as Lubin's choicest perfume compared with ex-
halations fit to strike a strong man down.   And
amid this sweetness I have spent the better part
of the last seven days.   Some things there have
been beautiful and appealing.   To hear Allegri's
Miserere in the Sistine Chapel with the awful
and mighty figures of Michael Angelo looking
down on one from the ceiling, to hear Guglielmi's
Miserere in St Peter's while the gloom of evening
was gathering in the lofty aisles and shrouding
the frescoed domes, was no humbug, but a deeply
affecting and solemnly beautiful experience.
Never can one forget the plaintive wailing of
the voices that seemed to float in the air and
to implore pity and pardon.   Then, again, in
the illumination of St Peter's the architecture
seemed as if traced by a pencil of fire in the
blue dark firmament.   First it looked like a
dream, when it was covered with the lanterns

—the whole body of the church being lost and only the lines of light gleaming along the outlines and ribs and cornices. Then when the second illumination came it was like a huge jewelled tiara, the gems of which glittered in the air. Bah ! how can one give any idea of such a spectacle ? Imagine a swarm of enormous *cuculli* gathering round the dome, or the stars falling like a snow of fire and lodging in every nook, or recall every brilliant and magical and fantastic image that your dreams have ever given you, and describe it for yourself. These things were worth seeing and cannot be forgotten. Browning and his wife are now in Florence ; Ida Hahn-Hahn is in Naples, and we shall see her, I hope. I am now thinking of going there, but as the time draws near I hate the more to leave Rome, so utterly exhaustless is it, and so strongly have I become attached to it. How shall I ever again endure the restraint and bondage of Boston ? Still there are a great many things there which Italy has not and which are great and good ! There is life, and thought, and progress of ideas, and political liberty ! "

And I cannot do better than place here the letter his correspondent had addressed him a few weeks earlier. The joke of it is prolonged, but not beyond felicity. Miss F., with whom the writer couldn't away — a significant mark for Miss F.—was of course Margaret Fuller.

J. R. Lowell to W. W. Story.

"ELMWOOD, *March* 10*th*, 1848.

"MY DEAR WILLIAM,—I begin with a cheerful confidence as near the top of the page as I can, trusting that Providence will somehow lead me through my three pages to a triumphant ' yours truly' at the end. Emelyn writes in good spirits, but I cannot help suspecting a flaw somewhere. There must be not a little of the desolate island where S. M. F. is considered agreeable. It is hardly possible that pure happiness should exist so far from Cambridge. One needs not to go as far as Rome to find an attic, nor should I prefer an Italian clime to an American one. As for ruins, you have there, to be sure, plenty of them, the work of [undecipherable] and Goths and other people with whom you have nothing whatever to do. But here we have an excellent ruin on Mount Benedict which we made ourselves. And, if you mention political changes, Italy has been getting herself born again ever since I can remember, and will have to be delivered by a Cæsarian operation after all. Besides, have not we ours ?

It is not a week since Sidney Willard was elected
to our Cantabrigian Mayor's nest in place of
James D. Green. · Mr B. has been dismissed
from the office as field - driver. We have two
watchmen, who, I have no doubt, could put to
flight the Pope's whole civic guard. Deacon
Brown has retired from business. Will not all
these things be as important to the interests
of mankind a hundred years hence as that
Noodle VI. sits on the throne of the two Sicilies
or Loafer XXI. in the grand - ducal chair of
Florence ? If you have your Pio Nonos, we can
also boast our Tommy Nonose also, whom I meet
every time I go to the Athenæum.

"Emelyn talks of roses in blossom. For my
part I think them no better out of season than
green peas. I could never enter fully into these
thermometrical and meteorological satisfactions.
Have you had three weeks' sleighing ? Have
you had the thermometer at 14 below zero ?
Have you stored twenty thousand tuns of ice ?
I presume you have not even so much as an ice-
sickle to reap such a crop with. But I will not
triumph, seeing that these are things in which
I had no hand, and it is not your fault that
you have no winter. We are not without our
roses either, and the growth of the open air
too. You should see them in Maria's cheeks—

roses without a thorn, as St Basil supposes them
to have been in Eden. . . . I confess I never
had any great opinion of the ancient Romans.
They stole everything. They stole the land
they built the Eternal City on, to begin with.
Then they stole their wives, then their religion,
then their art. They never invented more than
one god of any consequence, as far as I know,
and he was a two-faced one, an emblem of the
treacherous disposition of the people. Niebuhr
has proved that they made up the only parts of
their history that are creditable to them. . . .
You may depend upon it that Americans will
be objects of suspicion there if there be any
outbreak of revolution. There are no warnings
round the streets, as in decent communities
where a Christian tongue is spoken, to 'Stick
no Bills here,' and you will doubtless be singled
out as an early victim. My advice to you is
to come directly home as soon as you receive
this. I have it on good authority that the
Austrian Government has its eye on Miss F.
It would be a pity to have so much worth
and genius shut up for life in Spielberg. Her
beauty might perhaps save her. Pio Nono also
regards her with a naturally jealous eye, fearing that the College of Cardinals may make
her the successor of Pope Joan.

"Mr Wetmore, I suppose, will bring you all the news, and I do not know anything to tell you except what he would not be likely to mention. Mr Palfrey has been shot in a duel with Mr Winthrop, and I have been elected to his seat in Congress. It is expected by my constituents that I should shoot Mr Winthrop, and I am accordingly practising every day with blank cartridges. Longfellow has written a poem which Sumner and Felton do *not* think superior to Milton. I have written one which has been popular. The American Eagle is anxiously awaiting the return of Miss F., whom he persists in regarding as the genius of Columbia. A public dinner is to be given her in Boston at which the Bird of our Country will preside. . . . Page has captivated all the snobs by the urbanity of his manners, and is fast making his fortune. To-day J. Q. Adams's body is received in Boston with great pomp. I am sorry that I cannot send you a programme of the procession, that you might show the Romans we can do a thing or two. The 'Eastern magnificence' of the theatres is nothing to it. The corpse will be followed by one consistent politician (if he can be found) as chief mourner. The procession will consist wholly of what the newspapers call 'unmingled' patriots, and will of course be very large. I have sent in a bale of moral pocket-handkerchiefs for the mourners and for wads to the cannon. The anti-slavery feeling of New England will bring up the rear of the cortége in a single carriage. There will be present on the occasion forty last survivors of the Boston Tea-party, and fifty thousand who were in the battle of Bunker's Hill. But it occurs to me that there may possibly be some kind of humbug in Rome also; so I will leave this part of my discourse and ask you what you do for cigars? I know that the Virginian nepenthe is so much esteemed there that one of the popular oaths is 'per Bacco!' but it does not follow that the plant is any better for being deified. I know that Vesuvius smokes, but do the people generally?"

The flight of Pius IX. to Gaeta and the establishment of the Roman Republic had marked the year of revolutions, for though these events belong to February 1849, it was the high political temperature of the previous months that had made them possible. When our friends reached the scene, for their second visit, a few weeks later, apparent order prevailed; but this was not long to last, and their predominant interests and emotions soon enough found a centre in that most incoherent birth of the time, the

advance of French troops for the restoration of
the Pope, the battle waged against the short-
lived "popular government" of Rome by the
scarce longer-lived popular government of Paris.
It was at this battle that foreign visitors "as-
sisted," as in an opera-box, from anxious Pincian
windows, and the brief diaries of Story and his
wife give us still the feeling of the siege. They
arrive in time to place themselves well, as it
were, for the drama, to get seated and settled
before it begins, and were afterwards, doubtless,
with whatever memories of alarm or discomfort,
to love their old Rome better, or at least know
her better, for having seen her at one of the
characteristically acute moments of her long-
troubled life. The flight of the Pontiff, the
tocsin and the cannon, the invading army, the
wounded and dying, the wild rumours, the flar-
ing nights, the battered walls, were all so much
grist to the mill of an artistic, a poetic nature,
curious of character, history, aspects. From
their arrival, March 2nd, at the Hôtel d'Angle-
terre, the moment was full of illustration. Their
felicity in this was greater than the comparatively small one with which, in years to come,
after alighting, for the first time, at the same
threshold, the writer of these lines, though gratefully enough indeed, had to content himself. I

remember of what good omen it seemed to me,
and how quite the highest possible note, that,
in 1869, touching the sacred soil at the end of
the old night-journey from Florence, then interminable and almost obligatory, I hurried out
heedless of breakfast and open-mouthed only for
visions; which promptitude was as promptly rewarded, on the adjacent edge of Via Condotti,
by the brightest and strangest of all, the vista
of the street suddenly cleared by mounted,
galloping, hand-waving guards, and then, while
every one uncovered and women dropped on
their knees, jerking down their children, the
great rumbling, black-horsed coach of the Pope,
so capacious that the august personage within—
a hand of automatic benediction, a large, handsome, pale old face, a pair of celebrated eyes
which one took, on trust, for sinister — could
show from it as enshrined in the dim depths
of a chapel.

I continue first, for a moment, however, to
weave matter for retrospective envy from the
indications of Story's second Florentine autumn;
making as I do, I fear, a positive fetish of the
fancy out of the image of that precious little
city as it might have been lived in and loved
before its modern misfortunes. I find I can live
in it again with any old ghost whatever who

will so much as hold out a finger. The adventures may be small, the gossip not great; but the precursors, as I have called them, muster in force, flitting across the page and catching the tender light. The page here, for instance, is Mrs Story's, who journalises with spirit. "In January one evening came the Cranches, and we sat over the fire and told stories, escaping, I believe, all dangerous topics, such as homœopathy and the respective attractions of New York and Boston. One longs for the "stories" that circulated in this conscious avoidance, and wonders whether they made them up as they went along, or plucked them, by the Florentine fire, as fine flowers of experience. The special experience of the Cranches, that comes back to me from later, from Parisian and other days, on lines of its own, bringing with it the conception of the somewhat melancholy blossom it might have yielded. Memory turns to *them*, indeed, as to precursors of the purest water, whose portion was ever to tread the path rather than to arrive at the goal. Christopher Pearse Cranch, painter, poet, musician, mild and melancholy humourist, produced pictures that the American traveller sometimes acquired and left verses that the American compiler sometimes includes. Pictures and verses had alike, in any case, the mark of his great, his

refined personal modesty; it was not in them at
least, for good or for ill, to emphasise or insist.
That was naturally—as always in such connections—much more the part of his graceful and
clever companion, who would have painted,
played and written with more effect than he,
had her hand been formed for the various im-
plements. There were those, in the general
company we are considering (as one now imagines
or recalls them), who didn't "go home," and
there were those who did; there were those who
wouldn't even if they could, and there were those
who couldn't even if they would. Each of these
classes still shines for me, thus late in the day,
with its special coloured light, but the light that
is softest and kindest, that most poetically veils
all plain particulars, hangs over the group last
mentioned. Some were not to come home, we
make out, till after death; they must have done
so—those who had most wanted it—then. The
Cranches came before, well before; which gave
them but the longer time to be sorry. Then
they could sit by New England fires and tell
stories, *not* made up, to good purpose. For there
were precursors, in those days, in the path of
regret, one might even say of repentance, quite
as in the path of curiosity and cheer. There
were experiments, all round, in every kind of

nostalgia, and those only, I daresay, who quite
escaped the disease were those who either never
"went" at all, or never came back.

Mrs Story, at all events, quits her friends to
repair, for some occasion, to Piazza Maria Antonia
—which again is a trifle that I respond to with
a thrill. Which of the new baptisms now covers
that sweeter identity? Not, indeed, that I
would for the world have the question answered
—leaving its pictorial virtue simply as a question
while we pass, an inexpensive tribute to the good
Grand Duke. The whole scene hangs together
—which is the pleasantness; everything is in
keeping with a proper honour to good Grand
Duchesses. Old Mrs Trollope, seeking a contrast, in a villa at Bellosguardo, from those
Domestic Manners of the Americans which she
had not long before so luridly commemorated,
comes, indulgently, to call; after which our
friends attend "skaiting" on the ice outside one
of the gates. They do the most usual things
—except for the skating—and it is not our fault
if, after all, these should affect us, absurdly, as
the most desirable. Never was the spell of
desire less elaborately produced. They go to
the Pergola Theatre, to a concert "for the benefit
of the Venetians." Which of us, in Florence,
at that time, wouldn't have done anything, with

passion, for the benefit of the Venetians? "The
Barbiere sung, the crowd enormous, with a
staring man in front of us, and Rossini enthusi-
astically called forth." Story meanwhile has of
course a studio, where he is modelling hard, and
his wife, sitting with him as he works, reads
aloud Monckton Milnes's Life of Keats, lent by
Browning. They go to the Pergola again and,
during the ballet, make a sortie to F. B.'s rooms
and have time to sup and come back to the
theatre before the opera begins again. Happy
days, happy nights, happy F. B., above all, thus
gallantly entertaining, and whose benignant
identity—earliest of all precursors, most grand-
ducal of Florentines, and still [1] living in honoured
and cherished age—it is all I can do to resist
the impulse to unveil. If I succeed at all, just
here, it is by reason of the great incident, on this
same occasion, of the sudden reappearance of
Frank Heath, of whom we shall hear more, who
multiplies my Franks, and yet to whom, as he
is more thrust upon me, though I happen to
know little about him, I cannot deny room.
Neither indeed, on the other hand, I must add,
can I to any extent offer it, since prompt reflection warns me off the subject. I could track
Frank Heath—I find myself quite yearning to

[1] 1903.

do it; but I let him pass (with the mild light of accident in which, as I say, we shall yet see him) lest, precisely, he should too much beckon us on. I could track him, for instance, with the aid of F. B., rich in that order of information, and who is enviably sure to have known him; and if I stay my hand it is not from fear of disappointment. It is from the sense, to be perfectly candid, that I am in danger, as it is, of starting but too many hares, and of their perhaps being pronounced, after all, inconsiderable game. I find one, at all events, in every bush, seeming to hear them rise with each turn of my small bescribbled leaves.

Mrs Story drives daily, for her pleasure, in the Cascine and elsewhere, with "kind Mrs Greenough," whom we should have thought of, for genial convenience, in Florence at least, as the wife of the *other* sculptor. The Americans of the profession were already several; yet of how many, even in Rome, at that time, were we to come to speak as the "others"? There were the names that one was brought up to—one of which, for reasons I now wonder at, but do not quite seize, was not that of Powers, and this in spite of the Greek Slave, so undressed, yet so refined, even so pensive, in sugar-white alabaster, exposed under little domed glass covers in such American homes as could bring themselves to think such things right. Crawford, in Rome, who was to transmit his name to so distinguished an association in another art, was essentially, on the spot, one of the others; but Crawford was, tragically, to die young, and, as Greenough was to do the same, the period of the two "others" was practically over, for Rome, by the time Story came to the front. There were, in a sense, numerous others, as I say, of both sexes—most of all, at one time, surprisingly, not of the sex of Phidias. Horatio Greenough, as I read the story, was at that time, at the invitation of the Washington Government, adding to monumental work already supplied to the Capitol. No group more than that of the Greenoughs, in any case—for they too were several—falls into step with our procession; lovers of all the arts, and of Italy, all of them; such persistent Florentines, in fact, that old houses by the Arno, old villas on the cypress-planted hills above it, are still haunted with their name. If we start another hare—one at the very least— when, in these weeks, Mrs Story goes to Casa Guidi to lend Mrs Browning her copy of "Jane Eyre," we feel that the game is on this occasion, all round, large enough. We also feel, with philosophic detachment at this time of day, that the volume, almost certainly of the American pirated

form, would have been contained in one of the
parcels arriving from Boston "per *Nautilus*," the
blessed little New England sailing - ship of the
time before tariffs, which, coming straight to
Leghorn, makes our friends, as they note, feel
nearer "home" than anything had yet done.
But they were well away from home again, we
must assume, when, according to Mrs Story, they
"went to Mrs Trollope's to see the fancy dresses
for the ball at Sir George Hamilton's. A strange
show of the shell without the soul to animate it
—a dull, heavy set of people enough!" They
were not less so, obviously, when, at the Cocomero Theatre, with Frank Heath and Frank
Boott — the latter name *will* out! — they see
Ristori "in a thrilling play of Scribe's." They
were always seeing Ristori, the Ristori of the rich
and various early period and of the yet merely
local reputation, and seeing her as youth and
gaiety and happy comradeship see. The play of
Scribe's, in this golden light, was "thrilling," and
we wonder, in the age of criticism, which it was.
It could only have been, I surmise, "Adrienne
Lecouvreur," shortly before produced in Paris.
There were other occasions when the play,
"written by a Genoese, was miserable, but
Ristori's acting very fine." Who of us wouldn't
have faced the miserable play to see the *young*

Ristori ?—who must have been, in the pride of her prime, a personality, as we nowadays say, quite by herself. "Written by a Genoese" has, moreover, a suspicious sound — perhaps it was only the grand Tuscan contempt, so easy, in Florence, to imbibe. The day was at any rate then distant (as it is now, alas! distant again) when another imbiber, on the same spot, now speaking for himself, was to see the great actress, even then no longer young—*altro!*—offer, on a wintry night, Mme. de Girardin's irrevivable "Lady Tartuffe," with supreme "authority," to some fifteen spectators.

That the year was, at the end of 1848 and the beginning of 1849, still that of revolutions was apparent enough, in a quasi-comfortable, semi-sociable fashion, even in the streets of Florence, where the beating of the *generale*, the ringing of bells, the prevalence of "confusion," the making, in short, of history didn't prevent repeated visits to the Cocomero and then "supper, after much seeking, at a *trattoria* in Via Vaccasecca." We enjoy with them, to this hour, the much seeking; we take from them, if we have a glimmer of fancy, the dim little image of their hunting up their little refreshment together, a company of laughing artists, of hungry exiles, of women young and charming, through

the old Florentine streets, where the lighting, as
well as almost everything else, was still scarce
more than medieval. The confusion of the days
indeed overflowed a little, on occasion, into the
evenings, for it befalls them to see "a stupid
tragedy, which was finally hissed down." It
would have been interesting to see, even amid
civic strife, the Ristori—if it *was* she—finally
hissed down. There were at other times other
lurid things—"The 'Duchesse de Praslin' was
acted. It was awful." The Duc de Praslin—if
our generation be oblivious—had done his wife to
death with knives, in her bedroom of the Fau-
bourg Saint-Honoré, and we were, in America,
even to the listening ears of tender childhood,
talking it over the more generally from the fact
that an innocent witness of the drama, a lady
domiciled with the tragic pair, fleeing after the
trial and the catastrophe, the murderer's suicide
in prison, from the great horror, had lately taken
refuge among us. Admirable surely, for appreciative näiveté, that prompt theatric sense of the
monstrous actual, among the Italians, which leads
them to clap upon the stage, with abounding
facility and, as we see, "awful" effect, the leading crimes of the hour.

There was always meanwhile, nearer home,
plenty of contemporary history. "In the after-

noon we went to San Miniato, but were obliged
to climb upon the wall to look upon the city, not
being allowed to enter the fortress on account
of the Revolution." Delightful Revolution,
which, we seem to see, promoted afternoon
drives and friendly parleys; promoted the sweetness of the little treasure-city as seen, from
above, nestling in her cup of hills; promoted
again, at night, the indispensable Cocomero,
where the great Modena, master of our Salvini,
was admirable as Luigi Undici. Leghorn was
in mild revolt, as to which Mrs Browning had
written to Miss Mitford from Casa Guidi in
October: "The child's play between the Livor-
nese and our Grand Duke provokes a thousand
pleasantries. Every now and then a day is
fixed for a revolution in Tuscany, but up to
the present time a shower has come and put
it off. Two Sundays ago Florence was to have
been 'sacked' by Leghorn, when a drizzle came
and saved us." Mrs Browning thirsted for
great events, but the Storys were less strenuous
and took things as they came. The weather,
in any case, with the turn of the year, had
been finer, for Florence had by that time put
down her foot on the question of a Constitution.
She has her Constitution now to her heart's
content. Story and his wife prepared, late in

February, to leave her very unsuccessfully
getting it, but they had before their departure
for Rome, on the 20th of the month, " a long
quiet evening with the Brownings." As to this
impression Mrs Story, for the moment, does
not otherwise journalise ; but she startles us
a little by overflowing, in however few words,
in another connection. They had been leaving
cards of farewell at various houses and " considered that we had done our duty by Florentine
society—which strikes us as worth very little
consideration. Vulgar and ignorant people."
We should write history, we should read it,
but ill if we didn't yearningly wonder what
people in particular she meant. For we drop
of a sudden from the golden dream. Were
there vulgar and ignorant people anywhere,
were there, most of all, such there, even *then?*
However, the touch is a discrimination, and
discrimination—which is nothing but curiosity
on the way to satisfaction — is the breath
of history. History continues to sweep our
friends along ; they go to Leghorn by rail on
February 23rd, and, starting at three o'clock
in the afternoon, arrive by half-past six ; which
was by no means bad for grand-ducal antiquity
—was indeed quite as good as to-day. It is
a point over which history seems for the instant

to pause, and the paternal, the patriarchal potentate expelled by too rash a population to give us, from among the shades, a reproachful, pathetic look. Yet it is only for the moment; the Muse, jerking us on by the hand we grasp, tosses an uncompromising head. Against Leghorn, afresh, we are invited to discriminate; against Leghorn, where we read of " a long stupid walk. The weather glorious, like summer; but the people here, even in their festa-day attire, look like pickpockets, knaves and fools. The women *mere* fools." The hotel and their quarters are bad; everything fails. " No boat! no books! no fire! And very little dinner. No prospect of relief from this purgatorial environment." Relief comes, however, they thank the Fates, who send along on March 1st a French mail-steamer for Civita Vecchia—their "third visit to this interesting port." After which : " Rome, Rome, Rome ! The dome of St Peter's is again actually before us, a fairer vision on this second than on our first seeing. How true a joy as we drove through the gates!"

Margaret Fuller, again, on the morrow, joins them in a search for rooms, and they are established that evening in quarters in the Porta Pinciana—the steep, the amiable, the so famil-

iarly Roman Porta Pinciana of the old days,
where at present ghosts again hover, but where,
anciently, the models, all beauty and costume,
all varnished eyes and daggered hair and swathed
legs and peaked hats, all attuned to the good old
romantic note, clustered thick, and the staircases,
on which you brushed by them as you went and
they gloomed at you for a painter indifferent to
their merits, opened upon who can say at this
time what scraps of Roman view, what glimpses
of yellow loggia, what patches of morning sunshine and of perfect Pincian blue? Our friends
breakfast immediately with the Crawfords at
Villa Negroni, where the irrepressible Margaret
again joins them. What has become of Villa
Negroni, dim, denied, engulfed, more or less,
to a certainty now, but where three small in-
habitants, dedicated each, by the admirable scene
itself, as we make out, to distinction, grew up,
or at least began to, and laid up memories?
Nothing will induce me, however, to insist on
an answer to my question; one must never, in
Rome at this hour, for penalties and pangs, insist on such answers. There were two little
girls of the villa, and there was one brought to
play, and *she* remembers well how they picked
up bitter oranges in the alleys to pelt each other
with. Thirty years ago, and later, in any case,

the place was there still, but with that indescribable golden air about it (according to my faded
impression) of a paradise closed and idle, where
the petals of the Roman roses in the spring, all
ungathered, might be thick on the Roman walks,
where happiness unmistakably *had* been.   Mrs
Story makes on March 11th the prettiest little
entry.   "To walk with William and Frank
[Heath] round the Prætorian Camp—after having had the usual difficulty in determining where
to go.   Thence to a grassy hillside, whence W.
made a sketch of old Rome as seen through an
ivied arch ; and afterwards to St John Lateran,
where we walked about the church and went
into the vault under the Corsini Chapel.   Coming home by the Coliseum we met the Crawfords.
Oh, golden day !"   She goes on the next "with
Mrs Crawford to buy Roman scarfs in Piazza
Madama."   Roman scarfs, and in Piazza Madama
—exactly the right place : it is as if they had
done it on purpose that we should, at the end of
time, find it quaint, archaic, delightfully *vieux
jeu* and of a touching good faith.

What completes it, however, is the sequel,
than which nothing could be more in the right
note.   "After which tea at the Cropseys', with
a Pulcinello representation" by two of the gentlemen present.   History has these inventions,

which fiction tries for and misses. For who indeed are ghosts, however thin, if not, precisely, the Cropseys?—thin, thin, and yet once thick enough, as thick as the luscious paint itself on those canvases, all autumnal scarlet, amber, orange, which were not the least of the glories of the "Hudson River school." That was an age in which American artists yielded to the natural impulse to paint American scenery—when they didn't paint Roman, and when no subject for landscape art was deemed superior to the admirable native "fall." The only question is of what the Cropseys can have been doing by the bare banks of Tiber; true as it yet may be that even in such presences the kindly old traffic in American effects drew support from the frequent nostalgia of the American absentee. Certain it is, however, that, on the evening in question, with Pulcinello and Roman tea, the Cropseys had every reason *not* to foresee a strange time when their country would bristle, to the exclusion of almost everything else, with pictures of little flat fields, little stiff poplars, little grey skies, the little homely, sober facts of France, products of a palette not to be recognised by any Cropsey *as* a palette. The vivid native palette, prepared for so ample a range, where were they to see it hung up, and, above all, *why* were they ? If the answer belongs to the history of taste, that makes this history (what it has always been) but the more thrilling. To live over people's lives is nothing unless we live over their perceptions, live over the growth, the change, the varying intensity of the same—since it was *by* these things they themselves lived. When and how, therefore, did the generations perceive that the Cropseys, generically speaking, wouldn't do? When and how, still more, did they begin to perceive that the Hudson River wouldn't, and doesn't?—that is if it be indeed true that the discovery has been made. The appearance rests upon every one's behaving as if it had. The fond inquiry would be (in the interest, as I say, of living over people's perceptions) as to how such things take place, as to how such dramas, as it were, with all the staked beliefs, invested hopes, throbbing human intensities they involve in ruin, enact themselves. Only this, really, is starting too great a hare ; and all we need feel is that, for the moment, in the little circle of easy artistry and sociability, both abroad and at home, the complication had yet not come.

It suffices that there are no complications, none at least obvious, in the scene before us, which is all friendly Campagna sunshine and Pincian

candlelight, intermixed indeed always, with the
smoky theatric lamp; no false note, I mean, but
the growing, yet not importunate, political. Our
friends are under the Republic, but they have
other things to think of; unless, say, when they
go to the Chamber of Deputies to hear Mazzini
speak. They do the regular old pleasant things
in the regular old confident ways; at the Rospigliosi Casino first, to see Guido's "Aurora,"
and then to the Barberini Palace, unconscious as
yet of their eventual long installation there, to
guess the strange riddle that the Cenci asks over
her shoulder. On the evening of this occasion,
at the Argentina, they listened, with Margaret
and her Ossoli, to "Beatrice di Tenda." They
had pleasures, provably, that we have lost.
"Beatrice di Tenda" is never offered us, and no
more, with any assurance, in the coved and gilded
ceiling, are the fair academic Sun-god and the
academic parti - coloured Hours. The Cenci of
course—the other Beatrice—has, as an occasion
for melting moments, been positively removed
from the feast; with the added objection for us
of our having to know that our prolonged sentimental consumption of the tenderest morsel, as
we have mostly felt it, in all pictorial portraiture
was, all the while, the act of eating (to maintain
my metaphor) one thing for another. We suc-

ceed to generations replete with Guido's tearful
turbaned parricide, but are ourselves never
honestly to taste of her more, inasmuch as,
tearful and turbaned as she is, she is proved,
perversely, *not* a parricide, or at least not the one
we were, in tourist's parlance, "after." These,
fortunately, were disconcertments not dreamed
of when, for instance, on March 24th, our kindly
diarist "went home with Margaret and sat with
her in her quiet little upper chamber all the
evening. W. came for me, and we stayed until
a late hour of the night." The unquestionably
haunting Margaret-ghost, looking out from her
quiet little upper chamber at her lamentable
doom, would perhaps be never so much to be
caught by us as on some such occasion as this.
What comes up is the wonderment of *why* she
may, to any such degree, be felt as haunting;
together with other wonderments that brush us
unless we give them the go-by. It is not for
this latter end that we are thus engaged at all;
so that, making the most of it, we ask ourselves how, possibly, in our own luminous age,
she would have affected us on the stage of the
" world," or as a candidate, if so we may put it,
for the cosmopolite crown. It matters only for
the amusement of evocation — since she left
nothing behind her, her written utterance being

naught; but to what would she have corresponded, have "rhymed," under categories actually known to us? Would she, in other words, with her appetite for ideas and her genius for conversation, have struck us but as a somewhat formidable bore, one of the worst kind, a culture-seeker without a sense of proportion, or, on the contrary, have affected us as a really attaching, a possibly picturesque New England Corinne?

Such speculations are, however, perhaps too idle; the *facts* of the appearance of this singular woman, who would, though conceit was imputed to her, doubtless have been surprised to know that talk may be still, after more than half a century, made about her—the facts have in themselves quite sufficient colour, and the fact in particular of her having achieved, so unaided and so ungraced, a sharp identity. This identity was that of the talker, the moral *improvisatrice*, or at least had been in her Boston days, when, young herself, she had been as a sparkling fountain to other thirsty young. In the Rome of many waters there were doubtless fountains that quenched, collectively, any individual gush; so that it would have been, naturally, for her plentiful life, her active courage and company, that the little set of friends with whom we are

concerned valued her.   She had bitten deeply
into Rome, or, rather, *been*, like so many others,
by the wolf of the Capitol, incurably bitten ; she
met the whole case with New England arts that
show even yet, at our distance, as honest and
touching ; there might be ways for her of being
vivid that were not as the ways of Boston.
Otherwise what she would mainly prompt us to
interest in might be precisely the beautiful moral
complexion of the little circle of her interlocutors.
That is ever half the interest of any celebrated
thing—taking Margaret's mind for celebrated :
the story it has to tell us of those for whom it
flourished and whose measure and reflection it
necessarily more or less gives.   Let us hasten to
add, without too many words, that Mme. Ossoli's
circle represented, after all, a small stage, and
that there were those on its edges to whom she
was not pleasing.   This was the case with Lowell
and, discoverably, with Hawthorne ; the legend
of whose having had her in his eye for the
figure of Zenobia, while writing "The Blithedale
Romance," surely never held water.   She inspired
Mrs Browning, on the other hand, with sympathy
and admiration, and the latter, writing of her in
1852, after the so lamentable end of her return-
voyage, with her husband and child, to America
—the wreck of the vessel, the loss of father,

mother and small son in sight of shore—says
that "her death shook me to the very roots of
my heart. The comfort is," Mrs Browning then
adds, "that she lost little in the world — the
change could not be loss to her. She had suffered,
and was likely to suffer still more." She had
previously to this, in December 1849, spoken of
her, in a letter to Miss Mitford, as having "taken
us by surprise at Florence, retiring from the
Roman world with a husband and child above a
year old. Nobody had even suspected a word of
this underplot, and her American friends stood in
mute astonishment before this apparition of them
here. The husband is a Roman marquis appearing amiable and gentlemanly, and having fought
well, they say, at the siege, but with no pretension to cope with his wife on any ground apper-
taining to the intellect." The "underplot" was
precisely another of the personal facts by which
the lady could interest—the fact, that is, that
her marriage should *be* an underplot, and that
her husband, much *decaduto*, should make explanation difficult. These things, let alone the
final catastrophe, in short, were not talk, but life,
and life dealing with the somewhat angular
Boston sibyl on its own free lines. All of which,
the free lines overscoring the unlikely material,
is doubtless partly why the Margaret-ghost, as

I have ventured to call it, still unmistakably walks the old passages.

But I have given perhaps undue extension to Mrs Story's brief entries; each of which remains, none the less, a touch for the conceived picture. They drive, our friends, out to the Fair at Grotta Ferrata, taking their dinner with them, and see—well, indubitably see a great deal that is to be seen no more. One desires to miss no moment of it. They pursue a particular view, but to get at it "were forced to pass through a house and go out upon a little terrace built over the walls of the town." We warrant indeed they were, and we pass through the house with them and also go out on the terrace, lingering even longer than they, thinking of many things, having to make an effort, positively, to come back again and overtake them on another occasion; the day—namely, March 26th—when, at the Baths of Caracalla, they "passed one of the happiest, balmiest, serenest afternoons that ever came to man even under an Italian sky." After dining at the Unione, the day following, they go to the Metastasio and see (they honestly lack for nothing) Molière's "Tartuffe." They seem to dine most nights at the Unione; so that where, which, in the name of forsaken beliefs and impossible loyalties, *was* the Unione,

at which we never can dine? April 7th is, as
a day, "glorious," and they drive out, early,
to the Fountain of Egeria. "Spent the day
in and about the Sacred Grove"—and they make
no more of it, for the irritated ache in us, than
that. *Such* a spending of days!—all the more
that, before it ends, there is more Piazza Madama, there are more Roman scarfs, during the
dramatic purchase of which I press them close,
treading upon the ladies' heels, crowding with
them into the low-browed old-time shop. The
next day, the 8th, is Easter Sunday, with but
a first allusion to the political regimen, which
did not affect, after all, either the charm of the
Fountain of Egeria or the treasures of Piazza
Madama. Our friends have seen the Easter
ceremonies at St Peter's the other time, the
previous year, "when the Pope was here"—
Pio Nono, penitent Liberal, being still at Gaeta
—and care little to see them again with a republican sauce. The great Ristori is, on the
other hand, by this time restored to them, and
they applaud her first appearance, for the season,
in Rome. The play, by Scribe, was "harrowing,
but not good": in respect to which, mystified
once more by the odd description, we yield again
to sympathetic curiosity; most of Scribe's plays
having, precisely, *been* "good" in the good old

sense—too good, in fact, in that beatific sense,
to harrow. However, we should ourselves doubtless, all the same, and with Ristori to help, have
been duly dealt with. They do at last enter
St Peter's, in spite of the Republic, but on their
own terms. "Went up into the ball on top of
the dome and there sat and heard the wind
roar." Story, in a vivid letter, as we shall see,
makes ingeniously much of this. April 21st,
Mrs Story notes, is, with the firing of cannon
and the ringing of bells, "the anniversary of
the natal day of Rome"; which is pleasantly
puzzling (though all in the key of the confused
booming and parading, the sunny flag-flapping
and balcony speech-making, that attends short
spring-time revolutions), inasmuch as the pro-
clamation of the Republic, which is what is
suggested, dated but from February 8th previous.

They go, at all events, to see the troops reviewed by General Avezzana in Piazza San
Pietro, and are afterwards, interestedly enough,
in the church. "Blind boy brought up to kiss
St Peter's toe; his heavenly expression went to
my heart—an expression I shall never forget and
that I would often recall." They lunch in the
"queer old *trattoria* at Monte Mario"—which is
again a pang; there having been no queer old
trattoria there, that I remember, in *our* time,

though doubtless there is a queer enough new one now. On April 25th Margaret came in to tell them "that all Rome was in a state of excitement, the news that the French had landed at Civita Vecchia having been received. We went with her to Piazza del Popolo to hear the addresses made to the people, and there we met, standing on a bench, the Princess Belgiojoso." But it all winds up again, for the evening, with Ristori in another play by Scribe. On the 29th, however, the plot once more thickens, and they go to watch the barricade-making at Porta San Giovanni, where they "vote the workmen too lazy to live." But this is doubtless all the better for Story, who, studious of movement and attitude, sits and sketches the scene from a pile of timber "destined to be used in the defence." They find, going home, great agitation in the streets ; they see the Lombard reinforcements enter—Milan having had, before this, its own short, smothered outbreak—and they walk about the city to look at the various barricades. The approach of the French, to reinstate the Pope, becomes a reality ; on the 30th General Oudinot and his army were hourly expected.

"All the streets have been deserted, and as we walked this morning through the Babuino we were forcibly struck by the pause and hush of everything, the lull of the city as before the storm presently to fall upon it. It was as if the hour had come, and one could only pray for safe deliverance. We met on our way the terrified H., who urged us to remove to Casa Dies, whither he proposed to summon all Americans and place them under protection of our flag. While we were walking home we heard the first cannon and went quickly to move the children to Casa Dies, whence we have been seeing the whole battle. All day long the great interest and excitement continue. The house was filled with Americans, and as Frank Heath's rooms, which we had taken possession of, commanded the finest view, they all flocked thither. Margaret Fuller, who had been at the hospital, came to tell us about the wounded, of whom there were already seventy. At five o'clock, as the firing seemed to have abated, we went to the Pincio, whence we could see that the French had moved their position and, having been repulsed at Porta Cavallaggieri, were now before the Vatican gardens. The streets were kept lighted all night and all things prepared for a night attack. Rumours of all sorts were flying about and many persons greatly alarmed. We remained at Casa Dies, as our own house was cut off from the rest

of the city by a barricade which would be disagreeable in case of an attack.   We kept looking
at the watch-fires of the enemy as they blazed in
the distance, and we got little sleep."

And Mrs Story's notes go on. On May 1st
" the French have retreated ; saw through the
glass a slight skirmish, but it was so distant we
couldn't make it out. Rumour that the Neapolitans are at Albano or Velletri. A glorious
day indeed. Margaret came in as we were at
breakfast. All is so unsettled about us that we
can do nothing but talk and speculate, wish good
to the Romans and ill to the French. Frank
Heath went to the Hospital with Margaret and
returned so full of interest and sympathy that
he at once set on foot a subscription." On May
2nd, " as we had determined to take rooms permanently in Casa Dies, we packed up all our
goods in our old quarters and made good our
retreat. We went with Margaret to the Pellegrini Hospital and gave our money, some 225
dollars, to Princess Belgiojoso. Then we went
to Spillman's to get ice for the Princess, and
while there saw the burning of a cardinal's carriage, the blaze quite lighting up the front of
the Propaganda." On the following day, the
mother notes, their first little boy, whom they

were to lose early and inconsolably, was two years old. They go to the Vatican gardens "to see Ossoli," engaged there in the defence ; and they "walked along the wall and saw the posts of the Guard who had fought so well, and the ground held by the French. As we looked from the wall this the third day after the battle we saw the monks under the black flag looking for the unburied dead who had fallen in the ditches or among the hedges. The French had retreated without an effort to bury their dead, and in one instance a living wounded man was found on this third day with the bodies of two dead soldiers lying across him." The entry is mutilated; she goes on, "Let no one say that the Romans did not" — but it breaks off; it is evidently some good word for the dear old Romans. On the 4th, however : "A continued suspension of all sorts of business. The Neapolitans, *si dice*, are still at Albano, and Garibaldi has gone to meet them "—the Neapolitans being the troops despatched by King Bomba to the aid of the French, and whose virtue, for this particular purpose, was subsequently to be questioned. Our friends settle definitely at Casa Dies, Margaret joining them, and they dine together — that is with Frank Heath and her ; "dinner sent in from a *cucina*. Pleasant days and evenings; the weather cloudless; our balcony, which overlooks the city, a rich source of interest." Margaret's personal situation, it comes to us, must have been more or less of the same; as I may mention that on the occasion, just recorded, of their going to see the martial Ossoli in the gardens of the Vatican, we have it that a relative, who was with them and who appears to have been either too much or too little informed, took the odd line of not giving the lady in question "a chance to say anything of a private nature" to the gallant volunteer. The sense of things of a private nature was unmistakably in the air.

However, these are swallowed up in things of a public when, on May 5th, Story goes to see Mazzini, who gives an order for a guard in their house in case of trouble. Thus they seem, gathered together, to wait; and it is always interesting to learn how besieged persons do wait. "Salad-making and conversation" is one of their resources, and, on their adjourning to the apartments of a friend in the same caravansary, "some very bad music." One likes every little fact of these abnormal hours, every characteristic detail. "We need not even take a walk, for the gardens of the Quirinal stretch out before us, and the footing in the streets

is most unpleasant, as they have all been strewn
with gravel, so that the cavalry may not slip."
On the 7th there is "moonlight, which we spent
on our balcony, talking, dreaming, listening to
the distant city sounds." On the 10th comes
news of the defeat of the Neapolitans by Garibaldi. " This infused new courage and zeal
into the minds of the Romans. *Generale* beaten
in the streets, as the French were said to be
coming on." They walked that afternoon, in
spite of this alarm, on the Pincian and turn
" heart-sick " from the sight of the destruction
of numbers of the fine trees in Villa Borghese,
hewn down, for the construction of defences,
to their stumps. They go on the morrow to
St Peter's, "just after sunset, as a sombre shade,"
Mrs Story mentions, " was settling in its aisles
and hiding all its ornaments, so that the great
lines of its architecture were all we felt and
saw. Never had I seen it so impressively,
wonderfully beautiful. We were there quite
by ourselves, and wandered silently about, subdued by the presence of some deep spiritual
influence. But at length we were called from
our reveries by the custode, who invited us to
leave before the church was closed for the night.
Then I bade it a final farewell. I felt this
to be my last visit, at least for many years.

And although I did again go, it was not in
the spirit, for then I heard a chant and saw
some mummery or other which could not move
my soul. This was the hour of my parting
from that which, next to the deep heart of
nature as seen in sacred spots, has had power
to move me." They are on the eve of departure,
and they begin to circulate again, see Modena
once more as a Louis XI. Italianised from
Casimir Delavigne, just as Casimir's figure had
been Gallicised from Walter Scott's. They walk
afresh on the Pincian and see the French en-
camped near Monte Mario. Then, on the 19th,
they effect an oddly timed sortie, driving to
Tivoli through Porta San Giovanni, and with
Avezzana's pass carrying them " through the
guards and over the flower - covered dewy
Campagna." They have chosen the occasion
but for an excursion and are in Rome again
on the 21st. " Ossoli came in the evening,
one of the last sad days in Rome." They get
off on the 24th, sleeping that night at Civita
Castellana. " Passed by the French camp at
the foot of Monte Mario, and under our white
flag had no trouble." They take their way
past Narni, Terni, Spoleto, Foligno, where the
hotels are filled with officers ; and through
Perugia, where they lodge " in an old palace,

the remains of splendour still lingering about
it," and sleep "in a state bed under a canopy
of crimson damask." On May 30th at Incisa,
while they were breakfasting, "we were called
to the window to see the Austrian troops pass
on their way to Perugia. A whole battalion,
whose stony, solid aspect quite made us tremble
for the fate of poor Rome."

At Florence, on the 31st, they "found Austrian
officers at the gates, whom we at once recognised
as such by their be-braided coats. . . . Florence
seemed less agreeable than when we left it even,
for the streets were filled with Austrian troops
and officers. The poor extinct *guardia civica*
was hiding its diminished head, and of all the
noise and bustle we had heard during the winter,
the talk of heroic resistance, fighting to the death,
'viva la Repubblica,' nothing remained, scarcely
the memory of it. The heat was overpowering
and Doney's and ices our only resource." They
see a review of the Austrian troops in the Cascine
by Radetzky. They bear hard upon Florence—
"in all our last summer's experience of the heat
at Sorrento we had nothing like this. In the
winter we froze here, in the summer we bake."
Things had gone ill with the Florentine Liberals,
and they find them rather abject. The Grand
Duke had been invited to depart, and had de-

parted, and then had been invited to return, and
had returned, or was just about to, the Austrian
ascendancy, with plenty of bayonets, having prevailed. The bayonets embraced the occasion of
the procession of Corpus Domini to show "the
trembling Florentines their superior drill. . . .
Florence appears to us now so fallen and abject
in her cringing submission to them that we can
feel no interest in her, and long to breathe a
freer air. Looking back at Rome we can't but
make the comparison unfavourable to Florentine
valour—and tell them of it too." After which
pardonably Parthian shot Mrs Story's animated
diary records their departure, by the middle of
June, for Bologna and their subsequent stop at
Modena, where the picture of Rogers's Ginevra,
ostensibly to be seen, sadly fades away from them
under the affirmation of the *valet-de-place* that
it is "the fiction of a poet." By Piacenza and
Lodi they reach Milan, where I pause with them
to avail myself of the fact that Story, meanwhile,
during their Roman days, had been memorising not
less sharply, as well as more copiously, than his
wife. Do we not already find in these unstudied
images of the siege and of the road, terrorised by
foreign troops, something of the poetry of

> " Old forgotten far-off things,
> And battles long ago " ?

This chronicler, at all events, desiring to miss no impression, since, evidently, to a sharpened appetite for figures and scenes, there was matter for impression—this chronicler trudges by the old travelling-carriage as it climbs the Umbrian hills, hangs about the inn doors, with the ear ringed *vetturino*, at Narni and Spoleto, at Incisa and Perugia, and wouldn't, frankly, for such sense as we may get from it to-day, have had a single Austrian officer absent or heard a scabbard the less trail along a stone-paved passage. I even retrace our steps, without scruple, to pick up any loose flower of this blood-spattered Roman spring that may be to our purpose.

Story had begun to journalise from the moment of their return to Rome, and is full of ideas and emotions about everything, of happy æsthetic response and expression. " I could not help thinking as we passed the Tiber " —at the end of March—" how like it was to the Italian character; turbulent without depth, violent and turbid in its current, full of whirl-pools, narrow, overflowing constantly its banks, subject to great rises and great depressions, and having at bottom unknown riches and precious things concealed by its violence and muddiness." He was to probe much further, before he had done with it, this particular

mystery, and, though not perhaps the most
patient of explorers, in any direction — rather
the most alert and confident—to learn as much
as he desired, before he had done, about the
Italian character. " In the evening I heard
some truly noble music at Charles Perkins's;
the grand septuor by Beethoven, which is enough
to move the heart of a rock, so deep and
exquisite and yearning. And a very beautiful
trio by Hummel, solid and various and noble.
To recline on a sofa and look at the frescoes
by which I was surrounded, and, with a cigar
breathing about its aromatic smoke, to listen to
the divine outpourings of the grandest music,
is a paradise of sensuous and spiritual delight."
An entry which has none the less sweetness
for us from its playing its faint lantern (as of
candlelight very especially, this time, in old
saloons) over one of the most appealing of our
ghosts. A master of all the amenities, an accomplished student of Italian art, the author
of the " Tuscan Sculptors," which was to be
long the prime authority on its subject, Charles
Perkins lives for us again both in such echoes
as these—echoes of hospitalities to which other
associated figures, those of his friendly house,
gave character and colour — and in the unfor-
gotten harshness of premature and accidental

death. "The news arrives to-day," Story immediately goes on (April 1st), "of Charles
Albert's utter defeat at Novara, with the
flight, on the first fire, of 1500 Lombards and
the loss of everything. These are terrible
news. The Piedmontese fought well, it is said,
but it is loudly asserted that Carlo Alberto
never meant to conquer and that the battle
was a sham to excuse his future action. He
has abdicated in favour of his eldest son, Vit-
torio Emanuele, who is in treaty with Radetzky.
. . . What a people! Never is a battle without a *tradimento*. Yet it is said that the King
exposed himself in action, and his son also, who
was wounded." But I cite without interruption,
for the charm of their freshness of impression, a
full series of these memoranda, beginning (for the
sense of what the subject has always endlessly to
give) with a vision of the interior of St Peter's
at close of day.

. . . "What a sweet open air breathes through
it, like a smile upon the face, like morning sunlight! How free and noble and simple and pure
swell up its arches and dome, so ornamented, yet
as if no ornament were there! So chaste and
subduing are its grand circular effects of architecture that, as a strongly pronounced tonic

dominates every [illegible] of the chord and every variety of note, they compel all incrustation and ornament to simplicity. So always the church has the effect of music, of unity interpenetrating and harmonising variety. The great keynote of the dome rules the whole fabric and is echoed in its circular arches and down its many aisles. I listened to the single soprano voice which chaunted mournfully and in minor modulations, with every pathetic tone, the lamentations of Jeremiah—floating out like a glass thread in the great interior and dying and rising in mournful strains. After this was over and the candles were extinguished came the Miserere, in solemn and wailing counterpoint, with passages of earnest imploring that sounded through the chapel, while the single candle burned in the dimness for the singers, like a hope in adversity, and the gathering shadows nestled into the dome and confused the upper outlines.

"*April 5th.* — At the Villa Albani, from its beautiful portico, where sit so many antique statues, I looked out at the view of the Campagna and the Alban hill on one side and the Volscian mountains in the far distance. In front were the gardens of the Villa, set squarely out and surrounded with box, with tubs of oranges and tall vases of cactus and aloes, and with a fountain playing in the middle. This, with the wall surmounted by two sleeping lions and with here and there an ornamented ball, formed the foreground, while just behind, on the left, were two beautiful clumps of cypresses standing dark and solemn, one at a little distance from the other, shaking their tall green plumes in the air against the pure blue sky. Near by, was an arch with a statue on a pedestal in its centre and a fountain gushing out below.

"*April 8th, Easter Sunday.*—In the evening came the illumination of St Peter's, of which the Republic assumed the direction in the absence of the church dignitaries. At 8 we were on the piazza, where were great crowds gathered. Over the church and the colonnade hung only a few lights. Suddenly a rocket whizzed up from the centre of the piazza, and instantaneously blazed out a deep crimson flame all along the great arms of the colonnade, flaming against every pillar and flushing over the whole façade of the church, climbing the cupola and leaning upon the cross. The columns stood like pillars of crimson fire and the intervals were filled with light like that which gathers round the dying sun as it sinks after a burning day. So the pillars round the cupola seemed to waver in their splendour and to open into intense chambers of gorgeous flame. The cross at top was like a series of immense jewels about to melt. The whole outer façade blushed and glowed with the same intensity of colour, reflecting back the splendour of the colonnade; and in all the inner hollows of the arches was a pale green light, exquisite and delicate as the inside of the mother - of - pearl shell, but intense as molten metal, which set off the crimson of the outer front. The circular cupola also flashed forth alternate rings of crimson and green, like crowns and circlets of the most wondrous jewels. It was as if the whole was bound about with molten ruby and ultramarine. Over the faces of the crowd was the same light, and as this wondrous enchantment grew into existence a thrill went over the whole assembly; they shouted till the sky answered. Pale, serious and distant looked the calm stars, and the great dark obelisk stood up in the centre of the piazza like the finger of fate and seemed to say, 'Shine while you may, you thing of a few years; but I, who have seen centuries and centuries pass, shall stand when you are nothing.' After about a quarter of an hour the great bell sounded slowly and the second illumination began. The fires began to whirl round and circle up and hurry about over the façade and cupola and colonnade, and before

the bell sounded twelve the whole architecture
was written against the sky in lines of light—a
pure architectural outline in dotted fire, all the
solid material gone and only the ideal frame
remaining. The whole structure seemed to
waver as the myriad flames fluttered in the
wind. Sometimes it looked like an immense
hive covered with an immense swarm of fiery
bees that fluttered around it, sometimes like a
splendidly jewelled crown.

"*April* 9*th.*—Worked at the figure of the
girl writing on sand and began in earnest with
it; had a sitting of two hours from Vincenza.
She is not as fine as last year; I find all her
proportions heavy and short. Her waist and
her legs are ruined. So it is with these Roman
girls; there is but a short moment when they
serve—as they top girlhood and bloom. For a
year then they are fine in parts—just full
enough; but a couple of years fattens and spoils
their forms, and they sink altogether. Generally
below the bosom they are good for nothing; good
only in bosom, neck, head and arms.

"*April* 11*th.*—Went up into the cupola of
St Peter's and there had a magnificent view of
the brick-world of Rome below, and of the Campagna and mountains and sea beyond; saw how
we are planted in the midst of the great Cam-

pagna sea, which stretched round on all sides its
level plain; saw also beneath us the complicated
buildings of the Vatican and its truly Italian
gardens, its long shady walks cut through
hedges, its playing fountains, its Belvedere
court, where once tournaments were held. We
ascended into the ball, a large copper ball in
which some 8 or 10 persons can sit and which is
cut through by several longitudinal slits. Here
the effect of the high wind which roared throughout and whistled through the crevices was wonderful. It seemed as if we were whirling off
into space in some strange engine that laboured
and panted as it cleared the blue air. Now the
wind sang through it like the faint tones of an
Æolian lyre, sweet as the rustling leaves of
forests or the sound of brooks; now it stormed
like a tempest and resounded hollow and terrible
as in the incantation in 'Der Freischütz.' Now
it went like thousands of looms in a tremendous
factory, whirring and whizzing, and now swarmed
and shrieked like wailing demons. Holding on
to the great iron bars, we felt as if we were loose
in the air, on some mad career, in the great
planet - world of the dance that speeds on in
space, with all the earth far below like a speck.
Never were there more delicate, tender tones of
love than sighed and moaned in our brazen air-

ship. . . . Tremendous waterfalls we seemed
to pass by, and sounding caves; we heard the
tempest, in the open, beating the back of the
huge swell and shrieking amid the shrouds and
cordage of foundering vessels; we heard the
groan of mighty forests, the breaking up of the
polar ice, the swoop of the avalanche into the
vale, the roar of immense furnaces. The gale
played on our ball as on a lyre.

"*April 25th.*—To-day comes news that the
French have landed 1500 men at Civita Vecchia,
and the city is in great agitation. No one
knows what are their intentions, but everything
is feared among the Romans, who are as easily
scared as a flock of sheep. An *affiche* proclaim-
ing that *La Repubblica è in Pericolo* was on
every wall this morning, calling the people to
meet in Piazza del Popolo at 11. . . . Sterbini
arose in a carriage and said that the *generosissimi
Romani* must be quiet, that the French had been
deceived into a supposition that there was an-
archy here, and that when they learned the fact
they would embrace the Romans as brothers. I
met the Princess Belgiojoso, grown much older
and negligently dressed. We walked along together up beyond the Pantheon, and I then left
her. She was very cordial and agreeable, and
pressed me to come and see her. In the evening

we heard Ristori in the part of a simple country girl. She performed it admirably.

"*April 27th.*— . . . To Porta Cavalleggieri and Porta Angelica to see the barricades, or rather earth-mounds, ramparts, stockades, which the Romans are building in the event of the French. They had been working at these some thirty hours, and in some places had done three feet. Bunker Hill ramparts were thicker. Here nothing is right earnest. The labourers were leaning picturesquely on their spades, doing nothing, and everything was going on as leisurely as if the enemy were in France instead of at a few hours' march of the city. I understand from Vincenzo Bassanelli that the Guardia are nearly unanimous in desiring the return of the Pope and the abolition of the Triumvirate and Republic, and that they will not fight. . . .

"*April 28th.* — Went early with Margaret Fuller to Piazza Santa Apostoli to see the Guardia Civica meet and be harangued. Sterbini asked them if at the cost of their blood they were ready to defend the city; to which they screamed 'Si!' and held up their hats on their bayonets, making the piazza ring with huzzas. But the enthusiasm did not seem of the right stuff—it was rather a *festa* demonstration.

"*April 29th.* — Barricades are erecting and

the people preparing as for defence; scores of labourers and *contadini* standing round and sometimes pitching a shovelful of gravel into a wheelbarrow, but taking about three days to do what an hour did at Berlin. The drum is sounding constantly in the streets, and soldiers are parading and patrolling. This morning we saw the Lombard legion of refugees march in at Porta San Giovanni.

"*April* 30*th*.—Expectation of the hourly approach of the French. All the streets deserted, gloomy and morose, as before some terrible thunderstorm. The women were all fled to the houses, save here and there one whom curiosity had led out. The shops all shut, with here and there a door half open and revealing the form of a soldier peering out. At the barracks the people were busily working, and all things taking a serious turn. As we returned at about one o'clock we heard the pealing cannon and knew that the battle had begun. We then went to the top of Casa Dies and from the balcony could see the smoke of the cannon and musketry quiver and roll out, and hear the boom and rattle of their reports come travelling slowly after. At almost five we learned that the French had been repulsed at Porta Pancrazia and Porta Cavalleggieri, and shortly afterwards that they had attacked the walls by the Vatican, and been also repulsed there. . . . Margaret F., who has been at the Ospedale dei Pellegrini, reports there 70 wounded, some very severely, all suffering terribly and groaning with the burning pain of the bullet. This is the shocking reverse of the picture of glory; these are the bloody ends of the threads that work up the tapestry of honour and war. One cannot, however, but be excited and interested in a struggle like this—to repel the most unjustifiable invasion and aggression. But a short year ago France struggled through a bloody revolution for free principles and government, and won republican institutions at the cost of immense blood and money and a shattered political system. And now almost its first political act is the invasion of the only republic in Europe, contrary to its own constitution and to all international laws and rights.

"*May 1st.*—The French have retreated, and though we have been spying from the windows nothing can be seen. The Romans are all elated and surprised even at themselves. . . . The report is that a large force of Neapolitans is marching on Rome and is now at Velletri or Albano. This seems most unfortunate, but there is such a deadly hatred between the

Romans and Neapolitans, since the return of the troops of the latter from Lombardy, that there is no doubt they will be successfully resisted.   Our *donna*, hearing that the French had retreated, threw up her hands as in gratitude ; but, on learning that the Neapolitans were coming on to attack Rome, said artlessly, with a disdainful sneer, 'That is nothing—we can beat them.   Son' *anche* pauorosi '—afraid, that is, as well as the Romans !

"*May 2nd.*— . . . We went to carry our money to the Princess Belgiojoso, directress of all the hospitals, whom we found sitting surrounded with men and women, giving her various orders with calmness and clearness and showing the greatest practicality and good sense in all her arrangements.   She has laid down strict rules and reduced the establishment to order and discipline ; for three days and two nights she has been without sleep and still is strong. Then we went to Spillman's to get her an ice-cream to cool her parched throat, and while we were there came screaming and hooting a crowd which dragged along two cardinals' carriages magnificently painted and gilt.   These with pickaxes and clubs they broke entirely to pieces and set fire to, crying out, 'This is the blood of the poor !'—'E il sangue dei poveri !' Going along, we met Garibaldi's party, which had met a French detachment and taken 30 prisoners. Returning to the hospital we carried our ice to the Princess, and she partook of it, giving part to her little child, into whose stifling room I went to give it to her. Then we went over the wards—but how horrible is this reverse side of war! . . . I wish Pio Nono could have been there to see the result of his irresolution and vacillation, or rather of his weak and cruel inconsistency. Here is a man who refused to aid by his word a war for the liberty of Italy, and to free his country from oppression, because of the blood by which it must be purchased, and who less than a year after invokes foreign intervention and sheds, indirectly, the blood of his people to regain his temporal power and reinstate tyranny.

"*May 3rd.*—At the Vatican gardens, where we went to see Ossoli and saw the whole plan of the battle, the men talked with great spirit, told me all the particulars and said the Romans were a little timid at first, but grew hotter and fiercer as the battle continued, and at last were full of courage and confidence, even to heroism.

"*May 5th.*— . . . Called on Mazzini the Triumvir, whom I found haggard and worn in appearance, with rather an agreeable face, dim

black eyes, full forehead, straight black hair and
grizzled beard. He speaks English and wished
that America could give the Republic its sympathy and adhesion. His practicality, I cannot
but think, has been veneered over his mind by
his English life. Essentially, like almost all
Italians, he is visionary. But he sees and understands the virtue of simple direct action. There
was a little the affectation of a busy man with
him, and he was of course oppressed with labour
and distracted by details. But he had an air
beyond this.

"*May* 6*th.*—Went in the evening to the
Trinita dei Pellegrini to carry the American
subscription for the wounded in the late battle.
Everything was in complete order, clean floors
and beds, good ventilation, attendants gentle and
without confusion. These the hospital owes to
the Princess, who has a genius for ordering and
systematising. She said that nothing was more
pleasant to her than to attend to the sick—it
was indeed a sort of passion, for she added that
in the sick-room one is *sure* of doing good. All
efforts of charity in other directions may fail of
their end—money given may be squandered or
do injury ; but the relief of physical pain is a
thing definite and certain.

"*May* 7*th.*— . . . At the gate of Villa

Ludovisi we obtained entrance, but scarcely had we advanced far when a self-sufficient and extremely impertinent person, who represented himself as the Principe, met us and told us the place was not public. Nothing more vulgar than his manner could well be imagined, and I cannot imagine him, from his behaviour, to have been Prince Piombino. He rather resembled an ignoramus grown suddenly rich and immensely elated by the fact. All the evening we leaned on the balcony and looked over the city bathed in moonlight—sleeping in a pale shroud of faint mist. Far away, like a dream, dim and delicate, stood St Peter's against the thickened horizon; near by the Quirinal tower lifted its silhouette square against the sky; the obelisk before the Trinita dei Monti held up its dark needle at the end of the Gregoriana, and a thousand domes and towers and arched loggias rose, all around, from the roofs. Every now and then came by a band of Romans singing, or we heard the measured tramp of the patrol, or the laughing voices of girls talking below. Afar, from the Palace of the Cæsars or the Coliseum, an owl kept hooting.

" *May* 8*th.*—I was successful in finding my old *tornatore*, Malpieri, for whom I have now waited more than a week. I found him in bed, in a

room without windows and containing three beds
—hot, close, stifled enough, with his head ban-
daged and in a fever. To my surprise, however,
he offered to come to-morrow and cast my figure
for me. Glad enough was I to find him, for the
figure has now been finished more than a week,
cracking and shrinking.

" *May* 13*th.*—Went to hear Modena in ' Louis
XI.'—every movement studied to the life and
with all the freedom of nature. The decaying
powers of an old selfish wretch, hanging with
despairing hope and convulsive energy over the
bleak precipice of death and losing his grasp on
life every moment—all this was terribly true.
A great piece of acting, as great as any I ever
saw, if not the greatest.

" *May* 19*th.*—This morning early set off for
Tivoli, having yesterday evening procured a pass
from General Avezzana to go out by Porta S.
Giovanni. Outside we found the vineyard walls
all battered down to prevent the enemy from
taking shelter behind them, and the road was
therefore filled with rubbish. Soon we passed
this, and were out on the clear Campagna, which
was beautiful, rejoicing in light and carpeted
with the wildest profusion of flowers. Myriads
of scarlet poppies slept in the sunshine, lifting

their tall nodding heads among luxuriant weeds
and grass.   There were companies of bristling
thistles, with their balls of purple blossom, and
blue strips of meadow crowded with star of
Bethlehem and purple troops of various flowers
of which I know not the name.   And wild roses
hanging out their sprays like floating wreaths,
and spears of bearded barley, and richest growths
of all sorts of large-leaved weeds.   Overhead,
fluttering along in the clear blue, trilled the sky-
larks, making the air liquid with their songs and
rising as they poured forth their soul to the
morning.   Sometimes the fields looked positively
painted, for the flowers were not only dotted
here and there and everywhere, but were sometimes so clotted and heaped together that they
seemed like sweeps of colour — blue, purple,
yellow, bright scarlet, pale rose — from a full
brush, across the sward.   The dews were on the
grass and covered this wild greenery, all the
blossoming and flowering, with diamonds.   At 11
we arrived at the Villa, having been but some
three hours in covering the distance which occupied Hadrian and his luxurious retinue two or
three days.   We passed a picturesque Ponte di
Lucano, which Poussin painted, with its stream
flowing through light willows and the old circular
tomb of Plautius Lucanus, battlemented in the

middle ages, watching over it, and behind saw
the dark cypresses and broad-spreading pines
grouped together."

We feel it a pity, may we not freely confess?
in respect to the foregoing, that we have so scant
a title to recruit for our faded company one of
the figures intrinsically the most interesting and
most marked we are likely to meet.   It would
unquestionably have taken, on the part of our
friends, but a slightly less limited acquaintance
with the Princess Belgiojoso to have made me
not hesitate to seek for our pages the benefit of
her remarkable presence.   Her striking, strange
name (which, in connection with her title, seemed,
always, of old, to scintillate, exotically, orientally,
for eye and ear) was in the air, when we were
young, very much as that of Garibaldi was to be
a little later, and with the note of the *grande
dame* added, for mystification, to that of the
belligerent.   The history of this extraordinary
woman and of her revolutionary career has lately
been written, in detail and with much vivacity,
by an Italian investigator,[1] whose portrait of his
heroine, vivid, elaborate and placing in a strong
light her many gifts, leaves us in depths of doubt
—which are yet also not without their interest—

[1] La Principessa Belgiojoso.   Raffaello Barbiera.   Milano, 1902.

as to the relation, in her character, of the element of sincerity and the element that we have learned, since her day, from expert neighbours, to call by the useful name of *cabotinage*. A Lombard of old race, a Trivulzio and essentially a great lady, an ardent worker for the liberation of her country, was she not, to a tune full of renewals of suggestion, at once a sincere, a passionate crusader and a " bounder," as we elegantly say, of the real bounding temperament? Nothing is more curious, as we read her story, than the apparent mixture in her of the love of the thing in itself and the love of all the attitudes and aspects, the eccentricities and superfluities of the thing; a mixture which, however, after all, may represent little more than the fact that she was romantic, so to speak, in spite of herself, that the romantic appearance at least, in a life of eminent exile, of conspiracy, of all sorts of adventurous fellowship, was forced upon her by the general connection. The incoherent facts of her origin and person, moreover, greatly added to it; the strange, pale, penetrating beauty, without bloom, health, substance, that was yet the mask of an astounding masculine energy; the " social position " so oddly allied with her perpetual immersion in printer's ink, with the perpetual founding, conducting, supporting, replenishing,

from her own inspiration, of French and Italian
propagandist newspapers.   Not the least interest
she would probably present to a near view would
be by freshly reminding us that the great political
or social agitator is most often a bird of curious
plumage, *all* of whose feathers, even the queerest,
play their part in his flight.   We must take him,
in either sex, as the wild wood produces him ; he
is not to be plucked as for preparation for the
table.   The Princess Belgiojoso, in any case,
welcomed and valued, among the wounded of
the siege, the offered aid of Mme. Ossoli, to
whom the biographer just mentioned—quoting
also, in memory of the hospital-service during
these difficult days, from Story's " Roba di
Roma "—devotes an eloquent commemoration.
" Gloria a lei, vera amica d'Italia nostra !
Gloria, o fortissima ! "

IV.

VENICE AND BERLIN.

STORY, at Florence, at the end of May, notes the town as "full of Austrians; the officers, in their white coats, faced with purple, in every café and jingling everywhere through the streets."

"To-day (June 1st) we went to the Cascine to see them reviewed, and I feared for our poor Romans when I saw how they marched and heard the thunder of their guns. We met a crowd of people who, although this was a review of enemies, were ready to make it a *festa*. Their taste of republicanism under Guerrazzi's infamous administration was indeed sufficient to disgust them, but how they can tolerate the Austrians here, how they, or any one, could have cheered them on their entrance to the city, passes my comprehension. Upon so fitful and fickle a people what hold is there? I hear them now justify the entrance of the Austrians by saying that Tuscany is a fief of Austria, and congratulate themselves that now they can sleep peacefully in their beds. Meantime the Guardia Civica is abolished and all are forced to surrender their arms under penalty of being shot, as several have been in Leghorn.

"*June 5th.*—At the convent of San Marco the corridors and cloisters turned into barracks by the Austrians and bestrewn with the straw of their beds and litters, while they, coarse, dirty, rank-smelling, lay sprawled around half-dressed, some of them asleep, some squabbling and shouting over their food, some polishing up their arms, some mending their clothes and shoes. Beato Angelico was in strange company, and the fragrance of his suavity much at odds with the odour of their perspiration. A dirty monk, strong as a bed of garlic, guided me round! . . . I stood in the cloisters filled with soldiers and remembered that through this courtyard the noble and unsparing Savonarola was dragged by a brutal mob on Palm Sunday just $3\frac{1}{2}$ centuries ago, to be racked, tortured and then burned. How much progress since then has been made? Should in this convent a monk preach against the abuses of the government and in favour of liberty as Savonarola against the

vices of the Church and in favour of liberty
and reform, would he suffer a much different
fate? Not the stake, but the prison, exile or
the musket-ball, would be his fate.

"*June 7th.*—Corpus Domini, and all the streets
between the Palazzo Vecchio and S. Maria
Novella, as well as a lofty staging all across
the Piazza, were covered by a canvas awning
at the height of the third storey of the houses—
under all of which the procession passed. The
covered way, on either side, was lined by soldiers,
Austrians on one side, Italians the other, and
military bands playing all the while the procession moved. First came the *compagnie* of
the churches, clothed in white with dark over-
shirts and with cowls on their heads, bearing
church banners; then different orders of monks
and priests, with torches, and croaking out
chaunts which sounded, in the intervals of music,
like the chattering of frogs; then the nobles,
richly dressed, with crimson capes, and finally,
under a canopy, the Host carried along. After
this came the soldiery, all kneeling as the Host
passed into the church. The order afterwards
was given for the troops to fire, and the Piazza
rang with the report of a thousand muskets.
This was repeated three times, and then the
procession reappeared, the Host was turned

round to all the audience, and it passed away
followed by the soldiery and the crowd as
before."

They have had, on June 8th, "these last two
days, the most melancholy news of the battle
between the Romans and the French." He
relates the temporary repulse of the latter,
of Oudinot by Garibaldi, and other matters,
but also the imminence of a fresh and a greater
attack. "What will be the end? Fatal, I fear,
for Rome. Yet how bravely and resolutely she
has acted; how glorious her position compared
with that of the French!" Fortunately, even
in those days, in Italy, one could lose one's self
in other questions. "How magnificent, at the
Pitti, are Titian's portraits! That of the unknown who looks straight forward with grey
eyes that go through one—so calm and personal
are they; so living and scrutinising that they
would never let one feel alone in the room.
And the fierce hard head of Aretino, full-bearded
—what noble portraits all of them, how simple,
strong, individual! And all that comes from
Giorgione has such a charm; he had all that
Titian lacked—soul. The Madonna della Seggiola
I cannot think so superior; the composition is
beautiful, and nothing could be more so than

the head of the Child, noble and prophetic ; but the Madonna is insipid and seems to care for nothing but the spectator. The colour is much injured and the glazing much gone ; so that the picture looks raw and faded despite the false glazing of the glass. Rubens' landscapes are as free as air. Still, there is no *love* in them." And then again, a day or two later, "Picture-hunting and buying all day long"— one of the penetrating notes of the good old time, even when, as apparently in this case, the golden quest (for the gold was far from *all* rubbed off, and Botticelli, practically undiscovered, wasted his sweetness) was on behalf of importunate friends. The note of the good old time is also, I cannot but think, in the circumstances attending, on the morrow, their departure from Florence.

"Passed Pratolino and in a couple of hours were among the Apennines. Stopped at Fonte Buono, a picturesque little town, where we took some wine. As the carriage jogged on I sat outside and dreamed, looking up and down the mountain while the shadows began to thicken in the valleys and the masses to grow confused. Now and then along the curving road we heard the jingling of mule-bells and passed groups of *contadini;* and as we stopped at the post-station to change horses we heard the full-throated nightingales pouring out their honeyed wailing and striking their quick-throbbing notes. Overhead hung a deep blackish-grey cloud and beneath it a burnished strip of yellow sunlight; the lingering colour of the sunset still shone through the cleft of the mountain. Wild and desolate and strange the mountains closed us in, and I amused myself all the way with the thought of the chances there were for banditti. I remembered the story of the innkeeper at Covelaio (a village we expected to reach by midnight) who used to murder travellers at his house and burn up all vestiges of them and their equipages. It was the type, all round, of the scenes that 'savage Rosa drew.' I was also reminded of Poussin's grim solitudes."

They were presently to cross the Alps, but I cannot better help myself to delay leaving Italy with them than by quoting a letter written a few weeks before.

W. W. Story to J. R. Lowell.

"ROME, *March* 21*st*, 1849.

"MY DEAR JIM,— . . . I see that in a moment I shall be telling you what Emelyn has

already : how, one night as I was going out of
the theatre, a stout fair German with a moustache
placed his hand on my shoulder, how this figure
resolved itself into F. H., and how I caught him,
brought him to No. 4272 Via della Scala, 2 piano,
back-room, gave him a glass of wine and stared
at him and talked to him until 2 o'clock in the
morning.   We had received your books that
very day, and as soon as we had got over our
surprise we took you into our company and
laughed heartily over your jokes, true as good,
and plunged into the deeper waters of your
poems, feeling that we were all three together
once again.   'The Biglow Papers' I used to read
to convulsed audiences at our weekly 'at home'
on Sunday evenings, giving them as well as I
could the true Yankee note, and one evening I
interpreted in the same tones one of them to
the Brownings, who were quite as much amused
and delighted as I.   The 'Fable for Critics' is
admirable and just what I think in almost all
points.   It is very witty and, as the English say,
'amazingly clever.'   Once or twice you were
biassed by friendships (how can one help being ?
it is so graceful an error) and once by prejudice ;
but you know this really as well as I.   There is
but one thing I regretted, and that was that you
drove your arrow so sharply through Miranda.

The joke of 'Tiring-woman to the Muses' is too
happy ; but because fate has really been unkind
to her, and because she depends on her pen for
her bread-and-water (and that is nearly all she
has to eat), and because she is her own worst
enemy, and because through her disappointment
and disease, which (things) embitter every one,
she has struggled most stoutly and manfully, I
could have wished you had let her pass scot-
free.   But you beat Butler at rhymes and everybody at puns. . . .

   " F. H. is as charming as ever—as Hamlet-
like in every respect ; his mind the same, but
enriched and developed and Germanised. How
much I enjoy his society and friendship here you
can easily imagine.   It was a dream I never expected to be realised, to have him and Rome
together, and now we are together every day,
riding on the Campagna, visiting the ruins, seeing
the Vatican by torchlight and the Coliseum by
Bengal lights, and sitting up to two and three
o'clock at night, talking over old days, philoso-
phising, criticising.

   " The Brownings and we became great friends
in Florence, and of course we could not become
friends without liking each other. He, Emelyn
says, is like *you*—judge from this portrait ? He
is of my size, but slighter, with straight black

hair, small eyes, wide apart, which he twitches constantly together, a smooth face, a slightly aquiline nose, and manners nervous and rapid. He has a great vivacity, but not the least humour, some sarcasm, considerable critical faculty, and very great frankness and friendliness of manner and mind.   Mrs Browning used to sit buried up in a large easy chair, listening and talking very quietly and pleasantly, with nothing of that peculiarity which one would expect from reading her poems.   Her eyes are small, her mouth large, she wears a cap and long curls.   Very unaffected and pleasant and simple - hearted is she, and Browning says 'her poems are the least good part of her.' . . . Once in a while *I* write verses, and I think I have written better here than ever before—which is not perhaps saying much.   I have hundreds of statues in my head to make, but they are in the future tense.

"Powers I knew very well in Florence.   He is a man of great mechanical talent and natural strength of perception, but with no poetry in his composition, and I think no creative power. . . . When I compare him to Page I feel his inferiority ; and, after all, I have met very few, if any, persons who affect me so truly as men of genius as Page.   Certainly there are very few *artists* like him."

If we talk of shades roused from their rest, this is perhaps the best occasion for saying that the interesting and ill-fated genius so appreciatively mentioned plays his part in such a company with really tragic plenitude, the work having been as interesting as the man and yet being by this time, as I have already hinted, almost as completely extinct. It adds to my own sense of William Page's having become, in this manner, fairly the ghost of a ghost that I can remember, from far-away New York years, the extreme actuality that, for impressed childish ears, he enjoyed in the talk of our elders, and how, during his period in Europe, at a date probably somewhat later than that of Story's allusion, he was felt, in the little American art-world, as a bright but absent and regretted light. The darkness that was altogether to supervene appears to have been the result of a technical theory, some fallacy as to pigments, some perversity as to bases, too fondly, too blindly entertained, and of which I am unable to give an account. In presence of such an accident we reflect, not without complacency for our own hour, that, had Page, as a young portraitist of genius, been a somewhat later fruit of time, he would have gone to school not in Rome, but in Paris, and so probably, under a finer discipline,

have been kept in the straight path. His fate
represents, after all, clumsy *waste*, unlighted
freedom of experiment possible only (for it comes
back to that) in provincial conditions. And his
idea of himself, all the while, was that he was at
school to Titian. The young person of other
years, in any case, may entertain the recollection
of a portrait hanging, here and there, in New
York and in Boston, which was even then as
dim as it was distinguished, was even still as
distinguished as it was dim. It is possibly the
glamour of time and of association, but there
seem to have been no other such portraits as
those, things that gloomed out sadly, above
Victorian sofas in incongruous "parlours," like
consciously imprisoned spectres of strayed, of
abused Italians. I am safe, at the worst, perhaps, to think of them so nobly, for the dungeon-
darkness must surely, in most cases, quite have
settled by this time. I may add that, as things
of the deepening twilight, they associate themselves in memory with the rare relics of Washington Allston, another victim of blighting
conditions, for whom Story's word, later on,
utters itself in sympathy. The Allstons, in the
old parlours too, and over the old pianos, seemed
(though not portraits) somehow to express genius
struggling with adversity, yet luckily less doomed

and originally less compromised by "style." The twilight is, however, over all, and an indiscreet lamp, held up, would perhaps betray me.

The letter I have just cited suggests to me that I cannot place better than here the nearest approach I find to an answer. It was not written, this supposititious answer, till six months later, but that is quite consistent, in friendly correspondence, with the nature of answers. A second missive from Rome, one of those candid offerings of affection, in the past, that were apt to consist of local "ware" or other contemporary handiwork, had meanwhile reached the correspondent.

J. R. Lowell to W. W. Story.

"ELMWOOD, *Sept. 25th,* 1849.

"MY DEAR WILLIAM,—A conversation kept up (as between two deaf persons, with pen and ink) across three thousand miles of ocean can hardly expect the merit of liveliness, however rich it may be in graver elements. It would be a good debating or controversial distance. The long space of time between the discharges of each would allow the smoke to clear away in whose gathering fumes the disputants are apt to forget the original matter of argument. Or perhaps a love-letter, as that kind of composition is singularly retentive of life (witness those of Heloise, in Latin too ; witness those of many a defendant in suits for the least defensible of breaches), might carry its vital heat across those weary leagues of salt water as easily as down through dry and cold centuries of time.

"But I am not holding a disputation with you —be thankful for that and read on with cheerful hope. Neither am I writing a love-letter; yet I will satisfy here an emotion which enters into the composition of every solid and honest one, and discharge at least the debt of gratitude, however small the amount of assets may be that remains for the liquidation of my epistolary obligations.

"How did you know anything about it ? How did you guess that I had been wishing for one? —that Maria had intended to surprise me with the New Year's gift of a Chinese one, and searched all Boston in vain? Yours came just in the nick of time to fill a gap of which I had precisely then become conscious in the furniture of my otherwise well-treated study. The very cigar I am now smoking came out of its kindly bosom—the hamadryad of that fortunate tree, smacking of Sorrento and giving me a feeling of regard for the olive, a shabby tree in the main and nowise comparable to our elm, and whose

better part we get in flasks and jars. Not so,
neither ; its fairest use is to be made into boxes
with initials tastefully inlaid upon the cover and
sent as a memento. Had it been mulberry I
might have added *mori*, and given a new turn
to that tombstone morality. Think of this if
you are sending one to any other friend and give
him a chance. I am talking all this time of your
beautiful cigar-box. It has given me, moreover,
a more favourable opinion of modern Italian art,
and so enlarged my mind. Knowing that they
had been so long in the habit of getting into
bad boxes themselves, I had not supposed them
capable of such an achievement. I was not so
ignorant of the natural productions of our
western world as not to know that all the
nests of boxes came from Hingham, and had
too rashly concluded that, as the nidification
took place there, that was also the singular
locality for incubation. But possibly I was
wrong in supposing this particular box to be
the production of art. Perhaps it was brought
into the world by mechanical contrivance, as
chickens in Egypt? The egg may have been
laid in Hingham and thence exported? I should
look upon it with all the more tenderness as
never having known a mother's care, and put it
in charge of a full-grown Hingham box, which I

have in my closet. But whatever solution of the problem we have recourse to, the box remains—like so many a poor devil's poems—an ornament to the centre-table. I do not scruple to call it the handsomest piece of furniture I possess, except the table Maria made for me.

"There is one of your foreign experiences which I grudge you, only one which I envy, and that is the meeting with F. H. If he be still within reach of voice or letter, give him my love, fresh as ever after so many years' silence—nay, seeming all the fresher, like a flower upon a grave. Yet for that buried friendship I live in the faith of a joyful resurrection—and in the body. Here I sit alone this chilly September morning, with the rain just beginning to rattle on the roof, and the writing of his name has sent my heart back to the happy hopeful past when one was capable of everything because one had not yet tried anything. The years have taught me some sharp and some sweet lessons—none wiser than this, to keep the old friends. Every year adds its value to a friendship as to a tree, with no effort and no merit of ours. The lichens upon the bark, which the dandyfiers of Nature would scrape away, even the dead limbs here and there, are dear and sacred to us. Every year adds its compound interest of association and

enlarges the circle of shelter and of shade. It
is good to plant them early, for we have not the
faith to do it when we are old. I write it sadly
and with tears in my eyes. Later friends drink
our lees, but the old ones drank the clear wine
at the brim of our cups. Who knew us when
we were witty ? who when we were wise ? who
when we were *green?*

"You talk about my being a man of leisure.
Why, beside what other writing I have done, I
have for fourteen months contributed a column
a-week and for four months a column a fortnight,
to the 'Anti-slavery Standard'; which is of
course advantageous to me, since columns, you
know, do not allow poets to be mediocre. You
are the man of leisure there in Italy, whose
climate makes loafers of all. Now I will give
you a commission. Leaving out Dante, Ovid
and Boccaccio are the best part of Italian literature. Boccaccio was probably the best *man*
of the three, and, moreover, we who have the
English tongue derive our poetical pedigree from
him through Chaucer. Now you shall make a
pilgrimage to Certaldo and make for me a
sketch of his little tower, doubly interesting
since Landor laid the scene of his 'Pentameron'
there. F. H. shall go with you, and as you are
both lazy dogs, and F. no doubt fattish by this

time, you shall perform your pilgrimage afoot;
and you shall besides compose a *canzone* in alternate verses; your moiety being written in the
most toothsome Tuscan and F.'s in the very
highest of high Dutch. This you shall engross
fairly on a sheet of paper and deposit with the
parish priest, directed to me, to await my coming
whenever it shall take place.

"I do not know what your movements are to
be, nor when you will set your faces homewards.
I heard that you intend a journey to Egypt with
Uncle Tom. Do not go too far up the Nile. *Ex
Nilo nihil fit*—nobody makes anything of it, and
beside, there might be considerable risk for Mr
Wetmore. There are savage tribes in the interior of Africa who devour white ants, and if
so why not white uncles? Do think of this, for
it is hardly probable that they are respecters of
age or sex. Go rather to London, where there
are quarters inhabited almost exclusively by
uncles with three golden balls over their hos-
pitable doors.

"It will seem a very old affair for me to speak
of the 'Fable for Critics.' You know me well
enough to know how it was written—the work
(literally) of a few days and without any *malice*.
I should have sent you a copy had I known that
you were accessible by packages of that kind.

Or rather I should not have sent one—it was so wretchedly misprinted. Set down the parts about Miss Fuller as errors of the press. You speak of her as poor. I did not know that she was so, but thought the departure of her uncle Abraham to his namesake's bosom had made her independent. I only knew that she was malicious, and it was not what she had written of me, but what I had heard of her saying, which seemed to demand the intervention of the satiric Nemesis. You may be sure I have felt more sorry about it than any one ; only I always reflect *after* the thing is done. Nevertheless I imagine the general verdict was 'Served her right,' though it was also regretted that castigation was inflicted by my particular hand.

"The only news I have to tell you about myself . . . is that I shall probably make an arrangement with Ticknor to publish a new edition of my poems in two volumes this fall. By this means I shall profit by what I write more than hitherto, which is certainly a desideratum. With an unfortunate faith in my own future appreciation (I believe that is the phrase) I have been in the habit of myself stereotyping my books, so that, although my sale is tolerably large, I have barely more than paid expenses. Under the new system, if I enter upon it, you see that

I have my plates already cast, and, the printing
being the bookseller's share, whatever profit
there is will be clear. Of my 'Fable' three
thousand copies were sold as fast as they could
be printed, but of that I had given away the
copyright. Nevertheless it acted as an advertisement, for the authorship was at once guessed.
'The Biglow Papers' also sold well, but cost me
over two hundred dollars in stereotyping.

"I only know a single item of news which you
will be interested in hearing. That is the lamentable end of poor Edgar Poe. He was
picked up in the streets of Baltimore stagger-
ing under *delirium tremens*, and taken to the
hospital, where he died. Sad enough and a
man of real genius too.

"I look forward . . . to your return home.
I hope you will remain fixed in the plan which
Emelyn mentioned of settling in Cambridge.
Or perhaps we and some other decent people
may choose some spot and set up our rests
there. At any rate I see no reason why we
should not renew a friendship to last as far as
the grave at least. I want somebody very much
who will not only sympathise with me in literary
and artistic matters, but whose early associations were the same as mine. You and I, with
our cigars in our mouths, can talk and laugh

over a thousand matters which would seem very
poor stuff to most, indeed to all, who had not
been actors therein or witnesses."

To cling to Italy, meanwhile, on whatever
pretext, is to meet our friends as promptly as
possible on their first vision of Venice, which
took place, with all the honours of fresh rapture,
in the autumn of 1849. They had travelled in
the interval, wandered through Switzerland,
followed the Rhine and pushed eastward as
far as Vienna, but it is all of questionable intensity till they breathe again Italian air. I
cannot forbear, however, to reproduce a note
or two—if but for mere envy of the old-time
freshness of the susceptible traveller's sense,
before this freshness had begun to yield in advance, right and left, in every direction, to
the diffusion of photography and chatter. At
Heidelberg, in September, Story was "never so
disappointed in the appearance of any place,
and at first thought I must have stopped at
the wrong one. Dull and shabby, with one
long street running quite through it." But he
changes on the morrow, after the castle and
the view from the castle.

" We hunted for rooms, as the town this morning, in the sunshine, looked so much pleasanter than it did last night, that E. has concluded to stay here while I go to Vienna, Venice, &c. After all, when one has great expectations of the beauty of any place, and utterly false ideas in respect to it, the best thing that can occur is an instant and thorough disenchantment at first sight, even a feeling like disgust. *Then* one has a good platform on which to form new ideas. . . . I saw a beautiful little balcony holding out from one of the old walls (of the castle) and through the dark arch looking into the court of sunshine. Beside the columns of the portico were two saddle-horses; the façade, richly glowing in sun and shade, stood beyond; vines waved across the opening; soldiers in groups were spotted here and there; it realised my notion of what a fine old baronial castle must have been—where some lady might look from the balcony at her lover in the court and throw him her glove, or a flower, as he rode off in the morning, and think of him as she paced, all day, the long suites of spacious halls."

At Frankfort the statue of Goethe by Schwan-thaler seemed to him clumsy and unfinished. "There is considerable dignity in the head, but the draperies are ropy and unanatomised, and so

unite with the support at the side as to deaden
the effect of the figure. The cloak has a put-on
sort of air which did not quite please me, and the
undercoat and boots were very tinny. . . . I was
so very lonely that, after having walked the
streets and gazed for some time at the roofs from
my window, I grew desperate and went to bed
at nine." On which he breaks into the inevitable
horror of the German bed of the good old sort.
And he adds a page about Danneker's Ariadne,
all of the most disapproving, and leaves the figure
we must not say not a leg to stand on, but not
an arm to lean on. "Nothing *internal* in the
work"; which is a suggestive criticism in the
light of Story's own subsequent labour. It was
for the "internal" that he was himself persistently to try, even as he was so often and so
effectively to arrive at it. He believed, ardently,
that sculpture may beautifully express it, and
it was in the light of this conviction, as well as
of others forming its happy complement, that he
worked to the end. He takes his way, on this
occasion, to Nuremburg and to Munich, noting
all he sees and reacting from it, full of impressions, and of ideas about his impressions,
hanging fondly over the feast of pictures wherever he finds pictures, airing his freshness thoroughly, in short, in the good old sunshine, in the

German autumn days. At Munich he hears his first German play, and he is always prompt for plays, for which, and for the whole question of the actor's art, in Roman years, under beguilement of the so-oddly theatrified Mausoleum of Augustus or the more private pleasure of staged Barberini saloons, his appetite was never to be sated. "It was stupid enough, but I understood it"—the play at Munich, "turning on the marriage of a black woman and a white man, and I could not but feel how free the audience was of prejudice against such a union." Rather indeed, the earnest, the bland Bavarians! After the play he goes to the great pothouse for supper and is much struck with the Germanic picture. "Here one could see German life—here were truly German groups and figures of every kind of extravagance; some fiercely gesticulating, some stupidly contemplative, some with frogged coats and wild hair, some with moustaches that reached to their ears. Huge beards were kissing each other, great fists were knocking their beer-glasses together, people were shaking up dice in a great leathern bottle. Women waited on us; very friendly and familiar, without any bashfulness and yet quite proper." He hangs about the Munich pictures and spends the rest of the time in writing verses and in reading Macaulay's "History of England," then gloriously new, " which is as interesting as a novel." He bescribbles very many little pages with a candid and pleasant insistence on the art-things of Munich, modernisms and others—the modernisms mostly already middle-aged, and to be, too composedly, middle-aged for ever only, never to wake up, in their impossible German beds, as antiques : the whole redolent of the unsophisticated time when the art-things of Munich were a theme. They exhale, ever so kindly, one scarce knows what faint fragrance as of our early perusals of " The Initials," of the Baroness Tautphœus, so adored and so forgotten, and of the milder, yet, to the liberal little mind, sensibly haunting charm of Anna Mary Howitt's " Art-Student" at the feet of Kaulbach. The Danube by Passau and Linz reminds him, becomingly, of the Highlands of the Hudson, " though the foliage is not so rich, nor the hills so picturesque, and the great Catskills which loom up along our river were also wanting." At Vienna, where Mrs Story, originally left at Heidelberg, appears, on an altered scheme, to have overtaken him, the theatre prompts him again to reflections. " The Germans, like the English, *over* - act. Nature is not enough for them ; it must have a dais and be falsified and exaggerated. How much better the Italian acting!" That is suggested by some farcical comedies, but he also sees Dawison in Schlegel's translation of "Hamlet"; his note on which combines with other expatiations, those on the Vienna museums, to revive for us the good faith of the young American for whom Europe meant, even more than now, culture, and for whom culture meant, very much more than now, romantic sentiment. He reaches Venice, with his wife and children, on November 5th, by Trieste, and the first assault of the place on his senses and his fancy is, naturally enough, above all the assault of romantic sentiment. Venice was verily made, in the great scheme of things, for this perpetration of the first assault on the recurrent victim—unless we should rather say that the romantic sense was evolved, in the order of the universe, that it should be, in its bloom, assaulted. Story appears to have taken everything in at a gulp; he revolves, like a fire-wheel on a *festa*, at the application of the match.

"All the old life of the terrible republic was here (in the court of the Ducal Palace). Here swept the purple robes of the dread Council of Ten; here gathered the Senators; above, in the palace, were the *sotto-piombi*, where the prisoners of State died; here were the torture-rooms, the

dungeons, the judgment-halls of the Inquisition.
And here, where the black coats of hundreds of
modern Venetians were moving about, walked
the purple and furs and gold of the ancient
aristocracy. It was a time for strange imagina-
tions, which came thronging around me. . . .
It was like a dream. I abandoned myself to the
luxury of visionary enjoyment. As we passed
the palace of the Foscari a strain of music came
forth and floated down the water ; it was magical,
it was as if the dance and pageant of old Venice
had returned, and almost involuntarily I looked
to see the dancers and the shining lights. It
was like picture-sailing, like enchantment, so
unreal and voluptuous. Under the fatal Bridge
of Sighs and over the subterranean dungeons I
kept saying and thinking, ' How many fearful
crimes, hid from the light, has this fair Venice
seen ! ' The thought of the Inquisition passed
before me like a black shadow ; I thought of the
many who had crossed that bridge from judgment
to death ; of the secret swords that struck in the
dark ; of the grave State's enemies found in the
dark prisons out of sight of the laughing waves
of the Riva, which flickered by and wound their
silver nets of light upon the outer walls ; of the
corpses that had found hurried burial in the
canals and lagoons. Here was the nightmare of

the dream. 'And I am now in Venice'—the
thought trembles livingly in my heart even as
the quivering lights reflected in the canal while
we rowed home at dusk. All my memories were
a confused cluster of splendours and horrors, as
the twisted globes of Venice glass in which are
tangled so many various hues. I cannot tell
what I thought, but I felt strange feelings."

He ends his throbbing day by the inevitable
evening in the Piazza, thronged and brilliantly
lighted, and remembers Schiller's "Geisterseher,"
"while the Austrian band played almost continually. This was luxury." They receive on
the morrow "a letter from Margaret Fuller declaring her marriage to Ossoli." They go to the
"Hôtel de la Ville"—"anciently the Palazzo
Grassi, a magnificent old palace on the Grand
Canal, with fine courtyard and hall, and stairs
over which all round are frescoes representing
the carnival of Venice. Figures in old costumes,
masked and unmasked, flirting and mysterious,
lean over painted balconies." We hover at their
heels; we look through their eyes; there is, alas!
no hotel like that to-day. "Near by is an old
tower; opposite is the old Foscari Palace." And
of course for the pictures he overflows, he
abounds. We have, most of us, by this time,

stood before them, stood beneath them often
enough ourselves—so often that, with the habit,
the power of doing so for others has been en-
feebled in us ; yet here and there, in my blurred
notes, the words glimmer out and stop us.
"There is no hesitation of touch"—in Paolo's
"Europa"—"but a dash does the miracle. There
is no concern about the detail, yet the detail is
all there. The bull's head seems as if the blood
coursed through it, and the bosom of Europa
heaves." On Tintoret indeed he has an odd
word—as to "some four" of his "very *clever*
pictures." Wouldn't one almost as soon so apply
it as to the frieze of the Parthenon? But he
has his view. "After the rich openness and
freedom of the Veronese, Tintoret always looks
to me tame as sentiment and flat in colour. His
nature is grosser and his senses less full and
fine." However, things but simmer and brew,
at the best, in the silver cup of initiation, safe
to clarify later in the less brimming, if more
precious, vessel of acquired wisdom. Why is it
that we also feel, for instance, that he was but
to *live into* impressions a little further to become
incapable of concluding on them quite so curtly
as in his mention of a visit to the great palace
of the Bourbons, then occupied with the possessions of the Duchesse de Berri? "Here we saw

a quantity of trashy French pictures, small in size and in spirit, all finished to death. Every room was filled with little knick-knacks of every kind scattered about on the tables or under little cases or in cabinets. One room contained a gallery of second-rate pictures with great names. Behind her bed was a Madonna with a quantity of little gewgaws hung up as an offering. I cannot think a woman whose taste is so small and trifling can have much mind!" He was still in time to see in its original place in the Pisani Palace—a place by which the impression must have been enhanced, though I rest in vagueness as to whether his allusion be to the huge, melancholy pile, all wasted and sacrificed, behind the exquisite Barbaro—the splendid Paolo of the English National Gallery which appears then to have been known by the charming, if slightly inconsequent, title of the Tent of Darius; in connection with which he repeats the graceful legend of the painting of the picture, brought secretly to completion, according to this tradition, in an apartment of the palace in which the artist was at the time enjoying the hospitality and bounty of the Pisani, and intended as an acknowledgment, on departure, of favours received: as we write our name to-day, for example, in the visitor's book. Story applies to

the manner of the present that indicated term
"gentlemanly" which falls in so completely with
the character of the principal figure in the composition. How, we feel, could the artist capable
of such *procédés* not make his Alexander the
perfect type, for all time, of the accomplished
"young gentleman," and how could the man of
the world who was to reflect himself in such an
image not have been, inevitably, graceful in
behaviour?

Such perceptions, such questions were, visibly,
for him, part of the delight with which "one
dreams away life here in the mere deliciousness
of existence." He dilates on the enchantment,
on the "magic," in the slightly *rococo* spirit
that we smile at kindly to-day, but that was
still, even at that time—certainly for our friends
of the tentative generation—one of the keys
to the complicated lock, one of the happiest
phases of initiation. "Old associations, the
splendour and the crimes of the past, strike
across the present like the fitful sunlight through
forest-trees. The air seems to echo with the
music and gladness that filled it in the days
of pride. The very names of the old people,
which seem so fitted to mystery and crime, to
passion and intrigue and love, haunt the imagination." And he enumerates the scenes that, as

in the old melodramas, pass before him—the
Venetian beauty, less candid than Desdemona,
say, who drops from the Gothic balcony into
her lover's arms at night. "I see the gondola
silently steal along beneath the balcony while
the guitar-string is lightly touched to awaken
her to whom the lover sings. Before me the
dagger of the cloaked bravo or of the jealous
husband gleams, and I hear the splash of the
body as it falls into the dark canal." He sees,
in fine, what we all used to see, or what was
obligingly seen *for* us (for consequent clearing
of the air); that operatic side of the picture in
which the idea of "crime" recurs very much
as one of the indispensable rhymes of the libretto.
The recurrence is, however, quite apart from this,
an interesting mark of that special turn of Story's
artistic imagination which was to make him, as
sculptor and poet (in his Medeas and Judiths,
his Cleopatras and Stephanias, his Roman
emperors and Assyrian kings), strike with pre-
dilection the note of passion let loose. It was
in their dangerous phases that the passions
most appealed to him, and, with his predisposi-
tion to see sculpture as, above all, expressional,
he recognised betimes, in a country where the
breath of the centuries of violence was still in
the air and where the fancy could still so taste

it, his strongest affinities in the matter of subject. So the lingering *lurid*, in Venice, did more for the charm than, taking one kind of rococo with another, the ghostly grimace of the Carnival.

It was just such visions, none the less, that he immediately proceeded to quench by a step rather obscurely prompted for us, unless indeed we read into it, a trifle "pathetically," just the least natural reasons. We make out, at all events, in doing this, that his plunge into Berlin, for the winter of 1849-50, would be exactly the most heartrending obligation that could fix its teeth into the tender conscience of a precursor not as yet fully in tune with his mission. Nothing, in other words, could be more charmingly characteristic of the old precursive spirit while at the stage of *tâtonnement* than to have imagined such a sop to an unbridled æstheticism (an æstheticism not simply of thought, but of life and act) as a period of discipline in the unregenerate Prussian capital. The lamentable logic, so to speak, lives again for us, and we see the odd part played by this episode in the particular pilgrimage that was to qualify the pilgrim for "Art." It was to qualify him for art as a consequence of qualifying him for culture in general, which might be looked to, under Providence, for keeping art in its place. Con-

sidered therefore in its calculated bearings on
this latter result, the Berlin months reflected
in our friends' memoranda and letters round
themselves as a passage of the pleasantest
comedy. Story, as we patch it up, had not,
curiously enough, even after two years of Italy,
burnt his ships; he was to saturate himself, to
the end that he might happily model, with
what Europe should give him, but he was
somehow, by the same stroke, and in some
interest to be felt better than named, to be
protected against the saturation. He was protected so far as Berlin went. He returns with
his wife to Vienna, and they take, by rail, the
plunge, which they find attended, in the infancy
of the process, by the discomforts of a ponderous
slowness of trains, of interminable waits, of
wretched nocturnal and otherwise mistimed
changes, of a universal density of smoke in
carriages closed to any air. "Somewhat it has
[Berlin] that makes me think of Boston and
gives me a home-feeling. I know not what it
is; not the buildings, for in vain we seek there
for such noble structures — the Schloss, the
Guard-house, the Arsenal, the Opera — which
line the fine street Unter den Linden. But
there is a sort of comfortable look which resembles
Boston, even as the hurry and vivacity of Vienna

recalls New York. The climate is our New England climate, and to-day particularly a true Massachusetts day. I saw a chaise in the street just like a Boston doctor's chaise—the first I have seen since I left America." And he sees, he finds, an added reminder in the look of the Berlin interior, even to the papers and carpets of the rooms, "the sofas and furniture" —which is a side-light, or, in the modern phrase, a "back-hander," of some intensity, for the eye that summons up, through the historic perspective, these purely Prussian accessories.

But there were better things, including the soul of music—always, for Story, the greatest luxury to spirit and sense. "In the evening we heard the 'Marriage of Figaro' at the Opera—full of liquidity and melody, running singing along like a brook, abounding in delicious themes that enchant the sense and in deep, pure, prayer-like strains that ravish the soul. Mozart's music has a lark-like thrill, a wild and simple naturalness beside which Rossini's seems affected and artificial. I felt my heart smile, as the Germans say, during the whole performance. The Prince of Prussia was there; he came into his box, pulled out a little comb and brush and began to make use of them for his hair before the whole audience. This is a peculiarity of the Germans

everywhere—as soon as they enter a public place,
a café or a dining-room. The Princess was also
there, but I saw nothing in either face in the
least interesting. He has a big, full, snub-nosed
countenance, and she a shrewish." And Mr and
Mrs F. of Boston were also there—or were at
least in Berlin. "The former is a stick and the
latter too weeping and woman-like." Another
notice of the Opera yields a deeply disconcerting
allusion to a ballet, called prettily "Die Blumen-
Fee," the Flower-Fairy, "in which Marie Taglioni, a woman whose ankles were as great as her
name, flung herself about clumsily enough." But
for this untoward stroke we might have invited
Marie Taglioni to flit across our stage, on the
points of those toes that we expected never to
see compromised, as one of our supernumerary
ghosts: in the light, that is, of our own belated
remembrance, a remembrance deferred to the
years in which, as a very ugly and crooked
little old woman, of the type of the superannu-
ated "companion," or of the retired and pen-
sioned German governess, she sometimes dined
out, in humane houses, in London, and there
indeed, it must be confessed, ministered not a
little to wonderment as to what could have
been the secret of her renown, the mystery of
her grace, the truth, in fine, of her case. Her

case was in fact really interesting, for the sensitive spectator, as a contribution to the eternal haunting question of the validity, the veracity from one generation to another, of social and other legend, and it could easily, in the good lady's presence, start a train of speculations— almost one indeed of direct inquiry. The possibilities were numerous—how were they to be sifted? Were our fathers benighted, were ravage and deformity only triumphant, or, most possibly of all, was history in general simply a fraud? For the Sylphide had been, it appeared, if not the idol of the nations, like certain great singers, at least the delight of many publics, and had represented physical grace to the world of her time. She had beguiled Austrian magnates even to the matrimonial altar, and had acquired, as a climax of prosperity, an old palace, pointed out to the impressed stranger, in Venice. The light of testimony in the London winter fogs was, at the best, indirect, and still left the legend, at the worst, *one* of the celebrated legs, so often in the past precisely serving as a solitary support, to stand on. But to read, after all, that she flung herself about, with thick ankles, " clumsily enough," is to rub one's eyes and sigh — "Oh history, oh mystery!" — and give it up.

Story gets over, meanwhile, his sense of
Bostonian analogies — " I find the furnished
apartments here ' very tolerable,' as Dogberry
says, ' and not to be endured.' They are sense-
lessly arranged." The Opera becomes apparently his main consolation ; he sees " Don
Giovanni " in Italian, again delights in Mozart—
" throughout there is a dramatic power as well
as a melodic sensibility which make this opera
the greatest ever written " ; and he overflows,
on another occasion, about Gluck's " Armida "—
" in the scene in her garden, where Rinaldo falls
asleep, the music is exquisite ; the wind instru-
ments breathe like soft airs, the stringed instru-
ments keep up a gentle rushing and murmuring
as of brooks and leaves." The theatre, indeed,
seems less sustaining. " ' Romeo and Juliet,' in
Schlegel's translation, at the Schauspielhaus,
wretchedly performed ; the Juliet a stick, the
Romeo nothing, the Mercutio swaggering and
ungentlemanly, and the nurse terribly over-acted.
Love at first sight, such love as grows in the
South, were utterly impossible in such cold-
blooded creatures."   He meets " a thoroughly
New York merchant, with that kind of pretentious off-hand style of treating all persons and
subjects. Mrs J. was also there with the
daguerreotype of J. (' Don't you know J.?' said

the New York merchant with an air as if not to know J. argued one's self unknown. 'He is of our firm—J. & Co.') Mrs J. sang, 'Is it *but*—a dream?' and a German sang with her from one of the Italian operas, he singing the words in French and she in English!" This at a party given, as I take it, by the then American Minister. He sees "Don Giovanni" again, and again overflows — "the very Shakespearism of music; the greatest opera, for everything, I have ever heard. It gives the trashy libretto the glory the sunset gives a damp dull cloud." He speaks, however, in the same way, journalising for two pages, about Mendelssohn's "Midsummer Night's Dream:" "Then last came a fine 'Hochzeits-Marsch,' broad, noble and rejoiceful. This seems the true translation of Shakespeare into music; the 'Othello' of Rossini, the 'Romeo and Juliet' of Bellini, are beside it nothing, mere sound and fury." After which he enters an odd judgment: "Read 'David Copperfield' and found it exaggerated and not very interesting. I am tired of Dickens; the stream seems dry and the style is forced." And he follows it up, on the occasion of reading Victor Hugo's "Derniers Jours d'un Condamné," which he apparently finds more interesting, by three pages of reprobation of capital punishment and judicial murder.

Throughout this winter he was studying German with a certain Dr Stadthagen and attending lectures, on History, the Civil Law and other matters, at the University and, incongruously enough, cultivating the practice of sculpture, though we do not discern that, on the banks of the Spree, he had a studio. His wife notes on February 12th that "W.'s statue is already beautiful," but the matter fades into mystery. The statue in question would seem to be the figure modelled as a memorial of his father and afterwards so successfully finished, were it not unlikely that he had transported this work from Italian to German air. He to some extent gives an account of himself in a letter which I shall presently quote; but the impressions there commemorated needed evidently such further propping as they might borrow from a few rather jejeune "social" contacts.

Mrs Story notes a party at Mme. von Savigny's, "where we had a pleasant, though rather stiff evening; the ladies scrupulously sitting down on one side of the room while the gentlemen as scrupulously crowded together on the other. William's sketches were there, and they proved the centre of interest for the evening, one old dowager after another passing them on and remarking upon them. As soon as the first carriage was announced the whole party took leave as by the wave of some fairy wand." They were most occupied, really, in learning the meaning of Heimweh — of which sentiment Boston was not the object. "I sat alone," Mrs Story writes of one evening, "and read Andersen's 'Improvisatore,' and I found it so interesting in subject as well as fascinating in style that I could scarcely make up my mind to lay it aside and take my solitary cup of tea. How attractive and beautiful seems from this northern distance every spot in Italy! Even the meanest little post-town through which I have again passed this evening with A. has a charm, a picturesque nameless grace that is to be found nowhere else. With Goethe I went to Venice the other day, but he is too cold for Italy; warmer natures are better companions there. In a gondola he is out of place," she quaintly adds, "notwithstanding his great artistic genius." Toward the end indeed, weeks later, she wishes to be just all round. "I begin to feel unpleasantly when I think of leaving Berlin. It is cold, prosaic and in some aspects dreary; its social life is narrow and contracted; but it is the home of scholars and philosophies, and its air has some of the enchantment that they have lent it. I like to think how good

an atmosphere it is for thought and study—
and I can *feel* even that, slight as my application
is. When therefore I look at my things, which
ere long must be packed and carried out of the
house, I grow a little sorrowful, and a little
affectionate even toward our greasy Frau
Rosener." The vision that was to remain most
vivid to her was clearly that of Bettina von
Arnim, the child-friend of Goethe's old age,
in relation to whom her diary contains, under
date of January 25th, an entry so animated
that I fully reproduce it.

"Mme. von Savigny having called to tell us
that her sister Bettina (who for a few days had
come to Berlin) would like to see us, we embraced the opportunity to go to her. She was
not in the city proper; her lodgings were just
beyond the Thiergarten and but a few moments'
walk from the Brandenburg gate. We took a
carriage to go to her, but left it to walk upon
the snow. In front of the house were large
trees whose branches swayed and sighed in the
January wind. Having been directed to the
first floor, we mounted and knocked, and a clear
voice from behind the glass door presently called
out to know whom we sought. Being answered,
the door was thrown open, and Mme. Bettina

stood there to welcome us.   Most kind and
cordial and hearty was her greeting.   Mme. von
Savigny had already spoken of us to her and
we did not meet as strangers.   After some slight
difficulty in opening the door of her little parlour,
we were soon seated within and on the most
friendly terms imaginable.   She spoke freely of
herself and friends, but not obtrusively; she
became sad on speaking of the condition of
political Germany, and referred to the heartrending tragedy of the Hungarians.   But these
things she did not dwell upon, for she knew
that William was an artist, and art being most
near and dear to her, it was most natural to
make it the burden of her song.   She was full
of nature and enthusiasm, and as she became
interested in conversation seized my hand, pressed
it and kissed me.   There is something strangely
magnetic about her, and I felt wonderfully fas-
cinated.   Her eyes are fine, large and deep-
seated, her brow is nobly developed and her
expression full of fire and genius.   I had expected to see her in some odd costume, perhaps
with her grey hair streaming down her back,
but she was quite simply and neatly dressed,
with nothing in her appearance either unfeminine
or untidy.   Something there is in her fine eye
that seems to penetrate and read the heart,

and as she looked at me and spoke with me, as she did most affectionately, I can scarcely express how near I felt to her.

"She showed us her designs for the bas-reliefs intended for four sides of the base of the statue of Goethe; in conception and spirit they were and seemed quite like the work of inspiration. In execution they were very remarkable, considering how late in life she had begun the mechanical part of the art. We asked her when the statue would be erected, and she sighed and said: 'You in America must take it in charge now; there is no longer any hope of it here, I fear.' She said also that at one time before the late revolution in Berlin the King had sent to ask her to give him the designs and allow him to have them executed. Dear as the object was to her she could not sell her freedom of speech, and did not wish to receive such a favour from his hands as should bind her to a sort of friendship with him, or at least keep her silent when he was in error. So she said No, and all the world was surprised that she should, seeing the darling project so nearly accomplished, reject the offer. But she simply said: 'I prefer to keep my freedom and to speak as I think of the King.' She had once occasion to apply to him for the life of some prisoner. She asked it as of one who had

power to grant it. He replied : ' You deny us
the possession of kind feelings, and then in an
emergency apply to us as having them.' She
answered : ' Of what consequence is it who asks
you or what are my sentiments ? You must
simply look at the thing itself and see if it be
right to do.' The King said : ' But a friend of
the prisoner has told me that he is an infidel,
speaks ill of Christ, &c.' ; on which she replied,
' The charge against him is as true as that the
informant is his friend.' The man lives, but it
is, as Mme. von Arnim says, rather through
the influence of the Queen than of any one
else. During the conversation or correspondence,
whichever it might have been, the King said :
' But the power of pardon no longer remains with
me ; I have given up the case to others.' She
said in reply : ' Then you have nothing left, for
that power is more than crown or kingdom to
you.' Her daughter came in, and I turned to
talk with her in my bad German. I found her
simple, natural and naïve, and liked her ; but the
mother was ever more attractive to me, and I
listened to her words whenever I might. About
her books she had a long talk with William, and
told him that ' Mrs von Otis' came to see her
when she was here and promised to see that her
edition of the letters to Goethe were sold in

America, and that the money which was to go toward the erection of the monument should be sent to her. She had up to this time received neither money from the sale of the books nor any word about the matter from Mrs von Otis. She had heard that there was an American edition and wished William to inquire about it. She was to leave town in a day or two, but promised to come and see us and give us her books. Then after a long visit of three hours we took leave of her and trudged home through the snow of the Thiergarten to the babies and the Persian poets. She did come to us" (Mrs Story adds as a kind of postscript) "with her arms full of books, and took off her bonnet, and stayed some hours, talking as fast as possible."

As for Story himself he was to leave a record, sufficiently compendious, of what Berlin had to give him; the interest of which, again, must plead for its length.

W. W. Story to J. R. Lowell.

"Berlin, *Jan.* 30th, 1850.

"My dear Jim,—Your letter from Elmwood, dated some day in September last, had not the same disinclination to travel that possesses *you*. It spent nearly two months journeying backwards and forwards, between Vienna and Venice, to each of which places it made three or four visits before it could make up its mind to come to me in Berlin. At last, however, about a fortnight since, it abandoned the occupation of wandering Jew and, worn direfully by travel, much battered and over-scrawled, arrived at 9 Schadow's Strasse, 'eine Treppe hoch,' the present den in which we are domiciled. Yet the prodigal, for all its wandering, had lost nothing of its welcome; it was warm and *geistvoll* as when it left your snug room at Elmwood, and a shout of gladness hailed its arrival. For a time we were with you as we used to be in staunch old New England; the wind was in the great elms, and summer and youth in our hearts. I longed to stretch out my hand to you, with my heart in it, and unburden my soul, and claim your friendly sympathy, and sail down into the past with you along those shores so beflowered with happy memories. Yes, happy, though to me so sad. I must ever ferry across the dark river of death in order to enter into the elysium of youth beyond. We have now arrived at that point—I at least have—where I find myself looking backward oftener than forward, and I doubt if life ever will render an equivalent for what it has taken. . . . Sometimes I think—

it is a dream, but a delightful one—that nothing
could be so satisfactory and so easy as that we
should make a little colony in Rome and there
live in that old old home. Of all places in the
world it is the true spot for us. I cannot tell
you why it so haunts me and taunts me. But
ever my heart goes back there in my dreams,
and the thought of New England life cuts across
me like a knife.

"It was truly a joy to me to meet Frank
Heath, and to meet him and be with him in
Rome. He was to me all that a friend could be,
so genial a presence, so unselfish, so noble, true
and simple, that the old affection which always
lay in my heart for him grew deeper and more
vital with our renewed intercourse. His nature
is so smooth and equable and deep that he was
a constant consolation to me. I am irritable,
quick, harsh, and am easily annoyed, but I could
live for ever with him. Your commission to him
and me to make a pilgrimage to Certaldo how
gladly would I perform! But here I am shiver-
ing in Berlin, and Certaldo is away in the south,
and I hear no toothsome Tuscan here, but only
the rattling of the German cart-wheels. I am
in F. H.'s old tracks, and his friend Dr Stadthagen is my German master. As we drink our
beer at Kneip's the Doctor recounts to me the

vagaries of F. and we drink his *Gesundheit* with clinking glasses. I have for some weeks been a real student, and devoted myself to German, and attended the lectures, and sat on the student forms, and felt again as I did in old Harvard. The sensation with which I first entered the lecture-room was as if time had slid off my back and I was a boy again. I know not whether you will be interested to hear about any of the noteworthies here, but I venture to give you a sketch of some of them. And first for Neander, their great man, in whom also your father will be interested.

"As you know, he is a Jew, and, as you don't know, is dirty and careless of externals. Small, with black clotted hair, very heavy, shaggy eyebrows and purblind eyes which seem never to have been used in seeing, he is completely absent-minded and abstracted from the world. He knows nothing of life or nature, cannot attend to his personal wants and necessities, can scarcely dress himself, and has been known to come into the lecture-room in his drawers alone. Some very good stories are told of him in this respect—of which take this as a specimen. One day he went home and complained of being lame, saying that he had hobbled all the way along the streets. On being asked if he suffered pain

he said, 'No, I feel no pain, no soreness anywhere, but I *am* lame, for I hobbled all the way
home.' His sister examined him carefully and
found no injury, and a physician was called, who
punched and twisted the poor old man all over,
but to no purpose—he could find nothing wrong
Still, Neander insisted that he was lame and that
he *had* hobbled. All were in perplexity till some
one who had seen him returning solved the
mystery by stating that he had walked home
with one foot in the gutter and one on the side-
walk. His style of lecturing beggars description,
and it at first struck me as so ludicrous that I
confess to have not been able to be decorous.
He has a high desk, reaching about to his neck,
behind which, when he enters the room, he suddenly darts and disappears, so as to be visible
from only one side. Leaning one elbow high up
on the desk, he steps back, crosses his legs,
droops his head down beside it lower far than
the surface, seizes a quill which is always prepared and placed there, and twisting this round
and round with both hands just about on a level
with his chin, and tilting the desk so that one
is in constant fear of its falling, commences his
lecture—every sentence beginning with a spasm
which convulses his whole body, stiffening it
sometimes for a moment into a nearly erect

position. His hands clench and his frame is in a paroxysm, but gradually, as the sentence proceeds, his body relapses and droops lower and lower, until at the middle of it he has regained his original position. His voice also accompanies this convulsion, loud at first and then lower and lower, until at last the conclusion of the sentence is utterly inaudible. There is a pause, he twirls his pen violently, spits five or six times, and then there is another convulsion and a second sentence. He literally punctuates his lecture by expectoration—once for a comma, twice for a longer stop. As he stands crouched down beside the desk and tilting it forward with one leg tied in a knot round the other and a long frock-coat coming down below his knees and swaying to and fro, he is certainly one of the strangest of spectacles. His lectures are good, though repetitive and technical. He likes, as all the Germans like, to use their magnificent metaphysical vocabulary, and very frequently they keep saying over the same thing in a different manner and without really adding to or developing the subject.

"I have also been hearing Ranke, whose style is the acme of flippancy, without dignity, grace or intelligibility. He is a little round-faced man, with a baldish forehead, a high voice and thin hair; his head just appears above his desk, and

he rolls himself round, looking up at the ceiling
and jerking out with the extremest rapidity and
nonchalance, and in a most equivocal tone, which
one knows not whether to take as jest or earnest,
little fragments of sentences. If Neander always
seems to be drawing his ideas out of a deep well,
Ranke seems, on the other hand, like a garden
fountain which keeps spurting up little futile
jets and then stopping. Von Raumer I likewise
have heard—dull, dry, hard in manner, and his
lecture consisting of the dry bones of history.
Rudorf on the Roman Law gave us a catalogue
of acts and laws without the least development
or explanation; I should have thought it impossible to be drier had I not heard Raumer
and some others. Waagen on Art was the
stupidest old plodder I ever heard; nothing at
all did he give us but a series of facts, and in
the most mumbling, slovenly manner. Ritter,
the celebrated geographist, I found interesting;
his lecture was devoid of all grace and delivery,
but it was interesting and full of knowledge.
Michelet, in Political Economy, was really clever
and also amusing. I do not believe at all in this
system of instruction. The professors year after
year repeat the same lectures. It seems to me
the relic of a past age, when books were rare
and what the professors gave orally was no-

where else to be found. The Germans are learned not in consequence, but in spite of, this system.

"Now I am on these old worthies let me add to my catalogue a few others out of the University, whom I have met and whose acquaintance I have made First there is Von Humboldt, truly a noble old man, full of knowledge, of a calm clear mind. of great capacity and of very equally - balanced powers. His knowledge is immense, even in respect to the most trifling subjects, and I was astonished, in the interview I had with him, to find that he knew everything in relation to our country, from the beginning to the end, in great and trivial things, as thoroughly as I did imperfectly. Common men I had never heard of, acts of our Government unknown to me, adventures of insignificant travellers, details of the gold mines, facts relating to the geology of every different portion, &c., all were to him 'familiar as his garter.' He is now eighty years of age and has a beautiful head and brow—full, expanded and open. He kept up a continual gush of talk from the moment I entered his room till I left it.

"Von Savigny, the celebrated jurist, I have seen repeatedly, and I can assure you that he is of all petrifactions the most remarkable I

have seen. He is as dry as dust. Very
courteous and affable and complimentary I
found him, but living wholly in a book-world,
and that book-world a law-book-world. He
held up both his hands when he found out that
I was an artist, and cried out, 'What, an artist
and a lawyer? That is impossible!' But if he
is dry, so is not Mme. von Savigny, who is lively,
vivacious, chatty, elegant, and of great simplicity
and kindness of heart. I always devote myself to her, and in return she introduces me to
Gräfins with ugly faces and unpronounceable
names, while the other men herd in one corner
of the room, dressed in black and speaking mono-
syllables. It is odd that we are obliged to go
to these parties in mourning for the Queen-
Dowager of England. We have serious thoughts
of inviting Lord Westmoreland to dinner with
our landlady for cook. She is a creature only
to be found here—with the dirt an inch deep all
over her and the colour of her dress not to be
distinguished below the incrustation of the same.
We live here in the most simple and the least
luxurious style—with two dinner-plates, at the
most, alike, but not even two tea-cups. We
help ourselves to soup with a tin dipper. We
have our gravy in a cup. We have one tumbler
that holds a pint and one that holds a quarter

of a pint. When we came our landlady proposed to us to have our bedclothes and linen
washed once a-month, and she offered us a towel
a-week apiece. I have a big pudding-dish to
wash in, with one bottle of water for my allotted
quantity in connection with it. . . .

"We have become acquainted with Bettina
von Arnim, who is just what you would suppose
from the 'Conversations with a Child'—just so
artless, plain, wayward, simple, frank and poetic.
She received us in the most friendly manner
and, taking Emelyn by the hand, said, 'You
are beautiful. You are lovely.' At which we
laughed, and then she said, 'Is not that English?' She kissed Emelyn and then shook
hands with me and asked 'if I was for Liberty.'
I cannot describe the conversation, but, generally, she talked about the King, and the horrors
of the Hungarian war, and the suffering of many
nobles who had been basely betrayed, imprisoned
and robbed of all their fortune. She spoke of
art, showed me her designs for her statue of
Goethe, and said that the King had wished it
to be made, but that she had declined because
it would fetter her speech. She also told us
the history of her book—how she had refused
to write it until permission should be granted
to her to say all she chose, how this *was*

granted, what a stir the book made, how it was condemned by all as improper to be written to a king (they are so servile here), and how the King said it should not be suppressed, it was laid at the footstool of royalty with so childlike a frankness. We talked about the æsthetics of art and agreed upon them, and she showed me her statue of Goethe, which she herself modelled and which is very clever, far better than Schwanthaler's at Munich."

V.

RETURN TO AMERICA AND TO ITALY.

THEY left Berlin the middle of March, and early
in the June of that year were in London, having
spent part of the interval in Paris. If we view
them, with interest, as suddenly steeped in that
medium of overflowing "town" which they were
not then or ever after to find, like that of the
social Berlin, "narrow and contracted," and if
I rescue from the "dark backward," with all
sympathy, such scraps of their experience as
the record yields, it is because the gentle ghosts
(almost alike gentle now) here indeed begin to
crowd, and the human, or at all events the
personal, picture to thicken. We are substantially met, in Mrs Story's journal, on the very
threshold. "Mr Parry's in the early evening.
Mrs Procter's at 11 for an evening party.
Crowded day!" To which the diarist adds
(July 8th) in reference to the young, the
delicately charming, the doomed first wife of

her husband's closest friend: "Maria Lowell's birthday. When I thought of this my heart was on the other side of the Atlantic." Mr Parry evades me, fortunately for my space, but Mrs Procter, wonderful lady, never evaded any one, and becomes again, at the first touch, the most vivid of presences. The Storys were to meet her often in the future, and they now saw more of her, as we shall presently see. They appear also, by the same token, to have seen not a little, at this time, of one of the interesting men from her so largely, so impressively contemporised relation to whom, an inordinate backward reach, she herself borrowed interest, as she borrowed it from many sources. "Early dinner and a long evening in Leigh Hunt's library"—which would seem to mark the shade of change in that matter of manners on which we keep our eye. Who in London, in 1903, makes dinners early in order to make evenings long in any one's library? So, similarly, "Went to 142 Strand to see Mrs Horatio Greenough." Who stays to-day, and when July comes round, at any number whatever in the Strand? "Dinner at Mr Prescott's," who can only have been, I surmise, the historian of Cortez and Pizarro. "This we found so agreeable that we spent the evening also with him and talked over our various English experiences." At present, when people dine, they do, as a matter of course, spend the evening — unless they be going somewhere else; and this especially if they be gathered Americans with English experiences to talk over. *That* theme of colloquy, at all times, *that* medium of exchange (for the thought of it becomes lively as we trace it back to its possible beginnings and early stages), is certain to have, by its many-sided charm, on such occasions, carried any company far. "Went in the evening to the Opera and heard 'La Tempesta' and one act of 'Anna Bolena,' in which Pasta sang." And Mrs Story mentions that Mr George Peabody, whose great memorial image her husband was, in the years to come, to seat so solidly in the shadow of the Royal Exchange, "sent each of us" (for there was some other lady) a beautiful bouquet; jotting also, as if with more to say about it, "Pasta's singing and acting." But the comment, alas! has dropped out, and we are without the impression. What does remain, attached to this entry, is a little note: "5 tickets, 7s. 6d." From which we gather that it cost in that happy day but that modest sum—and it is a question evidently of the stalls—to partake, in this order, of supreme satisfactions.

And the satisfactions, verily, abounded. "Went with Mr Chorley to a morning concert at the Opera and heard Pasta, Castillan, Viardot, Tamburini, Mario, Ronconi and Grisi, besides the finest orchestra I ever listened to. W. went in the evening to see Rachel." They dine with "Mr Black," who also looms up for me as one of the hovering shades—a friend of Italy and of art, a friend of Rome, of Florence, of Americans, of F. B., of many persons, the light legend of whom, holding it only by hearsay, I rather fear I have lost. I cannot deal with Mr Black, though our friends deal with him frequently and pleasantly enough. They note an evening at Dickens's, as well as a visit to Carlyle at Chelsea and to Leigh Hunt at Kensington, and they mention another evening at Mrs Procter's. It is difficult, on meeting the marked figure of this latter lady again in our path. to resist the temptation to enroll her in our little company of the appealing and the evoked—or easy at least only because, somehow, her strong personality, than which none was ever, in any way, more impatient of attenuations, breaks, even over-much, through the rank. One would like almost to feign, on behalf of our friends, for the pleasure of seeing her image respond to the overture or the pretext, a closer connection with them than

appears to have existed; and this because, among
other reasons, she strikes us as having been—
for what she personally and socially was—singularly uncommemorated. No sign more striking
could there be, I remember thinking at the time
of her death unhonoured and unsung, that no
footprints are sharp enough for the great high
cold London tide not to wash them away without a pause. It is not of course literally that
song should have dealt with her, or that she
was a name to prompt the elegiac note ; but
that she was in an extraordinary degree a subject
for portraiture, which approached her no nearer
on any occasion than if it had been as afraid of
her as an afternoon caller whose welcome was
uncertain or his place in her drawing-room indefinite. Yet even to skirt her no more closely
than we are doing now is to wake her up.
Whatever may have become of her spirit, it
has never, we feel, consented to death ; it revives
at any mention, just as, we are sure, it must
have resented the unmannerly omissions. She
suffered the direct pencil-stroke, or something
in the nature of it, to my knowledge, but once
—when Kinglake, dedicating "Eothen" to her,
addressed her as " Our Lady of Bitterness"; and
her humorous acceptance of that title, under
which she had never winced—under what indeed

had she winced ?—was to become precisely one of
the strong marks of her aspect. Step-daughter
of Basil Montagu, the most accomplished editor
of Bacon prior to Mr Spedding; widow of Barry
Cornwall the poet, the intimate friend and the
biographer of Charles Lamb; mother of Adelaide
Procter the poetess, the ornament of anthologies when anthologies are not, as we may say,
pedantic; friend of a hundred eminent men and
perpetuator, for our age, of the tone of an age
not ours, she requires, no doubt, some introduction to a mistimed generation. Introductions of
Mrs Procter, however, are difficult; they were
in her lifetime all but impossible; they assumed
ignorances on the part of others, just as they
assumed preoccupations on her own, that were,
on the whole, less of a nature to clear the air
than of a nature to cloud it.

For the present perhaps too easily and too
variously solicited chronicler she had at all events,
as an admirable friend, during her latest years,
a value that he always qualified, to himself, as
historic; and not at all, moreover, in the comparatively superficial sense of her associations
and accretions, her extraordinary names and
dates, her long backward span and her persistent
presence, but in the finer one of her being such
a character, such a figure, as the generations

appear pretty well to have ceased to produce, quite as if the technical secret of the "paste," like that of some old fabric or mixture, had been lost to them. "There are no more made"—that might well be the answer given across the social counter to an inquirer curious of reasons. It was her tone that was her value and her identity, and that kept her from being feebly modern ; her sharpness of outline was in *that* in the absence there of the little modern mercies, muddlements, confusions and compromises. English to the core and thoroughly of her class, of her social affiliation, infinitely humorous and human, with perfect distinctness of wit and dauntlessness of opinion, a partisan to her last breath (which meant, on her part, an admirable constancy of favour and of its opposite), she testified somehow to a stouter and harder world than ours, an order more decreed and accepted, one in which the temper had had more at once to give and more to take, more to reckon with, but also more, within its rights, to maintain. Mrs Procter's rights were, to her own view, of the sharpest, but they included, delightfully, the right to be, however inconsequently (if that was the only way), pleased ; which she employed with the finest effect. I remember her once telling me, in answer to some question, after Dowden's Life of Shelley

had come out, that she recalled, from her girlhood,
an occasion on which Leigh Hunt had said, in
her father's house, that he was going up to
Hampstead to see what Shelley's "new wife was
like"; and that she also recalled his saying, on
her asking him, at the next opportunity, for news
of his errand : "Oh, she's like a cross baby."
This reminiscence, I further recollect, had been
determined by my asking her if she had known
Mrs Shelley on the latter's return to England.
"Oh dear, no—one *didn't* know her ; she wasn't
received" : that was a picture, I recall, precious
for the old tone.   But it was on my marvelling,
a little irreflectively, at the antiquity of her
having had such an acquaintance at her command, that she had said, "Oh, that's nothing
—for going back," and then had gone back to
the grey eld that was so much anterior to
Shelley's death and *a fortiori* so much anterior to
Byron's.   I retail this anecdote, however, precisely to emphasise my point that, interesting as
her anecdotes might be, her attitude and her
spirit (facts quite as definite, and certainly quite
as "quaint" as her anecdotes) were things more
interesting still.   More even than the anecdotes
they seemed to make a light, as to the social
world which had been not as ours, on the question
of human relations.   If one arrived at something

of a sense of such relations one sniffed up the
essence of history—to which in the absence of
that sense one remained blackly a stranger.
And it glimmered before one as something the
precious possession of which might bring one
nearer to the ancient reality. Without it one
was, at any rate, in respect to any reproductive
grasp of the ancient reality, a "muff." All this,
however, is a far cry from the fleeting vision
vouchsafed to our friends in the summer of 1850
—albeit, at the same time, that connections are
not wanting. There was, for instance, no more
"regular" friend of the trenchant lady's final
period than Robert Browning, who was also, with
a deeper shade of intimacy, an ally (as we have
seen him already begin to be) of the Storys.
She was, in addition, thoroughly well-affected to
Lowell, who was equally so to her; and these
facts would have in some degree constituted a
relation with her, her friends not being non-
conductors, for others, so to speak, of her relation
to *them*. This last truth, I may perhaps add, is
lighted for me, with some intensity, by my own
last reminiscence : a grey, wintry day and the
company, in a mourning - coach, during slow
funereal hours, of Browning and Kinglake, my
companions of the pilgrimage. That was an
occasion, verily, for as fine an appreciation of

shades of intimacy as one might have cared to attempt. Browning was infinitely talkative, and Kinglake, old, deaf, delicate, distinguished, perfect, infinitely silent. Mrs Procter, whose displeasure he had incurred, had not spoken to him for a quarter of a century. She was magnificent.

Story and his wife, who had spent the summer in England and Scotland, were in London again, the same year, early in the autumn. Let me not omit, in reference to the interval, a short entry in Mrs Story's diary at Edinburgh on August 6th. " Came home to find letters and the saddest of all news of Margaret and her child and her husband. How deeply I felt it, how sad I was made, I cannot here say ; but pale was the sky, dull the face of nature when I thought of the friend I had lost. Of course we were in no mood to meet our engagement, but stayed at home to be alone and write." Then a little later : " My mind, last night, was so filled with thoughts and memories of Margaret Ossoli that I found no refreshment even in sleep. The vision of her as I saw her last on the steps of our house, and the memory of those troubled days in Rome, kept coming back to me, and I felt so deep a sorrow that I could look neither before nor behind." They had had, on the other hand, in the country,

some measure of the society of one of their
American friends, not the least valued or distinguished—and far from one of our ghostly
chorus, happily, he—Charles Eliot Norton, of
Cambridge, Massachusetts, whom we shall, to our
advantage, meet again. It is from the September days in London that Story's long friendship
with Robert Bulwer Lytton, the late Lord
Lytton, whom we shall also meet again, was
pleasantly to date. "Found at Kenyon's John
Forster and Maclise. Forster told me that a son
of Sir Edward Bulwer wished to go to his uncle
in America and asked me to take charge of him;
to which I willingly consented. He also invited
me to dine with him and meet Bezzi, Kenyon,
&c., on Wednesday week." Sir Henry Bulwer,
afterwards Lord Dalling, was then British representative at Washington, and the Storys' first
stay in Europe was drawing to a close. He goes
to see his friend Black, of the Italian days, who
offers him, out of "pretty little gardens, some
wall-fruit, nectarines, of high flavour," and gives
him occasion, in the house, to observe that "one
of Landseer's pictures looked strangely out of
place between [copies of] Guido's and Guercino's
'Auroras.' The English school," he adds, "looks
hardly respectable beside the old works of the
masters." Harkening, as we must, for the lighter

notes of the time, we cull that one as we pass;
finding perhaps another as well in the fact that
the amiable Mr Black presented E. "with a
beautiful papier-mâché portfolio." There hangs
over the day, partly from these matters, the
sense as of old suburban September Sundays in a
more golden air than ours. "Walked to Clapham
with Black to see George Catermole. We had a
pleasant walk of five and a half miles and passed
by Clapham Academy, where Hood went to
school, and Black went also, and which is now
an orphans' asylum. Catermole I found a most
agreeable full-natured man, mild and humoursome
in conversation, and with a peculiarly oldish
choice of language." He notes a few contacts
with celebrities not of the first order; he goes to
see Frank Stone; he dines again with Black, in
company with Catermole, "who fell foul of the
Transfiguration and said many severe and true
things about it"; he reminds himself of anecdotes, rather faded now, of Hogan, the Irish
sculptor, of Forster, of Dickens: the golden air,
the September suburban Sunday hang over it
all.

He dines with the then little American world
of London, and lays the foundation of the friendship that was to be the most valued of his life
and to constitute for him, in after-years, a close

tie with London, with England; a tie never
strained, though again and again tested. These
were the early years of the long residence in
England of his loved and honoured countryman
the late Russell Sturgis, afterwards senior partner
in the house of Baring Brothers. The weak
wand of evocation rises of itself, I feel, to play
over Mr and Mrs Russell Sturgis's name, their
aspect, their so involved connection with this
record — over the large, bright, comprehensive
story of their career, character, hospitality, general bounty and benignity. The subject has—
and would have for many a memory beside my
own—a noble amplitude; but I am conscious
that it need not be, of deliberation, in relation
to our other matters, brought in; the deliberation would have to be, much rather, to keep
it out.   Story dines with John Forster and meets
Talfourd, "a thinnish, smallish, hard, wiry man,
very ambitious and spasmodic, and, though nice,
limited and wanting the freedom of genius.   Certainly, however, with the keenness of polish and
education.   Not an elegant man at all, nevertheless, and ate with his knife.   Mr Justice Hardwick, Bezzi, Kenyon, who drove us there, Maclise,
a quiet, ratherish dull, but pleasant, fellow, and
Forster himself, a jovial roaring blade.   We discussed Webster's case" — that of the Harvard

professor who had startled the world just then
by doing to death a Boston physician and cutting
up and burning his body : the first "murder-
case," of public interest, projecting its red light,
at that time, into the consciousness of small
American partakers of the shocks of their elders.
Story retails some of the talk at Forster's dinner.
"Hardwick told of Turner that, on a fishing excursion, when there was a fine sunset and his
companions, studying and delighting in the splendour, turned round and looked for him, they discovered him seated with his back to the view and
picking shrimps out of the lap of an old woman.
Forster showed us a beautiful letter from Hamp-
den to Sir John Eliot in the Tower.   Landor had
a similar one, and, on my saying that our language seemed not to have its old elegance, Forster
said : 'Charles II. and his age spoilt the language.
As soon as a grammar is printed in any language
it begins to go. The Greeks had no grammar
when their best works were written, and the
decline of style began with the appearance of
one.' " He devotes several little pages to an
excursion to Knole with Black ; he goes, for the
first time, to Oxford ; on September 28th Sir
Edward Bulwer calls, with Forster, to present
Bulwer's son.   But his face is turned homeward ;
the spell is broken ; I find under date of October

5th : " Off from Liverpool ; bright day. Forster
went down with us to see us off." In respect to
which I am uncertain if the record should stand
that the biographer of Goldsmith and Dickens
made with them for that purpose the then so
long railway journey from London. People do
not, nor ever did they, assuredly, go "down"
only to Euston. Forster's company on the way
is eminently, delightfully credible; it is simply
that, on the other hand, we have on our mind
his lonely return. Still, it was even then a
stouter age than ours. The ship of our friends
was, auspiciously — if not indeed, as more
promptly determinant of reactions, ominously—
the *America,* and they passed Cape Race (oh
the memory, as through the wicked light of wild
sea-storms, of those old sick passings of Cape
Race !) on October 13th.

Story mentions, in a statement from which
I have already quoted, that on his first return
to Boston he remained there "eight months";
this, apparently, however, was not exact to
within a few weeks, inasmuch as toward midsummer of 1851 he had still not taken his fresh
departure. He had exhibited to those concerned
his matured design for his statue of his father,
which had been viewed with favour; he had
again, nevertheless, with some incongruity,

renewed vigorously his connection with the
Law, and he took up in particular, at this time,
the preparation of his father's Life. In respect
to which, and to many other things, I must
again profess my inability to encounter a letter
of Charles Sumner's without yielding to the
desire to reproduce it. His letters prompt that
disposition, in as marked a degree, though not
on the same ground, as Lowell's. The grounds
in question in the two cases differ, in fact, I
think, diametrically. Irresistible in Sumner is
the way he gives himself out, irresistible in
Lowell the way he (with a still greater abundance, still more expression of it) keeps himself
in. Sumner, writing on July 4th from "the
steamer for Newport," had been reading with
Story the proofs of the Life. "I have read two,
which I received just as I was leaving Boston,
and I shall direct them to you at the Nahant
post-office. So, if you have not received them,
please call there. Do you not seem too much
to apologise for your father's early confidence
in Humanity? My faith in this is so constant
and fixed that I think him more right in those
early days than in his later life. Who can doubt
that hereafter, and before not many years are
passed, we shall all regard distrust in the Future
of Man on earth as little better than Heathenism?

The Future is secure; the Present alone is uncertain. Study the proofs well." From another friend meanwhile Story had also been hearing.

Robert Lytton to W. W. Story.

"WASHINGTON, *March* 10*th*, 1851.

. . . . "The so-called gaieties are over, everybody going away. In a week or two there will be nobody in the streets but the cows, and they look as if they would like to go too if they could. In the meantime I remain learning order and large text-hand in the Chancellerie, and my ambition oozes out at the tips of my fingers; for it is easy to make fine day-dreams and think about fame or fortune as if one had the future in one's pocket—but so hard to realise them, and the way seems so long, and we go with such little steps. For my own part, seeing the knaves and fools who get the great prizes in the lottery, and the wise and good men whom no one knows anything about, I think I shall be content, like Horace, with my salt-cellar, and laugh at all the rest of the world who bustle out of life as if they could not get rid of it quick enough. I have heard of a Secretary of State who was asked why he did not promote merit, and replied, 'Because merit did not promote me!'—and I think that

is just how merit gets kicked out of the way
by men who get on not for their good but for
their bad qualities. . . . I heard from my
father that there is going to be a dinner given
to Macready and he is to take the chair;
Dickens too will be there. What are you
doing in Boston? It would give me great
pleasure to have a letter from you, with all
the news, at least such as relates to your circle.
There is so much I would wish to have said to
you and heard from you while you were here,
and it seemed so short a time. Are your old
recollections of Washington sufficiently vivid
to compare them with your last? and does it
not strike you that here are social phenomena
wholly unlike anything else in this or any other
country?

"It reminds me of a picture I remember having once seen in which the hares roast the cooks
and the horses ride the men; a sort of *bouleverse-
ment* of every existing state of things. For here
are young ladies who seduce the men, sometimes
under promise of marriage (that is, if heiresses),
and old fellows who play the *joli cœur*, and young
men who marry and live steadily and wear spectacles, and sham Juans and sham Haidees talking
sham sentiment. But no one who stays long
here could, I think, help liking Washington,

for there is so much *laisser aller* and such a
fund of kindness and hospitality. Then too
it is the focus of so much intellect, though an
idler like myself sees more of the 'young and
thoughtless' than of the grave and reverent
seniors. And as for variety, it is a sort of continual Pentecost, with 'Turks, Jews and dwellers
in Mesopotamia all speaking one tongue.' Clay
has been making some somewhat fiery speeches,
which I think rather unworthy of him. I cannot
but think it bad taste even in one who has so
mighty a prestige to keep crying out, 'I am
Sir Oracle, and when I ope my mouth let no
dog bark!' You will have seen Allen's (?)
attack on Webster, which I am glad to see has
met almost universally with the scorn it merited.
I know of no more news. An Hungarian lady
who was Kossuth's *aide-de-camp* has arrived
here and created some interest. You see the
Government is going to send out a ship to bring
him over here. I hear from this person that the
Russian influence is so great at Constantinople
that he is now in great danger. I don't know
how I shall ask you to pardon me for having
bored you thus long, but I write to make you
write.

"*P.S.*—News! news! the Government is out!
Am I not a good prophet? Did I not say this

would happen while you were at Washington?
I hear it is not to be a Peelite Government, but
Sir James Graham as Premier and Lord Aber-
deen for Foreign Affairs. I wait with the ut-
most impatience to see which lot, for good or
bad, we over here shall get out of the raffle.
. . . What a singular thing it seems, the sudden break up of the Governments over Europe!
The Spanish Ministers have been turned out, and
General Narvaez is an exile at Paris. The
Belgian Government too has just gone out of
office. The French Ministers have all within the
last few weeks shared a similar fate, and now the
Whigs have crumbled away at last at home.
So, while the slides shift in the lantern, we, the
children, stare at the picture as they pass and
laugh or cry as our humour suits us. Well,
better do that, I cannot but think, than be the
gentlemen who manage the lamp and burn their
fingers!"

It would take us too far, unfortunately, to
read a little between the lines of the foregoing
and try for a moment to win back a vision of the
" old " Washington of those years ; the Washington of long " before the war," of a political and
social order that has passed away, and—as it has
occasionally lived again for us in anecdote and

echo—of an incomparable *bonhomie* of provincial-
ism. It was the Washington, as we so see it, of
an almost paradisiacal ease of intercourse, of an
unblushing ignorance of cold conventions, of a
winning indifference to imported standards; the
Washington of the Southern ascendancy, the
Southern luridity, but also, we must suppose, the
Southern sweetness, as the special field of the
"Southern belle"; the Washington of evil roads
and early springs and shabby houses and short
purses, of a more obsequious "niggerdom" and
of an uneradicated prejudice in respect to that
convenience. It was doubtless, with its queer-
ness and its anomalies, as of a great gay political
village or crude civil camp, the Washington
evoked for me long ago in the talk of an old
foreign diplomatist who had served there in his
younger time. "Je vous assure que lorsqu'on
sortait, le soir, de dîner chez le Président on
trébuchait sur les vaches couchées à la porte."
This indeed was probably when one had dined
thoroughly well. We must, however, but sigh
and pass. The situation in Boston, at any rate,
appears meanwhile to have been that, having
undertaken to prepare a new edition, already
invited, of the law-book he had published before
his absence, Story had his task to achieve, which
he did excellently, working against time and

ripening for a real rupture. The book in question, "Contracts," had reached by 1874 a fifth edition. It speaks unmistakably of his various ability and facility, the mental agility, the insistence in the direction of the hour, with which his life, his talk, his work and his play ever abounded, that he could keep himself in two such opposed relations at once, could take hold afresh even while really giving up, and give up even while really taking hold. This was to show in him as markedly later on, during the time of his second return, when he again simultaneously took hold and gave up—all of which, however, only characterised his variety. Of all victims (so far as victim he was) of the famous "artistic temperament," he was the least detached from other cares of the mind. His æsthetic sensibility, active as it was, was not a jealous, not an exclusive housemate. His mind begot ideas about everything, opinions, convictions, things that at the moment were passions; which things, in their turn, kept him perpetually at the pitch of communication, expression, discussion. He spent his life in the happy condition of never being without a *subject* (for affirmation, irritation, emphasis, for free development of some sort), there being one or two—such, for instance, as his inexpugnable view of the French nation,

French scenery, French products and character-
istics, of whatever sort, a view that fed, in an
odd but traceable way of its own, on his great
love of Italy—that might have been noted as
keeping him company most of his days : a provision for our happiness, in general, it may be
said, than which fate makes none better.

If, at all events, he was, during 1851, as I
have hinted, ripening for a real rupture, the
rupture shows as real enough in the next of
his letters.   There are none before me that
take him up at a shorter interval; there is
only the legend, preserved in his house, of the
intensity, the ineffability of the joy with which,
in the September of this 1851, he found himself
approaching Genoa from the sea.   He had embarked, at Boston, with his wife and children,
on one of the old sailing-packets, the *Kepler*,
and it was part of the legend that the captain
of this vessel always spoke of Civita Vecchia,
one of its usual ports of destination, as " Vetchy-
Vatch "—his seamanship being supposedly better
than his Italian.   Our friends, however, for some
reason, quitted the ship at Gibraltar and re-
embarked for Genoa; a touch or two more,
in relation to their journey, still clinging to the
legend.   Or I should perhaps say, rather, that
it is I who still cling to any touch—any echo

of an echo, for instance, that shows us, no matter for how few seconds, something of the old, the more human, way. They had got at last to "Vetchy-Vatch" and thence taken *vettura* to Rome; where, by night, Mrs Story sat in the carriage waiting while the exhibition of their passport went on in the neighbouring guard-house, or whatever, to which her husband had carried it, and whence she saw him, in time, return escorted by two gendarmes and two candles. He had shown first, with some effect of mystification, his old passport, the one prepared for his former visit; but he was provided with a second, in which (as apparently not in the other) he figured as Esquire, to the final illumination of his companions, in whose faces, between the candles, apprehension was seen to dawn. "Ah, Esqui-*re!* Re degli Esqui—sua Maestà!" with deep obeisances and a prompt liberation of the vehicle. It was not, as entries into Rome go, one of the least effective. But this is the next letter.

W. W. Story to J. R. Lowell.

"Castel Gandolfo, *July 8th*, 1852.

. . . "Well, from the Alban Mount I hail you. We are perched just over the lake, with the vast sweep of the Campagna stretching out

from our feet and the old castello looking grimly
down over the Pope's gardens opposite. We
have taken the Villa Ceni and we are here
with Cass,[1] or rather he is here with us. A
villa more to my mind, as far as the house
goes, I have not seen. Every bedroom free,
a magnificent salon, sixty-three feet long and
twenty-five high, with a billiard-table at which
I spend quite a third of my time playing with
Cass. Then a grand dining-room and a beautiful
loggia, looking over lake and mountains and
Campagna. And three handsome girls, with
their mother, are in the *mezzanino* below and
are 'so sociable.' I would that you were here
to saunter with us in the grand Barberini villa,
with its grove of pines, or to drive (for Cass's
carriage is here, stabled below, and always at
our command) through the galleries which lead
off in all directions, or to make excursions
to Gensano, Lariccia, Itri, or heaven knows
where. Cass really walks, by the four or five
hours together, and abjures carriages while we
are here. We find him very pleasant, not
obtrusive, and though not genial (that's beyond
his nature), agreeable. His wonderful stock of
stories is never empty, and I have had an opportunity of verifying some which were exceedingly

[1] General Lewis Cass, 1782-1866.

ill *trovati*, and been obliged to reserve the proverb. What we don't believe amuses us as much as what we do—perhaps more; and we have never found them untrue where we had an opportunity to know.

"Thank you for remembering the messages and inquiries in respect to a marble worker. Powers is in a fog as to all persons' interest except his own; in respect to the latter it is always clear day with him. I am glad, however, to know that he has ceased to trouble himself about my marble, as I shall now look out for it myself. It is quite preposterous to tell me that, had he wished, he could not in *four* years have obtained a block for me. He promised with such earnestness and so repeatedly to do this thing for me that I believed him—more fool I. . . . During our last days in Rome we had the glorious illumination of St Peter's and the Girandola on the Pincian—the latter of which we saw from Cass's windows. On St Peter's Eve were *vesperoni* in the great church by both choirs, which were very fine. The old bronze San Pietro was robed in a splendid costume with the triple crown on his head. Flowers heaped the altars and were scattered on the pavements and the whole well, where is Canova's kneeling Pope, under the balustrade of chandeliers, was exquisitely mosaic'd with the richest flowers. This ceremony was not among the humbugs. Crawford has returned and is now making a small model of his Washington monument. Tell Page he must come here next winter. No place is like Rome; I have seen them all and I know it. Florence is nothing but a Continental Boston in its spirit."

Such a letter as that, or as another, of the end of the same summer, with which I must follow it, is, besides being delightful in itself, delightful also in proportion to any old memories, impressions, visions of one's own, that one may read into it. And what indeed may the lover of Italy, the survivor of changes, extinctions, young intensities, the spirit haunted by the sweeter, softer, easier, idler Rome, the Rome, so to speak, of greater and stranger differences—what may so fond an embroiderer *not* read into almost any faded sketch in which there are enough of the old elements to " compose " ? One can in any case but speak for one's self, and in some cases, doubtless, even, be able little enough to give connections and reasons. Why for instance does it minister to tenderness, to wonderful little images, but all merely melancholy and merciful (so that they are droll as well as grave), to

caress, as moving in these scenes, the fancied
figure of the well-marked General Cass, who becomes interesting, or at all events vivid, among
them, precisely by reason of his incongruity?
Rich and curious, for that matter, would probably
be, from beginning to end, the series of portraits
of the diplomatic representatives of the United
States at foreign Courts up to the time of the
Civil War—especially as presented in the general
diplomatic picture. The *effect* would probably
always be there—the effect as we see it produced by General Cass in the Roman ilex shade,
among the watching blank-eyed busts. To the
strong, special, unusual nature of this effect,
establishing altogether a new measure of character, attitude, tone, and many other matters not
insusceptible of deterioration by flatness, the
jaded senses of potentates and premiers must, on
the whole, have owed a refreshment that was
none the less real for not having been registered
in protocols and gazettes. Incontestably, we
must add, the American imagination, engaged
with these pictures, does not yearn for a sallow
senator, either square-chinned or lantern-jawed,
as a *contemporary* contribution: we melt over
the phenomenon only as we see it conditioned
by time and distance and by the consequent
accessibility, in us, of the romantic spirit. I

seem, exactly, to see it so conditioned in a
document, as I am tempted to call it, that is
before me as I write—a photograph of the admirable statue of General Cass produced, for a
public position, by Mr Daniel French, a master,
in his art, of character. The massive, large-
headed, dress-coated American statesman of our
early day stands there planted on his feet with
convincing truth and yet with an aboriginal
erectness and dignity that has been paid for in
no concession to statuesque grace. This personage, we feel, has for the pedestal of his monument the "floor of the House," and never was
better rendered that manner of resting on the
legs which defies the push of parties. General
Cass, so preserved, rests on *his* for ever, reducing
time itself, in its certainty of not making him
budge, to a sense of political feebleness. Didn't
he wear, in the Roman summer mornings, the
dress-coat, blue with brass buttons, of his effigy;
didn't he hang about in it in the Barberini
gardens, and wasn't he there, with its aid, in
the *villeggiatura* season, of a rich exoticism of
aspect that the Swiss Guard of the Papal villa
alone could rival? We fondly build upon it; we
fill in the picture with more touches than I have
room for; the historic sense insists and persuades.
I feel indeed in still another connection that

there is no keeping it down.   It prompts me to
record how one of the survivors of that season,
then a very small child, remembers having been,
during the previous Roman months, "in a little
blue frock," taken by the kind old representative
of her country to call, as it were, on the Pope at
the Vatican ; so that, meeting his Holiness afterwards in the gardens of the villa, where she and
her brother were allowed to play, she enjoyed
the benefit of her introduction.   One day, while
they were, with their nurse, in one of the
galleries of shade that lead to Albano, they met
his Holiness taking a walk; which gave the
nurse—a thrilled Irishwoman from the States—
the opportunity to kneel and kiss his hand.   My
informant has not to this day forgotten the
penetrating Papal smile.   "Ah then, you're not
little Protestants to-day !"   Such things ought
doubtless to be trifles to the historic sense, but
I feel that in this general connection there is no
point at which it can be brushed away.   Melting
to visions and memories quite independent of
those I have just noted, I wander again myself
in Barberini gardens, I hang, at this villa, from
the windows of the painted *sala*, from between
the arches of the loggia, over wide Campagna
and deep Alban lake ; I partake of hospitalities
more recent and never forgettable ; hanging too,

very much as with the other contemplations, over the cradle of a work of literary art, a work itself all richly reflective of the conditions (and now well open to identification),—a work, in short, which was to enjoy a splendid maturity. But these are perhaps too many meanings to read into the single letter I have cited; so that I make haste to prop up my case with another. Lowell had spent in Rome the winter of 1851-52, and was supposed by his correspondent to be in England and on his way home.

W. W. Story to J. R. Lowell.

"Sept. 20th, 1852.

. . . "Such a summer as we have had I never passed and never believed in before. Sea and mountain breezes all the time, thunder-showers varying with light and shade the Campagna, donkey-rides and rambles numberless— a long, lazy, luxurious *far niente* of a summer, such as you would have thoroughly enjoyed. And how often have I wished to have you here; what excursions might we not have made together into the Abruzzi, where I long to go; what games of billiards at home! All that I wanted was to have some old friend with me. As for heat, we have not felt it; there has always been a breeze, and in the long, shady

galleries roofed over by ilexes one can walk even
at noon for miles. Just now the Pope is here
and all is *festa*. Every day he makes a new
excursion with all his *cortége*, and every town
he visits has a rumpus to receive him. You
cannot imagine anything more picturesque than
all these mingling costumes and bright-coloured
crowds and fairs such as we saw at Gennezzano,
with sales of squash-seeds and pigs stuffed whole
and *ciambelli* and spring-knives and false jewelry
and glaring bandana handkerchiefs; with spout-
ing fountains and almond-eyed children and
cleanly-dressed girls crowned with the white-
peaked *tovaglia*. Up at the castle *portone*
stand the striped Swiss Guards with their long,
glittering lances, and the square is gay with
soldiers and *canonici* and *monsignori*. When
the Pope rides, or drives in his great gilt coach
with his four black giants of stallions, what
kneeling to his benediction as he enters the
square, while tapestried hangings wave from the
upper windows of the castello and boys cling
to the gratings of the lower! And the band
bursts into a clash of music, and the organ inside the church, which is strewn with flowers
and box and lighted with pyramids of candles,
groans and thunders softly. I never tire of
these doings. Then the dancing to thumping

tamborellas, and the laughter and gaiety and
screaming, are really reviving. But why talk
of this to you? You saw enough of it to spur
your imagination at Gennezzano. . . . You
never were *here*, were you? Poor fellow, been
to Italy and never saw Castel Gandolfo! How
will Gurowsky[1] growl, aiming that fatal eye
over his nose at you, when he hears this! You
had better swear, when you return, that you
have been where the descendants of Æneas's old
white sow and thirty pigs, now coal-black, ramble
round the streets and are tied out to posts, and
where, with exquisite felicity, to the accompani-
ment of squeal and grunt, they snarl themselves
up with the legs of the donkeys that come to
visit them and are screamed and howled at by
a score of ragged boys.

"In a fortnight we intend to make a mountain excursion for a few days, and then shall
return to Rome, where we have taken a beautiful apartment in Piazza di Spagna, 93, just opposite to Hooker's Bank. I am anxious to be
at work in my studio, which is now completed
uniformly with Crawford's. You see your grand
schemes about the Palazzo Albano have fallen
to the ground; but we like our new quarters

---

[1] Count Adam Gurowsky, 1805-1866, Polish author and revolu-
tionist, long resident in New York and Washington.

better. They are more fitted to our republican condition, although perhaps even they are a little too florid. How we shall miss you and M. in the winter evenings! There is nobody to supply your place. . . . Since we have been at Castel Gandolfo we have seen only Italian friends, some of whom we find very pleasant and *simpatici*. Frank Boott writes me from Florence that he is preparing an 'Inno' to contend for a prize offered by some musical academy there. This however, I suppose, is a secret. He calls Rome by all the bad names he knows, and yet I'll engage that he longs to be back here. Crawford swears boldly to us that it is ridiculous to go out of Rome into the country, that he and his family find the villa (Negroni) good enough for them — to which the gentle Watson sings a feeble echo; but at the same time sweet Mrs C. confides to E.'s ear that Crawford is determined never to spend another summer in Rome, because he thinks it wears upon the constitution. At the Correa is a circus, and during the summer I have heard some admirable playing from a new company of actors.

"Your motions have been so erratic lately, and we have been in such confusion as to your whereabouts and whatabouts, that I have not sent you the letters of introduction that I prom-

ised.   But herewith I send one or two, and
could send more but that I doubt whether you
can establish yourself for a year or two and we
can go to the East together and make pilgrim-
ages to the many nooks and spots of Italy
which both of us have left unseen.   We must
take some untravelled paths which the English
have not spoiled, and go into the wildest fast-
nesses of the Abruzzi, perhaps to Sora.   Every
day that I live here I love Italy better and life
in America seems less and less satisfactory.   All
that I want here is a few old friends.   I've sealed
these two notes to Forster and Leigh Hunt because I have availed myself of the occasion to
write more than the introduction, and also for
fear that they may not arrive in time to serve
you."

A letter of the following winter to the same
correspondent, and in no less "launched" a
strain, must speak for itself save in so far as
we are able, dotting a few of its *i*'s, to clear up
a dimness or two.

W. W. Story to J. R. Lowell.

"ROME, *February* 11*th*, 1853.
. . . . "Here the winter until the last week
has been almost fabulously fine—clear, sunny,

and so warm that as yet we have had no fires until the evening. The grass is as green as in the spring, the birds sing constantly in the open air, and already the trees are putting forth their blossoms. But the Carnival has been a decided failure. It was so broken up with intervening *festas* that one never got into the humour, and the weather was quite unpropitious. For the first time almost for a year we had four or five days of rain—which meant mud and soiling of pretty *contadina* dresses. I sought out our handsome *contadina* of last year, but she was not to be found. Another very pretty one gave me one day a jumping-jack and a Roman smile, which were both highly satisfactory. We had a balcony under Clarisse's, and I longed for you and sulked all day at my studio because you were not here. If one could get rid of the ghosts of old times would it on the whole be an advantage?

. . . "Apropos of which you are creating at this time a furore at 28 Corso—W.'s harem (scarem) as I call it—among the emancipated females who dwell there in heavenly unity; namely, the Cushman, Grace Greenwood, H., S., and Co.; not forgetting the Bayne, who is here without her antidote. And for fear I should forget them, let me tell you of them. They live

all together under the superintendence of W.,
who calls them Charlotte, Hatty, and so on, and
who dances attendance upon them everywhere,
even to the great subscription ball the other
evening. Hatty takes a high hand here with
Rome, and would have the Romans know that
a Yankee girl can do anything she pleases, walk
alone, ride her horse alone, and laugh at their
rules. The police interfered and countermanded
the riding alone on account of the row it made
in the streets, and I believe *that* is over, but I
cannot affirm. The Cushman sings savage ballads
in a hoarse, manny voice, and requests people
recitatively to forget her not. I'm sure I shall
not. Page is painting her picture. He is well
and happy and delights in Rome, and I am glad
enough to have him here. He has made some
very fine copies from Titian which I suppose you
have seen, and is now Titianising the Madonna
della Seggiola. Frank Boott is also here; I told
him when he returned to Florence that he would
repent, and so he has. There are a great number
of Americans here this winter, but I have kept
out of American society, having exchanged it for
Italian, which I find agreeable. My life has
been very uniform. In November I began on
my large statue of Father, and it is now about
finished. Before this letter can reach you it will

be in plaster.   My marble for it is also purchased
and my *abbozzatore* engaged, so that there will
not be a day's delay in carrying forward the
work.   I am also putting into marble by bas-
relief 'The Flight of Youth,' for F. S.   My next
work will be the Arcadian Shepherd Boy in large
—so much for *me*.

"I have been so consumed by interest in my
statue that I have been nowhere and seen nothing
by day.   The Barberini faun still spouts his fine
column of water into the sunshine, and I stop
every day as I walk to my studio to admire it.
In about nine weeks I shall be at leisure and
mean to go into the mountains that seem to woo
me to them as I see them in the distance whenever I drive out on the Campagna or over the
Ponte Molle, as I frequently do after the day's
work is over.   The more I live in Rome the more
I love it.   All that I want is a few choice old
friends, and especially do I long for you and
Frank H.   How you would have enjoyed this
divine winter here !   Do come back. . . .   For
Dr Hosmer I did what I could, but he did not
like to be done for.   I got Miss Hosmer a place
in Gibson's studio, but W. took the credit of it.
Miss Homer is also, to say the word, very wilful,
and too independent by half, and is mixed up
with a set whom I do not like, and I can there-

fore do very little for her. She is doing very
well and shows a capital spirit, and I have no
doubt will succeed. But it is one thing to copy
and another to create. She may or may not
have inventive powers as an artist, but if she
have will not she be the first woman?"

Ghosts enough, verily, with a little encouragement, would peep out of the foregoing : I feel
indeed that were I to take an unconsidered step
to meet them they would fairly advance upon us
in a swarm. Old manners, old fashions, old
standards, old provincialisms, prejudices, inno-
cences wrap them about, after all, with the kind
historic haze—leave them, for the most part,
" funny" but vague, as we find the portraits,
the contributions, the verses, tales and other
ornamental literature, in turning over the back
numbers of superseded magazines. Story's
" Hatty" is of course Miss Harriet Hosmer, the
most eminent member of that strange sisterhood
of American " lady sculptors" who at one time
settled upon the seven hills in a white, marmorean flock. The odd phenomenon of their
practically simultaneous appearance would no
doubt have its interest in any study of the birth
and growth of taste in the simmering society
that produced them ; their rise, their prosperity,

their subsidence, are, in presence of some of the widely scattered monuments of their reign, things likely to lead us into bypaths queer and crooked, to make us bump against facts that would seem only to wait, quite in a flutter, to live again as anecdotes. But our ramifications might at such a rate easily become too many. One of the sisterhood, if I am not mistaken, was a negress, whose colour, picturesquely contrasting with that of her plastic material, was the pleading agent of her fame; another was a "gifted" child (speaking by the civil register as well as by nature) who shook saucy curls in the lobbies of the Capitol and extorted from susceptible senators commissions for national monuments. The world was good-natured to them—dropped them even good-naturedly, and it is not in our fond perspective that they must show for aught else than artless. Miss Hosmer had talent (it would be to be remembered that her master, John Gibson, dedicated her to renown, were it not that John Gibson's own renown has also by this time turned so to the ghostly), and she was, above all, a character, strong, fresh and interesting, destined, whatever statues she made, to make friends that were better still even than these at their best. The Storys were among the friends—my memory of later Barberini days, Barberini dinners, testifies to that, as well as to the more mature, but no less prompt, wit of the lady. My memory, if I may continue to press it, testifies also, in its degree, to the once great "actuality" of Miss Cushman, though not as to her Roman time nor as to her part in private life. When I wish to feel ante-diluvian I live again over a small incident of childhood—very young childhood it must have been, contemporary, quite, with the prehistoric, that is with the palmy days, as I take it I ought to call them, in New York, of the old Park Theatre. I recall the bent heads of two small boys, extracting of a winter's night, by the lamp, till nine o'clock, from such auxiliary fiction as was proper to their years, the fabled "lessons" of the morrow, and then the sudden infinite widening of this little lamplit circle, to soul and sense, through the irruption of the most generous and most impulsive of parents, who, present, that evening, as one of the parental pair, at one of Miss Cushman's moving performances, and im-pressed with its probable still greater impressive-ness for the candour of childhood, had driven home, at a rush, from the far "down town" of the Park, to snatch up and carry off my elder brother.

This as near as I came in infancy to seeing the celebrated actress in "Henry VIII."; I was to wait for that privilege to a much later time, the short period of her melancholy reappearances, impoverised and infirm, within a year or two of her death.   But the scene, that evening, at which, through my being inadequately estimated, I did not assist, is one of the most ineffaceable in my tolerably rich experience of the theatre.   I recall it as a vivid vigil in which the poor lonely lamplight became that of the glittering stage, in which I saw wondrous figures and listened to thrilling tones, in which I knew "Shakespeare acted" as I was to never know him again, in which, above all, I nursed my view of paternal discrimination.   Miss Cushman's career, properly examined, would probably vivify for us some of the differences, for better or for worse, between the old theatre and the new.   Markedly destitute of beauty or of the feminine - attractive, and thereby reduced to the interpretation of a small number of parts, she had yet found it possible, by the simple aid of intelligent art, the austere charm of "thoughtful acting" unenhanced and (save by other thoughtful actors) unsupported, so to "draw" as to have amassed in no great compass of time a considerable fortune and to have been able to retire with it to the easy winter watering - place that Rome had already then become, or rather had not yet ceased to be.   It was interesting, I remember, on the *other*, the long-subsequent occasion, to get the measure of the potency of mere premeditated art—from which there has consentingly remained with me but the recollection, however, of great beauty of voice and tone. To these were to have been added, I believe, as an element of the prime, some special mastery of the romantically gaunt and grim—if this be in fact the property that such successful efforts as her Meg Merrilies and her Nancy Sikes, in the emaciated versions, respectively, of Scott's novel and of Dickens's, may be conceived to have had in common. Whatever they had, are we not, with our eye so restlessly on the history of taste, rather left wondering at this *reine de théâtre* whose queer little kingdom, yielding a princely revenue (as the theatre of that age went), consisted of the three heterogeneous provinces of Queen Katherine, Meg and Nancy, to which might be added the outlying insular dependency of Romeo? And since we are asking such questions may we not also wonder to what particular barbarisms of the present such barbarisms as the "Guy Mannering" and the "Oliver Twist" of the early Victorian stage would correspond? Have we, after all, for platitude of poverty, anything to match them? I can myself dimly remember the early Victorian

"Nicholas Nickleby," with the weeping feminine
Smike of the young actress who was afterwards
to become Mrs Charles Mathews, and the sense
of incoherence, the flop and flutter as of perpet-
ually-shifting canvas, that could disconcert even
the sharp appetite of childhood. I believe, to be
just to Miss Cushman, that she had been known
to play Wolsey as an alternative to her Katherine,
as she had been known to play Juliet as an alternative to her Romeo. It is all, however, a little
gruesome, so I hurry on.

I hurry, if it may so be called, but, with our
restless eye, not too fast also to pause an instant
before the literary, the social shade of Grace
Greenwood and the memory of the odd association that, for a young imbiber of her friendly
prose and verse, could cling to her elegant name.
One knew it was somehow not real—wasn't it in
fact too beautiful to be ? yet why then, if feigned,
an adoption of the funereal note familiar to New-
Yorkers of the tenderest age in the style and
title of their great suburban Cemetery ? One
had a vision, I believe not incorrect, of a marble
brow, of dark sententious eyes that were like the
inscription on the fair slab, of drooping ringlets
that were like the gentle mortuary willow. A
sense, further, of that incipient discrimination
which is the soul of criticism attached itself to

the intelligent consciousness that Grace Greenwood must be somehow finely differentiated from
Fanny Fern, a contemporary New York glory;
difficult though it might be to decide, for preference, between the two lovely names, one so
sweetly, majestically sad, the other fairly inviting
you to tumble with its bearer in the woodland
undergrowth. Fanny, assuredly, was not Grace
and Grace was not Fanny—a perception of which
truth (at a season of life when confusions do
occur) may well have represented, in a small
mind, the earliest stir of literary discernment.

To what degree was that faculty concerned
with productions, with other and more eminent
shadows, evoked in the next of Story's letters
that I am able to quote? I must presently try
to say, mentioning meanwhile that I must let the
interval here jumped account, easily enough, for
itself. After the winter of 1852-53, spent in
Rome, he had again, for the summer, gone into
villeggiatura. The malady of travel was in those
days, blessedly, a milder fever than now, when
that noted "whip in the sky" which good Bostonians used to be prone to acknowledge in
another connection has reached its climax of
agitation. Spoken of, anciently, by an acute
member of that community (a member too of
our own present circle and a particular friend

of our friends), as the suspended *fear* in the old,
the abiding Puritan conscience, the lash cracked
by the New England Jehovah about the ears of
all plodders on the path of conduct, it is now
more than ever in its place, only applied, as
would seem, with a different intent. The image
holds generally, at any rate; the whip in the sky
descends on the backs of those who happen not
to be "going" and makes it a necessity that they
go. Where and why have ceased to matter; we
move, with scarce a question, to the arbitrary lash.
From the Italian sky of those days the whip was,
in respect to all of its functions, blissfully absent;
the journey northward, for the summer, was long,
arduous and costly; people moreover who were
there for love felt a scruple at leaving Italy when
Italy was most Italian. They went nearer, and
fared no worse; they did, in the time, by way of
refreshment, what they could; and for proof that
their experience was easily not to be wasted for
intimacy, for intensity, curiosity and beauty, we
find ourselves referred, it is scarce needful to say,
to some of the rarest promptings of the muse of
Robert Browning. Our friends were not all
Brownings, but they were almost alike deep
drinkers of the summer-sense of Tuscany.

W. W. Story to J R. Lowell.

"BAGNI DI LUCCA, *Aug.* 10*th*, 1853.

. . . "Your letter was brought to me by a smiling penny-postman in a tawdry chapeau. I was then alone in Rome, living with Crawford (both being temporary bachelors), and your handwriting looked so like you, so friendly and so redolent of old days and home and Cambridge, that when I read it I felt half-way between tears and smiles. How I longed to have you again on this side of the water! How indeed I always long for you and Frank. What is there that supplies the place of old friends? After reading your letter I slipped off the covering from your bust and placed it in its best light and stared at it a full quarter of an hour—after having lighted a *baiocc'-e-mezz'* cigar. I confess to having had a severe twinge of conscience that the bust still stood in the studio. It ought to have been in Cambridge before now; but I only finished my father's statue in time to allow me to complete the Piper by strenuous working before the summer heat, and as I could command no workman sufficiently trustworthy, I was obliged to postpone the bust until I could return in the autumn. Then I will finish it at once and send it off to you. Indeed it is almost finished now. I thank you for your kindness in inserting the complimentary paragraph about my statue of Father in 'Putnam,' and though I have not seen it I have no doubt that it is better than my deserts.   I do believe you will like it despite its faults, and I really think that it is not stupid. I am waiting to find an opportunity to send a photograph of it to my mother, and when that arrives it will give you some idea of the mode in which I have treated my subject, although a very imperfect and unflattering one.   This, by the way, reminds me that Macpherson has taken out a patent from the Papal Government for a new invention by which he lithographs and engraves photographs, making the sun itself engrave on the stone and copper.   The Government has after examination granted him a patent.   This makes Mac. look up in the world, and he grows his hair and beard six inches longer in consequence.

"We are all at the Baths of Lucca now, high up on the hills, amid the thick chestnut-trees, retired from the bustle of the Ponte below, where gossip simmers round the café, and we are leading the most *dolce far niente* of lives.   The place is beautiful.   All about us tower the mountains, terraced with vines and noble groups of chestnuts, and through the valley below sings our mountain-brook river as it sweeps under its one-arched bridges, turns picturesque mills, and goes winding along through its rocky bed to the Mediterranean. Every evening we drive along the richly-wooded banks of the wild, roaring Lima, or else beside the rushing Serchio, where Shelley used to push his little boat, to the Devil's Bridge. I have never lived an idler life. While the wind blows through the windows coolly we sit and read and fall asleep over our books — and feel intensely virtuous when we achieve a letter. Of society there is none we care to meet but the Brownings, who are living here. With them we have constant and delightful intercourse, interchanging long evenings together two or three times a-week, and driving and walking whenever we can meet. We like them very much — they are so simple, unaffected and sympathetic. Both are busily engaged in writing, he on a new volume of lyrical poems and she on a tale or novel in verse. These they would like to make some arrangement to have printed or reprinted in America, so as to secure some portion of the proceeds, or at least so as to derive some pecuniary benefit from the republication. . . . Both B. and his wife seemed greatly to have taken to you and M., and we all join in standing on the ramparts and waving our handkerchiefs for you to return.

They go to Rome this winter. If you were only to be there also! B. tells me that Clough has a position in London as superintendent of public schools, or some such office, to which he has just been appointed—you having some weeks before told me that he was settled in Cambridge and dining every Thursday with you. How is it? He had to me a sort of shagbark nature, with a smooth hard shell and a sweet kernel inside. It was hard work to get out the kernel.

"Putnam's Mag. I have heard of, but not seen. I am delighted to hear that you are writing for it, and am quite disappointed not to have received any of 'our own.' I shall of course be interested, and I long to see everything. What about the novel? You say nothing in your last letter. And 'The Nooning,' when is that? George Curtis's 'Best Society'[1] I saw in part, and thought it far the best thing I have yet seen from his pen. He did not seem to have been as particularly pleased with the dancing-girls of New York as with those of Esne. This very morning I have been reading an article in the N. Y. 'Tribune' on the sculpture in the N. Y. Exhibition, which is very clever : who writes their articles on art? I wish we had more criticism of the same kind, to prick these

[1] The Potiphar Papers.

inflated reputations of the most mediocre men. Nothing is more disgusting, nor more injurious to art, than the ignorant and wholesale adulation with which the most ordinary works of sculpture are lauded in our public prints. Can anything be more utterly without artistic merit than that abomination the equestrian Jackson by M. ?— and yet see what parade of praise and solidity of cash it has brought! Was ever a farce enacted more ridiculous than its inauguration? It makes one sigh to think how low the standard of excellence must be which is more than reached by such a work. Crawford is going on with his big thing admirably. . . .

" Page is just recovering from a fever he caught at Naples, and has returned to Rome, which is to him home. He has become enamoured of Rome and puts no other place in comparison with it; and he has taken an admirable house on the Quirinal hill, where the air is excellent, for which he pays some 35 or 40 scudi a-month. Of his pictures he has yet shown me none save the portrait of Miss Cushman, which is wonderfully fine—the finest portrait, I think, I *ever* saw! The picture of Mrs Crawford is nearly done, but he will not show it. And he is painting a head of Emelyn. He will find more to do in Rome than he can possibly attend to. I have a great impulse now to light a cigar, but as dinner is almost ready I will postpone it. Browning does not smoke; it is his greatest defect; but he tells me that Tennyson does excessively, and that after he got to Florence, on his way to Rome, he was so disquieted because he could not find a particular tobacco he liked that he turned back to England and never went to Rome. His brother Frederick is living in Florence, having married an Italian wife. B. says he is full of poetry. Lytton, by the way, is turning up a poet. I saw a couple of poems by him at B.'s, which were quite full of promise and richness. Frank Boott is at Pratolino writing quartetts."

A letter of Lowell's, of 1852, published in his correspondence, refers, with emphasis, to Page. "I have studied Art [in Italy] to some purpose, and like Page's pictures better than ever. Him I first saw in Florence. I went to the Uffizzi and passed him without knowing it. All his beautiful hair was cut short and the top of his head getting bare. After I had passed I heard him step back from his picture and recognised the tread. He was copying Titian as he was never copied before. . . . He is just the same noble great man, and as fanatical about a certain person's poems as ever. He has become something of a Swedenborgian." Meanwhile the conditions noted in Story's letter live again for us in the rough notes that I extract from another of the little pocket-books. Our friends had gone to the Baths of Lucca from Rome, the Brownings had come thither from Casa Guidi, and Robert Lytton had returned from his brief diplomatic novitiate at Washington and been appointed to a secretary-ship of Legation at Florence. I know not what happy air of the golden age, of dead summers, of easier terms, of genius and friendship in soft solution, rises from the record, slight though it be, of their various simple sociabilities. For myself, there is not an item noted that I would wish to pass. I find a richness, to begin with, in the very first entry, that of August 19th. "Took tea with the Brownings and stayed until nearly twelve, B. accompanying us home—a delicious moonlight night. Heard a letter from Miss Mitford there, which was admirably written, giving an account of Haydon the painter, whose Life is just out." "The Storys are at the top of the hill," Mrs Browning writes on August 10th to Henry Chorley; "you know Mr and Mrs Story. She and I go backward and forward to tea-drinking and gossiping at one another's houses, and our husbands hold the reins." And later the same month to Miss Mitford: "Then our friends Mr and Mrs Story helped the mountains to please us a good deal. He is the son of Judge Story, the biographer of his father, and, for himself, sculptor and poet; and she a sympathetic, graceful woman, fresh and innocent in face and thought. We go backwards and forwards to tea and talk at one another's houses. Last night they were our visitors, and your name came in among the Household Gods to make us as agreeable as might be." Which was obviously the occasion of Story's just-recorded mention. They hear together, the next day to this, "a series of recitations by M. Alexandre, the master of Rachel, a hump back full of cleverness and spirit." It is all, in its Arcadian setting, delightfully ancient, queer, obscure. Story expatiates with interest on the entertainment in question; but what was M. Alexandre, the master of Rachel, doing in the Tuscan mountains in August 1853? We see again indeed the little humpbacked ges-ticulant Parisian; we see also the Grand Duke's villa perched above the swift Lima; we make a connection as between some small court of the Renaissance and one of its salaried monsters or jesters, the little French dwarf, say, the unthinkable deformed tragedian. We fill out the picture, in short, in all sorts of ways, as we inevitably do, with our added "ell" whenever an inch of Italy is given us. Browning tells them one evening, at length, "the story of Basil Montagu," Mrs Procter's step-father; which was in other words the story of the *cause célèbre*, late in the eighteenth century, of Lord Sandwich and Miss Ray, Montagu's romantic progenitors, and of Hackman, the infatuated cleric who murdered, in a passion of jealousy, the nobleman's mistress. They go, the middle of September, "to Prato Fiorito, to picnic, our party consisting of the Duppers, Brownings, Lytton and ourselves. The day was glorious, and after climbing an hour we arrived at a little old church, near by which the view was magnificent. The grand limestone mountains spring sharply up, with deep patches of purple shade and little grey towns perched here and there on the lower spines. Under the trees here we spent nearly an hour, and then took our donkeys and horses again, and, after an hour and a half, passing over wild and grand scenery, with mountain-streams dripping and tumbling, and now and then over beds of red-veined jasper, we rounded a height bold and rugged as the Alps and saw before us the soft green velvety

dome of Prato Fiorito, adorable name, covered
with its short golden grass. Here we lay for
half an hour and talked and gazed at the
tumbling waves of mountains below." There
is more, but more than I can use. They spend,
on another occasion—they had done so for the
previous three days—"the morning down by
the brook, in a shady little hollow below the
house, drawing and listening to the gurgling
of the brown stream. To-day we dined there
on a smooth grassy table under the trees and
rocks. After dinner we sat on the rock by
the stream and sang, and I made me a long
pipe-stem of a cane-pole and smoked and smoked.
And thus the day went by till evening, dampen-
ing down the valley, sent us home. Seen from
here our house seems to hang in the clouds,
and I make a sketch of the place in pencil.
Down in the stream, knee-deep in water, were
contadine washing, whose splash we could hear."
Or again : "The whole day in the same woods
with the Brownings. We went at ten o'clock,
carrying our provisions. Browning and I walked
to the spot, and there, spreading shawls under
the great chestnuts, we read and talked the
live-long day, the Lima, at our feet, babbling
on, clear and brown, over the stones, and the
distant rock-ribbed peaks taking the changes

of the hours. In the afternoon we took a long walk through the grove and found wondrous *fungi*, some red as coral. . . ."

These weeks represent the first of three Italian summers spent in neighbourhood and intimacy by the principals of the good company concerned, and we shall fail of no mild light on the others that we can, however thinly, recapture. It was very much in search of mild light, so much of it at least as might abide in the old look of things, in the deep valley and the chestnut-covered heights, in the mountain-river in the little *villini* of the "Arcadian" time, clustered at their bridges, perched on their heights, and awaiting alike, apparently, in either position, some return of the tide of fortune, modest of old at the best; it was exactly, I say, under the impulse to recover any echo of an echo (as I might have held a sea-shell to my ear) that a certain time ago, early in the Tuscan summer, I went out from Lucca to where the blest Bagni—blest, I mean, to memory, but rather blighted otherwise—nestle in the deep fold of the hills. I have no right, I acknowledge, to reflect elegiacally on the fact that the Baths have now been made (had then but just been made) accessible by steam; inasmuch as, shrinking unworthily from the shadeless drive, I on this occasion took the train—only making a point, later on, in the interest of the old echo, of returning by road. The distance from brave little old Lucca of the russet ramparts is in truth, at the worst or the best—since a couple of hours suffice for it—no great matter. If, however, it both partly bettered my case and confounded the new enterprise that I seemed, in the first flush of the latter, the sole "superior" pilgrim, this had also the effect of making the little superseded spa appear to look more wistfully still, through the old crooked spy-glass of its scarred gorge, into the modern world, the only quarter from which patronage can come to it. To this quarter it can appeal, alas!—very much as a humble person in a back-seat at the play—only by a wearisome twist of the neck, the effort, as it were, to look round a corner. "Sister Anne, sister Anne, do you see nothing come?"—*that* was perhaps the sound one most distinctly heard in the murmur of the chestnuts and the plash of the river, sister Anne being conceivable as anxiously perched on some commanding summit. One felt ashamed, under so much public expectancy, to have "come" one's self for so short a stay; ashamed, positively of an opportunity again publicly declined, an opportunity with all its sweetness so visibly in the scale. Oh, the sweetness of the summer in long days on the higher hills, the sense of rambles, of afternoons, of siestas, of *prati fioriti* propitious to them, of views opening out into violet and silver, of villages perched in the shining spaces like old grey cities! It is a corner of the world where amiability reigns, but amiability, as we mostly see to-day, is everywhere driven to the wall, and the Bagni, with their back to their practical *impasse*, can only sit and confess to no other ground for being liked. The ground in question, poor Bagni, too rarely operates as sufficient now. Nevertheless, let it be said, the lovely land persists : what could be more amiable than little Lucca itself behind the russet ramparts once so formed to be forbidding? They are as sweet to-day—which indeed everything in the place is—as the smile of a resigned grandmother. It plays there so placidly, the smile, and withal so expressively, that it lightens the severity of interest, the slightly grim purity of character, of the fine Lucchesi churches, and suffuses even the somewhat hard historic face of Elisa Bonaparte (for her brief hour, by her brother's high hand, Grand Duchess of Tuscany and Princess of Lucca and Piombino), or that of some later Bourbon proprietress who figures on a pedestal before the Palace. Large ladies in stone and metal, in wind and weather, with magnified " charms," cheeks,

noses, bosoms, sandalled feet and dimpled hands,
are rarely objects to which the fancy warms;
but the tread of these heroines is now pleasantly light in the great apartments at their
back, in which, as well as almost anywhere, you
may still feel the wave of the feathers and fans,
the rattle of the scabbards, the dice, the diplomatic laughter, of a small old-world Court. The
Palace is large, as is also, I have said, the statue
of its whilom mistress, but the Court affects us,
in our musing walk through great bright rooms,
stiff and square and classical, and up and down
a stone staircase where we move, for all our
modern humility, like a "party" arriving and
retiring—the Court affects us as of just the right
size to keep rustling away, in a mass, as we
follow it; keep swimming, in advance, over the
polished floors, with a ghostly click and patter,
and, through whatever door we enter, whisking
out of sight by the opposite. Its shrunken
presence, however, here, suffers nothing worse
than this pursuit from a vain curiosity. The
small old grand-ducal villa at the Baths, on the
other hand, opens its doors now as an almost
indecently, if not pathetically, beguiling hotel.
The welcome made me wince for lurking shades,
which I honoured perhaps the more by running

up — though with the delicacy, after all, but rueful—so brief a bill.

The following letter brings back, a little, the time. The Storys, having departed in advance, were spending a month in Florence before their return to Rome.

Robert Browning to W. W. Story.

"BAGNI DI LUCCA, *October* 1853.

" We shall follow your track as exactly and as soon as we can, but it will not be to-morrow, after all. On Monday we do go, however—so it is fixed ; and what a joy to see you all again after such a weary while ! If you don't believe in Monday, after so much promise-breaking, here is our method of driving disbelief out of you very effectually. Will you please (prompts Ba) tell that identical old porter he is to see that we find (English) bread, butter, milk and eggs laid in by Monday afternoon, from the accustomed pur- veyor of the same ? This poor place has given up the ghost now, and we really want to get away. So you have good apartments ? That is very well. I hear more about the fever at Rome than I care to infect this paper with. It rained yesterday and to-day, or did a few minutes ago, and I have taken to write, in default of

anything better to do—wanting to make a sketch
or two (in emulation of your pencil, so happy at
bridge-sides and bits of rock and water) that
may bring back this last happy time when the
darker days arrive, as they will, I suppose."

Story journalises in November at Leghorn—
" Off at last in the old *Maria Antonietta*, a tub
of a boat, with no go in her." They make for
Civita Vecchia, where the difficulties raised by
the police, the *dogana*, the passport people,
render the place, he notes, a perfect hell for a
traveller.   He is three hours getting through
the *dogana* and feels like a bird whose feathers
have been plucked.   They are late, after starting, for Rome, so late that they stop that night
at Palo.   "The moon came out, the sea thundered
on the beach at the foot of the old posthouse and
foamed high over the ruined arches that reach
out into the water.   The old turret-cornered
fortress of the Odescalchi"—he questions the
attribution—"looked grimly out above its sea-
wall against the sky.   All was lovely and wild
and deserted, a fitting spot for some legendary
tale.   I walked on the shore and watched the
spray and great gleaming surf and waves.   It
was just such a scene as that where Schedoni
has the terrible interview with Elena on the

shore.   Inside, groups of soldiers and *dogana* officers and police-dragoons clustered round the narrow tables in the vaulted smoky rooms and drank and talked.   The post - carriages and diligences, now and then rattled up and after a hurried change were off again.   The Rospigliosi horses and carriages, stabled over the whole place, also woke it up like a stone thrown into a pool.   The night passed away easily, and I then framed a story for a poem on the place. The morning came up clear and glittering across the sea.   All the scenery is flat and desolate, with only thin grasses and here and there a shrub, or a shorn haycock with its pole.   Long tongues of tree-feathered land stretch out, into the sea, and landward the view is bounded by climbing hills, darkened over in patches with black foliage and softened into heavy purples and blues by the distance.   The seashore is a soft sandy beach, shelving gradually, with, at intervals along the coast, square watchtowers, turretted, that stand boldly out on some jutting bit of land or rock.   The old Odescalchi fortress, with its moat and turrets and its thick wall shutting in the courtyard where a fountain dribbles under the high steps surmounted by a stone sarcophagus, is lonely and gloomy enough. A wretched old broken - down soldier haunted this place, as ruined and rusty and out-at-elbows as the fortress itself, which rattled a wooden shutter in its gloomy turret while I talked to him. He prowled round, in and out of the barracks in the court-yard, like an old rat round a fallen house."

The Brownings spent in Rome, at 43 Via Bocca di Leone, the winter of 1853-54, to the events of which an undated letter of Mrs Browning's refers.

Mrs Browning to W. W. Story.

" When Robert and I parted this morning on our different ways of attaining to the Pope's benediction, he bade me, if I returned first, to begin a note to you. . . . Now, I do hope, that as there's a tide in the affairs of men the turn has come to *you*, and the salt water and bitter seaweed will dash back from you henceforth. May you never be wounded again through the objects of your love—the only wounds which *tell* in this life. The rest are scratches. . . . A change into a better air will abolish the lingering effects of this pestilent climate. Oh, you will let me say so now — you know it *is* full of physical and moral miasma, and when I have seen the Vatican twelve times, I shall go on to say so twelve times twelve. Meanwhile, of

course, I don't 'boast of having seen Rome'—
no indeed. I am properly humiliated for all my
disadvantages or defects, and confess meekly in
writing to England that I am the most ignorant
of travellers and have seen just nothing. We
are going to visit galleries, however, villas, ruins,
and crowd as much sight-seeing into as little
space. We heard the wrong Miserere, I believe,
on Friday, but it was very fine, wrong or right,
and very overcoming in its ejaculating pathos.
I sat that day in the Sistine Chapel for the first
time. Then we have made various Campagna
excursions with Mrs Sartoris and Mrs Kemble,
dined in bosky valleys, and pinewood forests, and
done the proper honour to your glorious opal
mountains in the distance. Castel Fusano pleases
me the best. . . . I shall not forget our
descent into Genoa from the mountains in the
supernatural moonlight, which touched my brain
with all sorts of fantastic suppositions. I remember Robert wondering whether I was mad
or not. That was in coming from Turin more
than a year ago."

Sorrow, for our friends, had at this time been
more sharply mingled with cheer than it was
ever again to be; their return to Rome had been
followed by an occasion of anxiety on behalf of

their two elder children which found its climax
in the death, at six years of age, of the boy, at
that period the most precious of their possessions
and ever afterwards to be remembered as such.
No person or thing, in their life, was again to
have an equal value.   Their little girl, taken ill
at the same time, had been removed to the care
of the Brownings : to all of which Mrs Browning, writing on December 21st to Mrs Jameson,
refers.   " Ah, dearest friend ! you have heard
how our fresh step into Rome was a fall, not
into a catacomb but a fresh grave, and how
everything here has been slurred and blurred to
us, and distorted from the grand antique associations.   I protest to you I doubt whether I shall
get over it, and whether I ever shall feel that
this is Rome.   The first day at the bed's head
of that convulsed and dying child ; and the next
two, three, four weeks in great anxiety about his
little sister, who was all but given up by the
physicians. . . . It was not only sympathy.
I was selfishly and intensely frightened for my
own treasures."   The death of the little boy was
followed, happily, by the recovery of his sister ;
in so slow and difficult a fashion, however, that
anxiety continued, an anxiety reflected to-day
in a series of singularly zealous and lucid letters
of Browning's—he apparently having mediated

between the parents and the great Roman doctor
of that time, Pantaleoni, at a moment when some
of the results of the physician's judgment and
treatment had caused them to doubt. They had
quitted Rome, with the convalescent child, for
other air, and he writes to them at La Posta,
Velletri. "I suppose your next will be from
Albano. I wish it had been Frascati, I think;
so beautiful did it seem last Saturday, when I
went there with Lockhart, whose temper got a
pain in it before the day was over. I'll tell you
at Albano, where I shall go on a much lighter
summons than the last. There are plenty of
small news we will talk and laugh over, Baths of
Lucca fashion, when we meet, if all proceeds as I
trust. Chorley has brought out *another* play,
with but dubious success I fear. Grace Greenwood has printed us flamingly in her book, it
seems." Concerning the early part of that
winter in Rome and the remainder of it, after
the dark cloud had discharged itself and the
Storys were restored to 93 Piazza di Spagna,
where they were then living, a pleasant legend
of kind, distinguished visitors still survives, one
of them incomparably benevolent to a languid
little girl who needed amusement and who was
to be for ever grateful. Hans Andersen, whose
private interest in children and whose ability to

charm them were not less marked than his public, knew well his way to the house, as later to Palazzo Barberini (to the neighbourhood of which the "Improvisatore" was able even to add a charm); where the small people with whom he played enjoyed, under his spell, the luxury of believing that he kept and treasured—in every case and as a rule—the old tin soldiers and broken toys received by him, in acknowledgment of favours, from impulsive infant hands. Beautiful the queer image of the great benefactor moving about Europe with his accumulations of these relics. Wonderful too our echo of a certain occasion—that of a children's party, later on—when, after he had read out to his young friends "The Ugly Duckling," Browning struck up with the "Pied Piper"; which led to the formation of a grand march through the spacious Barberini apartment, with Story doing his best on a flute in default of bagpipes. But the tenderest recollection is of Thackeray reading "The Rose and the Ring," as yet unpublished (a book of plates, so to speak, "before the letter"), to the little convalescent girl who was always so happily to remember that, chapter by chapter, the immortal work had, in the old Roman days, between daylight and dusk, as the great author sat on the edge of her bed, been tried on her. The first

edition of the book has been known to contain
a memorial of this charming relation in the form
of the image of an obsequious flunkey presenting
a little rose and a little ring on a salver, with,
above, in facsimile of the author's beautiful hand,
his "most respectful compliments to Miss Edith
Story": to all of which—the "foreign city where
there were many English children," the futility
of attempted purchase of Twelfth Night characters, the substitute thence excogitated with
Miss Bunch, and the other associations, some of
them so toothsome, with the Piazza di Spagna—
the preface prettily alludes. The happy relation
was moreover, in ceremonious form, to be renewed; both parties to it were during a part of
the next winter in Boston, and their later friendship is confirmed in a little old American copy of
"Ballads," presented with "the author's profound
respect."

Story quitted Rome, with his wife and children,
early that summer; to which we have, again,
testimony.

Robert Browning to W. W. Story.

"FLORENCE, *June* 11*th*, 1854.

. . . "We left Page (in Rome) fighting off
his fever; a little more effectually perhaps, but
far from well. I shall surprise you by telling

you—now that I *may* tell—that he painted a
magnificent portrait of me, the finest even of
his works, just the head, which he wished to
concentrate his art upon, in a manner which
would have been impossible had the canvas been
larger. The result is marvellous. I hate keeping secrets, but this was Page's, not mine; he
even wished my wife to be kept in ignorance of
it, which of course was impossible. And the
end is that he has presented the picture to her.
Both of us would have fain escaped being the
subjects of such a princely piece of generosity;
but there was no withstanding his admirable
delicacy and noble-mindedness, which made the
sacrifice of such time and labour even easy. I
wished him to keep the picture for a year at
least, but he sent it to me on the morning of
our departure. So it is here, the wonder of
everybody; no such work has been achieved in
our time—to my knowledge at least. I am not
qualified to speak of the likeness, understand,
only of the life and effect, which, I wish, with
all my heart, had been given to my wife's head
or any I like better to look at than my own.
Lytton goes to England in a few days; we have
had some pleasant evenings together. I am trying to make up for wasted time in Rome and
setting my poetical house in order. Mrs Kemble

left Rome on the same day with ourselves ; not
in our company, unfortunately, but circumstances
were too strong for our wishes. She left Florence as soon as we arrived. Mrs Sartoris will
be here, or at Lucca, presently. . . ."

Our friends, betaking themselves to France,
spent some weeks at Dieppe ; after which they
settled for the ensuing winter in Paris. There,
as was their nature, they found, they attracted,
promptly enough, their circle ; of which, with M.
de Tocqueville, were Mme. Mohl, the universal,
the irrepressible, her erudite husband and more
others than can here be recalled. Robert Lytton,
by that time transferred to the British Embassy
and engaged in writing "Lucille," was again a
valued visitor. It is to this period, I take it,
that an undated letter from him belongs.

R. B. Lytton to W. W. Story.

[PARIS, 1855.]

"MY DEAR STORY,—'A friend in need is a
friend indeed.' I came home only very late last
night, and did not get up till very late this
morning, so that I have only just read your
most kind letter, although I believe it has been
here all night. I cannot lose a moment in telling you how truly touched I am by the cordial

warmth and friendliness of what you say, nor
how heartily I reciprocate it.   The singular delicacy as well as frankness of your letter, and the
ready friendliness with which you have met
mine, makes me, I assure you, feel almost grateful to the unpleasant circumstances which have
procured me this noble evidence of what my
friend is.   I shall endeavour to get away from
the Chancellerie and follow this letter to your
studio.   But if I should find myself unable to
do this I will be there to-morrow *early*.   Meanwhile shall you be at home to-night, and if not
when will you?   Every night I am disengaged
except Friday, and I long to hear what more of
your poems you will read me.   But I should feel
of course very sorry if I thought you likely to
make any interference with other arrangements
on that account.   So I shall keep myself clear
for this evening until I have seen you.

"*P.S.*—My uncle is very anxious to be allowed
to see your Beethoven.   Is it too late for him to
hope to do so?   I think you said it was casting."

To which I add another, related by its date
to the same season.   J. R. Lowell, who had left
home the previous summer, had just quitted Germany; having prepared there, in our good old
way, for the Professorship to which he had lately

been appointed at Harvard, very much as Story
had been qualifying in Italy for the sculptorship
that he had embraced only to feel considerably
concerned to give it up.

J. R. Lowell to W. W. Story.

"PARIS, *July* 1855.

" MY DEAR WILLIAM,—I ought to have written
to you yesterday, and that is the only good
reason I can give for not having done it.   But
the truth is that I went to Versailles to see the
monster squirts which play there every other
Sunday, and as I got up rather late, I had not
time to write and see the *Granz-O* also.   I trust
you give me credit for enough human nature not
to expect me on the day I said I should come.
There are so many last things to do that though
not 'loath to depart' I am 'still taking leave.'

" I saw the Jardin Mabille and the Château
des Fleurs when I was here before, and have
been again—but found them rather stupid.   The
lights and all that are pretty, but the dancers
seem to me like a French vaudeville made out of
Dante's 'Inferno.'   The flavour of hell is there,
but every drop of poetry that would spoil the
punch is left out.   I have seen all I wish of Paris.
. . .   If I wanted to be 'wicked' I wouldn't be
so here as some of our compatriots, I believe, are,

but at home where the thing would have a great deal more *tang* to it. Smoky London suits me better, and we will go and dine at the Cock— yes, and see the Tabard also, and old Gower's tomb close by at St Mary Overie's. We will have rational amusement, which means a beef-steak and a pot of porter.

"Don't expect *us* (for Cranch comes too) till Wednesday. If we should arrive Tuesday it will be something to thank God for, but I know my own habits too well to think it possible. I shall rescue the watch and shall ransom it if necessary. In these sad days one can't get to-gether his retainers (I don't speak of lawyers) and go drub a tradesman into reason, nor am I facile enough (in French) to quarrel to any advantage. Cranch has just come in, and we debate the several routes. We want to see the cathedral at Amiens. But we are coming anyhow."

The Storys, in London at receipt of this, were once more on their way back to America—in obedience to considerations that, added to anxiety for his mother's health,[1] strike us (in view of the months just sacrificed to Paris, and though the

---

[1] He was greeted, on the ship's touching at Halifax, with the news of his mother's death.

letters in which we might trace their growth are absent) as now having begun to creep, a little after the manner of the disconcerting snake, into the general paradise of Italy. It is indeed true that the most insidious of these serpents had become, for Story, simply the question of his own future as an artist—a question which, after such continuity of experiment as appeared adequate, he had found himself impelled to answer with a negative. He had, to his view, either not the root of the matter in him, or else it required, for the promise of full growth, more watering than even the loved Italy could give. He had lost heart, in a word, under influences of which we have not the record, but which are sufficiently imaginable; though we shall see to what extent, and with what appetite, after he had carried his remedy into effect, he was to regain it. His remedy had been to return again to Boston; which, for a doubting sculptor, was naturally not the most direct one. He had had to come round to the indirect, the recovery of confidence in another profession; but this indirectness acted, precisely, as the situation developed, in the interest of the fonder dream. Story's real remedy, it may frankly be said, would have been, at any moment, to do what he was never to do, what he was to have failed, from the first, of favouring

time and place for : to go, namely, to school, in
the simplest meaning of the term. He had
served no apprenticeship to his craft and mystery,
had not only not been through the mill, but had
not even undergone preparation for that discipline. It is difficult, in truth, to see what mill,
at that season, and in all the conditions, would
have struck him as turning for him, what
apprenticeship, to the deeper initiation, he could
conveniently have served. He had started too
late for this, and we may take it to heart if we
like, as one of the lessons of our history, that in
having been, by his essential conditions, as one
may say, fairly doomed to miss the rigour of a
technical education, he was the victim, all innocent at first, and unconscious, of an order of
things from which standards were absent. His
own nearest approach to them had been to go to
Italy so that he might feed himself with impressions, and so that, in the light of these impressions, he might then produce ; but what he
appears to have ended by perceiving was that,
though it is in the nature of such delightful
matters to hover about us, on the up-hill path of
art, like cooling airs, this rude ascent gains from
them, in strictness, little smoothing or straight-
ening. That process is for quite another engineer,
the earliest riser of the escort, whose offices, in

their beneficent morning, Story may very well have had a season of feeling, not without despair, that he had lost. Still, when so much is said, none of his impressions were to be wasted; what befell in the event was that his susceptibility, curiosity, agility, facility, felicity, to say nothing of his plain power of hard work, were signally to help him. If Boston was to clear up his tangle the clearance that took place was, after all, in the sense of the greater inclination.

He was not to know till he had tried a second winter there how little his Roman doubts mattered. He might live as an anxious, even as a misguided, artist, but he could not, apparently, live as anything more orthodox. The anxiety, at least, might, so to speak, still be beguiled, but the habit of conformity was not to be acquired, was not, at any rate, to be found bearable. The unsuccessful effort to acquire it, and the resulting consciousness of not having found what he wanted, and of not wanting what he had found, is reflected, inevitably enough, in the pessimism of his letter. He missed too much what he had learned to love, and he missed in particular his correspondent, then out of reach, with whom at least he could have talked. Very special and very interesting to catch in the fact— even if not of the order of things "eternal"—is the state of being of the American who has bitten deep into the apple, as we may figure it, of "Europe," and then has been obliged to take his lips from the fruit. The intensity of the case depends of course on the inward energy of the bite and the kind of susceptibility involved in the act of tasting. There are small kinds and there are great kinds, and when these latter have been engaged the subsequent sense of privation is of course proportionate. The apple of "America" is a totally different apple, which, however firm and round and ruddy, is not to be (and above all half a century ago was not to have been) negotiated, as the newspapers say, by the same set of teeth. The inward drama of this perception on the part of the repatriated pilgrim has enacted itself in thousands of breasts and thousands of lives, and doubtless goes on doing so without coming to light—that is to any such light as permits us, as we say of dramas that are typical, to assist at it. It has never been noted, reported, commemorated, in a manner worthy of its intrinsic interest. That interest of course differs with the quantity of feeling, of passion and reflection involved ; and these differ, not less, with the quantity of experience assimilated, the number of possibilities missed, the number of actualities to be faced and the special savour of these

actualities. There is often, at all events, a conflict of forces as sharp as any of those in which
the muse of history, the muse of poetry, is usually
assumed to be interested. But the conflict, we
have noted, has mostly remained, for the critic's
eye, obscure and ambiguous. It has in fact
never been presented at all at that tribunal;
it has failed of its sacred poet, unaccountably
unconscious of its merits as a "subject." That
makes us the more keen in presence of examples
accidentally revealed.

W. W. Story to J. R. Lowell.

"BOSTON, *December* 30*th*, 1855.

"You and I want an audience which is intelligent and sympathetic, which can understand and
stamp what is good and what is bad; we do not
write for idiots or for bores; we gather strength
from sympathy; we must have our sounding-
board to give effect to the tune we play. Allston
starved spiritually in Cambridgeport; he fed
upon himself. There was nothing congenial
without, and he turned all his powers inward
and drained his memory dry. His works grew
thinner and vaguer every day, and in his old
age he ruined his great picture. I know no
more melancholy sight than he was, so rich and
beautiful a nature, in whose veins the south

ran warm, which was born to have grown to
such height and to have spread abroad such
fragrancy, stunted on the scant soil and withered
by the cold winds of that fearful Cambridgeport.
I look at his studio whenever I pass with a
heart-pang. It's a terrible ghost—all is in fact
ghostlike here. There's no such thing as flesh
and blood; we hob-a-nob with spirits freely.
We love nothing, we criticise everything. Even
the very atmosphere is critical. Every twig is
intensely defined against the sky. The sky itself
is hard and distant. Earth takes never the hue
of its heaven. The heart grows into stone. The
devil-side of enthusiasm (irritability) possesses us.
There is no hearty love of anything, for we are
afraid of making a mistake. We love unhappi-
ness. . . . You think we are honest, but I find
Boston changed greatly in this respect. You say
at least in the home-relations we are right, and
tell a horrible exceptional story. Well: it is
only some three weeks ago that two husbands,
under false pretences, inveigled two handsome
youths . . . to their houses, at separate times.
The husbands attacked each; drove —— down
cellar and beat him terribly, ending by kicking
him over the wall in the back yard. The poor
youth is since dead of the wounds he received.
The cause of this brutal cowardice is that the

two wives, &c., &c. . . . I disbelieve in the
superior honesty of the Americans. They have
little blood and few sensual temptations, but
they do not resist what temptations they have.
What do you say of S—, Q— and B—? They
are exceptional? Why then are they not caught
and punished as Strahan and Paul are in
England? We are not shocked at these things;
they are a day's wonder and that's all. Society
is scabbed over with pretences, but it's not
healthy for all that. Carter and I have terrible
growls over America in the little back room at
Little and Brown's. He says we are the greatest
and best of people. I do not agree. But what
a growl I have given *you*. I didn't mean to
when I began; . . . but if ever there was a
Little Pedlington!

"One great charm that America had to me
was that it held you within its limits, and I
feel the want very greatly. How I daily wish
you were here! . . . It is my brain that gets
so over-excited. What do you think I have
been about these three months? Why, writing
law—in Little and Brown's back room. I have
actually written about 400 pages in that time
to add to a new edition of my 'Contracts,' and
I feel like a wet rag after it. Now it is nearly
over, and I am thinking of making a basso

rilievo of the Pied Piper with the children
flocking after him. But what encouragement
to do it? Nobody will buy it, nobody cares for
it. There would be real interest if I had imported a cargo of saltpetre.

"Yesterday we had a great snowstorm, and
the snow is heaving like great surf-waves over
the walls in the country and the roofs of the
houses. All along the eaves are *friezes* of icicles,
jagged as a wolf's teeth, and now and then comes
down a thundering avalanche. For the last few
days we have had a crystal world, trees of pure
glass, and electric wires of spun glass stretching
for miles. The country looks like an enchanted
land; the sombre green pines crusted with
diamonds and bending 'neath their weight, the
slender birches bowing to the ground in arches
of gleaming ice, all the weeds like crystalline
fingers. . . . The spectacle is magnificent.

"Heaps of new books are out, but nothing
American of any importance but Prescott's
'Phillip II.,' which everybody is reading. Stories
and novels of wretched quality swarm. . . .
Longfellow's 'Hiawatha' has raised a row, a
free fight into which all the editors have rushed,
and in the meantime some eight or nine thousand
copies have sold. It is in many respects excellent, graceful and simple, but diffuse and

lacking in power. Thackeray has been lecturing here to crowded houses, but people did not want to be pleased, and he was severely criticised. He was not heavy and instructive enough, for Boston, and only a few dared thoroughly to like the light and genial sketches of manners and society he gave us in his inimitable way. Oddly enough, *our* people objected to him that he pitched into the Georges and called them names. . . . P. M. objected to them on the score that he could find all the facts and anecdotes in books he had in his library. I told him I was astonished to hear him say so, for I thought Thack. had invented them all. But this was too deep for P. Thack. has been far from well here, and I'm afraid that he's in a bad way. George Curtis begins on the 15th his course of lectures on the Novelists before the Lowell Institute.

"I was delighted to read what you wrote of Ristori. It was pleasant to see in Paris what a weight and value her character gave to her acting. Rachel seemed a sham after her. The Italians have the real *clou* of passion; the heart forces them into pathos and ‑moves enthusiasm and sympathy in others. They are the most naturally powerful of all actors; the heat of their natures melts the covering of artificial rules. But I am no judge of Italy and Italians; the very names fire me. My taste is spoilt for everything else—foolishly enough. Shall I ever again be as happy as I was then? Ah heaven, we never can repeat. Ardently as I desire to return, I *fear*. Things are so changed, *I* am so changed. Sometimes I dream I am there and life is glad as it once was. I take great drafts of beauty and awake to find myself in Rowe Street and to drudge the day out.

" Do you hibernate with a great white ghost of a stove? Do you talk the horse-language to unkempt professors? Have you got through the swamp of a dictionary yet? Do you put and answer daily those admirable Ollendorffian questions?—' I have been to Paris, but I have not broken my sister's wooden table.' You do not seem to over-like Deutschland. Yet there is good there—a homely picturesqueness of life and customs which is good material for art. Our imitations here are very brummagem. Our Christmas tree here is a ghastly sham. I wish you could send me the whole series of the ' Jugend - Kalender.' . . . The drawings are so free and clever and full of Germanity. M. has been staying with us all Christmas week and we had a great time together; such romping at night, with the wildest of shrieking, was never

known. We carried her out to Mrs Howe's
(Julia's) where was a Christmas tree and a dance
and tableaux from 'The Rose and the Ring' by
us great people. . . . Rachel made a great
sensation here; everybody took a book and read
to follow her; nobody understood what she said;
but everybody thought her wonderful. . . .
Nobody cared for her character. She was
wretchedly supported by a set of dirty Jews,
and they too were taken into the general admiration. She was jewier than ever and tried
to skin a flint in Boston, which created a little
reaction. But you know we go by fashion, and
it was the fashion to consider her unequalled.
It was as much as one's life was worth even
to make a question. I have not yet bought
any house or land, but if I do not I shall
never return to America. Let us . . . all
go to Newport and live there—or go somewhere and live together."

His chagrin, it need scarcely, after all, be
added, was eminently "subjective"; he was
sick and sore with his defeat, as he supposed
it, for the time, to have been; some of his
generalisations were assuredly whimsical and
some of his links missing. What it all came
to saying, however, was that, with an alienated

mind, he found himself again steeped in a society both fundamentally and superficially *bourgeois*, the very type and model of such a society, presenting it in the most favourable, in the most admirable light; so that its very virtues irritated him, so that its ability to be strenuous without passion, its cultivation of its serenity, its presentation of a surface on which it would appear to him that the only ruffle was an occasionally acuter spasm of the moral sense, must have acted as a tacit reproach. Hovering shades again, for the rest, peep out between his lines; it would be for instance, with more of a margin, scarce possible not to pause for a parley at the sight, behind the bars, of the handsome, the attaching younger face of George William Curtis. We have met G. W. Curtis's name, with an allusion slightly occult, in another letter; the allusion having been there, apparently, to his recent return from a journey to the East, followed by the publication of the "Nile Notes of a Howadji" with which his so variously responsive youth was regaling New York. The East was more distant then and Nile notes were less frequent; howadjis were more portentous, New York was more susceptible, and youth, above all, when not inevitably commercial, familiarly financial, when by exception addicted both to ideas and to the polka, was more easily brilliant. The reason is the better accordingly to rejoice in a personal impression (however immature at the time, or even however abnormally precocious the perceptive plate,) of the friendly little phase in which poetry and pleasantry could operate together, like a master-juggler, with few preparations. At an age so tender that I had then read neither " Eothen " nor, *a fortiori*, " The Newcomes," as yet unpublished, the howadji of the Notes seemed to exhale sandalwood and cinnamon with the last potency; just as " The Potiphar Papers," succeeding them from the same hand, seemed to pour upon New York society satire of the finest distillation. The book was an ingenuous tribute to the genius in whose projected shadow—for it was the time of Thackeray's own first advent—we were all living, and I mention it to-day but for the quaint ghostliness of the note. We liked to think that, on our reduced but still respectable scale, we were ripe, socially ripe, both for satire and for the fine degustation of it. We liked to think that we too had our wicked worldly side, our types and our hierarchy, our great people and our less great, our raddled dowagers behind their fans, our Major Pendennises at their club windows, our snobs and parvenus, in fine, our

themes for the easy moralist, our amiable vices.
Our vices in "The Potiphar Papers" will have
been, I surmise, of a really childlike amiability.
All of which indeed was soon, even then, to
become very ancient history, so that if I speak
of the ghostly quaintness of the note it must
not be without immediately adding that George
Curtis's own became, promptly enough, a much
fuller and deeper thing, that of the public voice
eloquent, persuasive, for more than thirty years,
in political and literary journalism and in that
art of the lecture-hall which, for given conditions,
the American people, inventors surely of the
modern *conférence*, had long been working out,
and were to continue to work out, with a special
ingenuity.

My earlier reminiscence finds itself in fact
easily overlaid by another; which, though of a
date still remote enough, lives in my memory
both as a charmed and as an ominous impression.
This—always in hoary eld and a matter of the
comparatively primitive, the provincial lecture-
hall—was also anciently to recur, in the light
of events, to a young mind just waking up to
a sense of contemporary history. The young
mind was to recall the particular occasion as
having caused it, at the very hour, to feel the
breath of public trouble then to come. This

marked—and with an uneffaced picture—the
first dim apprehension; for when the Civil War
began to loom as a reality I said to myself,
still with the complacency of youth, that such
was the argument I had in fact attributed, a
couple of years before, to the beautiful beguiling orator in the none too brilliant auditorium
of the Newport "off-season," even he who, pleading the cause of "The American Scholar," under
a dimmish illumination and with his back to
a solemn burgess or two, had shown us the
straight way to apply the great lessons of antiquity.   The great way was to stand up, at
every point, to the invading Persians, the
arrogant Slave Power—"these are our Marathon
and our Thermopylæ, these are our heroic fields."
The heroic fields were indeed little enough to
be wanting, any more than the connection of
the beautiful beguiling orator with them was
to fail of closeness.   In addition to which I
make haste to remind myself that sympathies
and loyalties of a certain order, reviving in
retrospect, are not properly a subject for a
parenthesis; all the more that there are meanwhile other faces — though considerably more
dim—behind the bars.   It looks at us, to my
sense, I confess, as a wan face, the one evoked
by Story's allusion to Washington Allston at

Cambridgeport. Irrepressible memory plays up again at this touch; not of the beautiful colourist and composer himself, withering in a cruel air, but of the indistinct yet irresistible inference that his great strange canvas, so interrupted but so impressive, at the old Boston Athenæum, used, at a particular restless season, to force one to draw. The unfinished, the merely adumbrated parts of this huge "Daniel before Belshazzar" would certainly have boded sufficient ill had it not been for the beauty of these other portions which shone out like passages of melody, of musical inspiration, in some troubled symphony or sonata; and the lesson of the whole picture, even for a critic in the groping stage, seemed to be that it was the mask of some impenetrable inward strain. On this theme the fancy —especially if the fancy asked nothing better— could embroider at will. It possessed few *data*; it was conscious, in presence of the work and of the temperament revealed in it, but of one *other* fact—the grim synthetic fact, as Story hints at it, of Cambridgeport. The picture itself was, in essence, the fact of Italy, of the earlier old Italy than Story's own, just as the fact of Cambridgeport was the fact of a Cambridgeport also earlier — which in this case meant newer. The theme for embroidery was thus in the mere collocation—and what indeed could the vision of the inward experience have wanted more? It was animated, the vision, as one walked back through Cambridgeport, with the remorseless analysis of the quiet painter's nostalgia. One lived it over—it had to have been, in the nature of the case, so much finer than one's own. To have seen what, in his divine *Wanderjahre*, he had seen, and to see, that period ended, what he did see — verily the intensity of the latter experience on one's own part acted, creatively, in one's mind, in respect to the former. And one didn't at the time know that, in the mystic, melancholy business, one was but treading in Story's steps. We trace these steps, more lightly, in another letter of the same winter.

W. W. Story to J. R. Lowell.

"BOSTON, *February* 18*th*, 1856.

"MY DEAR JAMES,—I must add my mite to the contribution-box going to a friend cast away in Germay, if it be only to congratulate him on being there. I dare say you think yourself worse off in Dresden than you could possibly be in Boston, for it is the peculiarity of man to hate what he has and cry for what he has not. But in this one instance you are

wrong—the arctic zone has slipped down like
a garter and got on to the temperate.   Kane's
account of his winter among the floes is not
an exaggeration of our Boston experience.
The city has spent no less than 20,000 dols.
in ploughing up and carting away the streets.
They are masses of hideous ice, with 'ruffian
billows' and pits — 'thankee-marms' as we
used to call them in the good old days—that
disturb the strongest stomach that goes over
them, as much as a steamer in a head wind.
. . . George Curtis's course of lectures on
the Novelists was very successful.   His manner
was charming, and his matter most genial and
pleasant.   Ticknor sat grimly beside me one
evening when the lecture was on Dickens and
remarked after it was over that he should
probably have been more interested in it if he
had ever read one of Dickens's books and knew
the *pearsons* alluded to; but that he had made
three unsuccessful efforts at the ' Pickwick
Papers' and had failed to find anything in
them.   All the girls fell in love with George
and said he was 'perfectly splendid.'   I thought
of you often, and all your friends spoke of *your*
lectures constantly as being so very admirable.
And, by the way, we drank your health in
good warm-hearted Hungarian wine the other

day at Longfellow's and wished you were with us, or rather we were with you. I am in hopes the Longfellows will go out with us in the summer.

"I have got almost through with my book on 'Contracts,' which has now swelled to two volumes of 750 pages each, and am preparing a volume of poems for the press; which, if I decide to publish, I shall ask to dedicate to you if you are willing to take so poor a gift. I do not think they are bad; at all events they are so very far ahead of the old volume that I think it may be as well to print. . . . Next week I prologuize the Beethoven statue, which is to be inaugurated with considerable circumstance of music, &c. I hate to do this, but for Crawford's and Perkins's sake I yielded—although I had sworn after the last [time] that I would never again publicly recite my verses. Consider all that Emelyn says. Resign your professorship and stay with those who love you."

Mr Longfellow's name, we need little reflection to feel, unfortunately does not—to a loss of honour for us—fall into even the most elastic of our categories. He has too much public substance and is of too direct a presence to

figure as one of our shades. Admirably, beneficently present, in the old days—with an urbanity all his own—he is yet not, I fear, even
reducible to a case of fellowship in nostalgia
with our friend : which indeed, at the same time,
would open for us a fresh scent and start a
fresh hare, had we conceivably time to follow
them up. For, complete and established, attuned
and settled, Mr Longfellow, precisely, was perhaps interesting for nothing so much as for the
secret of his harmony (harmony of situation and
sense I of course mean) and for the way in
which his " European " culture and his native
kept house together. Did he owe the large,
quiet, pleasant, easy solution at which he had
arrived (and which seems to-day to meet my
eyes through the perspective, perhaps a little
through the golden haze, of time,) to his having
worked up his American consciousness to that
mystic point—one of those of which poets alone
have the secret—at which it could feel nothing
but continuity and congruity with his European ?
I put the question—for all it is worth—without
quite seeing how it is to be answered, and in
fact merely as a manner of recording an individual impression of something in his liberal
existence that was like a fine (in those days, at
Cambridge Massachusetts a delightful) ambiguity.

If it seemed a piece of the old world smoothly fitted into the new, so it might quite as well have been a piece of the new fitted, just as intimately, into the old. What is mainly incidental, however, to the letter last quoted is the reply.

J. R. Lowell to W W. Story

"DRESDEN, *Jan.* 28, 1856.

. . . "As to what you say about Boston, I will drink up Essel and eat a crocodile with you on that subject any day—you can't scold worse about it than I would. I know that the finest political institutions in the world don't make a country pleasant to live in, and that one may find unlimited freedom frightfully oppressive. I would gladly subscribe toward *offering* (a judicious phrase) a handsome reward to anybody who will find a cure for the (*small-*) potato-disease with which Boston is fearfully infected; but——! For example, here you are asked to deliver an address or something at the inauguration of Crawford's Beethoven—which you can do very handsomely, as you have made a better one yourself: well, give 'em a rousing orthodox discourse, give a distant panoramic view of the lake of fire and brimstone that is prepared for all nations who don't love art, or who don't love it

rightly. You have got plenty of fight in you—
let it out so. You can do the people good : there
are plenty of them who would be glad to think
right if they only knew how. But to think of
liking any country when your experience is such
as you describe is preposterous. If Little and
Brown had a shop in Elysium and I were shut
up in a little back room of it to write a law-book,
I would do something or other that would get
me transported to hell—where, by the way,
one would be much more likely to meet the
booksellers.

"But the truth is when I wrote to you I was
suffering under a horrible homesickness and—
shall I confess it ?—longing for Italy. I am going
there ! in a month. I got absolutely sick under
it, and I've only begun to mend by agreeing with
myself to let the real part of me go, if the professional part works hard enough in the meanwhile. When I wrote to you, I was trying to
reason myself out of it. I couldn't sleep, I
couldn't eat, I couldn't endure to be spoken
to ; in short I was very badly off, and my
nerves are still not what I like.

"I agree with you as to the wants one feels at
home. When I look back and think how much
in me might have earlier and kindlier developed
if I had been reared here, I feel bitter. But on

the other hand, I prize my country-breeding, the
recollections of my first eight years, my Hosey
Biglow experiences, as something real, and I mean
to make a poem out of them some day that shall
be really American. But we were born at an ill
time; we must fight; we can't merely live, and
unluckily we can't be born over again. But I
like America better than Germany in many
respects. They have too *many* ideas here; so
many tools that they only handle them without
doing anything. The beauty of Greece was that
they had very few ideas, and those simple and
great. The Germans try to recreate Greece by
studying themselves into it and acquiring a bee-
hive of notions small and confused. The wise
Goethe has talked as much twaddle as any man
I know. When people jabber so much about Art
as they do here and have all their terms so cut
and dried they are only playing cards on Art's
coffin—just as Aristotle's Poetics was the funeral
oration of Greek poetry. But I must quit that.
'Take your hat and come out of that!' That
reminds me how many good times we have had
together. It was one of our old catchwords.
But I must not think of old times either,—it
makes me sick. I will think of what is to come,
and namely of your Pied Piper. . . . It is an
admirable subject, and you must make something

out of it fit to go up beside Luca della Robbia's
Singing Children.   There is a very good version
of the story, by the way, in Howell's Letters,
which may give you some hints if you have it
not already.   Why doesn't Charley Perkins
order a Mozart for the other niche? or it
ought to be an Italian, Palestrina, perhaps.   Do
you remember our ride and the nightingales?
Well, we shall meet some day or other I hope;
if not here on some Italian planet."

The ride with the nightingales had of course
been to the Palestrina of the Roman hills during
Lowell's visit to Italy four years previous, the
spring of 1852, spent by him, with his first wife,
in Rome, as has been mentioned, and marked by
the death there of his little boy.   The occasion
had already, in 1854, been commemorated, with
a charming play of humour and fancy, in one of
the episodes of " Fireside Travels."   If Story,
meanwhile, during the winter of 1856, was doing
his best to turn his back upon the plastic arts,
he had at least, in Boston, to venture a look over
his shoulder at his friend Crawford's fine bronze
Beethoven, then about to take the place it was
for long years so impressively to occupy in that
interesting, that infinitely historic old Hall of
Music which, after signal service as one of the

worthiest temples of the art, has been lately superseded. I recall vividly, from various scenes and occasions, — from which the gravity and dignity of the place never seemed absent, and to which they even, at hours, seemed quite nobly to contribute,—the effect of the great composer's image, erect but absorbed, meditative, mighty, and as if dimly gilded, holding the note, guarding the idea, so to speak, of which the whole place was the expression. Short of having been able to indulge the dream of himself creating the figure, nothing could have made Story happier, to a certainty, than to celebrate in verse the creation of a colleague. He was happy, all his life, in his command of these alternatives, and I think that day at the Music Hall gives something of the measure of it. Sculpture, poetry, music, friendship—those were his fondest familiars, and it was a sacrifice to them all in one.

MIDDLE ROMAN YEARS

VI.

THE PALAZZO BARBERINI.

IT was early in the summer of 1856—on July 2nd, to be exact, and in the old *America* of the Cunard line—that Story left Boston, on his way back to Rome, "for good." I glean from a confused little *carnet* that the local thermometer, a few days before, had marked 98 degrees in the shade; by which *carnets* might well have been confused. I further glean that his friends R. H. Dana (no longer "before the mast") and T. G. Appleton, the much revolving —the latter doubtless as an effect of that "whip in the sky" which his wit, locally famous, had been the first to denounce—were of the ship's company. By the end of the month Lowell, quitting Dresden, had joined him in London, and, though the little *carnet* presently fails, it first holds out a finger or two. "August 1st, dine with Thackeray and the 'Punch' men"—one could at need find worlds in that; just as, more

specifically, I could find worlds in the entry—
" Out to Mount Felix and spent the day there "
—of July 30th. He spent that summer at
Walton-on-Thames, close to the beautiful and
bountiful Mount Felix; in which happy neighbourhood, in September, his youngest son was
born. These English lingerings, with more be-
guilements of friendship than I can name to-day,
were not, however, to his main purpose; in pur-
suance of which latter he settled himself in Rome
later in the autumn. But before following him
there I find a place, the least inconsequent, for
a letter he had received a few months before.

J. R. Lowell to W. W. Story.

"CATANIA, SICILY, *May 7th,* 1856.

" MY DEAR WILLIAM,—Your and Emelyn's
letters followed me to Florence, and I have been
running about so ever since that I have not had
a quiet day for answering them. I wrote you
that I had resolved to go to Italy. Well, I came
and found myself so much the better for it that
I am already the first week of my third month.
Having got to Rome, my sister would have me
go on with them to Naples, and being in Naples
she advised me very strongly to make the tour
of Sicily, which I have just been doing with
Black, Norton and Field. We have come hither

from Palermo on mules, I believe about two
hundred and odd miles; tremendous work, but
worth doing at any cost and discomfort.   Enough
discomfort there is—such inns as it never entered
into the heart of man to conceive; so nasty, so
fleay, and all that.   But one lives and likes it.
I am staying at home to-day in the hope of ac-
complishing Etna to-night; but I am afraid I
shall funk, as I do not find myself very well,
and unless I feel better this afternoon shall not
try it.   We are getting old, my dear boy.   Black
and Field will go at any rate, and Norton and
I as far as Nicolosi.   Thence we go to Messina
and so back to Naples.   In Italy proper I have
done one or two places I skipped before—Ravenna, Parma, Mantova, Orvieto and the like.
I cannot tell you how well it has been with me
till now—when I was getting a little down-
hearted again.   Now I have given you a notion
of my track, and you know Italy too well not
to be able to fill it out.   The great days, of
course, never come back; but Italy is still Italy.
I dreamed night before last of being at Nantasket
with M. 16 years ago, and it has made me sad.

   " When I read about your book, my dear
friend, and your offer to dedicate it to me, it
brought the tears into my eyes—it brought back
so much.   How could I be anything but pleased?

I am sure the volume will do you honour, as the dedication will me. We are long friends, and we shall be more to each other as we grow older. I am glad to have our names united in any way.

"I hear in a roundabout way of your Beethoven-statue inauguration. It must have been at a good time, but your own letter is the last I have received from home, and I wait to hear directly from you. . . . But what things one sees in sculptors' studios, side by side with all that fulness of old art! The want of fancy in decorative parts quite perplexes me. I begin to believe that even Greek breath in frosty air took gracefuller forms than ours."

The letter winds up with a reference to a subscription then on foot among the friends of William Page for the purchase of a wonderful Venus lately painted by him, and of which it was bravely desired that the Boston Athenæum might become possessor. Whether or no—as well might have been—that institution was shy of the gift, the idea was to be crowned with no consequence perceptible to later generations. What with the immateriality of the welcome to the "consummate" nude on the one side and the evanescence of the offering itself on the other, the plot of the little drama (the actual develop-

ment of which might have presented a various
interest) was never to thicken.   Story was moreover now to breathe, at his ease, an air in which
the interest of the consummate nude had never
been denied.   At his ease, I say, though it was
not for a year or two that his Roman existence
took the form it was so long substantially to
keep.   There is meanwhile another letter or two
from my too-scant store of Lowell's.

J. R. Lowell to W. W. Story.

"DRESDEN, *June 7th*, 1856.

"MY DEAR WILLIAM,—You will see by my
date that I have got back here to Germany
again.   The first sheet was written in Sicily,
but I found the safety of the post thence very
questionable and so kept the letter by me; and,
having travelled like a courier ever since, by me
it has remained.

"Pray write me here as soon as you arrive in
London.   I shall be here for a month longer, and
then for home.   Shall you make any stay in
England?   Or, if you go straight to Paris,
couldn't we make some little excursion thence
like that we made in England?   I should like
of all things to have you come here.   Have you
seen *our* Saxon Switzerland?   It is worth a
journey; but write and we'll arrange some plan

or other. I am sensibly better in body and mind than before my journey, only dreadfully bothered by having let my correspondence fall into arrears.

"I must be at home by the 1st September. I have orders. But I hope to be there by the 1st August. *Then* I shall have to work like—a professor on leave. I know no extremer comparison. . . . Rest assured that Messina is duller than Boston. We had to wait a week there for a steamer."

His friends were meanwhile, at receipt of the following, on their way back to Rome.

J. R. Lowell to Mrs Story.

"Hôtel de France, Rue Laffitte,
Paris, *July* 16th, 1856.

"My dear Emelyn,—Here I am back again just where I was a year ago at this time and as delighted to hear of your being in England as I was then disappointed to find that you had decamped thither—for in England I shall be in a few days. It is rumoured in diplomatic circles that you are at the White Hart, Windsor— which has a very comfortable sound. But are you to stay there? Shall we go and see another cathedral or two together?

"What I wish you particularly to do now is to write and tell me where you got the *doll* which has so excited Mabel's cupidity. If you can't remember the exact address can you tell the street or the quarter? Also whether it is a gal of wax? Moves her eyes? About how big? Cost *environ* how much? Has a wardrobe? I see ruin staring me in the face, and have just got a letter from M. ordering shoes, stockings and what not for the young foreigner. You see what a predicament I should be in were I to go home with the wrong baby. It is not a case for a warming-pan, for the features of the child are already known to the expectant mother by vision — nay by actual touch of the twin sister of elder birth. Not *every* supposititious child would answer. . . . I am already tired of Paris where *ich langweile mich immer fürchterlich*. You think I am suffering from the hyp-complaint? Very well, the result is the same. But I have really been ill, mind and body. Mind is better—body so so.

"So the Longfellows are coming? Won't they have a nice time! Over here it is more of a reputation to *know* Longfellow than to have written various immortal works. Gather your laurels while ye may, old Time is still a-flying! and old times, too, more's the pity. We will

have one more, though, in England, I trust.
Since I wrote, I have seen William's Beethoven,
which I like extremely, both sentiment and style.
It must have been very effective, and is short
enough to make one wish for more—a rare merit
on such occasions, when poets generally hang all
their wardrobes fluttering on the lines. Is W.
as savage as ever against that wretched town
of Boston? Since George Third nobody ever
treated it so. Well, I give it over to him. I
entrench myself in Cambridge; it is a good
kind of place. For the country in general, with
Kansas and Brooks and what not, I don't wonder
you were in haste to get out of it. . . ."

Story's face, notably in a preliminary residence
or two (before settling at Palazzo Barberini), was
now frankly turned to all the pleasantness of the
coming years—none the less copious a quantity,
to the spectator distant and wistful, for having,
even in the golden Roman air, its usual human
admixture. The Roman air, for us, insistently
pervades and tinges; so that—to make my own
confession at least complete—I see no circumstance too trite, no image too slight, to be bathed
by it in interest and in beauty. At this rate
and with this intensity do we feel our picture
glow. Wonderful, at the threshold, the charm

of the tradition, consecrated and classic, the
general hospitality and facility of the legend,
into which it all falls. As a question of the
"artist-life"—happy invention!—how or where
could that life have awaked to more charmed
a consciousness, have so surrendered itself to an
endless easy rhythm? The fact that the conditions had verily, since Claude, never, among
the northern invaders, flowered into the grand
style made little enough difference when they
had begotten we may perhaps not say so many
grand substitutes for it, but at least so many
happy dreams of it, so many preparations, delu-
sions, consolations, a sense of the sterner realities
as sweetened and drugged as if, at the perpetual
banquet, it had been some Borgia cup concocted
for the strenuous mind. The mind addressed
mainly to the great plastic question had, in such
an air, to lapse rather easily from the strenuous; it did so, in general, markedly enough, in
spite of an Overbeck, of an early Ingres, of other
academic phantoms, unless stiffened, as in the
case of the Niebuhrs and even of the Ampères,
for some effort of the quite heroic sort. The
very interesting "Roman Diaries"[1] of Ferdinand
Gregorovius, lately published, give, in a highly

[1] Diari Romani, Milano, 1895. I know but the Italian translation.

interesting manner, the measure both of how such an effort might be sustained and how it might find itself on all sides, countermined. Gregorovius had set himself the huge task of writing the history of the City during the Middle Ages, and this boat, on the river of oblivion, he pulled steadily, up - stream, from 1852 to 1874. His journal, even though written but little from the point of view of the "picturesque," represents vividly, for the seeing eye, the degree to which the obsession protected by that much-abused name could constantly work, and at the same time the degree in which it could be kept, so to speak, in its place. A man of this order, a man of rare distinction, managed merely to put his lips to the insidious liquor, tasting but not swallowing, and setting down the cup with a smile all courteous and wary. But the sensitive soul in general drained it, and, for the most part, at first, in innocent delight, without a misgiving or a reserve. Moreover, as most of those who sickened or died of it never knew they were either ill or dead, the feast had never the funeral air, and the guests sat at table to the end. All of which, not to be too cryptic, is but a manner of saying that Rome was, no doubt, during the golden age (wherever we may place the golden age) better,

mainly, in the process than in the proof. The
artist hovered there in the interest of concentration—which was so much, in the matter, to
the good; but the medium was one, in fact, in
which that hard grain was apt richly to dissolve,
and the result remained a delightful ambiguity.
Concentration ceased, as it were, to be a pill—
it became a liquid element in which one could
bathe and splash. In such an element, in fine,
one could—certainly for a long time—sit up to
one's neck, quite as the convinced patient sits
in his particular prescription at a German bath.
The place was the æsthetic antidote to the
ugliness of the rest of the world—that is, of
Anglo-Saxondom in especial—and to become intimate with it was the warranted cure for taints
unhappily contracted. Assuredly, as far as it
went, it was a cure for many things. The
faculty for dryness and dreariness peculiar to
our race could never be quite the same after.

This was an admirable lesson, and there were
plenty of others scarcely less so. It was all
right, as might have been said, if you reacted,
and Story, fortunately for him, was a man of
whom that could always be presumed. Drugged
or not with the Borgia cup, he could keep on
his feet and move. Nobody in fact moved more,
from subject to subject, interest to interest and

relation to relation; so much so, indeed, that for a relation to pass before him, in some example, as possible to any one, was for him immediately to wish to make it possible to himself. He proposed not, certainly, to write the history of Rome, but, besides proposing to give free substance at last to the forms that haunted him, he constantly strained to know, and to prove he knew—knew for himself, for others, on the spot—either the history of Rome or whatever else might be. He did, for years, what he desired—expressed himself with the rewarded pertinacity of the seeker, the finder, of the rare. He sought and found the secret of beauty, of harmony and, so far as these things went, of truth, for himself—as every artist worth his salt finds it; with that good faith which has the odd double property of leading to "success" and of consoling for the want of it. So it was that his worried experiment of somewhat perversely "commencing" sculptor and poet, as used to be said, justified itself in the mixed manner of human undertakings. He was of course various enough and ingenious enough (without which no man is finely interesting), never to have shut his door once for all to the knock of the vagrant *question;* it was, rather, positively his temperament to keep his head at

the window for such of this tribe as might
happen to pass. He therefore never failed of
any plenitude in feeling—in the fulness of time
and on due occasion—that a man always pays,
in one way or another, for expatriation, for detachment from his plain primary heritage, and
that this tax is levied in an amusing diversity
of ways. He had the sharp as well as the soft
reactions, and could, in the multiplied years
which can be years of disillusion even for the
dull, view the sweet æsthetic surrender, the
ancient Roman spell, the fine foreshortened past,
at any droll angle that the play of his humour
might determine. He could suspect, on plenty
of evidence, the definite, the homely proof of
the pudding—the show, as to *value*, of the
general heterogeneous production to which the
general charmed life could point. He could
suspect it—which was all that was necessary
for the prime lucidity—at the same time that
he could do it justice and feel how things happen
and how the case stood and how, if Boston had
never been Rome, so Rome could never be
Boston; and also how, in a word, they had all
danced to good music and·in the noblest ballroom in the world. Which is all, precisely, that
we need dream of demonstrating. The ballroom,
the music, the dance—they suffice for outsiders

who gather at the windows and flatten their
noses on the panes. It is not with any analysed
treason in the golden air that we are concerned,
nor with the ultimate lesson and the strained
moral of consenting absence, of perverse presence
—since who knows, in their finality, anything
of these? Our picture is not of pondered
finalities, but of happy processes, accidents,
adventures, a generous acceptance of generous
goodly appearances—all sufficient, in their order,
unto the day.

The day then (to the eye of the poor flat-nosed
spectator) was to draw a blessing, regularly, from
those elements that cluster still where, in the
course of time, he gathered them together—in
the great cool studio, or series of studios, on the
high, cleared and reclaimed ground of the quarter
known as the Macao, which, though actively and
fruitfully occupied by his son,[1] are practically a
museum of his own work. Everything that came
from his hand is there in some form of duplicate;
the place is peopled by the number and variety
of his productions; the vivid idea, the expressive
image, appeals straight, on every side, from
pedestal and table, yet looking back, at the same
time, with blank eyes, at all the pleasantness, all
the stress and struggle too, of the past. These

----

[1] His elder son, the distinguished sculptor, Mr Waldo Story.

things sit there now with calm faces and free
limbs, but they touch us, all together, as the cold
residuum of ardent hours. Taking them, as we
may to some extent do, in their order, they
testify—certainly for any other artist-mind—to
the travail and trouble in which fine things are
born ; besides seeming to speak, indefinably (and
with an eloquence perhaps essential, sooner or
later, to any sculptor's studio,) of a lost com-
panionship, a figure missing, among them, as the
absent leader is missing in the orchestra or the
absent shepherd in the flock. Is it not to such
a presence, genial glowing, particularly familiar, in
Story's case—signally loveable as the presence of
creator for creature—that they must feel they
once owed a season of warmth ? The effect is
doubtless a matter of the golden air again, of all
the old enacted but unrecorded æsthetic history
with which it is so heavily charged ; the travail
and the trouble are as if they had never been,
and the mere charm of association, of the accidents and accessories, the sense, always at hand,
of the poetry of life in such conditions, rules the
scene. Is it the poetry of the life that makes the
beautiful things, or is it they that—almost as
much when less beautiful as when more so—make
the poetry of the life ? One doesn't ask, and one
doesn't care ; the poetry of the life fills the view,

so that, even as a mere wistful visitor, one
partakes of it and lingers in it.   It is in the
slight dimness of the high rooms, lighted from
above and with a *tone* for all their figures; it is
in the space and sunshine of the garden outside,
where a vague, easy pressure of business flickers
and drops, where odd morsels of marble shine and
shade as in their natural light, where happy
human adjuncts make labour look like leisure,
like luxury, like love, like something independently sweet.   A door stands open to a court
(there are glimpses, vistas everywhere,) and impressions so multiply that you go to meet them
—meet them in the form of workmen of the
pleasant race, delightful, one would say, as partakers of one's thought and diviners of one's
intention; propitious with their fine hands and
mild handsome faces and light hereditary skill
and general amenity and practicability.   A group
is having its dinner in the warm shade of a clump
of wind-stirred trees, and a small boy in a paper
cap sings as he brings them, across the grassy
yard, something savoury in a tin pot.   There
could be no better centre for the comings and
goings of the imaginative *maker*, for the prosecu-
tion of mysteries and the entertainment, the
invocation, even the very endurance, of moods.

Scarcely less harmonious a home, however, for

such matters, was that admirable Palazzo Barberini in which Story took, in 1856, his final
Roman stand, and which was, to the end, the
main scene for him of an overflowing personal
and social life, a life in which security and
intimacy never grew prosaic, in which satisfaction never quenched eagerness, in which curiosity, hospitality and variety never ceased to
renew themselves. There are drawbacks of sorts
in old Roman palaces, in the employment of
which, as a class, our current generations suffer
from finding themselves at once not grand
enough and too "particular"; but they cover
their deficiencies with such a general amplitude,
and carry their incongruities with so high a
front, that they seem to remind us of the honour
they do us by admitting us even to such family
secrets as are matters of the back-stairs.   In
such a house as the great Barberini residence—
built by Urban VIII. "out of the quarry of the
Colosseum," on the design of Bernini—the type
has been so solidly seated that the centuries
revolve without wearing it down. The original
lucidity of the idea abides, its original insolence,
one may almost say, triumphs; it keeps the
place, always, as great when you see it again
as when you saw it last; it faces you, as so
many of the Roman monuments of the first

order do, with the assurance of some great natural fact; and it brings you round, in especial,
to the conviction that, taking one thing with
another, it may rank as the first of its company.
Something in its position on the sharp slope of
the Quirinal, half-way down the valley formed
by the opposite slope of the Pincian, something
in the way it stands reduces perhaps, till you
get nearer, its noble scale and mass; but many
admirers, for long years, were always getting
nearer, either on their way into the left wing,
to be sad over the turbaned Cenci, or into the
right to climb, more gaily, though a good deal
more steeply, Mrs Story's stairs. Then the scale
and mass loom nobly, just as the strange, clean
old yellow of the porous travertine shows deeper,
and you marvel once more, under your impression, at the revolutions of time. It was the
name, the race, the power, that, in other days,
made the palace; it is the palace that, in our
own, has to make, stiffly and ponderously, what
it can. But such a general presence even shrinks
and straitens with majesty. To the Storys, at
all events, the occupancy of a voluminous apartment of the second floor was proposed by a
member of the family, whom they had known
in Paris during the winter of 1854-55. Don
Filippo Barberini had been destined for the

church, but it was not in Paris, I take it, where he afterwards died, that he was preparing himself for any such career. He lived at any rate long enough to see his friends installed in the rambling, many-roomed *suite*—many-windowed, thereby, as well, and with every window a view of something ineffably amiable and Roman—that was still spoken of as "Miladi Coventry's": consecrated to this attribution by the somewhat sinister fact that the personage in question, occupying it some years before, had been stabbed there (whence, naturally, an immense commotion and a proper weird legend,) by a treacherous servant. She had been found, in her blood, on certain steps at the door of one of the rooms, and, having forced the blade of the knife with which the man had attacked her back upon his hand, had herself inflicted a wound by which her assailant was identified.

The legend, however, was not of a nature to be oppressive—there were plenty of others (born from day to day, for that matter, of the perpetual play of picturesqueness, of sun and shade, even of current history and current curiosity, in such a place,) to overlay it. Other Roman palaces have mostly, with their grandeur, their gloom; the only fault of the Barberini is perhaps the large brightness of its face, a note almost

of modern gaiety in its complexion and its open
approaches ; the note repeated (for happy tenants)
in all the heterogeneous pleasantness and poetry
of rearward, sideward views—blue, Claude-like
distant things and brown, yellow, amusing near
ones : iridescent horizons, accidental pictures,
unsuspected revelations and possessions, waste
Barberini courts, terraces, treasures of space,
precious Capuccini gardens, Capuccini bells,
Capuccini figures, Capuccini quaintnesses of
every sort.   With these impressions the place
is all invested—or *was*, since what Roman view
is not, at some points, now changed ?—so that,
for the pilgrim of occasions, the right observer of
opportunity, they play (or used to) richly into
each other, giving to any friendly recurrent
relation a touch of the romantic.   That sense
used to deepen on the admirable great staircase
that mounted to where Thorwaldsen's grand lion
—"really" grand, I should say, but that here
one somehow drops patronage—seems at once so
to guard the spot and yet not to bar the way ;
and it can surely nowhere in Europe reach a
finer, clearer maximum than in presence of the
picture made, above the couchant beast, by the
great confronted doors, surmounted with papal
and princely escutcheons, that admit to the
piano nobile.   State and style, nakedly enough,

but with the conscious art of greatness unadorned,
express themselves in these dispositions; and
nothing was more interesting, as one slowly
passed, than to ponder again the old mystery of
the strong effect that resides in simplicity and
that yet is so far from merely consisting of it.
Great lines, great spaces, great emphasis, great
reserve — if the grand style abides in them all
they yet scarce suffice to make it. And the rest
of your way up, a steep straight vista, gave you
time to puzzle out, if you could, the essence
of the insolent secret. It was all really, with
the very swagger of simplicity, a wrought refinement, a matter of the mixture of the elements,
a question, like everything else indeed in the
whole place, of the mutual relation of parts.
It was through such impressions as these that,
in Rome, at every turn, you were met by the
sharpest reminder of all, that of the old social
appearances, old manners, figures, features, the
delightful, dreadful old conception of conduct,
of life. What the grand style for the few involved in the way of a small style for the many
—this and many other ancientries had arts of
their own for popping out or becoming vivid.
Manners in fact—manners as they *had* been—
could, of old, as the first impression of pilgrims
with a sense for them, hang upon the very house-

fronts and perch (in the special Roman light into which, of afternoons, high things emerge from narrow streets) on the very cornices. They stood on the steps and at the doors of the churches, they stalked in the great Renaissance naves, lurked in the florid chapels, fairly bloomed in the general smell.

But these are memories, these are openings, that would take us too far; we are concerned, and but for the instant, with one of the openings that yawn majestically on the Barberini stair-case. Acceding to fifty high chambers it gives us, this glimpse of a vista, exactly what it should (during the years we go up and down,) as the characteristic image, the concentrated, typical scene: old Cardinal Barberini playing cards every evening with two or three obsequious priests, on the inveterate note, for the con-clusion, of the triumph that his Eminence's humility and simplicity have had to accept as the mysterious order of Providence—the intelli-gent resigned smile of the others when *Sua Eminenza ha vinto!* It was perhaps indeed rather the new manners that were in question when, of an evening, as one approached, from above, the bottom of the wondrous stair and felt the mild breath of the court, one inevitably caught the sound of rain and regretted, with a momentary vulgarity, the absence of the London cab-whistle. It was always (that is it was often) but the plash of the great fountain, that babble of water from somewhere which is ever the most Roman note of all: as if, precisely, in one of the most bloodstained of cities, fate had provided for it a proportionate washing away. There is plash enough, at any rate, at the Barberini, to cleanse, for the fancy, the threshold on which poor Lady Coventry bled, and even to send up its cheer into the other wing, where generations of tourists, with Hawthorne's beautiful novel in their hand, still fancy they find in the sweet face of Guido's picture the plea of justifiable parricide. The access to the place from the left as you approached was much the more majestic, but I am not sure the possibilities of impression in the opposite quarter were not, in their way, as fine. This latter approach was in any case queerer and quainter, and not least because of the odd dangling cardboard, inscribed as by a conscientious *portiere*, which anciently marked the means of summons for the keeper of the Gallery. The admirable ascent, circular but ample, was in the nature of an inclined plane, and the little doors in the wall, widely interspaced, found their climax, at the top, in the grave entrance to the great Library, acces-

sible to the public but one day in the week,
though doubtless more freely opened to the rare
special seekers for whose musty errands, in the
clear blue air, amid the deep-toned old wood-
work, the melancholy leather, the labelled vellum,
the antediluvian maps, one had the consciousness
of an envy surviving even the chill of awe.

Easier feelings attended another threshold, the
lurking door, the door of ghostly tinkles, between
the Gallery and the Library, though such feelings, to-day, in truth, encounter difficulties, delicacies, once scarce knows what to call them,
vague scruples of statement, just indulgences of
memory. As the art-life was led everywhere,
so, inevitably, it was led in the adorable little
old *rococo* apartment to which our ghostly tinkle
would admit us had we time to follow it up
There too American art—that of the landscape
in the manner of Claude, the stone-pine, the ruin,
the sunset—flourished in its day, having both
its noon of glory and its evening of eclipse ; but
there, above all, "luck," the admired of every
comer, could hold, for years, its discreet revel—
the luck of a lodging that was a minor master-
piece of early eighteenth-century *tarabiscotage*,
of contorted stucchi, mouldings, medallions, reliefs
of every form, a small riot of old-world elements.
Robert Browning and his wife, at a time when,

in view of Mrs Browning's health, an alternative
to their Florentine winter seemed urgent, had
been in treaty for this apartment, but the arrangement had failed, and it was to be peopled,
for my own eventual recollection, with more
troubled spirits.   Ghostly enough to-day the
career of Story's neighbour Tilton, the American
painter of Italian and Egyptian landscape, who
had his season of delusive fame, his flush of
Turneresque eminence in London, for a year or
two, at the Academy, on the "line," and who
not unnaturally supposed that, in the well-worn
phrase, his fortune was made, whereas it was
but to remain, for the long after-period, quite
sadly, publicly, permanently unfinished; yet with
such compensations of setting, of background, of
incident, of imputed, of possible association and
experience, a kind of Roman felicity of *in*felicity,
in the whole dim little drama.   Its dimness gives
out—as what old Roman dimness does not?—
broken pearly lights to the lingering mind, and
I find, at all events, that, for memory, the names,
the facts, the misfortunes involved produce no
vision of dismal things, but only and insistently
an image of the situation lurking, between the
Gallery and the Library, on the edge of the
old mild ascent; a recall of the charming *rococo*
shell of the story, the plaster scroll-work, the

delicacy, the floridity of the little consolations or exasperations, whichever they may have been. For they produce as well the wonder again, after all, of whether troubles may best be borne in plain places which appear to leave the question of happiness out, or amid the ornaments and graces that are supposed to contribute to it. Platitude has been known to irritate not less than pomp, and the question doubtless defies settlement, though it is one that must so often come up for exiles and absentees (it must have come for our friends and too-often uneasy precursors,) in the lovely land of Italy.

Once more, however, such matters are not our note, nor, fortunately, have cause to be : the brave Roman years, in our circle, were the reign not of labour and sorrow, but of labour and pleasure, of application and reaction more happily commingled, surely, than at any other time or in any other place. The fineness of the charm of Rome was exactly in the quality of the amusement ; always so associated with something beautiful and great, so interfused with perceptions and impressions, with the character, the accent, the dignity (one scarce knows what to call it) of the medium itself, that it became not a waste, but a positive gain of consciousness, an intensification, at its best moments, of experience.

The Campagna alone, for the satisfaction at once
of sense and of soul, for rides (most of all), drives,
walks, excursions of whatever sort, feasts *al
fresco*, pictures *ad infinitum*, archæology lively
or severe—

> "Winged Persuasions and veiled Destinies,
> Splendours, and Glooms, and glimmering Incarnations"—

the Campagna was an education of the taste,
a revelation of new sources both of solitary and
of social joy.   Who shall say that, in the fond
artist - life, the line of division ever could, or
needed to, be clear between the world of ab-
sorption and the world of effusion, or whether
as much fortunate work was not done in the
one as in the other?   Nowhere, in fine, so much
as in all these conditions, can it have seemed
light to be serious, and serious to be light—and
with a wonderful particular levity, or intensity,
as one chose to consider it, for every day in the
winter.   Was there not always a meeting, a
junketting, an excursion in order—some church-
feast, some curiosity of colour and sound, not to
be missed, some new "find" in some admirable
scene of excavation, some Cervara *rendezvous* of
fraternising artists, costumed, polyglot, theatrical, farcical, delightful; something new finished,
reported of, in somebody's, poor fellow's, clever
chap's studio; some actor, some young Salvini

worth seeing at the Mausoleum of Augustus; some singer, somewhere else, singing for sixpence an old opera never heard but in Italy; some hospitality, for the evening — the concern of some of the company—offered at a painted and storied palace? The whole matter, at the present hour, is rather phantasmagoric; the artist-life, in the romantic conditions and with the romantic good faith, is a thing of the past; the Campagna, near the walls of Rome, has been for the most part cruelly curtailed and cockney-fied; the hotels, huge and overflowing, the paradise now of the polyglot element, much more copious than of old and more strident, outface the palaces and entertain, gloriously, themselves and each other. But the softer tone lives still, on the spot, in a fond memory here and there, and echoes of the old evenings in especial, of the Roman balls, say, before the days of mourning, even yet fall upon the ear. At these festivities the early evening was quiet and dancing in suspense; nothing was done till the Cardinals had arrived, preceded up the great staircases by the four torches to which they had a right and which preceded them, in a like manner, on their urbane departure. Then, beneath the great lustres that clarified the rich old ceilings, the dancing broke out. The *vice-principi*, as

the major-domos were called, stood behind the
princesses, on occasions of multitude, to indicate,
when necessary, the identity of arriving guests
or other vague persons, with a further hint of
the degree of salutation required.   There were
cases, apparently, in which the degree was high:
"*Due reverenze, tre reverenze — reverenza pro-
fonda!*"   And there is an echo, a very interesting echo, that bravely generalises: "The princes
themselves were mostly stupid."

Central and splendid, meanwhile, of course, for
any full vision of the artist-life, would be the
Villa Medici, that massive, monumental Académie
de France which nestles, among dim nymph-
haunted groves of its own, at one of the entrances
to the public Pincian.   The Roman school, the
"finishing" school, the grave temple of consecration of the happy young prize-winners—in both
the plastic arts, in architecture, in music—of the
Beaux Arts in Paris, it would easily engulf our
handful of shadows, had it the opportunity, in its
fine crepuscular influence.   Our good fortune is
that, in our retrospect, it but indirectly competes;
it was a world in itself, with its own cluster of
stars, and doubtless is still, even though the
Roman finish may have lost, in an age of im-
pressionism, so much of its credit.   It is *we*
indeed rather—the barbarians at large—without

our temple and our priest, who didn't compete ;
the day for this was, in its manner, to come, to
come with the creation of an American temple.
The art-world was indeed a collection of little
worlds of contrasted origin and speech, bands
almost as numerous and as separately stamped
and coloured as the little promenading "nations"
—black, white, red, yellow, purple—of the Propaganda college.   They had, conspicuously, their
Cervara masquerades and other chances of re-
ciprocity ; but the Académie de France represented, with all the genius that had conceived
and maintained it, an organised and domiciled
life which reduced the other collective existences,
æsthetic groups, in comparison, to the level of
gipsy encampments.   It sat enthroned, in fine,
on "State aid" ; only, as it was grand, it was also
—rather solemnly—amiable, and dispensed hospitalities, carried on dim Sunday evenings (under
high *lambris* and attention to delicate music, in
the presence of Poussinesque tapestries and an
occasional bland great lady), that had all the
benevolence of a great example offered.   Profiting by the example as (or at least when) I could,
I seem to remember to - day that it was all a
scene the general artistic conscience was free to
feel as central — as attesting, that is, with a
stately ceremonial, the beautiful collective faith.

It is possibly because of one's thus thinking of the Villa Medici as the special temple of the worship that one falls into alluding to it as crepuscular and solemn; quite particularly pleasant and profane as was obviously much of the young life lived there. Its great garden of ilex vistas, where statues and busts unfailingly "composed," diffused doubtless a shade and seemed to give the pitch. Everything made for majesty; nothing fell below the academic—neither the fancied nymphs at twilight nor the candle-lit attitudes at the music. The nymphs doubtless, at certain hours, stood more revealed; yet remaining in their degree Poussinesque, draped with some shadow of style, on the smooth canvas and in the caressed clay of the workrooms. It was all, at any rate, noble, harmonious and interesting; it presents its particular ghosts with a perfect art.

A letter of Story's of May 21st, 1857, makes a date definite, though there are still references for us to matters previous to it.

W. W. Story to Charles Eliot Norton.

"ROME, *May* 21*st*, 1857.

. . . "We are off next week to Burnt Sienna, but what will most interest you is that we have almost ' combined ' to take the second story of the Palazzo Barberini. The Principe has shown very good will to have us come, and will put the whole apartment in complete order and let it to us for 250 dols. less than the rent we receive for our little house in Bussey Place. I never saw anything more rambling than the upper rooms above the apartment, which are to be included in our lease. They are legion in number and crop out at every new visit. I should think there are some twenty at least, of every kind and shape, going oddly about, up little stairs, through curious holes, into strange lumber-rooms, and then suddenly opening into large and admirable chambers."

It is with this moment in the life of our friend that I should be glad to connect, did I but enjoy the liberty, a small but charming group of letters in which the interesting shades we interrogate fairly swarm; fairly flitting through them as over the stage — before the soundless orchestra—of a theatre of ghosts. This privilege, however, is denied me, and I must content myself with recording, in the light shed by the documents, a relation and an episode that were evidently alike delightful. Mrs Gaskell, the author of " Cranford," " Sylvia's Lovers," " Wives and Daughters," admirable things which time has consecrated, takes up, from Manchester,

in the autumn of 1856, an acquaintance made,
or rather, apparently, renewed, in Paris in 1855.
"I like to think of *our* Sunday breakfasts in
Paris, and your Sunday bunches of violets, and
the dear little girl, and the magnificent baby,
and the Italian nurse, and the Etruscan bracelets,
and the American fish-rissoles; and then of Mr
Story, high and far above all, with his ——
Island ghost-story and his puns. Oh, weren't
we happy!" She inquires as to the identity of
"a very agreeable American Kennedy, whom I
met a good deal in London this year, and a very
charming Mrs Edward Twisleton and a Miss
Dwight, her sister"; at which the faint echoes
begin more or less to sound and the dim scene
to people itself. The island of the ghost-story
eludes us, as does also the very agreeable
Kennedy, but we recognise the rosy dawn of
the "international" marriage, destined subsequently so to flourish, in the writer's other
reference. Images of fair and elegant girls trans-
planted to English soil, briefly and charmingly
blooming there, then early extinguished and long
mourned, peep again through the closed window
—with clever Boston sisters, eminent and trenchant, and reserved, in their time, for happier fates,
but now at last shadows as well, looking at us
also, if we like, through the clouded pane. Mrs

Gaskell's letter of 1856 mentions as "the vaguest idea in the world" the possibility of her going to Rome with two of her daughters at the winter's end. "I hope to have finished my Life of Miss Brontë by the end of February, and then I should like to be off and away out of the reach of reviews, which in this case will have a double power to wound, for if they say anything disparaging of *her* I know I shall not have done her and the circumstances in which she was placed justice; that is to say that in her case more visibly than in most her circumstances made her faults, while her virtues were her own." The Storys passed the winter of 1856-57 at 43 Via Sant' Isidoro, and it was in the spring of the latter year that this correspondent carried out her plan of a couple of months spent near them and under their immediate wing—a season the perfect felicity of which was to feed all her later time with fond memories, with renewed regrets and dreams. Mrs Gaskell had clearly, in an eminent degree, the sentiment of appreciation (*as* a sentiment); reading her letters suggests, singularly, the charm of such a relation with her as would spring from having had occasion to contribute to her pleasure, her rest, her relief. Clear echoes of a "good time" (as we have lived on to call it) break out in her full,

close page ; making us ask ourselves what could
have been more delightful, in those days, than
to be in any degree able to see that she had it.

"I want just, if I can," she again wrote, "to
leave England on the day of publication of my
book : this will be, I expect, one day in the first
half of February ; and I believe it will take us
eight days to reach Rome—somewhere about
Feb. 20th at the earliest. It might even be a
fortnight later. I have still 200 pages to write,
but they begin to print to-morrow. I shall bring
you a copy with me, if it is out, in memory of
our happy Paris Sundays. I think you'll be
interested in it—I am so much so." But there
was, however, inevitably, a delay in her starting,
and she writes again, undatedly, but apparently
in March : "I must first of all thank you for
all the kind help you have given us, and then
accept most gladly your charming invitation to
spend our first few days with you while we
choose our lodgings and get a little initiated
into Roman ways." To the happy conditions
of the pilgrimage when it at last took place we
have her testimony, from the "cold dim grey
Manchester," in the following September. "It
was in those charming Roman days that my life,
at any rate, culminated. I shall never be so
happy again. I don't think I was ever so happy

before.   My eyes fill with tears when I think of
those days, and it is the same with all of us.
They were the tip-top point of our lives.   The
girls may see happier ones—I never shall."   She
read all poetry into almost any friendship, and
she now looked back at the Roman felicity across
an interval that had bristled with disagreeable
things.   She had gone forth in the joy of having
finished her vivid Biography, but the book, though
in the highest degree " successful," had sown her,
at the same time, a crop of dragon's teeth (the
effect of an apparent mistake of fact as to the
history of Bramwell Brontë,) which had bravely
to be gathered in.   Of this unpleasant business
she gives a full and interesting account, which
is not, however, unfortunately, to our present
purpose ; besides which some of us still remember
the nine days' flurry, which was to attach a
" fancy" value to the first edition of the book.
What it had, at any rate, especially done was to
embitter the aftertaste of the pleasure she had
taken, in Rome, with so good a conscience.   Still,
the aftertaste was to recur irrepressibly.   "Oh,
I so long for Italy and Albano that it makes me
ill !" she sighs in another letter, apparently of
1858 ; in which her first allusion is to the
removal of her friends to Palazzo Barberini.   " I
am glad Domenico is with you.   It is bad enough

your having changed your house; I don't like to think of your changing a single servant. Have you still Serafino? Our remembrances to Luigi and Clarke. Speak of us to Amante and Domenico. Have you still little birds for dinner, and the good 'dolci,' the creams of which it was necessary to be forewarned, lest we should eat too much previously?" Writing at another time that she has been for a while at Whitby, whither she had gone for impressions preparatory to "Sylvia's Lovers," she mentions that Hawthorne was at the same time, on the same coast, at Redcar, ten miles off, engaged in finishing "Transformation," the subject of which she sketches as she has heard it narrated. Then touching on that outbreak of the faun nature, the animal, in the strange hero, which moves him at a given moment to the commission of a murder: "For all of which, somehow, you like Donatello the better!"

For all of which—that is for all, from her hand, that I have before me—we like *her*, Mrs Gaskell, so much the better that we would fain keep her present with us as long as we may, as long as we feel her spirit, over all Roman matters, willing to linger. We must let it go, however, on a couple of the inevitable notes of home-sickness. "I think Rome grows almost

more vivid in recollection as the time recedes.
Only the other night I dreamed of a breakfast—
not a past breakfast, but some mysterious breakfast which neither had been nor, alas! would be—
in the Via Sant' Isidoro dining-room, with the
amber sunlight streaming on the gold-grey Roman
roofs and the Sabine hills on one side and the
Vatican on the other. I sometimes think," she
goes on, "that I would almost rather never have
been there than have this ache of yearning for
the great witch who sits with you upon her
seven hills."   After Hawthorne's romance has
come out she expresses to her friends her supposition that they will have read, as every one
in England had, the "Cleopatra chapter," and
assures them that she is proud of being able
to say to people that she had been acquainted
from the first with the statue commemorated.
"I feel funnily like Quin, who, when George III.
made his first speech before Parliament after
his accession, said, 'I taught the boy to read!'—
for I come in crowing over my having seen the
thing even in the clay and describing more fully
what every one is asking about. I can't say,
unluckily, 'I taught the boy to imagine beauty.'"
And in relation to a collection of tales, promised
to her publishers, but with which, for the time,
she is disinclined to proceed—"I could *tell* the

stories quite easily. How I should like to do
it to you and Mr Story and Edith, sitting over
a wood-fire and knowing that the Vatican was
in sight of the windows behind! . . . You
don't know how a scrap of paper from Rome
is valued in this house." And then at the
last : "Please don't forget you have my 'Tolla'
with you somewhere—left to be bound in the
pretty Roman vellum binding. But if it is
lost never mind it; only if you come upon an
old shabby copy remember it is mine. I am
very loth to shut up this letter—it somehow
seems like closing up Rome for ever." Which
allusion I strain my licence to quote for old
acquaintance' sake—because of the impossibility
of not vibrating a little at a touch of reference
(for rare to-day *is* reference) to Edmond About's
first, and truly beautiful, little novel; a master-
piece of the pathetic, as we used at least to
think it, just as we used to think several of
its successors masterpieces of the ironic and
the comic. Strange often indeed are the fates
of little books—and stranger still sometimes
the fates of little authors.

I remember how, during the first walk I ever
took in Rome, "Tolla," though even then of
respectable antiquity, seemed so recent and fresh
to me that I was half the time occupied in

wondering which of the palaces had stood for
the Palais Feraldi—in which of them the exquisite Tolla had lived, loved, wasted, died;
the palaces really having, as it struck me under
that violent and irreproducible impression, more
to say about everything Roman than any other
class of object. And I was already wondering
why About's tragic tale, read in extreme youth
as a permitted, a quite encouraged specimen
of French "grown-up" fiction, had ceased to be
a work frequently mentioned, had not in fact
become a classic of the same order as " Manon
Lescaut " or the history of Paul and Virginia.
I might indeed have found an answer to my
question in a re-perusal of the book; which,
none the less, I have never to this day—and
quite also for old acquaintance' sake—read over.
That has left me free to think as tenderly of
it as I like—and of the far-off hour of young
sensibility, of young subjection; as fondly and
musingly as may be of these innocent things
and others besides : the odd, abrupt extinction
of the writer's bright star in the eclipse of the
second Empire; the warning, lesson, morality,
conveyed in so sharp a turn of the wheel, so
fickle a fortune; the ferocities of fate that such
transitions represent; the question of who is to

be sure, if About could not have been ; the fact,
above all, that a great literature may be thought
of as rich indeed when it can afford to sacrifice,
as one may say, not consciously and publicly
to *wear*, so clear a talent. All of which remarks
may possibly figure a pyramid resting on its
point. The point of my pyramid is that the
little old Roman love-story, Mrs Gaskell's and
mine, was a thing to be cherished—as it was,
most peculiarly and insistently, a thing to be
bound in the little old parchment and gilt. Was
it, *is* it, a small full-blown flower of the story-
teller's art ?—does any one in the world to-day
really know ? But to find out, I remind myself,
is possibly to expose to danger the most delicate
literary grievance of one's collection. One's
collection is precious, the haunted chamber,
the innermost temple, of Taste, the air tonic
beyond any other for that principle. Therefore
let us bind in ivory vellum the slim idyl of
our fourteenth year, and let us keep it always
on some shelf of good credit. But let us decidedly never open it again—referring, of course,
when I say "again," to the antediluvian few.
The many who are now fourteen have enough
with the late Mr Henty, a classic whom our
own literature will *not* sacrifice.

These things we might well take, had we
margin for it, as stirring up for us another
mute company. It is hard indeed—as with a
positive heartlessness—to pass over names into
which one would fain for the moment read, or
at least write, some of the pleasant meaning they
have to give. Hamilton Wild, whom we have
already amicably encountered, had left Rome
with Mrs Gaskell and her daughters, on their
departure, and befriended them, in complications,
by the way ; they having desired to put in, on
the road to Florence, the vision of Siena—which
offered some difficulty on which they had not
counted. Mild enough and dim enough are such
adventures after such intervals, but consorting so
with the remembered figure, the character, charm,
talent, production, of the man of many friends,
who painted, who talked, who travelled, who in
particular endeared himself, and on whom also
rests something of the soft light of the old
Arcadia. Where are his pictures now ? They
were not vulgarly numerous, and to ask the
question, for that matter, is immediately to feel
sure that they must have incurred the happy
fortune of that special shade of indulgence which
is spoken of as " friendly keeping." He painted
them very much for himself, and it is logical

that for himself—that is for his memory—they should be kept. But have they not the further felicity that when, at this time of day, they are shown for *him*, for the so amiable man, they strike, they surprise, a little, on their own account, produce the brief, belated, benevolent "Really?" which, as an eventual crown of glory, is the best that most of us may hope for? I recall Hamilton Wild, at all events, as, with two or three others—with T. G. Appleton, with Arthur Dexter, the "mio amico Arturo" of the dedication of Story's "Grafitti d'Italia"—of the small, select company of the bachelors of Boston, a group so almost romantic in their rarity that their "note" would suggest, their title verily adorn, a light modern opera. I fail, at all events, to resist the disposition to commemorate him to the extent of a short note addressed by him from the heart of Arcadia and which has strayed into my collection, though belonging to it only through reference. It has indeed more than on reference, and another haunting shade, an Arcadian of the Arcadians, slips from it into our path. I can scarce express the regret, or the gentleness, with which I brush by this latter apparition.

"They [the Storys] start for somewhere near

Siena on Monday, and wish me to go in their carriage. Mrs Tappan and suite go on the same day to Florence by Perugia, and she has likewise invited me ; and as I have never seen that route I am strongly tempted to go with her. Wouldn't you ? I have finished my pictures for ' Belmont,' as you may suppose. Rome is now most lovely, all full summer splendour ; every wall covered with roses, and the Campagna like a great garden as you look over it from the Cæsars' Palace. We have had a succession of hot days lately, and one crept into the shade as one walked in the city. People sit out of doors in the evening, and all Rome goes quietly to sleep at mezzogiorno. Shops are shut, blinds closed, and all take a snooze ; you hear only the cry of the lemonade-vendor, with his basket daintily lined with cool green leaves over which nods a bunch of roses, as he bawls 'Aqua freschis-s-sima ! Limo-o-o-one !' I haven't told you what a jolly time we had in the Abruzzi ; it was really splendid."

There would be other scents to follow ; but there are luckily, in the interest of concentration, deterrents. The eminently social (as well as the eminently individual) figure of Mme. Mohl, with its high antiquity and its supreme oddity, would be a signal instance, for she looks out at me, characteristically, from one of Mrs Gaskell's letters. But this remarkable shade has enjoyed, copiously, the honours of commemoration—walks in fact with a public effect with which no light touch of private testimony can hope to compete. In spite of which, I may add, I shall not resist the opportunity of reproducing a brief entry of Mrs Story's inspired by her in the course of some notes on the Parisian winter of 1853-54. What a fortune indeed, I may here boldly parenthesize, would have assuredly awaited any chronicler able to produce her image, by the light of knowledge, quite intact and as a free gratuity to his readers ; produce it in its habit as it lived, in its tone as it talked, with its rich cluster of associations, and above all with the mystery of the reasons of its eminence—a mystery admirable, almost august, from long duration, and enhanced by the complete absence, at any moment, of any weak attempt on the lady's part to clear it up. Mrs Story had however, in a manner, her explanations. " Mme. Mohl used to drop out of an omnibus, often into a mud-puddle, at our door, and delight us with her originality and freshness. I can see her now, just arrived, her feet on the fender before the fire, her hair flying, and her general untidiness so marked as to be picturesque—since she showed a supreme indifference to the details of dress. Her talk was all her own; nobody was like her for a jumble of ideas and facts, which made her mind much like her clothes, topsy-turvily worn. If she came to urge me to go to the theatre or a concert with her it was after her own fashion; she elbowed her way through the crowd with wonderful success, and enjoyed the plays, from some *balcon* or *fauteuil* that she had wrested from the box-office, in complete indifference to her surroundings. She cared for nothing but what she was hearing or seeing, and her racy comments were always worth remembering. Her little dinners were amusing beyond any others, thanks to the quantities of clever talk. She was always at home on Friday evenings, which were occasions we so liked that we never, when in Paris, omitted one, and in fact often timed our arrival or put off our departure not to miss them. She knew how to manage her clever people—it was what she was most remarkable for, putting them always on their strong points and effacing herself except for appreciation."

In addition to a more meagre note on Alexis de Tocqueville ("He often in 1854 came to

breakfast with us on Sundays; the most charming of men; sensitive and fastidious, full of ac-
complishment, spirit, grace of mind,") I find in
the same little cluster of memoranda an affectionate reference to Thackeray, written apparently in some later year, but connected with the
same winter. She says, after noting that he had
been at this time a frequent visitor: "I took
Annie [1] to her first ball at the Hôtel de Ville,
and his interest in her dress, appearance and
enjoyment was delightful to see. He sat up for
her, to have the details of the evening before she
had lost her fresh impression, and enjoyed to the
full her enthusiasm over the splendours we had
seen. He often looked in upon us during his
afternoon walk, talked with Edith as she liked,
and looked with her over the wardrobe, counted
even the rows of socks, of *mon petit frère*, in
whom he took great interest. The next winter
he was with us in Boston, and dined with us,
in Rowe Street I remember, on Waldo's first
birthday, calling him 'Henry the Eighth' and
tipping him with his first sovereign." And she
goes back to the sad winter in Rome, the time
of the death of her eldest son, when "we often
urged him to forget us and not to be drawn

[1] Mrs Richmond Ritchie.

down into the depths of our sorrow, but rather to disport himself in the cordial sunshine of appreciation, among his own people, to which he had so good a right. But he would not hear of this, and came again and again, listening to our tale of grief as if it had happened to himself, with a kindness and sympathy never to be forgotten. Once he surprised me when I had in my hand a little worn shoe which had for me an intense association; he shed tears over it with me and understood what it meant to me as few could have done. . . . Under what people called his cynical exterior and manner, his was the kindest and truest heart that ever beat, large in its sympathies and gracious in its giving. I think he must have liked us—we liked *him* so much and took such endless pleasure in his society. When alone with us he talked abundantly, but when people were numerous he seemed to have little to say."

Had I been able to make further use of Mrs Gaskell's letters I should have sought a connecting link in saying that the few of Mrs Browning's that I have before me might well, in their perfect amenity, keep them company; all the more that my scant handful of brief notes from the latter source refers itself obviously to the same general season. The first alone perhaps is of slightly earlier origin.

Mrs Browning to Mrs Story.

[*Winter of* 1853-54.]

"When Pen, fresh from your kindnesses and his happy day yesterday, brought me, my dear Mrs Story, this too beautiful gift from you, I felt for a moment embarrassed; but it is better, I think, to tell you at once that a brooch *identically the same* has been already given to me and accepted. What am I to do? I can't wear two brooches exactly alike, can I? Perhaps you will set us down as ungracious about gifts, and it is true that the sincere clasp of hands (which you spoke of in an answered note) is better to us than the best gifts. But my reason for begging you to appropriate otherwise this lovely trinket is *too* reasonable to run the least risk of being untenderly interpreted, or, what would be worse, of vexing you. So I take heart to entreat you to fasten it into dear Edith's collar and to let her feel that it is not spoilt by having just passed through my hands. The sentiment of the Christian symbol, so significant and touching to us all, remains with me, while the innocent unconscious Dove, floating whitely in its atmosphere of rose, suits indeed her years rather than mine. I thank you much, and I shall thank you more if you understand kindly, which you will, I think.

"We count on you to-night, and would fain be exacting for to-morrow night also if we thought that Mr and Mrs M. might draw you. Believe that among the warmest wishes of your truest friends at this season of wishes, there is none, &c., &c."

Two others are of trivial occasions, but there is scarce a scrap of a letter of Mrs Browning's in which a nameless intellectual, if it be not rather a moral, grace—a vibration never suggesting "manner," as often in her verse—does not make itself felt. She writes, apparently in 1860, to the little girl whom she had taken care of in illness several years before—"by Pen's desire. He is not well, and prays you to send him for solace a certain 'Family Robinson,' says he, 'by Mayne Reid,' and to be sure not to remember against him his having 'blotted a book of yours last year.' I doubt the connection between Mayne Reid and Robinson, but speak as I am bidden. Poor child, he wants a book of some kind." And on another occasion she addresses the same young friend in the same interest: "Dearest Edith,

I am very sorry, but papas are more particular than mamas, and this papa of Pen's wants him for his music, he says, and does not like the whole day to be idled. There are lessons, besides, for to-morrow. Dearest Edith, forgive us. Another day, with less obstacles, you see. And thank you for your goodness." It is impossible to disappoint a little girl more mercifully.

END OF THE FIRST VOLUME.

WILLIAM WETMORE STORY

AND

HIS FRIENDS

FROM LETTERS, DIARIES, AND RECOLLECTIONS

BY

HENRY JAMES

IN TWO VOLUMES

VOL. II

MIDDLE ROMAN YEARS

CONTINUED

WILLIAM WETMORE STORY
AND HIS FRIENDS.

VII.

SIENA AND CHARLES SUMNER.

THE Storys spent in 1857 the first of the several summers they were to spend at Siena, but this one passed without the company of the Brownings, which on other occasions they were to have there. Siena, like the Baths of Lucca (where, with Robert Lytton, of their former party, the Brownings again spent the August and September of 1857), is peopled for us to-day with wandering shades—impalpable phantoms of lightly-dressed precursors that melt, for every sense, into the splendid summer light, when, on the chance of making them confess by some weak sign to acquaintance, we take our way out of one of the open gates (great mouths in the old walls, overbrowed as with high pink foreheads,) to the region of the haunted villas.   How can one hope to find the right word for the sense of rest and leisure that must in olden summers have awaited here the consenting victims of Italy, among ancient things all made sweet by their age, and with Nature helping Time very much as a tender, unwearied, ingenious sister waits upon a brother, heavy of limb and dim of sight, who sits with his back against a sun-warmed wall.   The lurking shades at present, on the spot, in the places they occupied and that must have changed ever so little, melt, for every sense, into the actual splendid light, the mere happy, indifferent, oblivious luxuriance of garden, vineyard and podere, into the shimmer of olive-slopes, the tangle of orchards and cornfields and long-armed flowers, springing up like embracing girls—the blaze of blue, the glow of tawny yellow and iridescence of far away violet.   Strange and special the effect, in Italy, of the empty places (and there are many) that we stand and wonder in to-day for the sake of the vanished, the English poets; the irresistible reconstruction, to the all but baffled vision, of irrecoverable presences and aspects, the conscious, shining, mocking void, sad somehow with excess of serenity.   There is positively no

great difference between the impression of the
Lerici of Shelley, that of the Ravenna of Byron,
that of the painted chamber of Keats by the
Spanish Steps in Rome, and the great, bright,
vacant, yet all so solemn smile with which, one
July morning, not long ago, the cluster of Sienese
villas met my unanswerable questions. These
questions — which were, for one's self, about
William Story and Robert Browning and Walter
Savage Landor, and other spirits of the general
scene not here to be named—renewed, in their
vanity, renewed, on the high terraces meant for
soft evenings and in the cool bare echoing rooms
where shutters were pulled open for me to violet
views, that pang, not so much of accepted loss as
of resented exclusion, of which the other more
or less violated shrines had pressed the spring.
There they still stand, at any rate, the old cool
houses — Meschatelli, Belvedere, Spanocchi-Ser-
gardi, Alberti, Gori, Borghese — on their com-
municating slopes, behind their overclambered
walls and their winding, accommodating lanes;
there they stand in the gladness of their gardens
(congruous haunts of delightfully-named young
gardeners, Adone and Narciso,) and in that
wondrous mountain ring which seems to contract and expand as, with the time of day and
the state of the air, colour deepens or swoons.

And there, at its distance, on its admirable deep-plunging ramparts—a presence as felt, perpetually, as marked for your spiritual economy as that of some great reduced personage on a prolonged visit to you would be for your domestic and social—stands the hard old fighting, painting, dwindling city, even yet as embattled for the eye, even yet as buttressed and bristling and frowning, with its tallest sharp tower in the sky, as some girt and armoured warrior who forever shakes his spear.

The Storys were in *villeggiatura* at the date of the following.

Robert Browning to W. W. Story.

"FLORENCE, *July 22nd*, 1859.

. . . "Our business is to keep what we have gained, and I don't know so likely a way as by getting our share in your pleasant Siena cool and quiet. Will you have the goodness to engage for us the Bargagli villa from August 1 to September 30 ? We must pay 35 francs a month if they won't take 30 ; you will do for us what you can, and we cheerfully abide by your bargain. We bring our own plate and linen.

"I am vexed at what you tell me of poor Mr Landor : I write to him, under cover to you, and will, if I can, prevent him doing anything so foolish as going to Viareggio. I had no notion of his meaning to go to Siena till he told me he had written to you : he would hear of no other plan. Now, through the happiest of chances, he finds exactly all and far more than he wanted, and he begins scheming in this fruitless way. His family take no notice of his letters, and, till I hear from England, which I hope to do every day, I cannot be sure that his agent or relatives will advance him a farthing. He must at all events stay till his means are assured, and were they ever so abundant he is manifestly unfit to be trusted alone. Nor can I engage to go about with him and be responsible for what happens — as to a certain degree I might in Siena. If Mr Landor is in earnest in preferring any 'two rooms,' with simple board, to living with his family, that arrangement may be made; but Viareggio, &c., are 'not in the programme.' I will make this as plain to him as is consistent with the delicacy of com-munication that he requires, and, no doubt, he will acquiesce. What a load you have im-posed on yourself, in your generosity; but you shall not long remain unrelieved of it, be assured. He will show you the letter I write."

To which this is complementary.

Robert Browning to W. W. Story.

"FLORENCE, *July 28th,* 1859.

"I wrote to you hurriedly the day before yesterday; since then two most kind communications have reached us from your villa. I told you that Forster had written energetically begging me to take every care of Landor till he could make new arrangements with the brothers and agents; the serious illness of the latter being all that prevented the matter from being very speedily terminated. I wrote on the same day to Mrs —— demanding in a mildly-gruff way clothes, books, plate, pictures, residue of cash; in short all that poor Landor, by a note just received, desired me to obtain through the good offices of the Commissary of Police. However, diplomacy being more efficacious than frank fighting, I simply wrote, as I say, and yesterday was favoured by a visit from Mrs ——, all butter and honey (save an occasional wasp's sting overlooked in the latter when she occasionally designated our friend as 'the old Brute!'). The end is she gives up all we require; the clothes this very day to Mr Kirkup, the rest as soon as possible. I will bring them with me, and the note I enclose may set our poor friend's

mind at rest on that point. But it will also
serve another purpose, I trust—induce him to
take that lodging you were so fortunate as to
place at his disposal. Of your own goodness and
generous hospitality you will not let me speak,
nor is it necessary; but it *is* necessary, not on
your account at all so much as on his own, that
Landor should now fairly try the experiment
which he was bent on making, and show whether
he can indeed live independently of the immediate superintendence of his family. The question
is not which of his friends will be happy and
ready to entertain him as a guest, but whether
he can ever be anything else; which Mrs ——
very emphatically denies. I should certainly
like to see how he sets about it, and I strongly
press on him in the note the necessity of taking
those lodgings for a single month and finding
how he likes the way of life he was determined to
adopt. In a month we shall know exactly what
his means are, and can contrive how they may
be turned to the best account. He must try
now, because a failure can be easily redeemed.
Had I supposed he would stay with you more
than a day, I should have made quite other
arrangements. . . . We mean to go to Siena
the first day that my wife is able to make the
effort; she is decidedly better, but still very

weak. We mean to be as happy as possible
for these coming two months, and therefore, to
avoid any precipitation and mistake we will
go to Siena, attack the triangle of villas in
succession, armed with those capital plans, and
establish my wife to her mind—as I know will
be soon done. Let us once arrive, and the rest
will be an easy matter."

But he writes again before starting.

Robert Browning to W. W. Story.

[1859.]

"My wife has been so ill, and the calls on
my time so incessant, that I was unable to tell
you—what would have pleased you to know
two days earlier—that I have had a very satisfactory letter from Forster, kind and conclusive.
He will make every effort to help poor Landor,
and entertains no doubt of being able to do so
effectually; he energetically bids me hold *himself*
responsible for all expense, insists on Landor's
finding every comfort, an attendant, and other
assistance I will tell you about when we meet;
but adds that he is sure there will be no need
of any such effort on the part of any friend, as
the brothers of Landor, with whom he will put
himself in immediate communication, are most

'noble, honourable gentlemen, and wealthy to boot, and will never bear indignity to their family's head.' They have all been under the delusion that the Fiesole people used the greatest kindness to our poor friend, spared no effort to make him at his ease, &c. The greatest inconvenience is that Mr Walter Landor, of Rugely, the cousin-agent, is seriously ill, dying in fact, and this may a little retard matters; but that eventually a satisfactory arrangement will be made we need not doubt, and meantime he and other friends just as zealous will gladly take all the engagements that may be necessary. I have communicated so much of this as seemed needful to Landor, beseeching him to possess his soul in peace and quietness—as your goodness to him indeed makes a very easy matter.

"And now, dear Story, the moment my wife can be moved to Siena we shall take the journey; but as there is a stop in our negotiations about [our quarters] let me profit by it to beg dear Mrs Story will let us know, before we decide, what I overlooked in my usual stupid way for the grounds and groves and other external beauties. My wife is tenacious of a ground floor—no stairs to ascend: now which of the three at our discretion is the *stairless* villa? I am able to satisfy her about the

coolness and picturesqueness of situation, but
I forget the rest. Can you help us again without finding the bore too exorbitant?"

The help, it is needless to say, was given, and
the following, from Florence, in the autumn,
was after the event.

Robert Browning to Mrs Story.

[FLORENCE, 1859.]

. . . "You need not be told how entirely we
owe you the delightful summer we have spent at
Siena. Its one fault was its briefness. Ba is
hardly so well as when she was let thrive in
peace and quiet in that dear old villa and the
pleasant country it hardly shut out. She is
forced to see more people and talk oftener than
suits her. I am very anxious to get away, and
see no obstacle to our doing so by the end of
the first week in November, when Mr Landor
will be finally established in his winter quarters.
We are papering and carpeting and doing things
superiorly. He is quite well; as gentle and
affectionate as ever; and I shall regret his loss
more than there is any use in dwelling upon,
now that it must be. Ba enters the room at
this moment, saying 'I wish we were in Rome!'
Tell us, for we count on your goodness, the day

you expect to be there, and, when you get there, any news about houses, sunny ones, and prices of the same : in short, as usual, trouble yourselves infinitely for the sake of us poor do-nothings-in-return."

To which Mrs Browning adds—

"Yes, I am very anxious to go to Rome. Nothing keeps us but the Landor necessity. The air here (since it has turned to damp) and too much talking make me feel more *unsound* than I have done lately, and the prophesied-of massacre at Rome (toward the imagination of which Dall' Ongaro contributed poetically two evenings ago) does not alarm me so much as thoughts of the tramontana. The Venetian poet threatened us also on other points. But I am steadfast in the faith that things are going excellently. Let us pray that the Pope and his Antonelli won't give up an inch. The danger is that they give up. Will nobody help the Pope away ? My kingdom for a horse, or rather a mule, or rather a boat from Porto d'Anzio. Then the emperor's last promise to the Tuscan delegates that there should be no intervention — *neppure Napoletano* — is worth something."

We have meanwhile Story's brief account of the summer.

W. W. Story to Charles Eliot Norton.

"VILLA BELVEDERE, SIENA, *Aug. 6th*, 1859.

. . . "Walter Savage Landor has been staying with us here for the last three weeks. The poor old man, you may remember, . . . left England and made a reconciliation, . . . and there at his villa (in Florence) with them he has been staying for a twelvemonth. . . . He was finally forced to leave the villa and take refuge in an inn in Florence. There Browning found him and brought him to Siena, he having expressed a wish to find a little cheap apartment here. Having previously written to me for information as to the villas and houses on lease, he came at once to me, and I persuaded him to stay; so shocked was I at the whole story of ingratitude which he told me and which Browning fully confirmed. He looked very much broken down when he came, but a cheerful life, with nobody to irritate him and plenty of fresh air, have made a new man of him, and he has taken a villa in the neighbourhood, where he will remain until we leave for Rome. It is a noble structure of a mind,

capacious and perfect still in all its main parts.
Here and there are cracks and flaws, and the
gigantic memory has begun to crumble away,
but the great imposing edifice shows much of
a grand front.   The old man is still strong,
though he has completed eighty-four years and
looks back on a long space.   Up early in the
morning, he reads and sometimes writes Latin
alcaics, and since he has been here he has
fired several Latin bombs into Louis Napoleon's
camp.   He is as stout for liberty as ever, a
great friend to Garibaldi and a real lover of
Italy.   We hope still to have imaginary conversations from his pen, as we have real conversations from his mouth.   We have found
him most amiable and interesting, with certain
streaks of madness running through his opinions, but frank and earnest of nature and a
hater of injustice.   He tells us stories of past
times, past men and past actions, and we are
sorry to lose him at last, after the long discourse, looking before and after, that we have
had.   He is now publishing a new volume
containing his Hellenics and additional new
poems.

"Browning too is at a stone's throw from us,
and every evening we sit on our lawn under

the ilexes and cypresses and take our tea and
talk until the moon has made the circuit of the
quarter of the sky. He is well and full of life
as ever, but poor Mrs Browning is sadly weak
and ill. She is intensely interested in Italian
affairs, and, as you know, believes in Louis Napoleon. When the news of the peace of Villa-
franca came she was very much overcome by
it, and, having unfortunately taken cold by
some imprudent exposure, she has been utterly
prostrated. We think she has passed the
dangerous crisis and is slowly moving on towards health ; but still she is terribly weak, so
that she cannot walk across the room, and is
afflicted by a racking cough which often robs
her of sleep by night. I have seen her only
once since she left Florence, for she cannot
talk, and every excitement must be avoided.
When she came up she was carried in arms to
the carriage and thence to the house, and looked
like a dark shadow. Browning is in good spirits
about her and has no fears now. Pen is well,
and as I write I hear him laughing and playing
with my boys and Edith on the terrace below
my window."

I find among my documents in relation to
this period two groups of careful and vivid

notes by Mrs Story, to which I cannot do
better justice than by giving them in their
order and mainly as they stand—that is with
few omissions — and with the application to
both of the heading borne, in faded ink, by
the one which is apparently the later in date.

"RECOLLECTIONS OF WALTER SAVAGE LANDOR;
WITH AFTER-DINNER TALK AT SIENA.

"We first made Mr Landor's acquaintance at
Bath, where we were introduced to him by Mr
Kenyon. He was living there by himself,
away from his family, who were in Italy. We
found him extremely cordial and kind, and he
induced us by his pressing invitation to pass
most of our time with him. He had his walls
lined with paintings of no great value, I believe,
but bearing high-sounding names of the Italian
schools. He was a fierce believer in things
and people who interested him, and a most
violent denouncer of whatever didn't. He in-
veighed against his wife and against his
children, but on the other hand told us the
story of his love for Rose Aylmer. He was
altogether most brilliant and entertaining.

"Later on, at Siena, when we were living at
Villa Belvedere, we were surprised by a visit

from him.[1] He arrived one sultry morning
with Browning, looking very old, and almost
as shabby and dusty and miserable as a beggar.
Browning had helped him to get away from
Florence, from great complications with his
belongings there, and had brought him to us
and to the perfect peace of Siena. He made
us a long visit and was our honoured and
cherished guest. During the time he was
with us his courtesy and high breeding never
failed him ; he was touchingly pleased and happy
with our life, and so delightful and amusing that
we ourselves grieved when it came to an end.
When the Brownings, who had taken the Villa
Alberti, about half a mile distant from us,
arrived to stay, a small villa close to them was
then engaged for him. To this he went, and

---

[1] . . . "One hot summer day towards noon his wife and children
turned him out of doors, with some 15 pauls in his pocket, on the
burning highway, and told him to be off and never to come back.
He was then past 80 ; and he wandered down to Florence a broken-
down, poor, houseless old man. There straying aimlessly about the
hot streets, exhausted and ill, he had the good fortune to meet Mr
Robert Browning, who was to him a good angel and who took him
under his protection and did everything he could to make him comfortable and happy. Shortly after this Browning brought him to
me at Siena, and a more pitiable sight I never saw. It was the
case of old Lear over again ; and when he descended from his
carriage with his sparse white hair streaming out, and tottered
into my house dazed in intellect with all he had suffered, I felt as
if he were really Lear come back again."—Story's "Conversations
in a Studio."

the legend presently grew that on the very day of his arrival he in a fit of anger with his landlady threw his dinner, plates and all, out of the window. [It has been variously related, of many of Landor's dinners, of many windows. It was a rate at which he must often have fasted, apart from his bill for crockery.] We constantly met him at Villa Alberti, and he often came to us, with the Brownings, for afternoon tea on the terrace. On Edith's birthday he came in his best attire, wearing a wonderful gay flowered waistcoat which, long years before, had been a present from Count D'Orsay. His laugh was a surprising inharmonious burst of sound with no merriment in it. I seem to hear it now in sharp quick discords.

" His habit of work was so strong in him that even then, when it might be called his holiday of old age, he got up early in the morning, before the rest of us, before even the servants were astir, and went out under the cypresses to write Latin verses, which he read to W. at breakfast. His memory for the far distant time was extraordinary ; he gave us details of incident and talk that had occurred iñ those years, with the greatest certainty and delicacy, while the ' middle distance ' was lost in a cloud and the foreground, the present immediately about us,

appeared to make little impression on him. His
judgments of *our* artists and authors were good
for nothing, as they were all the prejudice of
the moment, rash and intemperate; but those
he had formed in the past showed the finest
perception about men and things, and he could
recall them as if written in a book and learned
by heart. What he most cared for was his
Latin verses; at that time he seldom wrote in
English—only a verse or two of satire and spleen.
As we sat on the terrace with our beautiful
view the interesting hours flew by, full of wit
and sense and all sorts of noble things. Mrs
Browning was often convulsed with laughter at
his scorching invective and his extraordinary
quick ejaculations, perpetual God-bless-my-souls,
&c.! But I find it too difficult to record the
strange charm of his talk. His stories were
admirably told, full of point and often of pathos.
His mention of Rose Aylmer — and he often
mentioned her—always brought the tears to his
eyes, if not to ours; for there with her he had
evidently buried his heart. The marriage he
made was to do nothing for his happiness. . . .
So it was that in extreme old age he was driven
out in utter poverty, with barely sufficient to
support life. To the last he couldn't resist the
impulse to attack and fight—to fight out with

them (his family), and with everybody, his points of difference. But he was full of generous instincts too, and having nothing to give, gave liberally; offering for instance several times his so-called Titians and Raphaels to W., and trying, later on, to force them *en masse* upon Browning, who of course didn't accept them."

The talk we may imagine to have fallen from Landor on the Siena terrace in the summer nights must atone by its vivacity for its disconnectedness, and perhaps even in a few cases for our impression of having already and elsewhere caught its echo.

"Lord Ward once paid me the highest compliment. Somebody took a book of mine to read him when he was ill. 'Oh, don't talk of books!' he said; but my friend managed to read him one of the 'Imaginary Conversations,' that of Cicero with his brother. 'Well,' said my friend when he had finished, 'don't you think that's exactly what Cicero would have said?' 'Very much,' said Lord Ward, 'if he could.'

"Our old housekeeper, Mrs Lockington, fell ill when she had been in our house 43 years, and my dear sister Elizabeth used often to go to see her. One day she went over and found

her groaning and very bad. 'Well, Mrs Lockington,' said she, 'what's the matter?' 'Oh
Lord,' says old mother Lockington, 'I've got
such a beating of the heart, Miss, that I can
hear it the other side of the room.' 'Now
Elizabeth,' said I to my sister, 'I don't believe
that. How could you keep from laughing?'
'Why,' said she, 'I did almost laugh out, but
I don't always laugh in people's faces, as you
do, Walter.'

"Keats is perhaps the most *wonderful* poet
the world ever saw. There are other greater
ones, but none so wonderful—and none more so.
They may talk of Chatterton. Well, he *was*
extraordinary; but he was nothing to Keats,
for Keats was simply a Greek. Wordsworth
said that the Hymn to Pan was 'a pretty piece
of Paganism'; but if Wordsworth had lived to
a hundred, and then had the advantage of a long
residence in heaven, he never could have written
'Hyperion.' You may take the what-do-you-
call-it?—'Excursion'—and find a dozen idylls
in it, but who can read it straight through? I
did so once, but it was a labour of Hercules.
He once paid me, however, a pretty compliment.
He was a malicious person—I had heard of his
malice, and we were talking of Southey. I said
I thought he was a much greater poet than

Byron—that Byron had more vigour than imagination. 'Well,' says Wordsworth, 'that's exactly what I've always thought. I never said
so perhaps, in so many words, but it was always
in my mind.' My friend Count Lecci said when
he saw the three Wordsworths together, the
poet, his wife and his sister, 'The Lord of heaven
never himself made three such ugly people, and
it's a satire on him to suppose he did.'

"Crabbe Robinson bored me to death with his
German talk. I said I hated the language, and
he said that if I knew it and understood it I
should be delighted with it. Goethe alone, he
said, would repay me for the trouble of learning
it. 'His epigrams,' says he, 'you're fond of
epigrams.' I told him I didn't care a farthing
for 'em. I said I knew many Latin and Greek
ones—also many French ones that were better
by far than either. He repeated to me one of
Goethe's, saying it was wonderful. When he
had finished I said 'Where's the epigram?'
'What, don't you see it?' says Crabbe. 'Well
then, here's this one;' and he tried me with
another. 'I don't call *that* an epigram either,'
said I. 'No? Good Lord, then I've done.'
'Thank God,' said I.

"Trelawney told me that when Byron was
once in company with some one who praised

something of mine he at first assented, but after a while said, 'The devil's in me if I like *any* of his things.' When Trelawney told me this I said, 'He's right—the devil *is* in him.' Trelawney was a great liar. I once said to him, 'You've said so-and-so in your book.' 'I didn't, did I?' says he; 'I don't think so, at any rate.' 'Yes,' said I, 'you did, and I can show it to you.' 'Sure enough,' says he. 'Well, I'm damned. But it's true, for all that.'

"I once heard Sheridan, Pitt, Fox and Burke speak at one sitting of Parliament. Sir Robert Adair took me. Pitt had a magnificent voice. Fox screeched and screamed. Sheridan was splendid. But Burke was the finest of all—yet with the House quite inattentive. Somebody said, 'There gets up that great fool Wilberforce' —he was a very mild-spoken man.

"I once sat next Lady Stowell at dinner, and I asked her to take wine, after trying to engage her in talk. 'For the love of God let me alone and don't bother me so, Mr Landor,' says she; 'I don't know what I'm eating.' 'Well, my lady,' said I, 'you're a long time making the acquaintance': for she ate like a tiger and in great quantity. . . . Don't suppose I'm proud of my family (when speaking of its antiquity). I'll tell you what it is. I don't care a farthing for any

of my ancestors, and I'm the cleverest of all of
'em ; so now you may believe I'm not very proud
of 'em. Old Wheeler the counsellor dined often
with my father and swore horribly. Vulgar
habit it is—that's luckily done away with. I
could see my aunt jump in her chair when he
came out with his horrid words. At last he
said something very bad, and I burst out laughing to see her. 'What the devil in hell are you
laughing at?' says he, naming not only the
padrone but the locality too.

"Queen Caroline died of taking medicine without advice. She was always taking it, for she
was half dead with the drink she took—a bottle
of madeira and one of champagne at dinner.
Lady Hood told me she came one day to the
Palace and the Queen said, 'I'm quite sick, and
I've just taken some magnesia, but it doesn't do
me any good.' 'Well,' said Lady Hood, who
was a great fool, 'try a little castor oil.' The
Queen took it, and as castor oil, or any oil, and
magnesia mixed, make a hard cement, it killed
her. I know this for a fact, for the Queen's
medical man told it me.

"When I read Chaucer I feel as if I were in
the fresh, open air, but when I read Spenser I
feel as if I were shut up in a room full of per-
fumes. I admire Molière more than any writer

of comedies except perhaps Aristophanes; but
Corneille, Racine——! Think of a nation that
calls An-dro-ma-che Andromaque. I once said to
a French lady who was extolling Corneille, 'Oh
yes, I like his comedies next to Molière's.' 'His
comedies? Grand Dieu, what d'ye mean?' says
she. 'Yes,' says I, 'all his tragedies are comedies
to me; I die o' laughing over 'em.'

"Hexameters cannot be written in English.
Longfellow seems to me never to have read a
Greek or Latin poet—at least with any sort of
care. Dryden's great ode, Alexander's Feast, I
never liked much. 'Fallen, fallen, fallen, fallen,
fallen from his high estate!' Four times is the
most a word can be repeated by a poet; only a
musician perhaps can do it a fifth time. . . .
Franklin was a very good writer. Lord Auckland was to receive him once about some business
with the Colonies, and a person who was present
at the interview told me that Lord A. stood
up all the time and cut short the conversation,
bowing out Franklin, who had come in full dress.
Franklin went home, took off his fine clothes and
smoothed out his grand coat on the bed. 'Lie
there. You'll see better days yet, old boy!'

"I met Tom Paine once at dinner—his face
blotched and his hand unsteady with the wine
he took. The host gave him a glass of brandy

and he talked very well; an acute reasoner, in fact a monstrous clever man. I went at that time into very grand company, but as I was a young man some of my relations who wanted to put me down said, 'Well, we hear you know Tom Paine—Citizen Paine we suppose you call him, with your ideas.' 'To persons with *your* ideas I call him *Mister* Paine,' says I.

"One day at Bath Louis Napoleon, who had a charming house there, came and asked me to dine with Lady Blessington, and I went, finding a capital dinner and rooms most tastefully decorated with flowers. After dinner Lady Blessington and I got into the carriage for a drive, while D'Orsay sat outside with the Prince, who drove —so that, you see, I've been driven by a prince. Louis Napoleon is an extremely clever man, talking well on all subjects. He always wanted me to like the first Napoleon better than I did. I told him I admired the King of Holland more than I did the Emperor. I used to spend a month at Gore House every year. Lady Blessington was a charming, kind, good creature, a great heart. I spent evening after evening with her at Florence and was quite the *ami de la maison*. No truth at all about D'Orsay and Lady B. All a complete lie. I remember she was always bothering me to write my life, and

one evening she said, 'If you'll do it I'll get
Colburn to give you 600 guineas for it to-
morrow.' 'No,' said I, 'I won't, for a pretty
figure some of you ladies would cut in it if I
told the truth.'

"I met Mrs Siddons once or twice at the
Duchess of Lancaster's; a mighty pompous
woman, mighty pompous — but wonderful on
the stage, *wonderful*. I knew Mr Kemble,
and once in the street he came up and said,
'Or I'm very much mistaken, *or* this is Mr
Landor.' 'It is indeed,' said I, 'but who could
ever mistake Mr Kemble?' On which he said,
to return the compliment, 'Allow me to introduce my friend M. Talma.' So I had some talk
with Talma, and told him that I didn't see how
they managed in France to break the necks of
all their verses so well, and that French poetry
had a villainous metre! He was very like
Napoleon the Great, had a charming manner
and was perfectly a gentleman. Rachel I
remember as brought to Gore House by her
mother. She was a great creature.

"I once happened to say in a conversation,
when out for a walk, that I didn't care what
people believed, so they were honest; whereupon a young parson, very forward, said, 'What
do you believe, Mr Landor?' 'I'll tell ye what

I believe,' said I ; ' I believe you're an impertinent
young prig of a parson !' ' Well, Mr Landor,' says
he, ' I call that personal.' ' I'm not talking over
the hedge,' said I (there were some men working
in the field close by,) ' I'm talking to *you*.' "

It is only in his own letters—and there but
allusively—that I find a record of the visit paid
at Palazzo Barberini by a distinguished American
visitor in the spring of 1859. Charles Sumner,
their friend of many years, was with the Storys
at this time from April 20th to May 13th, and
he wrote back, after departure, while completely
under the charm of his impression. But I like
to give first a note they had had from him nearly
two years before, written during the early part
of the long stay in Europe which remarkable
events in America had imposed on him. His
health, it will be remembered, had been almost
fatally shattered by the furious assault made
upon him in the House of Representatives at
Washington, in May, 1856, during the now so
scarcely credible heat of the Southern campaign
for the further extension of Slavery, by his Con-
gressional colleague Brooks of South Carolina.
It need scarce be recalled even to the new
generations that, on the morrow of Sumner's
delivery of an impassioned, somewhat rhetori-

cal, but signally eloquent denunciation of the
Southern claims, the perusal of which may
still, after these years, stir Northern blood, he
was approached by his assailant from behind
(while writing, out of session-time, at his desk),
and so, taken unawares, struck down with a
bludgeon, helplessly floored, and, while unconscious from the force of the first quick blows,
mercilessly beaten about the head. The impression of the event, which was like a welt
raised by the lash itself across the face of the
North, is one that memory has kept, for this
careful chronicler, even though the years of a
life have overlaid it. I recollect, from far away,
the "terrace" of a little ancient house in Paris
—a "pavilion" in the Champs Elysées, the
site of which has long since ceased to know it;
and the sense as of a summer morning on the
edge of the wide avenue, then heterogeneous
and queer, with other old pavilions, vaguely
seen as survivals of old _régimes_, with the Jardin
d'Hiver opposite, with a beautiful young Empress
to be watched for over the railing of the terrace,
with a little Prince Imperial, sublime, divine,
driven past in a gilded coach surrounded by
brilliant bobbing Cent-Gardes grasping cocked
pistols, and, finally, with the slow-coming
American papers and the great splash in the

silver lake—the reverberation in parental breasts, in talk, passion, prophecy, in the very aspect of promptly-arriving compatriots, of the news which may be thought of to-day, through the perspective of history, as making the famous first cannon-sound at Fort Sumter but the *second* shot of the War.   To very young minds, inflamed by the comparatively recent perusal of 'Uncle Tom's Cabin,' it was as if war had quite grandly begun, for what was war but fighting, and what but fighting had for its sign great men lying prone in their blood?   These wonderments, moreover, were to have a sequel—the appearance of the great man, after an interval, in Paris and under the parental roof, with the violence of the scene, to one's vivid sense, still about him (though with wounds by that time rather disappointingly healed), and with greatness, enough, visible, measureable, unmistakable greatness, to fill out any picture.   His stature, his head, his face, his tone—well do I remember how they fitted one's very earliest apprehension, perhaps, of "type," one's young conception of the statesman and the patriot.   They were as interesting and impressive as if they had been a costume or a uniform.   Mr Sumner was to remain abroad in search of health; with improvements and relapses, experiments and alarms.

Charles Sumner to W. W. Story.

"IVREA, *Aug.* 31*st*, 1857.

"I am in Italy and must write to you. Do you know this place? A mountain stream is now rushing under my windows with the noise of Niagara. Two days ago I came over the St Gothard, down Lago Maggiore to Turin, all of which was new to me. I have been tempted as never before, to go still further, to Florence, to you and to Rome; but my brief time would fail me; and so I turn back by the Great-St-Bernard, inspired by 'Excelsior,' the monks and the dogs. The Val d'Aosta I shall traverse to-morrow, alone. . . . Ah! you have a happy time here in Italy—particularly *Dove il 'si' suona.* But seeing my country from abroad gives a new detestation of Slavery and a new determination to fight the battle."

The following also speaks for itself.

Charles Sumner to W. W. Story.

"HÔTEL NEVET, MONTPELLIER, *Dec.* 11*th*, 1858.

"You cannot, my dear William, be more surprised at receiving a letter with the above date than I am at writing it. But the physicians have willed it, and I am here. On reaching Paris, after my autumn rambles, there was a consultation on my case : present Trousseau, the eminent practitioner, Brown-Séquard, my attending physician, and an excellent Dr Hayward. They were unanimous in urging that I should not return to my public duties this winter, and prescribed a treatment which, though painful, is most pleasant in comparison with my tortures by fire. To carry this out under the most favourable circumstances I have left Paris and come to this quiet place, where I devote myself to my health ; beginning the day with *ventouses sèches* and *capsules* and *pilules*, and amusing myself by moderate walks and by tranquil society.

"But I turn toward Washington, and every day regret this enforced absence. This of itself is a torment. Two years and a half have passed during which I have had trial of pain, ache and smart of every kind, and at times have halted between the grave and hospital. For two or three days I have felt very well ; but on my way here, at Avignon, I was struck by a sudden relapse, which for a while promised to throw me back two years. This seems now to have passed away. But it has left me in great distrust as to my real condition and the amount of fatigue and excitement which I can bear. But for this I should take my flight

at once to America. Next after my seat at
Washington is Rome; but to enjoy Rome I
must be well, and without a constant care for
my health. Besides, you have about you there
men who, if not accessories *before* the fact were
so after the fact, to an act of assassination or
have made themselves its compurgators. . . .
Remember me kindly to all friends—especially
those who hate Slavery. Ah, what barbarism!"

It was his good fortune to be in Italy at
the time of great events, into which no visitor
could have entered with a larger sympathy. He
paid a visit at Palazzo Barberini in the spring
of 1859. That Future in which he had so
general a faith—on the whole so easy a confidence—was all in the air and tremendously
in the balance. Magenta and Solferino were
of this summer. He writes just after leaving
Rome.

Charles Sumner to W. W. Story.

"*May 14th,* '59. On board *Lombardo.*
"It rained, dear William, torrents all the way
to Civita Vecchia, and at sea till seven o'clock
in the evening, when the sky was bright with
moon and stars. There was no American aboard;
most were Italians. *Tanto meglio.* The captain,

in reply to my inquiries, tells me that everything
is most tranquil at Florence and Leghorn and
with *la gente del popolo*. He does not venture
yet to say that the Austrians will be chased out
of Italy, which I let him know I longed for;
but he declares with a good deal of pride that
recent events, particularly in Tuscany, have
shown the capacity of the Italians to govern
themselves. The chief news at Leghorn was
the arrival of Louis Napoleon at Genoa, and
three days of *festa* thereupon. What I have
left undone at Rome haunts me even more
than all that I enjoyed. I think perpetually of
pictures and statues unseen; but more than this,
I am unhappy in beautiful opportunities I let
slip. Why did I not press you to go *with* me
to the Capitol and the Vatican? And why did
I not press Wild to a similar service in the
picture-galleries? You know that I am always
a learner, and such tutors, with such means,
would have added for ever to my knowledge and
to my pleasant memories of art. But this is lost.
But I have stored away much. Rome now, as
when I first saw it, touches me more than any
other place. Then I have been so happy with
you. Perhaps it will be long before we meet
again; but I cannot forget these latter delicious
days. The captain promises that we shall arrive

at Genoa at 8 o'clock this evening, where I shall
close this scrawl, by telling you what I learn
there."

This last promise he handsomely keeps.

Charles Sumner to W. W. Story.

"Turin, *May* 18*th*, 1859.

. . . "And yet it [the journey from Genoa]
was full of interest.   At every point where the
common road was visible there were French
soldiers without number, all daubed with mud
and draggling in the rain.   Several thousand
were sheltered in the station of the railroad at
Alessandria.   The train, as it entered, seemed
to penetrate this living mass; and yet all was
order and tranquillity.   Nobody knows the
counsels of the Emperor.   I should think the
rain, which had lasted the last three days, must
have damaged the enemy much.   Their course
is one of pillage and robbery.   They live upon
the people. . . .   Yesterday I passed half an
hour with the Comte de Cavour.   He received
me in his bedroom, where he was writing.   Let
me say that a note which he kindly wrote me
in French was in the clear round hand of his
country, so different from the French, which is
small and flowing like their language.   This

national peculiarity of handwriting is curious to observe, particularly in its relation to the languages. He was calm, as if he felt himself master of the situation, and asked me to observe the tranquillity of Turin with not a soldier to be seen. To my inquiry if he thought the Austrians would be driven from Italy this summer he quietly said 'Je l'espère.' And when I dwelt upon the strength of the fortifications at Verona he said that he thought they could be taken. He seemed to understand the condition of things at Rome — that Lady William Russell is *très-autrichienne*; that the people there are right; but as he spoke of the Saint-Père I thought the *subrisus* of his face seemed to expand. It is evident that he does not doubt of the result.

"I've also passed several hours at the house of the Contessa de Coligno and at that of Mme. Arconati. This I owe to Miss Weston; pray let her know how completely her introduction has been honoured. There I learn that everybody is full of confidence and anticipating victory. They say that this is to be their last war and that great armies will no longer be needed. But nobody seems to understand the plan of campaign. All, however, are sure that the Austrians are to be beaten. Mme. de Coligno seemed much moved at the thought of the blood that must be

shed to dispossess the enemy of those immense
fortifications.   It seems that in the hospitals
of Turin is a solitary Austrian soldier, wounded
and taken prisoner in a recent skirmish.   These
humane ladies, who speak German, had visited
him, but he could not understand them.   He
turns out to be a Hungarian.   The property of
Mme. Arconati is near the Ticino, and of course
is now in possession of the Austrians.   She
describes their conduct as barbarous.   But in
the present deplorable condition of their finances
they can only live by turning highwaymen. . . .
Tell our friends they will find Turin more
tranquil than a Washington hotel.   The Savoy-
ards are showing their monkeys in the streets,
the boys playing marbles, the theatres thronged,
the table at the hotel served with abundance;
although the Austrians are within a few hours
of the capital.   I have been charmed to learn
that Manzoni, who is in his house at Milan under
the hoof of the enemy, is Italianissimo.   From
one of his grandchildren here, Count Bentivoglio,
who has called on me, I have learned the sentiments of the distinguished author.   The weather
is execrable, but I trust it will make the
Austrians suffer.   Thus far it has prevented me
from going to the Superga, where Lord Aberdeen
told me he enjoyed the view of the Alps more

than from any other place. To-night I am to
meet a party invited expressly to put me *au
courant* of events here."

To which the following, late in the evening,
is a postscript.

"I have just come from the Marchesa Arconati's, where I have met familiarly a considerable
circle, all full of Italy, and I write to let you
know in one word the spirit which prevails.
Nothing can surpass the courage and hope which
I find in all. I cannot say that they seem even
to be anxious, so assured are they of the result
and so necessary as well as glorious do they regard it. The Austrian ultimatum, which was
practically a declaration of war, was welcomed as
a solution of their perplexities. Without that
they would have been delivered over to the
uncertainties of diplomacy. Cavour himself was
happy to have the knot cut. The Austrian officer
who came on this message is said to have addressed the former in the most courteous terms,
assuring him that the message he bore had at
least one pleasure for him, as it gave him an
opportunity to make the acquaintance of the
first statesman of Europe. . . . Turin is a
magnificent lordly place, with spacious houses

which make me understand why Alfieri, as he records in his autobiography, found Paris *mesquin* when he first entered it coming from Italy."

He continues his report with characteristic abundance.

Charles Sumner to W. W. Story.

"SUSA, *May* 20*th*, 1859.

"Thus far I come, dear William, and to-morrow morning I shall quit Italy. I am unhappy at the thought, for I shall never see it again. My travels will soon end. Rome haunts me perpetually, and I wish to ask you a hundred questions which I forgot. I believe this is my fourth despatch. Since my last I have been in the way of hearing something more of opinion in Turin, particularly from a leading deputy of the gauche. He looks for sympathy from the King-that-will-be of Naples, and counts upon at least a great northern Italian kingdom. I am astonished at the warmth with which the King is spoken of. He is said to be not only the *bien-aimé*, but the *adoré*. He mingles with his people without state or ceremony. Only the other day, when Cavour returned from Paris and a crowd assembled under his windows to cheer him, it is said the King was among them crying

Vive Cavour! But the representatives of the gauche are not strongly attached to Cavour. They say that he has adopted his present opinions as the means of advancing himself, and that he allows no first-rate talent to be associated with him, in the Cabinet, which might impair his pre-eminence. The news has continued to arrive of the barbarous conduct of the Austrians in subsisting their troops at the expense of the provinces where they are. . . . Three cheers for Italy, and may the Austrian empire cease to exist !"

He was again, on leaving Italy, in the hands of the doctors.

Charles Sumner to W. W. Story.

"BAINS FRASCATI, AU HAVRE, *Aug.* 11*th*, 1859.

" Your generous letter, after travelling to London, found me here, enjoying seclusion and sea-bathing. Since I wrote you last, great events and changes have occurred. The programme of the Emperor has not been carried out, but much has been done. Look at it. (1) Lombardy wrested from Austria. (2) The Duchies, Parma, Modena and Tuscany, given to themselves ; for I assume that this is done. (3) The idea of Italian unity and independence crowded upon the attention of Europe. (4) New means established in Italy for the support of these ideas. (5) An impulse toward reform throughout all Italy. These are not small conquests. Out of these I hope for the great result. I have recently been reading the 4 vols. of the writings and speakings of Louis Napoleon. Much as I dislike him I confess to having risen from them with a higher idea of his intelligence and of his character. During his exile and imprisonment he occupied himself with topics many of which are intimately associated with human welfare. Two or three of his speeches seem to me masterpieces ; particularly that at Bordeaux, where he said l'Empire c'est la Paix, and that where he announced his marriage. But I have been disgusted at seeing his repeated declarations in favour of the Republic followed by its most treacherous assassination. I sympathise with you completely in all your aspirations for dear Italy and grieve with you in her discomfitures. But I doubt not that her good time will come at last. Most happy should I be on your lawn. But do not tempt me. The movement and unrest of travel are not the best conditions for me. I have already passed three weeks in London, where I saw much of the great world ; but daily breakfasts and dinners

were not so good for me as my private life
here, where I go to bed at nine o'clock. . . . At
times I think of starting for Madrid, merely
to see its gallery and then turn back.   But I
say ' Get well, get well, for work next December,'
and then I banish all such ideas.   Looking
only yesterday at the second vol. of the magnificent work entitled ' Moyen Age et Renaissance,'
I fell upon the chapter on ships and the drawings
of a Spanish caravel in the time of Columbus.
I thought what beautiful materials Rogers has
for filling up the vacant space about his doors.
Remember me to the excellent and noble
Brownings."

With all of which he continues the best of
correspondents, as well as the most characteristic,
surely, of letter-writers.   He has, as I have
already observed, his *tone*, of which he never
any more fails than a great actor fails of that
of a great part.   Yet he was no actor; he was
himself the person represented.

Charles Sumner to W. W. Story.

"BAINS FRASCATI, *près du* HAVRE, *Aug. 15th*, 1859.

. . .   "To-day the wind is strong, and the
sea is heavy, and I lose my bath.   But this
seclusion here is profitable and not unpleasant.

Yesterday, however, I broke away from it to
see the entry of the troops, with the Emperor
and his marshals—the most remarkable triumph
since Paulus Emilius mounted the Capitol on
his return from Greece, and I doubt not the
most imposing spectacle ever seen in Paris. Why
not say in the world? The arrangements and
appointments were perfect. I was in a balcony
au premier, near the corner of the Rue de la
Paix and the Boulevard—a most excellent place
to see; price of my chair 50 francs!—and I
looked closely at all that passed. The Emperor
was for some time at the corner near me. He
was superbly mounted, and sat his horse well;
looked in good health and bronzed by the sun.
More than any marshal or general, he held his
head down, bowed only occasionally and seemed
to crawl along. While near where I was he
was occupied in twirling and smoothing his
moustache. As he passed there was a hush
of silence, and intense curiosity, but no enthusiasm. MacMahon looked more like an American
than an Irishman. Canrobert had a joyous look
as he turned to the right and left to receive the
applause.

"The news from Tuscany is inspiring. Pray
help them to be firm. The Brownings must work.
The Ducal family has ceased to reign; let this

be the decree. If they consent to take back the son the battle is postponed to another day. In London I met one evening at Lady Granville's the runaway Prince Corsini, and heard him say that he was going to join his Grand Duke. I understand that he announced the ministry that would be formed on the Grand Duke's return to Florence. An amusement of exile! Lady G. asked me if I noticed his most excellent Tuscan. I see by the late papers that 'Roba di Roma' again appears in the 'Atlantic.' Oh, I do love Italy, and wish that I were there, to lap myself in its Elysium. But I shall be in another place, in scenes very different, amidst tobacco-spitting, swearing slave-drivers, abused by the press, insulted so far as is possible, pained and racked by the insensibility about me to human rights and the claims of human nature; finding little true sympathy, but cheered, let me confess, by the dignity of the cause I serve. . . . Did I tell you that I saw H. in London? —once in society, trying to be eloquent, as if with Mrs Ticknor. He seemed so little at ease, so like a *manant*, that I asked if it could be he."

The following was practically his farewell. Theodore Parker, mentioned at the end, as full and eloquent a voice from pulpit and platform (on the same agitated ground) as Sumner was to remain, or in strictness still further become, in the Senate, reached Italy scarcely less battered and spent with the fray. But, less fortunate, he was not to recover his strength, and in Florence, the next year, he was to sink to rest.

Charles Sumner to Mrs Story.

"PARIS, *Oct. 9th*, 1859.

"My paquets are made and in an hour I leave Paris—which never was more beautiful. Latterly I have been devoured by desires which were stimulated in Rome. Here it is choice engravings, bronzes and manuscripts on vellum. The gentle Wild is partly responsible for the bronzes, for he gave me the address of Barbedienne, whose bill runs up to 2500 francs. But my treasures are three MSS. most exquisitely illuminated—superior to anything in all Boston!

. . . "Sartiges, who came to see me yesterday, said that he expected to see me in Paris *au moins dix fois encore!* But I turn my back now upon all such expectations and return to my country and my duties there. In following my career I have indeed a higher pleasure even than in art. But art will cheer the graver life which I pursue.

"It is too true—I cannot write a letter like yours. I am dull and plain. Often with envy I thought of those delicious Tuscan evenings on your lawn, with Browning and the immortal style of Landor. Till it became cold I followed my baths at Frascati's, and then made a little tour in Normandy and Brittany with an old acquaintance of William's, Hamilton Aïdé. He thinks William a very accomplished person. So do I.

"You have seen in the papers that a subscription has been started for a statue in bronze of Horace Mann, to be placed in the State House yard. I have written to insist that William must do it; first because he is the first American sculptor, secondly because he would especially appreciate the character and life of Mann. Tell him to write me at once his ideas on this matter —what of portraits or photographs he would need, and how he feels about undertaking it.

"I sleep to-night at Amiens and to-morrow touch English earth. I have already accepted country invitations more than enough to fill all the time until sea-sickness begins.

"[Theodore] Parker will winter in Rome. I fear the excitement and strain of art, antiquity and history there will not leave him his needed repose. Pray watch him and send him home

strong and well, to preach great sermons and
hold aloft the scales of justice. Hillard I hear
of in Paris, but see him not. He must be
ashamed of himself."

We feel by his first words from Washington
(January 27th, 1860) that in his absence the
plot has indeed thickened. "What a difference
between this place and Rome! I feel it keenly.
And yet there is a delight here which you have
not. It is the standing up for truth and liberty.
The slave-masters seem to me more than ever
barbarians—in manner, conversation, speeches,
conduct, principles, life. All things indicate a
crisis. Society is dislocated. The diplomats cannot give a dinner without studying their lists
as a protocol. There is little or no intercourse
between sides." And he breaks out again, on
March 23rd, in a note from the Senate Chamber.
"A walk in the streets of Rome, a stroll on
the Pincian, a visit to the Vatican, a sight of
St Peter's—oh, for an hour, one brief hour, of
any of these! And oh, better still, for a talk
with *you!* I have so much to say on art—
and on our politics here, which have none of
the refinement of art. Never was such a horror
put into bronze as this recent statue by Clark
Mills, unless you except his other horror. Motley

is in the Institute (of France). *A la bonne heure!*" And as of the same year I give the following, dated Boston, August 10th, and forming the first half of a letter of which the second is occupied with requests and orders for reproductions of busts in the Vatican, columns in the Forum and other Roman relics.

Charles Sumner to W. W. Story.

"Boston, *Aug.* 10*th*, 1860.

. . . "Yesterday I was at Mount Auburn especially to see the statues in the Chapel. I had not been there for years. I was pleased with them all; but yours seemed to me more beautiful than ever both as portrait and as art. I doubt if there be a finer portrait-statue in existence. . . . Your bust of Theodore Parker is spoken of with admiration. It ought to be ordered in marble for the Public Library. I shall push this idea. But what a loss was there! Daily I feel the immense void which his death has made, and I know not where to look for any one to fill it. I know well how earnestly he would have sustained me in my late efforts. . . . I am charmed with the news from Italy. The sooner the old is rung out and the new rung in the better. I hope to hear very soon that Bomba has fled and Pius after him. Meanwhile I imagine you at Siena. I wish that I were there. I should like to feast my eyes on an Italian landscape, with glimpses at Italian art, and to feel that I was in Italy. But life is real, life is earnest—does not Longfellow say so?—and I have hard work here which I mean to do."

The Brownings spent again in Rome the winter of 1859-60, and for the summer returned to Siena, to which the following, from Florence, was prefatory. The friends were to be together again for the last bright season, as it was to prove, of Mrs Browning's life. The journey had been pursued, after the stages enumerated, to Florence, and the return to Siena and the Villa Alberti was made in July. There attaches to the letter something of the charm of a document on the old romantic method of progression at a date when such documents were becoming rare. This is one of the last of them.

Robert Browning to Mr and Mrs Story.

"SIENA, *June 8th*, 1860.

"I said I would tell you how we found things and fared on the Orvieto road. We arrived at four yesterday afternoon and preferred resting

here for four-and-twenty hours to going forward
at once. We travelled 48 or 50 miles delightfully the first day and reached Viterbo early.
Next morning we began the new part of the
journey—continued 30 miles at a stretch and
got to Orvieto through a pleasant placid country
(much work of Luca Signorelli at the cathedral).
On Wednesday we advanced to Ficulli; but
for Ba's fatigue it would have been better to
push on to Città della Pieve, where a fresco
of Perugino's is worth the trouble of a longer
journey and the comfort of the inn would have
been much greater. But it was our own choice
to divide the way so. We reached Chiusi
early, having travelled all day through exquisite
scenery. We felt the heat — not intolerably,
however, nor before this third day, and there
was never any dust to mention. We left Chiusi
at nine, or later, yesterday (I got up early
every morning and saw sights for an hour or
two), and reached Sinalunga by one o'clock.
Had there been an endurable inn Ba might
have rested sufficiently to proceed to Florence;
but she was forced to choose between the
kitchens and the carriage, and preferred the
latter — so here we stopped, as I began by
saying. We were perfectly served throughout,
the *vetturino* caring for all things, and his

charge for the three days and a half amounts
to 19 scudi, 2 pauls. I paid the service myself;
only this was not much. The end is, we have
had a delightful journey which Ba has borne
very well on the whole, though the whole
business is far more fatiguing than by the short
stages on the Perugia road. . . ."

Before the return to Siena, meanwhile, Browning had again written.

Robert Browning to W. W. Story.

"FLORENCE, *June 29th*, 1860.

. . . "I was going to answer you leisurely,
when there is a sudden occasion of writing to
Nencini, for Landor determines at last to accompany us, and I want the old quarters for
him, where you helped to make him so comfortable last year. So I just write a word, without
prejudice to the other few words I mean to write
before we set out, to say that, for ourselves,
the best news is that we start for Marciano, and
you all, to-morrow week,—as I have just ap-
prised Alberti. Won't you like to see another
month or two of dear old Landor and Can'-
Giallo (he has just come to me for picture-
money—such pictures !). . . . Would you have
the goodness, whenever you engage your piano,

to secure for me the same that I had last year,
at the same terms? And beg that it may be
transferred to the villa on the 7th, so that we
may find it on arriving."

He brought his dying wife in the autumn
back to Rome—they were settled in September
at 126 Via Felice; and Mrs Browning mentions
in a letter of the autumn that her husband "has
taken to modelling under Mr Story (at his studio)
and is making extraordinary progress." These,
it is needless to say, were months of deep anxiety
and suspense for lovers of Italy; public events
had hurried over the stage like the contending
armies of Elizabethan plays; the "cause" and
its issue hung, as never before, in the balance:
with the sense, and the alternations, of all of
which Mrs Browning's correspondence flushes
and turns pale. Her letters, of this and the
previous time, while the pulses of her companion's
much more clearly throb, reflect her passion, her
feverish obsession, with extraordinary vivacity
and eloquence; but it is impossible not to feel,
as we read, that to "care," in the common phrase,
as she is caring is to entertain one's convictions
as a malady and a doom. Her state of mind
on the public question, as her letters present
it almost from the first of her residence in Italy,

is an interesting, an almost unique *case*, which
forces upon us more than one question; so that
we wonder why so much disinterested passion,
so inflamed a desire that the right (and for a
people not her own, a people only befriended
and admired) should not leave us in a less
disturbed degree the benefit of all the moral
beauty.   We wonder at the anomaly, wonder
why we are even perhaps slightly irritated, and
end by asking ourselves if it be not because her
admirable mind, otherwise splendidly exhibited,
has inclined us to look in her for that saving
and sacred sense of proportion, of the free and
blessed *general*, that great poets, that genius
and the high range of genius, give us the impression of even in emotion and passion, even in
pleading a cause and calling on the gods.   Mrs
Browning's sense of the general had all run,
where the loosening of the Italian knot, the
character of Napoleon III., the magnanimity of
France and the abjection of England were involved, to the strained and the strenuous—a
possession, by the subject, riding her to death,
that almost prompts us at times to ask wherein
it so greatly concerned her.   It concerned her
of course as it concerned all near witnesses and
lovers of justice, but the effect of her insistent
voice and fixed eye is to make us somehow feel

that justice is, after all, of human things, has
something of the convenient looseness of humanity about it—so that we are uneasy, in short,
till we have recognised the ground of our critical
reaction. It would seem to be this ground,
exactly, that makes the case an example.
Monstrous as the observation may sound in its
crudity, we absolutely feel the beautiful mind
and the high gift discredited by their engross-
ment. We say, roughly, that this is what
becomes of distinguished spirits when they
fail to keep above. The cause of Italy was,
obviously, for Mrs Browning, as high aloft as
any object of interest could be; but that was
only because she had let down, as it were, her
inspiration and her poetic pitch. They suffered
for it sadly—the permission of which, conscious
or unconscious, is on the part of the poet, on
the part of the beautiful mind, ever to be judged
(by any critic with any sense of the real) as
the unpardonable sin. That is our complaint :
the clear stream runs thick; the real superiority
pays; we are less edified than we ought to be.
Which is perhaps, after all, not a very graceful
point to make (though it must stand), while I
avail myself of the last fine tracings of her pen
that I encounter. One is but a scrap of a note
to Mrs Story, which sounds for the first time—

that is my reason—a name I must not let slip. " Dearest Emelyn : I wrote to Miss Blagden to-day about the Pantaleoni apartment. Thank you twenty times. Wish for me, *will* for me, mesmerise for me, that I may indeed go to bed early to - night. For Mr W. is here talking down art in Italy ! " This other fragment, from Florence, undated, and as a postscript to a note of her husband's, belongs to some moment of the previous couple of years.

. . . " Here are fanatics of all colours, now-adays. News from Naples are threatening in this ' Monitore' just opened. Whoever goes mad among the enemies of Italy she gets the advantage of it. May they go mad therefore. As soon as the rain ceases and I can get out I will go and see your charming little Duchess (di Carigliano). I like her and honour her house —here in Florence I mean. Robert hasn't told you that whatever Can'-Giallo may be doing poetically his master is active. Robert *might* tell you that a poem on the goddess Diana was produced the other day, for instance, which had the peculiarity of being so exceedingly indecent (for Diana or any other goddess or woman) that it might be objected to by less prudish critics than Monckton Milnes."

There were to be, at any rate, no more missives in the delicate but so definite little characters. This of Browning's, in Rome, must have been of May, or thereabouts, 1861, and have preceded but by a few days their last return to Florence. The plans for the summer were to have no sequel.

"I meant to go down to you to-day and thank you—but Ba, who caught cold in some strange way two days ago, suddenly became much worse, and last night was alarmingly attacked by the old obstruction at the chest. I had to fetch a doctor in the night who stayed with us till morning; it really seemed as if she would be strangled on the spot, and that for six hours together. At five o'clock she began to get through it, and since then has been much better. I shall be forced to leave this burning place as soon as she is able—*where* do you go? I will write to-morrow and tell you how she is. In your letter you incline to Viareggio, do you? Or the old Siena? Or the Baths? Or any place in the mountains, such as Corvigliaio, 30 miles hence in the Bologna mountains, said to be cold as Switzerland, with one inn and no resources beyond its romantic scenery. Let us be together if we can. Such a fright this attack has been.   Suppose we had been pleasantly travelling!"

There was to be quite another sequel to the hopes so expressed for the coming weeks, but that these hopes persisted until shortly before the catastrophe I gather from another letter, from Florence, undated, but which can scarcely belong to another moment, and which refers again to pleasant possibilities. The allusion to the negotiation attempted for the Brownings in Rome has a reference to the small *rococo* apartment in the Barberini which I have already mentioned, and which was in the opposite wing of the palace from that of the Storys. The hope of acquiring it, as "just the place," had been the more fondly entertained as the Florentine winter had, at the last, definitely become impossible to Mrs Browning. It would indeed have been just the place, with that luxuriously mild inclination of its staircase designed as if for the ascent of an invalid. But the question, with so many other questions, dropped.

Robert Browning to Mr and Mrs Story.

"FLORENCE [1861].

. . . . "There's no doubt you can have Villa Orr how and when you please. Nencini said the owners wanted money, would never have

refused an offer; in short, I took it for granted
that any conditions so reasonable would be accepted unless I gave too early notice of the
possibility of your return. Should you incline
to the Baths of Lucca? I hear of the propitious emptiness of that place also, how any
terms will be caught at. What do you think
of Viareggio, which seems rather attractive to
folks this season, and is praised for its sea and
six miles of sand?

"How kindness's self you have been in all
that troublesome negotiation for the apartment!
It will all come to nothing, we begin to fear,
as the days go by and bring no tidings. As
the chair could be appended without disfigure-
ment to the house, one sees no other reason
against it than that fears and scruples shake
the Prince and we shall probably drop off in
the shake—a great pity though!—Yes, very
good news, good symptoms on every side, for
Italy. The main of it is affected, let us hope—
tutto è salvo, and the less of delay in these
plaguy *dettagli* the better. How hot, how
unpleasant to be so far away from you, how
pleasant to hope soon to see the good summer-
time again as of old in your company! We
all want the same things exactly—can it not
be? Ba is stronger and better, but has not

left the house. Landor has cut off his beard—
treasure your photographs! We hear less of
American news than when we were at Rome,
and abundantly despise our own mean newspaper
articles."

The sequel that did occur in June forms part
of a long and very interesting letter of Story's—
so full that I give it without curtailment. Like
Browning, he, that year, with his wife and
children, left Italy.

W. W. Story to Charles Eliot Norton.

"DIABLERETS, *Aug. 15th*, 1861.

  . . . "We are immediately under the bare
and broken heights of the great Diablerets, in
whose rocky bosom, almost, as it seems, within
reach of our hands, though in fact there are
miles of air between us, lies the flashing glacier
with its soiled edges. This valley is a long level
studded with black pines and with the lighter
green of maples, hazels and willows, and through
it are all sorts of little grassy paths leading
you into depths of woods or up mountain heights
or through groups of cedar-brown *châlets*. As
I look out from my window I see the slopes
of the mountains towards Sepey, whose vast
meadows of bright glad green are sprinkled all

over with *châlets* and darkened here and there with parliaments of pines—or rather platoons of pines, which seem to be marching like black rangers, or Lützow's wild hunters, down into the valley. The great torrent called the Grandes Eaux, which intersects the valley, rushes to empty itself in the great lake below with a joyous, tumultuous sound, as if glad to be free from the glacial torpor above. Plant me here then and imagine me looking one way down the laughing valley, brilliant in the sunshine, and the other way up the grey barren cliffs of the Diablerets, covered with eternal snow and grim as despair. . . . We were skilful enough to land here the other day, after excellent fishing, our friend Mr Gaskell, whom we had never before seen. He spent a week with us, and we enjoyed his society extremely. What a sweet, broad character he has! I was really glad to see him in the flesh, for he had been but a name before. We talked of you and of all our friends of the Italian campaign, and it was pleasant to find how truly he shared our friendships. Yesterday morning we walked down the valley with him and said good-bye with real regret.

"But to turn to sadder things. You have before this heard of course of the death of Mrs Browning, though the news had not reached you when you wrote. This was sudden and unexpected at the last, for though she had always been so frail that one only wondered what kept soul and body together at all, we had become so accustomed to thinking of her as different from all others in the matter of health that we began to think that she might even outlast us. Fifteen years ago her physicians told her that life was impossible, yet she had lived and borne a child and written immortal verses and shown an amazing energy of spirit and intellect. But last winter I had many fears that she was failing. The death of her father had struck her a hard blow; then her sister's death struck her again, as it were, when she was down, and I feared that her vital energy, great as it was, might not resist. Yet she revived and, as spring came on, went out to drive, and, though weak, began to gather herself together again, even at one time projecting a journey to Paris. This however was impossible. Yet she went to Florence by *vettura* and did not suffer more than usual, and we were all hesitating, at Leghorn, whether we should not abandon our scheme of Switzerland for another summer together in Siena when the fatal news of her death reached us. Browning was to have come down to spend Sunday with us, but on Saturday night she was attacked

with difficulty of breathing, and at dead of night
he was forced to run for a physician, Dr Wilson,
who remained with her all night and took a
very gloomy view. The morning brought relief,
and, though weaker, she declared she was otherwise as well as ever. They talked over their
plans for the future, decided to go to Siena for
the summer with us, agreed to give up Casa
Guidi and take a villa in Florence to return to
in the spring and autumn. Being in treaty for
an apartment in Palazzo Barberini at Rome for
six years, they discussed the question of how
they should furnish it. During the subsequent
days she constantly came into the salon and lay
on the sofa there all day—until Friday, when
Lytton stayed all the morning there talking with
B., so that she did not come out. On Friday
evening they had again a long talk about their
future plans, and she went to bed as well as she
had been in general respects, though there were
some few symptoms which troubled B., such as
raising now and then her hands and holding
them long before her, and also a slight wandering of the mind at intervals and as she was just
about to doze. But this wandering he attributed
to the morphine, which by order of Dr W. she
was obliged to take in larger quantities than those
she was accustomed to. At about three o'clock

he was startled by her breathing and woke
her, but she said she was better, and reasoned
so quietly and justly about her state that his
fears were again subdued. She talked with
him and jested and gave expression to her love
for him in the tenderest words; then, feeling
sleepy, and he supporting her in his arms, she
fell into a doze. In a few minutes, suddenly,
her head dropped forward. He thought she had
fainted, but she had gone for ever. She had
passed as if she had fallen asleep, without pain,
without thought of death. After death she
looked, as Browning told me, like a young girl;
all the outlines rounded and filled up, all traces
of disease effaced, and a smile on her face so
living that they could not for hours persuade
themselves she was really dead.

"We went immediately to Florence, and it
was a sad house enough. There stood the table
with her letters and books as usual, and her
little chair beside it, and in her portfolio a half-
finished letter to Mme. Mario, full of noble words
about Italy. Yes, it was for Italy that her
last words were written; for her dear Italy
were her last aspirations. The death of Cavour
had greatly affected her. She had wept many
tears for him, and been a real mourner. This,
agitation undoubtedly weakened her and per-

haps was the last feather that broke her down.
'The cycle is complete,' as Browning said, looking round the room; 'here we came fifteen years
ago; here Pen was born; here Ba wrote her
poems for Italy. She used to walk up and
down this verandah in the summer evenings,
when, revived by the southern air, she first
again began to enjoy her out-doors life. Every
day she used to walk with me or drive with
me, and once even walked to Bellosguardo and
back; that was when she was strongest. Little
by little, as I now see, that distance was lessened,
the active out-doors life restricted, until walking had finally ceased. We saw from these
windows the return of the Austrians; they
wheeled round this corner and came down this
street with all their cannon, just as she describes
it in "Casa Guidi." Last week when we came
to Florence I said: "We used, you know, to
walk on this verandah so often—come and walk
up and down once. Just once," I urged, and
she came to the window and took two steps on
it. But it fatigued her too much, and she went
back and lay down on the sofa—that was our
last walk. Only the night she went away for
ever she said she thought we must give up
Casa Guidi; it was too inconvenient and in
case of illness too small. We had decided to

go away and take a villa outside the gates.
For years she would not give up this house, but
at last and, as it were, suddenly, she said she
saw it *was* too small for us and too inconvenient. And so it was; so the cycle was
completed for us here, and where the beginning
was is the end. Looking back at these past
years I see that we have been all the time
walking over a torrent on a straw. Life must
now be begun anew—all the old cast off and
the new one put on. I shall go away, break
up everything, go to England and live and
work and write.'

. . . " The funeral was not impressive, as
it ought to have been. She was buried in the
Protestant cemetery where Theodore Parker lies;
many of her friends were there, but fewer
persons than I expected and hoped to see.
The services were blundered through by a fat
English parson in a brutally careless way, and
she was consigned by him to the earth as if
her clay were no better than any other clay.
I did what I could, but I had arrived too late
to assume the arrangements. . . . So I carried
two wreaths—it was all I could do—one of those
exquisite white Florence roses, and the other
of laurel, and these I laid on her coffin. She

is a great loss to literature, to Italy and to the world—the greatest poet among women. What energy and fire there was in that little frame; what burning words were winged by her pen; with what glorious courage she attacked error, however strongly entrenched in custom; how bravely she stood by her principles! Never did I see any one whose brow the world hurried and crowded so to crown, who had so little vanity and so much pure humility. Praise gratified her when just—blame when unjust scarcely annoyed her. She could afford to let her work plead for itself. Ready to accept criticism, she never feared it, but defended herself with spirit when unjustly attacked. For public opinion she cared not a straw, and could not bear to be looked on as a lion. Her faiths were rooted in the centre of her being.

"Browning is now with his sister in Paris. The house at Florence is broken up, and I have lost my best friend and daily companion in Italy. You cannot imagine how I shall miss him. For three years now we have been always together; never a day has passed (with the exception of two months' separation in the spring and autumn when he went to Florence) that we have not met; all the long summer evenings

of these last summers at Siena he was with
us, and we sat on our terrace night after night
till midnight talking together, or we played
and sang together above stairs. All the last
winters he worked with me daily for three
hours in my studio, and we met either at my
house or at his or at that of some friend nearly
every evening. There is no one to supply his
place. Returning to Rome, I have not one
single intimate ; acquaintances by hundreds, but
no friends, no one with whom I can sympathise
on all points as with him, no one with whom
I can walk any of the higher ranges of art
and philosophy. This for me is a terrible
want. I must have some one to sail with me
over deeps that So-and-so and So-and-so ignore.
But at Rome who is there ? Only such rubbish
as M., R., and Co. among the artists, fellows
whose brains are an inch deep and who are
animated by all sorts of meannesses. . . .
Englishmen who think are very rare ; they
are generally ganglions of prejudices, which they
call opinions, and what ideas they have are
generally narrow and bigoted or developments
only in a single direction. Their education is
never general, but special, and outside their
speciality they are terribly barren. There was

for instance Newton, the British consul, with whom I was in very close relation on questions of art, who thought, felt and dreamed with me most harmoniously, and with whom I had real sympathy in these matters. But he never had heard John Webster's name, asked me who Thomas Middleton was, knew nothing, cared nothing for poetry, music, painting, and was most curiously developed in literature : an admirable Greek scholar, who quoted and knew, who admired Æschylus and Plato and yet knew nothing of English poetry beyond Shakespeare, or in modern philosophy beyond Locke. He never projected himself into philosophy— he needed to be pushed along. You and I know hundreds of such men. They are planted on their ground and can't speculate ; they say 'Ouh! ouh!' to you when you hazard a theory or state a principle. The English mind is not a philosophic one ; they are not of the air, but of the earth ; in the good sense of the term, but still of the earth. Browning is by nature not an Englishman.

. . . "The last thing I did before leaving Rome was to make a bust of him which his wife was good enough to call 'perfect.' It was made for her as a present, but, alas! you see

the end of that. Since you were with us I
have made several statues—one of Judith at
the moment she makes her prayer before killing
Holofernes. The right hand is thrown up to
heaven, the left holds, a little behind her, her
sword. In this I endeavoured to express passionate religious enthusiasm and the summoning of
all one's energy to do a great patriotic act, thus
putting out of view the crime. It is not to
kill Holofernes her betrayer, but Holofernes
the tyrant, the oppressor of her country, that
she asks the help of God in a great duty and
a great sacrifice. All other representations make
Judith a criminal, an assassin, and it is only
before the act that she is poetically and artisti-
cally grand. The deed done she is a woman
who has killed a man—and with Holofernes'
head repulsive. The painters represent her thus,
for sake of colour and contrast, but this conception of her is low. The only other time
is when she holds the head up to the people,
a grand subject for a grand painting. Next
I made for contrast of sentiment a boy Bacchus
on a panther, which is purely lyrical in treatment. Then this last winter I finished what
I consider as my best work—it is so considered
by all, I believe—the Libyan Sibyl. I have

taken the pure Coptic head and figure, the great massive sphinx-face, full-lipped, long-eyed, low-browed and lowering, and the largely-developed limbs of the African. She sits on a rock, her legs crossed, leaning forward, her elbow on her knee and her chin pressed down upon her hand. The upper part of the figure is nude, and a rich simple mantle clothes her legs. This gave me a grand opportunity for the contrast of the masses of the nude with drapery, and I studied the nude with great care. It is a very massive figure, big - shouldered, large - bosomed, with nothing of the Venus in it, but, as far as I could make it, luxuriant and heroic. She is looking out of her black eyes into futurity and sees the terrible fate of her race. This is the theme of the figure—Slavery on the horizon, and I made her head as melancholy and severe as possible, not at all shirking the real African type. On the contrary, it is thoroughly African—Libyan Africa of course, not Congo. This I am now putting into marble, and if I can afford it shall send to the new Exhibition in London. . . . If it is returned on my hands I shall abandon sculpture, or at all events shut up my studio."

I give without interruption, as adding to the

record, two more letters to the same correspondent.

W. W. Story to Charles Eliot Norton.

"ROME, *May 3rd*, 1862.

. . . "My winter is over, Rome has broken
up, and we are off to England in a couple of
weeks. I have been hard at work and have
just finished a statue of Sappho seated—a love-
lorn lady dreaming of *him*, whoever he was,
Phaon, Anacreon, or any other *on;* very tender,
very sweet, very sentimental. In this statue I
have gone into Greekland, as in the Sibyl I went
into Africa, and in the Cleopatra into Egypt.
I fancy just at this moment of time that you
would think it my best work—I have put all the
Love into it I could. The Sibyl and Cleopatra
are gone to the Exhibition [London 1862], and I
must go and look after them. But I have little
will to go to England, and were it not for
these statues nothing should persuade me to the
journey. Once there, it is just within the bounds
of possibility (and nothing more) that I may go
over to America for a few weeks and set my
house in order, following the example in that
respect of good king Hezekiah. But this too
will go terribly against my grain, and nothing
but necessity will drive me across the ocean.—I

hope you received a little pamphlet of mine on the American question. We are in a great state of excitement here as the telegrams arrive containing news of battles. All seems to be going on well, but I am sorry not to see more strong indications of Union sentiment in the South. The course pursued toward McClellan by a portion of the press and by a large party is disgraceful. We are an impatient and ungrateful people. But I feel confident that McClellan will overcome at last all his enemies. . . ."

The house from which the following is dated, at Walton-on-Thames, long occupied by Mr and Mrs Russell Sturgis, was to be in a manner, for years, Story's headquarters during his visits to England. His various sojourns there, with the innumerable incidents of an irresistible hospitality, would be almost matter for a chapter, one of the pleasantest, by itself.

W. W. Story to Charles Eliot Norton.

"MOUNT FELIX, *Nov.* 10*th*, 1862.

"Herewith I enclose to you, or rather Frederic Locker will enclose to you, a copy of a little volume of his poems to which I beg to call your attention. They are of a light humoristic character. . . . Many thanks for your kind (as

usual) letter, which I should have answered at
once but that my time has been so completely
occupied with visiting and correcting for the
press my 'Roba di Roma,' which is finally to
appear. As in my art so in my literary efforts,
I get the best appreciation in England. The
publishers at home rejected my book. . . . It
is of no use in America for me to hope for anything. I do not expect to find a public there
until I have obtained it elsewhere. They will
resist to the last considering me as anything but
a poetaster, dilettante and amateur.

"My visit to England has been delightful;
everywhere and from everybody I have received
the warmest kindness and hospitality—such as I
never can forget. People have vied with each
other in generous expressions and acts, and I
have been greeted with a praise which, grateful
as it is, I cannot feel to be quite deserved. However, some day I hope to deserve it. . . . I
hope I have established myself on a new footing
as an artist. I am going back to Rome full of
good intentions and strong for work."

VIII.

THE CLEOPATRA AND THE LIBYAN SIBYL.

THE year 1862 was a date, *the* date, in Story's life; bringing with it the influence, the sense of possibilities of success, the prospect of a full and free development, under which he settled—practically for the rest of his days—and which was to encounter in the time to come no serious check. The time immediately to come was to have its dark days—which were the dark days of the American Civil War, that weary middle period of anxiety almost unrelieved, especially for spectators at a distance whose sympathies were with the North and to whom it sometimes seemed that the issue scarce hung in the balance. Story was in England each of these years and inevitably in contact with much feeling and expression, in this connection, that was not of a nature to soothe patriotic soreness. His own sentiments and convictions relieved themselves by a demonstration on which he was distinctly to be congratulated and of which we shall presently encounter evidence. But meanwhile his artistic and his personal success were of the greatest, and, as the shadow of the War slowly cleared, life, activity and ambition opened out for him in a hundred interesting ways. The effect produced by his work at the Exhibition of 1862 was immediate and general, and would carry us back, should we follow the clue, to a near and suggestive view of the taste, the æsthetic sensibility of the time. The clue would take us, however, too far; we can only feel, as we pass, a certain envy of a critical attitude easier, simpler and less "evolved" than our own. "Critical" attitude is doubtless even too much to say; the sense to which, for the most part, the work of art or of imagination, the picture, the statue, the novel, the play, appealed was not, in any strictness, the æsthetic sense in general or the plastic in particular, but the sense of the romantic, the anecdotic, the supposedly historic, the explicitly pathetic. It was still the age in which an image had, before anything else, to tell a story, and that had much to do with the immense welcome offered to the Sibyl and the Cleopatra of the new American sculptor. In living over these enjoyments, these enthusiasms and responses, the pleasantness, the felicity, the intellectual comfort of it all are, I confess, what most strikes me, and to the point really of wishing we might again have our pleasures, in this order, on terms on the whole as easy. Story, as we have noted, was frankly and forcibly romantic, and with a highly cultivated quality in his romance; so that he penetrated the imagination of his public as nobody else just then could have done. He told his tale with admirable emphasis and straightness, with a strong sense both of character and of drama, so that he created a kind of interest for the statue which had been, without competition, up to that time, reserved for the picture. He gave the marble something of the colour of the canvas; he in any case offered the observer a spectacle and, as nearly as possible, a scene. It was a question if not always absolutely of an action perpetrated, at least of one meditated, prepared, remembered or prompted, and, with that, of a state of feeling, a state of expression, to which association could lend a glamour. He chose his subjects, for the most part, among figures already consecrated to the imagination — by history, poetry, legend—and so offered them with all their signs and tokens, their features and enhancements. He created thus, ingenious and

abundant as he was—created it, that is, above
all for the English taste—a tradition of sculpture
quite distinct from that tradition which previous
generations, haunters of dim Academic shades,
gropers in queer crepuscular cellars, were excusable for never having, at any moment,
markedly "warmed to," for having in fact
quite positively looked at askance, shyly,
coldly, unpersuadedly. Strange, starved creations glimmer before us in that early Victorian
limbo, shining with a light too pale for identi-
fications, yet wearing the fetters of the academic
without suggesting its possibilities of "style";
meagre maidens and matrons, earnest, respectable males, nymphs and heroes equally without
temperament or attitude, pomp or circumstance,
and all, somehow, blank, bereaved, disconsolate,
as if deprived of their proper lachrymal urns
or weeping willows. If the section of sculpture
in the old exhibitions was mainly a desert, there
were thus, with all respect to occasional exceptions, memories and warnings that accounted
for the mistrust.

Little wonder accordingly that Story's new
note so promptly "took"—the new note that
was distinctly not English, and yet was as little
French (as the French note was remembered
or conceived); and, still again, was not at all

American on the lines of Mr Powers's Greek
Slave, the only piece of American sculpture
then known in England. He "drew," almost,
like a successful play; he peopled, at a stroke,
a quarter of the desert; he showed, in a word,
that marble could be made interesting even to
the many. On the same lines, accordingly, from
that time on, he continued to make it so; the
rest of his work is in germ in the two statues
of 1862. The admirable Libyan Sibyl indeed
he, on the whole, I think, never surpassed—
never perhaps even quite equalled, for his subject here was a treasure to him and his vision
of it wholly felicitous. If it be sometimes given
to parents to have a child whom they recognise
as born happy and who is to remain for them
under the protection of that star, so artists—
and perhaps, fortunately, oftener—produce works
that have come into the world exactly as they
should, that bear the stamp of it all over, and
that have been provided for, solidly, from their
birth. By which I mean that the individual
producer has been blest when he has known this
complacency once or twice. We may really
say of Story that he knew it as repeatedly as
he might; since the Cleopatra, exhibited for
the first time on the same occasion as the Sibyl,
ranks almost equally as one of the happy children,

creatures of inspiration and prosperity. Well may these figures, with their calm intensity, have been found expressive and living, and yet, by the happiest art, tranquil in their beauty in spite of the quantity of story they were addressed to telling. The Cleopatra in particular is admirable for this, for the way in which line and form, a composition interesting in itself, control and condense the historic, the romantic hints. At the same time, no doubt, not less than its companion, this figure would have sown the seeds of a critical objection that was to express itself, freely enough, later on — the restrictive view of the artist's fondness for the draped body and his too liberal use of drapery. The Cleopatra is practically a dressed heroine; the Sibyl is covered, voluminously enough, from the middle downward; and so, in many a case, their successors were to be, in a manner, costumed. The fact, however, suggests more than one reflection—the first of which is of the sort that, bearing on the question of the current taste, of what, in relation to the public, was possible and not possible, has always an interest. Story's work as a sculptor speaks, incontestably, of the public it had to confront and involves a view of that public. There are things in the arts, of a truth, that have more eloquence and value for us by

that reference than they offer in any other way;
so that positively, at moments, we find ourselves
turn insistently from the work itself to the evoked
spirit of its place and hour, which become, in its
light, almost as concrete as itself.   Such, so many
and so perverse, are the solicitations to which
the critical sense is open.

It might easily here, for instance, be drawn
into wonderments that would carry it far;
wonderments, say, as to what the felt *demand*
for drapery, in the mid-Victorian time, may
really have been, and then, conformably, as to
what coherent terms the demand would have
been expressed in.   There was apparently no
case against sculpture — as, for that matter,
there is no case to-day against painting; yet
there presumably both was and is a presentable
case (though never presented) against the nude,
to which these arts are of necessity beholden
for so much of their life.   Story, visibly, was
preoccupied with this supposed interdict—which,
as reflected, for better or for worse, in his labours,
might thus, as I say, had we space, invite consideration.   How far was he right, how far
was he wrong?   how much would the world
about him have "stood," had he insisted, or
what scarce imaginable revelations of shockability
might we, on the other hand, have been treated

to ? Story kept, for all sorts of excellent reasons, one of which I will presently mention, on the "safe side"; but it is possibly not open to question that the fond critic (critic, I mean, of the peculiarities of publics,) may have been deprived by this circumstance of precious lights on significant abysses. There might, for all we know, have been pleas, arguments, documents; and the documents might have been curious; by which I mean that the case against the nude might have been, for once in a way, presented— with consequences calculable, or perhaps rather incalculable, for the earnest observer, to say nothing of the genial satirist. Story, obviously, at all events, loved the nude, as the artist, in any field, essentially and logically must; and he paid it, in marble, in verse, in prose, such frank tribute, on occasion, as he might; and I hasten to add that if his relation to it is visibly enough governed by influences, mistaken or other, one at least of these latter operated not only quite lawfully, but, from his point of view, quite happily. Drapery, that is, folds and dispositions of stuff and applications, intimations of ornament, became a positive and necessary part of his scheme from the moment that scheme was romantic; nothing being more curious than the truth that though the nude may have a dozen other convincing notes it is eminently destitute of *that* one—or possesses it only when conscious, contrasted or opposed. To borrow from the list of Story's productions alone, we no more see, for romantic illustration and conviction, a naked Saul, a stripped Sardanapalus, a Medea without her robe or an Alcestis without her veil, than we see a dressed Agamemnon, an accoutred Antinous, an Apollo protected from the weather or a Venus rising from the sea in a bathing-suit. The "story" of the most beautiful of legends is (at least pictorially speaking) not in Andromeda, isolated and divinely bare, but in the mailed and caparisoned Perseus, his glorious gear, his winged horse and helmet and lance.

It was in elements of this order that, even with his interest in the endless human body, Story found a constant charm, recognising how much, in almost any case, they might do for his conception. His imagination, of necessity, went in preference to the figure for which accessories were of the essence; which is doubtless a proof, one must hasten to recognise, that he was not with the last intensity a sculptor. Had he been this he would not, in all probability, have been also with such intensity (so far as impulse and eagerness were concerned) so many other things; a man of ideas—of *other* ideas, of

other curiosities. These were so numerous with
him that they were active diversions, driving
him into almost every sort of literary experiment
and speculation. It was not that he failed to
grasp the plastic, but much rather that he saw
it everywhere, and that, wherever seen, it
tempted and challenged him. It tempted him
perpetually in the form of verse, and he is
singular in having apparently, in respect to
some alternatives, never really made up his
mind. He was as addicted to poetry as if he
had never dreamed of a statue, and as addicted
to statues as if he were unable to turn a verse.
Add to this that he constantly overflowed, by
spoken and by written talk, into an extremely
various criticism, and we see that, if the approach to final form be through concentration,
he was not concentrated. If sculpture be a thing
of supreme intimacy he was not supremely intimate. He had, in a word, too many friends
for any one of them ever to have succeeded in
establishing absolute rights. It was, æsthetically
speaking, a wonderful all-round sociability. All
of which considerations, however, in this connection, solicit me less, I feel, than the mere
side-issue—comparatively—of the echo started
for us, a while back, in Mrs Gaskell's letter.
She was full of her Hawthorne, she had been

reading "Transformation," and she sets us, so
far as our connection is concerned, reading it
again for ourselves.   Then it is that a much
pleasanter thing occurs than even being sure
we are right in estimate and characterisation—
then it is that we are contented and charmed to
be, in the matter, whatever the good Hawthorne
was in the golden air of his Romanised vision;
then it is, in fine, that we assist, ever so consentingly, at the odd, delightful business of the
practical *consecration* of a work of art, and are
moved, over and above, to brood genially on
the shy phenomenon.   That is perhaps easier
than to express it, to say exactly how it is that
in such a case we are affected by the poetry of
association, the beneficence of perspective, the
antiquity, as we may almost say, of tone.   It
is all a matter of the writer's singular sweetness,
which embalms and enshrines, for the responsive
mind, the figure round which it plays.   The
mysterious Miriam, in the novel, it will be remembered, comes, in her sad unrest, to the studio
of Kenyon, the young American sculptor, and
makes acquaintance there with the image of a
grand seated woman, a personage royal and
wonderful, who is none other than a fine prose
transcript of Story's Cleopatra.   Immensely impressed, she questions her host as to the source

of his vision, and his admirable answer may doubtless stand for the artist's only possible account of the origin of any work. "I kindled a great fire in my mind and threw in the material —as Aaron threw the gold of the Israelites into the furnace—and in the midmost heat uprose Cleopatra as you see her." She saw her, Miriam, as romantically as the artist himself could have wished, weaving fine fancies about her in the gentle Hawthornesque way; as a result of which, and of the talk, of the scene, of the whole charming context and confusion, the beautiful light mantle of the book, all loose and soft and ample, is thrown over the statue. It is not exactly, of course, as if the protection had, in advance, been needed, but when once the phenomenon, as I have called it, occurs—the phenomenon of a recognition, an assimilation, which is not as that of criticism, but something tenderer and more fraternal, and which fairly gains by being " old-fashioned"—we take it in for our edification. Such is the quality, such the diffusion, such the magic of the sweetness that we impute; an element that so constantly clears and disinfects Hawthorne's so-called gloom, making it light, pictorial, digestible, and in which the whole thing floats as through a pleasant September haze. "Transformation," in short, with

its laxities of insistence, its timidities of indication, its felicities of suggestion, its sincerities
of simplicity and, most of all, its total vague
intensity, so curiously composed of all these, is,
more than anything, a loveable production—
which, in its wandering amiability, holds up for
a moment a mirror to another work, a little
magic mirror from which the reflection, once
caught, never fades.

Story's liveliest sympathy meanwhile, it need
scarce be said, had followed Browning to England,
and he and his wife were constantly present in
spirit at that work of building up a new life
from the very foundation to which their friend
was now committed. Browning's existence had
sharply broken and had, in conditions completely
changed, to be, as it were, repaired and made
practicable.   There would be perhaps no more
interesting chapter in his biography than that
of his return from his long Italian absence,
stricken and lonely (save for the place henceforth
taken in his thoughts by his young son), to
address himself to a future indefinite and obscure.
It was almost a fresh beginning; he had quitted
London, fourteen years before, sufficiently young
and sufficiently unknown to have left his possibilities in general, his maturer contacts and
relations, still to establish, themselves, his im-

pressions, mainly, still to condense. His early letters to his Roman correspondents reflect, vividly enough, this phase; they are in themselves very nearly the picture of a situation and the history of a period. The writer's London period was in fact to be rich and ample, was to be attended with felicities and prosperities, of every sort, that cast the comparatively idyllic Italian time into the background and seemed, superficially, to build it out. But thus, really, was generated, in the personal, social, intellectual way, the wonderful Browning we so largely were afterwards to know—the accomplished, saturated, sane, sound man of the London world and the world of "culture," of whom it is impossible not to believe that he had arrived somehow, for his own deep purposes, at the enjoyment of a double identity. It was not easy to meet him and know him without some resort to the supposition that he had literally mastered the secret of dividing the personal consciousness into a pair of independent compartments. The man of the world— the man who was good enough for the world, such as it was—walked abroad, showed himself, talked, right resonantly, abounded, multiplied his contacts and did his duty; the man of "Dramatic Lyrics," of "Men and Women," of the "Ring and the Book," of "A Blot on the

'Scutcheon," of " Pippa Passes," of "Colombe's Birthday," of everything, more or less, of the order of these,—this inscrutable personage sat at home and knew as well as he might in what quarters of *that* sphere to look for suitable company. The poet and the "member of society" were, in a word, dissociated in him as they can rarely elsewhere have been; so that, for the observer impressed with this oddity, the image I began by using quite of necessity completed itself: the wall that built out the idyll (as we call it for convenience) of which memory and imagination were virtually composed for him stood there behind him solidly enough, but subject to his privilege of living almost equally on both sides of it. It contained an invisible door through which, working the lock at will, he could softly pass and of which he kept the golden key—carrying the same about with him even in the pocket of his dinner-waistcoat, yet even in his most splendid expansions showing it, happy man, to none. Such at least was the appearance he could repeatedly conjure up to a deep and mystified admirer. Our point, at any rate, is that we see him vividly, during the early " sixties," in the letters before us; see him without mystery or attitude, with his explicit sense and his clear, full, masculine tone, the tone, ever, of reason and cheer. He is always, to our conceit, on the hither side of the wall.

Robert Browning to W. W. Story,

"*Chez* M. Chauvin, St Enogat, *près* Dinard,
Ile-et-Vilaine, France,
Aug. 20*th*, 1861.

"My dear Friends,— For so let me write to you all as I was used to talk in those days which already seem so good and old. . . . I *did* leave Florence at last—on the 1st of this month — accompanied by Miss Blagden, who has devoted herself to me and P., disregarding health, inconvenience, and all other considerations. We took the straight road, and reached Paris at last—for, being encumbered with P.'s pony, we could not travel by express. I had meant to cross over to London for a day or two's talking with Arabel Barrett, but the prospect of going over the old ground, stopping at the old house, was too much, and I found it impossible to go further. Paris also is unbearable to me, and I only breathe freelier since we arrived at this wild, primitive and lonely place—Saint-Malo—with a solitary sea, bays, sands and rocks, and green, pleasant country. Miss Blagden left Paris on the 10th, in a very indifferent state of health, for London. I shall stay here till the autumn sets in, perhaps a month longer; and then, after just a day or two spent in Paris, shall finally settle in London for the winter and spring. I mean to get a very good English tutor, capable of preparing P. for the university without, if possible, necessitating the passage through a public school; and if I delay this, as my original notion was, I may lose the critical time when the English stamp (in all that it is good for) is taken or missed. I have written to various friends about my projects, and shall be glad to profit by their experience. Such a school as dear E. described would have been desirable had he been brought up in England from the first, but I distrust all hybrid and ambiguous natures and nationalities and want to make something decided of him. I find, by myself, that one leans out the more widely over one's neighbour's field for being effectually rooted in one's own garden. . . . London may suit me better than a brighter place for some time to come; but I shall have no ties, no housekeeping, nothing to prevent me from wandering about if circumstances permit. I want my new life to resemble the last fifteen years as little as possible. It is idle talking just yet, however.

"I deeply feel with you about the disaster

at Bull's Run, so far as I know anything about
it from having glanced at a single newspaper.
I only know that the good cause has suffered
and that we all suffer with it.   As to scurrilous
articles in the ——, I have had the satisfaction
of never seeing the outside of that paper ; but
quite sure am I that its habit of deliberate
maligning will have found exercise in this and
every other matter interesting humanity.   How
can you mind such writing ?   I look to the end,
to success, with every confidence ; but, as I said,
I have missed all the details of this misadventure.
You must and will do better, and best, another
time—and meanwhile the fewer big words on
all sides, in any sense, the better !

" ' Tannhauser ' is written by Lytton and
Julian Fane ; the latter's are the songs,
which are poor.   Julian Fane wrote a volume
years ago which the —— reviewed much in the
way you now describe : I conclude that his
father's being ambassador to Austria and his
brother Earl of Westmorland now, has some
little to do with the ——'s admiration.   Lytton,
to whom the best part of the book belongs,
has no such influence.   He gave me the book,
told me Fane was publishing the secret everywhere, and spoke modestly enough about his
own estimation of the thing.   I have just heard

from him, by the way; he must be at Vienna
by this time.

"And now it is hard to say good-bye, which
of late years has always gone along with 'we
shall so soon meet again, and so merrily.' Go
you, dear Story, on in your admirable way—
nor altogether without me, who shall continue
as interested in your work as when I could see
it in progress from the little door of the room
by the garden."

I cannot (with any fidelity to our law of
salutation of hovering shades) fail to take up
the mention, in the above, of the devoted little
friend who ministered to Browning at this time,
who had been, in Italy, not less devoted to his
wife, who came with him to England, who held
herself at his service during so much of the
after-period as she was herself, somewhat sparely,
to enjoy on earth, and who, in particular, mingles
her small, responsive, expressive presence with
old Florentine memories. My own part in them,
in this connection, is scant, yet such as it is it
remains — the impression still has sharpness;
so that I pause an instant before it even though
over the shoulder of this particular ghost, and
on the very spot where it stands, other ghosts,
intenser, but necessarily nameless here, look out

with eyes that seem to ask if they too may
not answer. Isa Blagden comes vaguely to light
in Mrs Browning's letters, some of which, in the
later Florentine years, are addressed to her;
she figured also, not with much greater distinctness, I seem to recollect, on the covers of
old Tauchnitz volumes, having contributed to
that series the inevitable nice novel or two of
the wandering English spinster. Above all, she
had befriended the-lonely, cheered the exile and
nursed the sick; given herself indefatigably, for
instance, to the care of Robert Lytton, during
a long illness, in the good old days of casual
tendance, before the dawn of the capped and
cloaked, the now ubiquitous "trained." These
friendships and generosities, in a setting of
Florentine villas and views, of overhanging
terraces and arched *pianterreni*, of Italian
loyalties and English longings, of shy literary
yearning and confessed literary starvation—these
things formed her kindly little legend, and they
still, after long years, melt together, for my
personal reminiscence, into the springtime air
of a garden at Bellosguardo. I feel again the
sun of Florence in the morning walk out of
Porta Romana and up the long winding hill;
I catch again, in the great softness, the "accent"
of the straight, black cypresses; I lose myself

again in the sense of the large, cool villa, already then a centre of histories, memories, echoes, all generations deep; I face the Val d'Arno, vast and delicate, as if it were a painted picture; in special I talk with an eager little lady who has gentle, gay black eyes and whose type gives, visibly enough, the hint of East-Indian blood. The villa had, as I say, a past then, and has much more of one now; which romantic actualities and possibilities, a crowd of international relations, hung about us as we lingered and talked, making, for the victim of this first impression of the place, a mere fond fable of lives led and work done and troubles suffered there. She had seen the procession, the human panorama, more or less polyglot; there were odd people—oh, "precursors" enough, in *her* list!—whom she had known, and of whom I knew; and then we had friends in common, figures of the Florentine legend, to my knowledge of whom she added; with which, moreover, there were wistful questions that were at the same time, for the passer-by, provocations of envy: the books she would have liked to read, the news she would have liked to get, the people she would have liked to see, amounting all, in their absence, as I remember ingenuously thinking, to nothing more than a sign of how deep one might be in Italy. She had come back there after her pilgrimage to England with Browning, and it was from there, I recall, that I received in the after-years (none too many of them) that other and last sign of her that was to match with my Bellosguardo morning. It was an invitation to be one of the friends contributing to a memorial placed over her grave. It was wonderful how much we had talked; I had become one of the friends in that one hour.

There is a glimpse of Miss Blagden, and of other matters, in another letter.

Robert Browning to W. W. Story.

"St Enogat, *Aug. 30th,* 1861.

"I had a very exact picture made of the room in Casa Guidi, after vainly trying to get it photographed; and of this picture I have photographs, giving a sufficient idea of it, which I will send you. I think I shall not examine the state of my invaluable [negative] till I get to London.

"You must know that I feel your affection, as I remember all your past goodness; but I can't write about anything. I could perhaps speak, if we were together. But to write freezes me altogether. Tell me about yourselves—whatever interests you will deeply interest me. I read no newspapers, know absolutely nothing of what has been going on the last two months. I feel impatient at doing nothing, and long to begin with P. . . . It will all come into use presently in our grim London. (It is ungrateful of me to say this, with so many kind friends proposing to put light into the coming gloomy winter, but I feel so, and may say so to *you*.)

" Miss Blagden will not return to Italy—at all events not before she has made an endeavour to live in England. She goes to Clifton, in all probability, where Miss Cobbe is to see her comfortably settled. I cannot believe she will bear the change. She has given up her villa, where she was counting upon a joyous summer with Hatty [Hosmer]. I blame her for all this, but unquestionably like her for it.

" Don't tell anybody about *those rooms*. I should hate to hear that the first who could climb the staircase had entered in and taken possession. This is very silly, I know. But I only think and write sillinesses just now. The staying at Casa Guidi was not the worst of it. I kept in my place there like a worm-eaten piece of old furniture, looking solid enough ; but when I was *moved* I began to go to pieces. I am getting ' mended up ' here, and shall no doubt last my proper time, for all the past. Landor remains under my care. Lytton is very kind— has written to me three times this fortnight : he is at Vienna."

Browning's letters, at this moment, were as interesting, as frankly and heartily personal, as they were frequent, and I give them as they come.

Robert Browning to the Storys.

"1 CHICHESTER ROAD, UPPER WESTBOURNE TERRACE, *Nov.* 10*th*, 1861.

"The last day I spent at St Enogat I remember I was bent on writing an answer of some sort to the letters, brimful of kindness, which I had received just before. I had to go to St Malo, however, and could not get a clear quarter of an hour. I meant therefore to write on arriving at Paris. The end is that all this while I have said nothing, and, as a consequence, heard nothing. But you do know my feeling to you all, and whether it is likely to grow less now. I have one of my old headaches this morning, cannot attend to Pen, nor go out for a walk (in the rain), a duty of religion forced on me at leisure minutes ; so I will chat a little with you, if you please, as if

I came in (in) the dear old way, taking my seat by the corner of the 'mobile,' whatever it should be called, where my elbow goes so well—and there you are in the customary places.

. . . "I had an adventure in going to Boulogne, was strangely misinformed as to the proper train—that which transports horses—and the people refused to take me. I proved the fault was theirs (having their printed paper to show, and also their officials'), and explaining the loss of time and money they would put me to unless I was suffered to take P.'s pony by the express-train (my own, that was to have been, went without me), I declared (in all good humour, for they were polite enough) that I would prosecute them : I was upwards of two hours in this weary work of battling with them. 'It could *not* be !'—but at the last moment, literally, it *was*. They pushed me into the train, put the horse-box on, which there was no time even to pay for, and so I got off, reached Boulogne in time to get the pony through the custom house, and consequently did not miss the boat to London which sailed two hours after midnight : missing, moreover, the accident which happened to the 'proper train for me,' which I certainly should have taken had they beaten me, which was run into by another train at Amiens—having '22 wounded and 10 or 12 killed,' said 'The Times' two days after.

"Another strange thing happened while I was in the train. I had been thinking much of the meeting I had had with Tennyson ten years ago, when he was the first person I chanced upon in Paris: I must have told you, for it always impressed me. Well, I, in like manner, not having seen an English friend since I left Florence, put my head out of window at the Amiens station, when out came Tennyson and entered a carriage. He was changed, had a great beard, but I could not be deceived. At Boulogne I met him in the doorway and was reassured, but I kept out of sight. When the luggage was disposed of Pen proposed to go and see the quay; the Folkestone boat was on the point of starting. I said 'I'll show you Tennyson,' and presently he came forward with his wife and two beautiful children. They seated themselves a few yards from me; I pulled my hat over my face—not that they would have recognised me; and so saw them off. Odd, is it not, to leave Florence twice, and twice meet, for the first English face, Tennyson's? I wonder whether he also had missed the afternoon train and its smash.

. . . "My own time (to end with all this
about myself) has every minute taken up: I
have much to do with the printers, and shall
have for some weeks more. I see nobody—have
only called on people about business. There
being what is called 'nobody in town,' there
was no need to inquire who made the exception.
I shall presently go about, I suppose, for people
have been very kind indeed. Miss Blagden is
opposite, in a house no further from this than
your ballroom from the green drawing-room.
She came last week and will stay three months
at least—pleasantly for me.

. . . "It is not because I do not feel the
deepest interest in the American news that I
rather turn from writing about it—particularly
to you who understand so much more, foresee
and perhaps apprehend more than can the un-
instructed here. The grin of the —— may be
hard to bear, but indeed the feeling of the few
people I see is altogether free from its malicious
self-satisfaction. I never hear a word for the
South even from those who think the North
underestimated its strength and despair of a
better issue than separation. *We* say fight it
out to the last; but for English lookers-on,
who abjure heroics, to say that, would be saying
'Do yourselves as much harm as you can.' The

Italian hope deferred again is also a weariness—
but not worse, I think. Dear friends, we feel
together, hope together—did so and will do
so! Here is a 'length,' as the actors used to
say. I can't stay longer with you in the cheerful
home. . . ."

The last lines of the above refer of course
to interests painfully present to Browning's correspondents; just as his next letter was to be
the act of response to a demonstration that had
broken, in all naturalness, from Story's irritated
nerves. For history then, as happened, was
making itself in relations markedly enough
distinct from its immediate concern with our
friends. There was a good deal of English
feeling on the subject of the War of Secession
with which Story was not, and could not be,
especially acquainted; whereas the feeling with
which he *was* acquainted, and which was then
patent and flamboyant, had no message of
comfort for his inflamed patriotism. The Roman
studio, the poetic visions struggling, with their
beauty and their indifference, into shape, soothed
him at these hours in vain; so that he was
moved, in their not very helpful company, to
draw up a statement of the case of the North
that might be brought before the English public.

He addressed himself to the task with characteristic vivacity and with an excellent result. Despatched to London, his paper—"The American Question"—appeared, by Browning's aid, in the form of three letters to the "Daily News" (December 26th, 27th, 28th, 1861), and was afterwards published as a pamphlet matching the pamphlet composed of the letters addressed shortly before to "The Times" by Mr Motley, the historian of the Dutch Republic, then United States Minister to Austria. Story's plea for the particular justice to his country that he had been so disappointed not to find is a remarkably lucid and temperate performance for a man whose affections were so much engaged. For a sculptor and a poet it is in fact a singularly methodical and reasonable document —of which there would be perhaps even more to say were it advisable to dive again with him into the deeps of the London newspaper-press of the time for the pearls of a tolerably turbid sea. Rich and rare are some of those produced by him in picturing the element of indignant virtue that was so striking a feature of the perversity against which he protests— an element that may surely now be felt, all round, to have contributed some of the rarest curiosities of "tone" to the queer museum of

history. It may be added that, on the dismal
"Trent" episode in especial, Browning is as
clear and explicit as his friend.

Robert Browning to W. W. Story.

"1 CHICHESTER ROAD, *Dec.* 17*th*, 1861.

" DEAREST FRIENDS, and dearer than ever just
now! . . . I will go this morning and see
with Edward Dicey what is to be done. I *much*
fear little or nothing, beyond some cost of
publishing, which you may expect, I should say.
Perhaps immediate circulation, even in a cheap
and popular paper, would put your thoughts
into thousands of heads at once, would be better
than any delay in trying for the more dignified
journals, and certainly than the pamphlet form :
this miserable affair of the ' Trent ' has so changed
the object of interest for the moment. I have
not even glanced at your writing, so anxious am
I to assure you at once on all the above-
mentioned points, but I know that we agree in
feeling *here*, as in other matters—and probably
do not differ even in appreciation of facts, as
in old subjects of disputes when our feelings went
equally together. I think English judgment of
the Northern procedures has been wrong from
the beginning—just as of the French procedures
(will you let me say ?) in Italy : our people ex-

pected in both cases that the pure and simple
rights in the case would be declared and vigorously carried out without one let or stop. 'Italy
shall be free, and Slavery abolished, absolutely,
at once and for ever.' At the first hesitation
in face of difficulties we cried out 'Italy will
not be freed, nor Slavery extinguished, after all';
and our sympathy stopped and irritation began,
as if the spirit of all we would have sym-
pathised in were not actively alive all the time,
and, taking the crooked road to walk, in this
poor world, is only reached by a straight one
'as the crow flies' — far above our heads and
rather near the heaven. The *spirit* of all Mr
Lincoln's acts is altogether against Slavery in
the end; but in apprehension of the result of
losing the uncertain States he declared his
intention to be quite otherwise.

"*You* understand this, and the English did
not, and so all the work of the —— was 'cut
out for it,' and, just as in the Italian case, every
measure now taken by the North in the direction,
plainer and plainer, of complete Emancipation,
will be considered as 'forced upon them.' It
seems besides as if no mistakes on one part can
be met without two or more mistakes on the
other, to make up for their coming late into
observation; so the malice of the —— provoked

abuse enough on your side, and threatenings
quite beside the question : because our neutrality,
poor, hard, cold thing indeed, was the worst you
had to expect and in no moment of the fear of
a terrible result for the cotton-operatives here,
did any one dream of taking part with the South.
This sad affair of the 'Trent' puts all this away,
however ; our people hold to the *bone* they have
got in their jaws this time, that a naval lieu-
tenant is not an admiralty-judge. If you put
things as they were, so far as possible, let the
prisoners be restored with an acknowledgment
that the seizure was wrong.   I think the 'Trent'
ought in fairness to be considered as taken into
one of your ports and subject to adjudicature :
if our lawyers are right you will have to re-
store her and pay for the detention; if your
authorities, the ship is yours, envoys and all.
There is remedy for our wrong in the legal way,
and no other ; but you are too likely to say
'The ship would be confiscated, the damages
infinitely greater ; this twitching the sum in
dispute out of the waistcoat-pocket is kinder
than issuing writs and imprisoning the debtor'
—while *he* demurs : 'If the debt be disproved
after all, the writ and expenses will all fall on
you; whereas carry off my money and I lose
that decidedly, right or wrong.   Moreover, you

treated me thus at Charing Cross!' So it seems
we may fairly say and *you* fairly do; but who
can be sure he sees clearly, with the bad blood
setting toward the head?

"Come what will, I, insignificant unit, can
make no 'war' in my soul with my truest
brother and friend. No one ever had cause to
love a country better than I, who have so long
been only not an American because people can
hardly experience such generosity except as
strangers; nor do I mean ever to go into the
matter again with you, dearest of all American
friends, which our respective lawyers will wrangle
out for some time yet, I *hope*. Here is a first
bitter fruit of the business, that this letter,
which I have been meaning every day to write
in reply to your two precious budgets of home
news that gave me pleasure like pain and pain
like pleasure, so recently — this letter proves,
as you see, something altogether foreign to what
it should be if true to my heart and responsive
to yours. It is all written, moreover, while Pen
is practising at my elbow on a grand piano in
a very little London room. My minutes (I don't
know whether I began by saying) are numbered
and disposed of from morning till night. I never
had so much to do or so little pleasure in doing
it, or anything. Having scribbled what I really

doubt whether you or anybody else can read or understand, in determination to say something at once, I will leave off for a day or two. All regards and remembrances from us both to the Abbé when you see him."

And the writer resumes, after a short interval, with the same excellent lucidity.

Robert Browning to W. W. Story.

"1 CHICHESTER ROAD, UPPER WESTBOURNE
TERRACE, *Dec.* 31*st*, 1861.

"You must have received the three numbers of the 'Daily News' (Dec. 25, 26, 27) containing your paper Dicey sent them; all your thanks are due to *him*. I put the MS. in his hands at once, and he succeeded in his endeavour, as you see; but unluckily there was no time to refer to Mr Adams. The editor said this 'slack week's' occasion must be seized, and so good an occasion was not let slip; for indeed every day puts the past question deeper in the background beside the terrible interest of the new question altogether distinct from it. The inaccuracies therefore must be corrected in the pamphlet, should you please to reprint it *so;* Mr Adams has been communicated with, and no doubt will explain if needful. Your position so far from London makes very excusable the slip to which you refer; those cases have been turned and tried, till they are dry dust now, and it is true that Americans and English *here* are of one mind about them. Oh, the pity of it all! Capt. Wilkes with his instincts and law-studies *extemporary*, and notion of 'embodied despatches'! To quarrel about such a man's 'notions'! And no words, nor love indeed, on this side, can help it all! Indeed you are wrong as to men's 'fury' here! I have not heard one man, woman or child express anything but dismay at the prospect of being obliged to go to war on any grounds with America; but every one felt there might be an obligation as stringent as a slap on the face in public from one's bosom friend. But I've done. . . . This new dear letter comes warmly into the grey cold corner where I am keeping alive this last day of my last good year. Next year, next hundred years will change nothing in my gratitude and love. I mean to go out and see friends as I used. I shall be able to gossip with *you*. Meantime I run in and shake hands and sit by the fire as of old, see you always and love you always."

It was all a question, a danger, at the over-darkened hour, that could not easily drop.

Robert Browning to the Storys.

"1 CHICHESTER ROAD, *Jan. 21st*, 1862.

"I wrote two hurried letters to you, weeks ago, about the American letter, and meant to say something more leisurely at the first opportunity—which is *now*, and not earlier; you shall hear why. . . . I at last write the word or two which your kindness will take as if they were worthier. First, I am very glad that, on the whole, the matter of the Letter may be pronounced successful through Dicey's energy and opportunities. It would have been better could the supervision have been given to Mr Adams, as he wished, but the great point was to secure such an advantage as the columns of the 'Daily News,' a first-class paper—and you understand that, no doubt. I don't remember whether I told you my own poor opinion of the extreme cleverness of the exposition of the question. The 'Trent' affair was necessarily less complete in its handling than we should have found it had you been nearer the law-books. Of my heartfelt delight in the issue of *that* thing, why try and speak? Don't mind the mean, vindictive ——; every one here understands the difficulties that have had to be overcome, and thinks the reparation complete and handsome too. The purpose of the North is also understood at last, and if the event of the struggle seems less certain here than to your politicians, there is no longer the notion that 'Slavery had nothing to do with it.' The 'Commissaries' will be received with the contempt they deserve, and the antecedents of both gentlemen are kept profitably in mind here. On the other hand, this blocking-up Charleston seems inconsistent with any hope of eventual success on your side; for what will you do if Charleston becomes loyal again? There may be better reasons for such a step than we can see; let us hope so. Dicey will be a good interpreter, at least, of Northern intentions and accomplishments; he is gone, you know, for some months. I gave him a few letters; you, however, will do whatever he wants in that way, and as hardly anybody else can. I am heartily glad he goes.

"Of myself—so little to say; my life is as grey (or yellow) as this sky, one snow-bank above head at this minute. I make up my mind from week to week—*next* Monday I will begin and call on my friends. But this fort-night of anxiety was a real excuse. *Next* week I still say. I see hardly anybody, but mean, I assure you, to alter all that for abundance of reasons. I have got, besides, a tutor to my mind—rather than to Pen's perhaps; but he is

sound to the core in grammatical niceties. . . .
My end of life, and particular reward for myself,
will be, one day years hence, to just go back to
Italy, to Rome, and die as I lived, when I used
really to live. If you knew—but you *do* know,
and can conceive, how precious every mud-splash
on the house-walls of Rome is, how every minute
of those last six months in Rome would *melt up*
into gold enough for a year's use now, if I had
it! But I have *not*, and must think of something else—as that you at least are there, where
you were, as you were. But come here, all the
same; for you can go back, you know. Surely
you will all come—will you not?—for the Exposition, which (I told you truly in my last note)
is to go on just as it was intended. Let me
know what you do intend, and how far advanced
is the Sibyl. And, dear Mrs Story, do *you*
please write me more of those letters that I
was so delighted to have and that stopped of
a sudden: why? I will try and make some
sort of return in my lame way by repeating to
you all the news that occurs when I go my
rounds and see people you know—whose very
letters are in a pile here unanswered, but not
always to remain so (observed for the hundredth
time).

" You may know—what I have left out in my

account of the daily work—that I have been
painfully engaged with the printers and am not
yet absolutely out of their hands.   The book,
advertised long ago by the publisher, will not
appear for a month at least.   I shall send it to
you the first thing.   (Since writing this paragraph arrives an invitation from Miss Wynn to
dine and meet Mr Maurice only, and I have
accepted it as I said I would.)   I have just
written to Cartwright—for the first time since I
was here.   Very black it looks when actually
put on paper.   Dear Story, tell me what you
can about the studio; let me smell the wet clay
once more and hear the birds and the goat
through that dear little door to the left.   I would
send my kind remembrances to M. Boncinelli if
he cared to have them, and he may, in his good
nature.   Have you to do still with that clever
Lombard artist?   Probably not; but as for your
being idle, I don't believe it.   By-the-by, Mrs
Cholmondeley wrote the other day and mentioned
the death of poor Gajassi: if there is a sale of
his effects and the cast of Byron's head by
Thorwaldsen (with his 'points' on it) is to be
sold for what you consider a moderate price, I
should be glad to have it—supposing that there
is no trouble to you and that Boncinelli attends
such sales as of old.   Keep it in your studio 'till

I come.' I want you to tell the many and true friends I have in Rome and elsewhere, when you write to them, how they are all like portraits in the one habitable room of a house ; I go in among them many a time in the course of the day and night. And now good-bye. If you knew how the minutest news of your daily life interest me you would register every chip picked up on the carpet. How is Wild ? I have his picture of P. facing me. Give him my true love. But you need no telling how I think of old friends. Don't forget to remember me most kindly and particularly to Mrs Dicey—to Lady William (Russell). How is *she?* The accident had just happened, and I have heard nothing, of course, since your letter. There is no protracting this final shaking of hands in decency."

This next has especial interest as giving us a small fact of biographic value not, I believe, to be found elsewhere.

Robert Browning to the Storys.

"1 CHICHESTER ROAD, *March* 19*th*, 1862.

" Three letters, from one or another of you !— and the pleasure they gave me I can't, honestly can't, tell you. Will it be told you in any degree by the fact that I sit down at once to obey the desire in the last (that carried by Miss Gaskell) 'that I should write just a word *at once'*? Here is the word, never minding the injustice it does the many things calling for many words; but my time is almost wholly taken up, first by work of a morning, then by going out of evenings. Did you not bid me do that too? I ought to be able to return your news by mine, and tell particularly *who* was where, as you do so pleasantly; but it really goes out of my head the next morning. Moreover, what a difference between your Roman names and such as I might remember! I *will* remember some. . . . I dine to-night with Emerson Tennent—but I can't go on with the week's work; enough is said to show you that I try and see old friends, when my true *treat* would be an evening over the piles of unread books, or a morning with the old coat and wet clay. Oh, the days! Well, Rossetti has had a miserable loss of his wife a month ago; she took an overdose of laudanum one evening— they had dined out, returned early, and he had left her for his class at the working-men's 'Institution.' Coming back, he found her in a stertorous, unnatural sleep, and presently found an empty bottle. He got assistance, but in vain. He is in trouble indeed, poor kind fellow. I met Dickens at dinner the other day, looking very well and young. Thackeray has just re-signed the editorship of the 'Cornhill.'

" Why should I not trust to you what I know you will keep to yourselves, but what will certainly amuse you as nothing else I could write is like to do? What good in our loving each other unless I do such a thing? So, O Story, O Emelyn (dare I say, for the solemnity's sake?) and O Edie—the editorship has, under the circumstances, &c., &c., been offered to *me!* I really take it as a compliment because I am, by your indulgence, a bit of a poet if you like, but a man of the world and able editor hardly! They count on my attracting writers—I who could never muster *English* readers enough to pay for salt and bread! My first answer was prompt enough—that my life was done for and settled, that I could not change and would not; but the conveyer of the message bade me consider, in a flattering way, and I took the week to do so accordingly. I can't be sure how I shall answer—that's the end; for I have rather an impulse, first to get the salary, which P. might find something to do with, next to figure as a man actually capable of choosing better articles from the quantity always on hand, and last to try what the business is like.

It requires merely editing—no line of my own writing (*that* would be another matter). On the other hand, the little to do ought to be honestly done, might take more of my time than I choose to part with—and what do I want with more money? I shall diplomatise accordingly—write for a full statement of what I am expected to do if I accept, and what, and for how long, I am to receive in that case. One farthing less than Thackeray got, apart from the price of his substantive articles, I shall not take, of course; and if I don't like the terms the publishers have my bow, I have my little piece of satisfied conceit, and *you* have what is amusing you dear three, I engage!

"Seriously, now that I care not one whit about what I never cared for too much, people are getting good-natured to my poems. There's printing a book of 'Selections from R. B.' (SCULPTOR and poet) which is to popularise my old things; and So-and-so means to review it, and Somebody - or - other always was looking out for such an occasion, and What's-his-name always said he admired me, only he didn't say it, though he said something else every week of his life in some journal. The breath of Man! . . . I went to Paris three weeks ago and saw my father to heart's content (in his eightieth year and strong as thirty years ago); saw no one else but Mme. Du Quaire, and came back on the eighth day. I wish the absence from London could be to-morrow: the little book [1] is to be published, and if books were to be distinguished as formerly by a great red edging, this ought to have something of the kind round it without help from the printer. Reviewers will have my heart in their rough hands for the next month or two. But I am not very formidable; witness Mr Thornton Hunt, who has *not* printed the letter of his father's which I meant to give him, but in place of it, without a word to me (as he confesses in his preface), is printed *our* letter to his father! He knew I should have refused leave to print such a thing in the most energetic terms possible—so he takes leave. It is hardly worth noticing further that he prints my writing, which he can't read, so as to make it pure nonsense in parts—as he also confesses in his preface. He has printed William's letter to him as well as the letter of his father, but there was reason for *that* in the nature of the communication. I ought to be angry, but can't. I shall simply, when quite sure of myself, write and say what I think of his proceeding, and

---

[1] The Selections just mentioned.

then propose to give his father's letter in exchange for the one actually printed, which he shall cancel. There's nothing in my letter I care about except the indecent nature of the exposure : it's just as if, being at my toilette, some clownish person chose to throw the bedroom door wide. There's enough of it.

. . . "Of friends, I rejoice heartily in the recovery of Lady William, and will write a word to her since you encourage me. I had indeed thought of doing so. . . . Mrs Procter was told by a believing friend that Mr Home 'particularly felt the annoyance of being perpetually confounded with the Mr Hume Mr Browning insulted and Mr Trollope abused— it was quite another man!' Eh, my friends? Thank the dear Abbé for his loving word. I will write to you again, but give me another drink of the Roman air when you can, to send me rejoicing through the grey, drear lengths of days here."

With the social ramifications of our friends (and of *their* friends) in England the hovering ghosts so multiply that to follow all our clues would lead us well over the limit of our subject. These allusions, these figures moreover represent in many cases lives but recently extinct. Other-

wise how pass Mme. Du Quaire without a greeting?—how not instinctively pause at her name
as we used to pause, whenever we did pass,
at the friendly little door in Wilton Street
behind which it was ever a reminder of her
art of entertainment that the tiny and much-
encumbered house, the little red drawing-room,
decorated not only, but practically furnished,
with miniatures, snuff-boxes and other social
relics (I give at least what seems to me, after
a long interval, to have been my amused impression), reconciled the generous amplitude of
her person with the boundless extent of her
acquaintance and the emphasis of her kindness
to those she judged most in want of it?   I think
of the circumference of her round table, under
the suspended French dinner-lamp, in the little
room densely garnished with old engraved portraits; I wonder again at the single heaped
dish of southern fruit in the middle, all yellow
and green and purple, vast as some embossed
tray held up by a blackamoor in a Veronese
picture; I recall agreeable and interesting folk
who lived in the light of their time, but each
of whom, as I pass from name to name in the
list, would now answer with silence if the name
were called.   Her friends were like a family
bred to harmony of intercourse and left in charge

of a strong, soft, humorous, mildly-mothering,
absolutely indulgent elder sister. And the
silence of the roll deepens when I go back to
still more distant Paris days and the old red
house on the river, that of a common acquaintance, opposite the Louvre, in which I first met
her. The salon of Mme. de Blocqville, *née*
d'Eckmühl, daughter of Marshal Davoust—*that*
is truly a cluster showing gaps that help it
to resemble, for the imagination, some riddled
Napoleonic array. Of old Northumberland race,
married to a Frenchman, then widowed, childless,
and loving the world, of which she took an
amused view, Mme. Du Quaire seemed in those
days, with a home on each side of the Channel,
to have had neither in Paris nor in London a
sacrifice to make. She had kept each intimacy
without giving up the other—which was really
to know how to live. But on the threshold
of the great chamber of London memories, I
remind myself, the step must yet a while falter
and the voice not be loud. I none the less
venture to recollect that this lady was a great
friend to Kinglake, who is mentioned, though
but in his character of historian, in the following
letter, and also a great friend to Mrs Procter;
and she was interesting on the subject of the
difference that had parted these two for years.

She knew how little there was "in it"; she knew the name of the lady—which was interesting, assuredly, when one happened to have knowledge to match; she appreciated the gentleman's embarrassment in presence of the condition exacted. "Tell me you're in *love* with her, and I'll forgive your resenting what I said about her. Without that you had no right to resent it. So if you weren't in love, there we are." There they were indeed, since Kinglake was neither in love nor, in the particular case, likely to be: whereby he was unable to meet the condition — which, distinct and final, was, quite in the grand manner, never abated.

W. W. Story to Charles Eliot Norton.

"ROME, *March* 19*th*, 1863.

. . . "To-day is San Giuseppe's *festa*, and in every square the *frittate* are hissing under the decorated booths. Besides, we make three cardinals this morning at the Consistory, and all our party are assisting at this ceremony by lending it the honour of their presence. They thought it fair to do this, as they were at the great reception of the new cardinals the other evening. Russell and Julian (Sturgis) are to join the rest here in about ten days, and I am really glad that he can get a run if only

for a month, so as to change the course of
his life.

"My winter ever since I returned from
England has been full of hard work, and to-
day, for the first time since December came
in, have I an hour which is free. My Saul is
finished, and the tornatore is at work upon it,
so that I am as vain and useless at my studio
as a partner who has been turned out of the
firm. I believe I have told you about my
statue before, but cannot recollect. He is seated,
and I have represented him at the moment when
the evil spirit is upon him and David is called
in to play to him. The action is all interior—
the struggle of a half-demented soul; one hand
clutching his beard and one fumbling at his
dagger. I think it my best work, but no man
is judge of his own. Did we not, however, believe in the thing on which we are engaged
we could never have the heart or enthusiasm
to go on with it. I should like you to see it,
but unless you come here you never will, for
it seems that no important work of mine ever
is to go to America.

"I hope you will ere this have received a
copy of 'Roba di Roma'—yet one never can
tell! The book seems to have met with success—it is already going into a second edition.

Yet I have not heard one word about it from America; like everything else of mine it drops still-born there. Perhaps they will wake up when they find it is liked in England.

"I received a lively letter from Hamilton Wild the other day, promising to return here soon, but I am afraid if he waits for exchange to go down I shall wait some time before seeing him. I was rejoiced to find that you look upon our War prospects with so cheerful a hope. From this side the water things look dreary enough, and I confess that at times my fears outrun my hopes. The Government at Washington has in my opinion nearly compromised our future by its course, and if we go on as we have been going for the last six months I am afraid it will all be up with us. Stanton and Halleck are completely inefficient, and the former seems to me to be devoted to feathering his own political nest. The only man in whom I have the least confidence is McClellan, and I think if he were not tied by the leg and the string hitched to the White House he would in three months change the whole aspect of things. Has not all he said and prophesied been completely justified? He was turned out for slowness, but have we made any advance since he left?

"Have you read Kinglake's book? It has

not arrived here, and I have only seen extracts, but his character of Louis Napoleon is said to be most masterly, and from all I hear and see I think I should entirely agree with him. My detestation of that man is unutterable; I never can forgive him his crimes. This poor people is under his feet, and I see no issue for the present from their difficulties. The Pope is in precarious health and may die any day—or may live for years. But I cannot see that his death would affect the question. I believe that L. N. has no intention, under any circumstances, of leaving Rome. Nothing would bring him to this but a revolution in France or a series of pistol-shots at him in Paris. Orsini forced him to befriend Piedmont, and another Orsini may compel him to leave Rome. We have had a gay and pleasant winter, warm and genial weather, and numbers of agreeable people. The Carnival was very dull because the Comitato asked the Italians not to go into the Corso, but balls and parties of every kind have abounded. Arthur Dexter is here with his mother. Secession has its allies in . . ."

The almost fanatical faith of which General McClellan was the object on the part of many persons at the North during the middle period

of the Civil War is fairly ancient history now—
and the more ancient from the fact that the
controversy was to die a natural death almost
immediately after it had fiercely raged.   But,
for those who can remember, Story's reference
gives it a spectral actuality, renews the "feeling of the time"—that feeling of the time which
so often makes itself intense as from the sense
of its only chance, of foreknowing that it will
scarce be the feeling of any other time.   This
indeed may still leave other times generously
tender to it—besides which Story was nearly
related, through his wife, to McClellan, who was
his guest in Rome at the close of the war.   After
which tribute to public history I feel a pang at
having to brush almost in silence by the bearer
of the name last pronounced in the above, perfectly private though the allusion.   One must
have perhaps almost a morbid memory—or certainly an extravagant interest in the mere
fellow-creature, the mere honourable gentleman
—to feel tempted by every clue held out by
handsome young men of leisure, of fortune, of
"artistic tastes," of clever conversation, of filial
piety; passionately devoted, that is, to admirable mothers and steeped, for the golden fusion
of effect, in the old Barberini air.   So I leave
this decorative figure—as that is how I seem

to recall it—to that Italian *envoi* of Story's "Graffiti d'Italia" which I have already had occasion to mention; taking up my tale with another letter, undated, but of the same or the following season.

W. W. Story to Charles Eliot Norton.

"ROME [1863 or 1864].

. . . "Rome has been filled to overflowing with strangers this season, and we have had a very gay and pleasant society, particularly among the English. They have done for me what the Americans would have seen me rot rather than do, and I must feel grateful. Among others Coventry Patmore has been and is here, and I see a good deal of him and like him very much. He and De Vere hunt in couples, and I suspect De Vere talks a good deal of Catholicism into him. But it does not take root. . . . Miss Cushman is mouthing it as usual, and has her little satellites revolving around her. Tilton has been improving remarkably, and has painted some really beautiful pictures this year. He is almost the only one of all the American artists with whom I can have anything to do. The American permanent society here is very low, eaten up by jealousy and given shockingly to cabal and scandal. Our Legation is no legation at all. —— is a pleasant enough man and his wife a pleasant enough woman, but their tongue is solely American, and they do nothing and see nothing, have no house—that is, never receive, never go into any society but that of the Americans, where he likes to play cards with M. and Co. The great Cushman patronises them, and Mrs —— nestles under her wing. Our real representative (do not blush and deny it, for it is the plain fact) is J. C. H., who writes himself on his card 'Secretaire de la Légation des Etats Unis près le Saint-Siège,' though he has not a shadow of right to do so as I understand, and goes to the diplomatic dinners as our representative and parades about in his diplomatic dress, with sword and gold lace, and introduces his friends into the diplomatic box at all the ceremonies, to the immense disgust of the diplomatic ladies, and in a word entirely supersedes our Minister, who cannot speak a word of French. Nobody refers anything to ——, and he merely economises here and says he cannot afford to receive. Of course everybody knows what H. is, and of course our Legation is in consequence at the lowest ebb, the jeer of the diplomatic circle. I assure you that my cheeks tingle sometimes to hear the remarks made, and justly made too, so that I cannot answer. I do not mean to say anything against the ——s, who, in their way, are agreeable and amiable. He is a very intelligent man—only entirely out of place.

" We had last night a great illumination in honour of the Pope and St Agnes, on the anniversary of the miraculous interposition of the Madonna by which his life was saved when the Church of S. Agnese fell. The Piazza Navona was a superb spectacle ; all across the square were great transparent globes of light ; from the windows coloured lanterns were suspended, and little lamps starred the eaves and façades, while crimson Bengal lights glared in the centre, round the fountains that seemed to pour wine, and reddened the churches and palaces. Of course the whole thing was enforced, but the spectacle was beautiful. I just hear that a bomb was thrown into the Piazza Minerva and a man killed. The condition of things here is turbulent ; the people are very weary of tyranny, and the Papal troops constantly come to blows with the French. The Pope is not well, has erysipelas in his leg, which grows worse every year, and was unable to perform the usual functions at Easter. But he may live for years yet. Until he dies there is no hope, and even then I see no prospect, for the French will not withdraw,

and until they retire what can the Romans do?
—I hear that Hamilton Wild is coming out in
May. So much the better; he ought not to
stay any longer in America; his place is here,
and he is wasting his life there. We shall be
delighted indeed to greet him again. Pray tell
him from me not to stay in America any longer."

Story had meanwhile, besides writing a great
deal of verse, been turning to literary account,
in prose, those impressions of the aspects and
manners of Rome, its current life, public and
private, which had had time, since his first
visit in 1848, to store themselves in his spirit.
This attempt had taken the form of papers contributed, at uneven intervals, to the " Atlantic
Monthly," and which now had so accumulated
as to make matter for a substantial book. The
book, in 1863, was about to appear, and Browning, helpful and wise, had undertaken to over-
look, in London, the publication. I have before
me the two volumes in which it thus came
forth, decorated with the book-plate—the name,
escutcheon and crest—of Anthony Trollope. The
book was eminently successful, and but that the
aspects it mainly celebrates have suffered more
alteration during the last quarter of a century
than for (one is tempted to say) many centuries

before, it would remain an all-competent and charming companion for the city in Europe in which we most find ourselves desiring a sympathetic fellow-rambler. It did indeed for many years play this part—as to its original happy performance of which in my own case I retain a memory so fond and grateful that I perhaps scarce can speak of "Roba di Roma" with proper detachment. The golden air, as I look over its pages, makes a mist; I read them again in the light of old personal perceptions and emotions; I read, as we say, too much into them, too many associations, pictures, *other* ineffaceable passages. I remember perfectly the consuming envy kindled, on my part, at first, by the sense of an impregnation with the subject at which it seemed to me I could never hope to arrive, and at which the writer must have arrived by all sorts of delightful steps and contacts, any quantity of exquisite experience. It summed up, with an extraordinary wealth of statement, with perpetual illustration and image, the incomparable *entertainment* of Rome, where almost everything alike, manners, customs, practices, processes, states of feeling, no less than objects, treasures, relics, ruins, partook of the special museum-quality. Story rambles through his multitudinous subject as from room to room, up and down its many staircases and through its endless corridors, quite as if showing a friend some crowded collection with which habit has made him familiar. His multifarious reading, his love of curious knowledge, of enumeration and detail, of discussing "points," historic, æsthetic, linguistic, literary, here overflows, shows the sense of "evidence" as a thing in his blood, that passion for small cumulative facts which made him, under pressure of his lore, amplify the chapter on the Evil Eye into the treatise subsequently published with the somewhat too merely-enumerative monograph on the Castle of St Angelo. But I used to think, I remember, that the great challenge to envy was in the little evoked visions of that out-of-the-season Rome to which one had one's self to be a stranger, the Rome of the Romans only, of the picture-making populace, both in the city and the small hill-towns, who lead their lives as the sun gets low on the long summer days and the clear shade spreads like a tent above the narrow, sociable streets. To read these passages over is to taste and feel again the very air of early rambles, when one was always agaze; to hear the sounds, to smell the dust, to give one's self up once more as to the thing that was ancient and noble even when homely or sordid, the thing that might be mean but that yet couldn't be vulgar, the thing condemned, in spite of itself, in spite of weakness or ugliness or other offence, to be mysteriously interesting. There is a long passage of the chapter "Villeggiatura" which gathers into a cluster the various different notes of the writer's observation—a passage too long wholly to quote, but which I would fain send the reader back to the book to find.

"There is a crowd round the fountain, where women are filling their great copper vases with water and pausing to chat before they march evenly home under its weight like stout caryatids. Broad-horned white oxen drag home their creaking waggons. In the distance you hear the long monotonous wail of the peasant's song as he returns from his work, interrupted now and then with a shrill scream to his cattle. White-haired goats come up the lanes in flocks, cropping as they go the overhanging bushes, and, mounting up the bank, they stare at you with yellow glassy eyes and wag their beards. Down the slopes of the pavement jar along ringing files of wine-carts going towards Rome, while the little Pomeranian dog who lives under the triangular hood in front is running about on the piled wine-casks and uttering volleys of little sharp yelps and barks as the cars rattle through the streets. If you watch the wine-carriers down into the valley you will see them pull up at the wayside fountains, draw a good flask of red wine from one of the casks and then replace it with good fresh water. . . . Nothing can be more exquisite than these summer nights in Italy. The sky itself, so vast, tender and delicate, is like no other sky. The American sky is bluer, but harder, more metallic. There is all the difference between the two that there is between a feeling and an opinion. As you stand on one of the old balconies or walk along the terraces of the Frascati villas, looking down over the mysterious Campagna and listening to the continuous plash of fountains and the song of nightingales, you feel Italy, the Italy of Romeo and Juliet. . . . The waves of the cool, delicate air, passing over orange and myrtle groves and breathing delicately against the brow and cheeks, seem to blow open the inmost leaves of the book on which youth painted its visionary pictures with the colours of dreams. In a word we say this is Italy, the Italy we dreamed of; not the Italy of fleas, couriers, mendicants and postilions, but of romance, poetry and passion."

It is interesting to meet in the following a passage that has something of the quality of the writer's studies of imagined or reconstituted character, some monologue of "Dramatic Lyrics" or "Men and Women."

Robert Browning to the Storys.

"19 WARWICK CRESCENT, UPPER WESTBOURNE TERRACE, *May 2nd*, 1863.

"DEAREST FRIENDS, — What a time since I have heard from you! I got a letter from Story nearly a month ago—a full chord; and then, instead of striking up myself, I began to count my how many bars' rest—thirty days of it about; always meaning to lead off with a fresh subject presently! If I had written *two* days after, and told you any little thing—for instance, how I went the day after to Chapman's and found that he had already printed off the first volume and was working double tides to despatch the second—you would have, some one of you three, replied to me as you will now. To go on — I easily reconciled myself to the perhaps fortunate impossibility of chopping and changing—a vile business. Your book has succeeded remarkably—Chapman told me two days ago that he was getting rapidly through the new edition. The praises have been universal and hearty; why not let 'well' alone? And we *must* this time. But so you will next time

if you take my advice. Next, 'Saul'—I wish
you and us all joy of it. I know it will be all
I hope. Arthur Russell speaks in the highest
terms of it, and other opinions in the same sense
have reached me. That is right. And now, the
new statue, what will that be? Give me another
to expect.

"I told Mrs Story what I thought about the
pleasant charge against that hardened reprobate,
Don Juan *redivivus* and so on, poor dear good
simple——. His sister's defection doesn't surprise
me one bit more than his wife's, though on quite
different grounds. I never knew but a very
little of Miss X., who was, had one cared to look
into the matter, a far more curious study than
her sister-in-law; for you had a person neither
stupid, nor vain, nor pretentious, nor scheming,
nor false in any discernible way, who yet, for
some inexplicable reason, chose not to see, or by
some miracle would not see, what must have been
perked in her face daily and hourly. You know
that those inventions about 'spirits,' &c., were
not at all more prodigious than the daily-sprout-
ing toadstools of that dunghill of a soul—lies
about this, that and the other. I am convinced
that even her husband caught a sight of these;
indeed more than once came full upon some
outrageous specimen and then resolutely shut

his eyes and said black should be white to the
end of the chapter.   But then *he* was in love.
I remember once inadvertently telling him something she had said about an invitation 'she had
reluctantly accepted to please *him*'—whereas, as
he cried in amazement, 'she had forced *him* to
go purely to please her.'   I saw his face change,
and was afraid he would go home and explode :
not he !   It was gulped down and ignored thence-
forth and forever.   But for his sister to gulp
and ignore—I can't explain.   But it must have
been so, and I shall continue to believe that *here*
has been a swallow of a camel, where no gnats
nor blackbeetles have been 'strained at.'   My
own fancy is that the intercourse with Lady Y.
has fired Z. with a noble emulation—the interest
and mystery of the 'injured wife,' the glory of
becoming a Lady—in 24 months ; and from the
wanting this to the oldest of old ways of *getting*
this was, as Hamlet says, 'as easy as lying.'
The more I discover the perfect ease of it the
more do I feel humbled before minds so made
that to them the immense difficulty of lying
appeared an impossibility ; made to accept Z. with
her wallet of wares for an angel laden with
roses.   *I* accept her now as a familiar blotch on
a picture of the past, and I solaced myself the
other day by placing two portraits of her on

each side of a delicious drawing of a 'model' in the costume of Truth, just given to me by Leighton. I should like above most things to have a good talk with her: no hurting *me*, alas!

"Lady William more and more dear and delightful. She suffers much, but recovers soon. I am hopeful as to the result, and that she will yet walk as she can talk. I dine with her to-day: she always asks (did ask two days since) 'when I heard last from you.' Let me tell her something soon."

The Storys meanwhile were returning to Siena for this summer.

Robert Browning to the Storys and their Daughter.

"STE.-MARIE, près PORNIC, BRITTANY,
Sept. 5th, 1863.

. . . "I shall only scribble a word or two and leave myself in your hands and hearts. Here are we in the old place, just as we left it last year, and I rather like it better on acquaintance. The barrenness of the country is not a bad thing—the silence and surrounding sea all one could wish. The weather, however, is broken up and autumnal; they say here that never was so hot and unvaried a summer—we came in for the end of it. Not that I object to the blusterous winds and bursts of rain, but the bathing gets colder. I bathe duly and fancy it is particularly good for me, body and spirit. . . . Rossetti I saw just before I quitted London ; he lives after an easy fashion in a large old house at Chelsea, amid carvings and queernesses of every picturesque kind. I will certainly give him your message and remembrance on my return. . . . Now I have done with England and all in it, let me breathe Siena to the end of my five minutes. It was indeed stupid to fancy you could have been unfaithful to the old villa, but the ' Orr '-name used to be enough for me. There is something in this place that brings Siena to my mind *always*. No two places were ever more unlike, but the autumn feeling, winter cares, comparative idleness and stoppage of one's life, besides the stillness—these are here as they used to be there. . . . Oh, (Louis) Napoleon ! do we really differ so thoroughly about him after all ? No understanding comes out of talk on such questions, because one presses to the support of the weaker points—not necessarily untenable, but weak ; and the end is *these* seem the argument. But I never answer for what any man *may* do, if I try and appreciate what he *has* done ; my opinion of the solid good rendered years ago is unchanged. The subsequent deference to the clerical party in France and support of brigandage is poor work, but it surely is doing little harm to the general good. As for the party of action one sees the main chance tolerably clear from this distance : Austria is uncommonly strong just now, and if Italy attacks her without France to help she will rue it, that's too likely. . . . Well, two of my English years have slipped away. If I live (and I am particularly well) I shall have plenty of Italy yet. I bring out two volumes of new things ('Men and Women'), but under some other name to please the publisher."

To Siena still, and doubtless longingly enough, went the following; with its visible reflection, however, in spite of all longings, of the form already more or less taken by the writer's London life—a life henceforth of multiplied contacts and impressions, "social" activities.

Robert Browning to the Storys.

"LONDON, 19 WARWICK CRESCENT, UPPER WESTBOURNE TERRACE, *July* 17*th*, 1863.

. . . "This scrap shall go to beloved Siena therefore, where I am better contented to fancy you than elsewhere. I cannot remember which the Belvedere villa is—tell me exactly. . .

This has been a busy season; I have gone out constantly, but not too much of my experiences stays in my head, except a general feeling of thankfulness and wonder at people's kindness. Lady William will be your first object of interest —very dear, and exceedingly clever, as well as admirably patient under her prolonged imprisonment. I much fear the summer is slipping away and will hardly find her prepared to make the effort of leaving home. Indeed she has not yet even left the house. The general health seems sadly affected by this vile indoor life. Still one sees little of this *late* of an evening, when visitors and their contribution of news bring out the old colour and quality—and you know how pleasant *that* is. Another invalid here is no less than A. Tennyson, who is kept in bed by an ambiguous sort of rash—supposed hay-fever and irregularly-acting vaccination; the learned don't know. I saw him and found him his fine self two days ago, affectionate and simple as ever. He has poems which will be printed soon; of one, 'Enoch' (the Fisherman or Sailor) friends speak highly. Ruskin is back from Switzerland, and well: I see him now and then, with Dickens, Ristori (I sat with her twice at dinner lately) and a few others you would care to know, and plenty you may guess.

. . . I could not go to Italy this summer, but next year I *must* go if I live. I confess I never think of seeing you again satisfactorily till the end of things here, till a few years more go by —and they *do* go like a dream. That it should be already two years, all but a few days, since I left Italy! I hope to end my life in the land I love best, and, what with work and troubles of great and little degree, five or six years will pass, if I don't pass them. So one day a very aged person will come knocking, &c., as in the story books. Who lives at the old villa, ours? And at Landor's and Orr's, if you are really not there? And the people—who is there dead or just the same? tell me, won't you? Last Sunday who came here but Annunziata? she is with Lady Duff Gordon. Remember—but I must have said this before—you cannot tell me the number of flies that buzz in your window without interesting me. I believe if you made mere crosses on the paper I could read the sheet full. Landor wrote yesterday; was very well. He has been ill, dangerously so, but seems likely to bear up against his eighty-nine years."

Browning continued, it will be seen, to give his friend his best service as negotiator, proof-reader, it may almost be said editor.

Robert Browning to W. W. Story.

"ATHENÆUM, *Nov. 20th*, 1863.

. . . "But to business, for Odo Russell goes
to-morrow. I forwarded the parcel to Lansdowne
House, at once, and I hope you know as much.
I did the same by Lady Ashburton's on her
return. And now listen. Chapman formally
asked me to do what you shall hear. He said
you had agreed to reduce the two vols. of ' Roba
di Roma ' to one for handbook use ; that your
abstractions were not sufficient, accompanied as
they were by new matter, and that something
more must be done to effect your purpose as
well as his own. I at first refused decidedly,
on the ground that you had pleased yourself,
and I could not and would not cut away what
you wished to leave. I bade him send me the
proofs, however, which I engaged to correct
thoroughly. He said somebody else must
attempt it in consequence. When the first
proofs arrived I bethought me, and made up
my mind that you would be safer under my
hand than any other's. I accordingly went
through the whole book again and, with proper
tenderness, have only touched a few corroborative
passages which do not interfere with the text
and may be supposed to answer the purpose of
notes—so can be producible at any time in

another shape. There was no removing any of your own descriptions or remarks, but some of the historical notices of early times are not so immediately to the present purpose of the book and may be postponed—let us say. Thus in the paper on the Jews, while all the part relating to the mediæval and modern state of things is retained, some of the more recondite and preliminary matter is removed. Also, I much fear, the final note on the Population of Old Rome must be given up. I shall see, at the very end; but, according to the project, something must be sacrificed—the volume would otherwise be too bulky,—and I preferred, as I say, detaching what might be used separately hereafter to breaking up the pictures and discourses in the book which are in immediate request. At all events I have done my best, and certainly better—inasmuch as more liberally to my author—than the regular man-of-all-work would have done; but the task is an ungracious one, and I don't like it, though I like you to judge of it, for you will understand and forgive. To make amends, be sure that what is printed shall be flawless and perfect as care can make it. This much said, I will *go on*, the first day I can find, and write in my old way—not having time now for the many things."

This delicate business, the reducing and re-touching of " Roba di Roma," meanwhile proceeds with a discretion and a harmony that are to the honour of both parties.

Robert Browning to W. W. Story.

"19 WARWICK CRESCENT, *Jan. 8th*, 1864.

. . . " I finished *last year* correcting the book. The delay in getting it out was none of mine, depend on it ; but there is a good deal of new matter, beside corrections, and the printer would do it no quicklier. You may have got a copy by this, for aught I know. If the printers attended to my corrections all is right now. I am sure you will forgive me if anything may seem *over*corrected, in some trifling matters ; but I wanted the book to be right—not merely blameless so far as my strict share in it goes. Thus I try at uniformity in the titles *Saint*, &c. ; since we say St Augustine I say St Bernardine, not San—St Anne, not Sta. Anna, &c. Also when an English expression or word is referred to as original, if *that* is Latin I give it rather than Italian—equally a derivative—when this last would look like a blunder ; *e.g.*, ' beaks of ships (*rostri*) ' I changed to the real *rostra ;* and so on. The book reads well throughout, and nothing is lost, you will see, except the early

history of the Jews. All the statistics are in
—so good luck to it! Always, if you are
satisfied with my doings, let me have the
correcting your labours of this kind.

. . . " G. writes to me about that impossible
Bust—it can only be from his little acquaintance
with the procedures of art, especially your art.
For a painter might give a few traits in full
and leave the rest to one's fancy, but a sculptor
must make a whole somehow, and for me at
least the result would be 'the better the worse.'
To strangers an idealisation might do very well.
In the Tomb now constructing the central circle
will contain no attempt at a portrait, much as
I should desire it, but a simple 'Poetry,' with
no pretence at anything but a symbol. G.
thinks there would be help in the magnified
reproduction of the photograph made at Hâvre;
he does not remember that it is an ambrotype—
beneath, or at the back, of glass — incapable
of being reproduced, as a picture would be with
a glass over it. Even the original is not in a
state to be sent to Italy, having been cracked
across the face in its passage thither—the least
motion would divide it. I can quite believe
that G., seeing what you can do,—'Saul' and
'Sappho,'—may hope that even this might be
within your compass; but I know it will never

be, and I hate that you should even try vainly
to do anything—and that, of all things.   Understand me, dear Story!   I shall write to G.;
the first disappointment will be easier to bear
than a later one.   If you made a beautiful head
which we could not bear to look on——!   (Poor
Thackeray!   I was to have met him on Wednesday
23rd at dinner—we talked about his empty chair.
He was to dine next day, 24th, at another
friend's where I was certainly to see him, and
where I heard, on arriving, what had happened
in the morning.)   He was no worse than I ever
knew him; in higher spirits than of old; I often
met him.   He never got rid of his way of doing
himself injustice by affecting—but never mind
now.   One has forgotten all about it. . . .
Love to Mme. Du Quaire particularly.   She
writes great things of 'Sappho.'"

This next, though of a date of several months
later, may find its place conveniently here.

W. W. Story to James Russell Lowell.

"ROME, *December* 10*th*, 1864.

"MY DEAR JAMES,—I was taken ill a month
ago at Paris, and while I was lying on my bed
E. read to me your delightful book of 'Fireside
Travels,' which I was fortunate enough to pro-

cure from London.   As she read it all the old
days revived, all the old passages of love and
hope and joy which we have known together
came before me, and my heart yearned toward
you as to one of the oldest and best loved of
all my old friends.   For years our correspondence
has ceased—why I know not ; but my affection
has never wavered for a moment, and I've eagerly
sought from all who had seen you news and information about you and yours.   But as I read
your book—so genial, so rich in humour and
fancy—I seemed as it were to be again talking
with you, and I determined, as soon as I should
be well and have a half hour of unoccupied time,
to write and break this long silence, and thank
you for the kindly mention of me which is
scattered through your book, and for the dedication of it to me.   I hear that there is a sonnet
or some verses prefixed to the American edition,
but this I have not seen, as it is omitted in the
English edition.

" How I wish you were again here as in the
olden times, and that we again could wander
about the streets of the city and through the
mountain towns, or sit long evenings before the
fire late into the night and talk as we used to
do.   There is one great drawback to me in my
Roman life, and that is the want of some friend

with whom I can thoroughly sympathise and whom I can meet on the higher ranges of art and literature. For the most part, and with scarcely an exception among the American artists, art is (here) but a money-making trade, and I can have no sympathy with those who are artists merely to make their living. As for general culture there are none of our countrymen here who pretend to it, and I hunger and thirst after some one who might be to me as you were. But nobody makes good the place of old friends. We are knitted together with our youth as we never can be in our older age. . . . Has the wild love of travel gone out of your blood as it has out of mine? Are you growing respectable, solemn, professorial and dignified? I figure you to myself sometimes as sitting in the academic robes on the platform at Commencement, and cannot but smile as I see you there. Once in a while I hear your trumpet sound through the columns of the ' Atlantic ' or the ' North American,' and more rarely I read some new poem. But why are the poems so rare? Do not let the dust of the University drop too thickly upon you. Do not yoke Pegasus down into the professor's harness. You see I have not touched your hand and heard your voice for so long that I cannot do more than grope after you in the dark, wondering about you and fearing and hoping, and getting perhaps everything wrong.

"This year I thought of going to America and seeing the old places again. But I hate to travel, and the expense, added to my dislike of worry, prevented me. Besides, I was not quite well in England, and loved better to lounge on the lawn at Mount Felix than to be tossed on the restless and roaring ocean—but it is just possible that next year I may brace myself up to this terrible voyage, and then I shall see you. If I do come I hope to bring with me some statue . . . to show as token of how I have spent my thoughts and my life here. At present there is nothing of mine in America of the best that I have done, and I should like that something *should* be there containing my best—which is nothing too good. I suppose as yet that nobody is convinced that there is much in me, and I fear that they are all right. They still pat me on the head and feebly encourage me now and then.

"Edith has grown up to be a woman, and so has Mabel. How I wish they could see each other and have the friendship their mothers had! But it has been ordered otherwise. Bobo you have seen; he is now ten years old and yesterday was his birthday. But Julian you

have never seen—who is going to be an artist,
I think. I let him work out his own way. If
the love of art is real it will domineer ; if not
real it is useless to foster it. . . . We live
in the Barberini Palace and look down from
our windows over all Rome, but there is not a
person in any house so dear to us as you are."

But meanwhile, that summer, Story had received the following. The bust in question
was his portrait, in marble, of Mrs Browning—
not the least interesting feature of that collection
of relics of both poets preserved during these
latter years, in the Rezzonico Palace at Venice,
the house in which Browning died. None,
among Story's busts, has a greater appearance
of delicate truth and tender characterisation.

Robert Browning to W. W. Story.

"19 WARWICK CRESCENT, *May 3rd*, 1864.
. . . "Of the Bust—I have told you : I could
not but fear and be repugnant, for reasons as
utterly removed from any suspicion of your
power to do anything short of miraculous as
one thing well can be from another. Miss
Blagden and you both think a miracle *has*
been done, and I believe in miracles, though
I don't count upon them. I may easily be

morbid, and the Bust is not meant for *me*.
That a beautiful work would come from the
genius I always recognised is a very natural
matter. One day I shall see—waiting hopefully
meantime. . . . Let me bury these under
the hopes of occupying any *ultimo piano* in
Rome one day. What do you mean by talking
about the ending of the lease in the P. Barberini? That you would ever, in any conceivable circumstances, leave Rome? I am
not sure, however, that I might not incline
to try the south, Naples or Sicily, when the
railways overhaul Rome, as they seem likely
to do. But don't let us think of that now.
I do not call the week or whatever it may be
which I suppose I shall have to spend in Florence
a return to Italy, any more than Father Matthew
called taking the sacrament wine-drinking. I
shall send you my Poems when they appear—
on the 21st. They have been delayed thus
long to suit the requirements of Mr ——, who
made such an offer as induced me to conquer
my repugnance and let him print some of the
things before publication. When he had got
them safe he informed me that the money should
be forthcoming—in better times! Suppose I
had reversed the process, required the money
first, and then announced that when my in-

vention was better I would remit the owing
verses with five per cent interest, meanwhile
praising extremely the quality of his cheque!
But enough of him."

And I insert here, for general congruity, this
last article of an interesting docket—undated,
but belonging to the years immediately following
the writer's return to England.

Robert Browning to Mrs Story.

"CAMBO, *près* BAYONNE, BASSES PYRÉNÉES [*no date*].

.   .   .   "We had a fancy to try a new place,
Arcachon by Bordeaux, and reached it in two
days' easy journeying only to find what was
a few years ago a beautiful pine-forest turned
into a toy-town, with boulevards traced through
the sand-hills, *tirs-au-pistolet,* a casino and
other French institutions, and the whole full
to the edge of strangers.   There was nothing
to be had, though I spent a couple of days in
trying my luck.   We looked at an adjoining
old town of a different sort, La Teste (?)—
nothing to let there; so we determined to go
on to Bayonne, and did so, hoping for rest to
the foot-sole at St-Jean-de-Luz.   This is really
an exquisite little place, with a delicious sea,
and great mountains in the background; (but

with) every house taken, every *one* of not a few. Last we braved the awful Biarritz, but liked the noise and crowd of it still less than Arcachon. The prices moreover were calculated for diplomatists, ambitious senators and so on. There seemed no course open to us—pushed up at the very end of France as we were— but to lie by in some quiet place till the bathers should begin to leave St-Jean; they never stay long, in France, but come and go in a crowd. So here we are at Cambo, a village in the Pyrénées fifteen or sixteen miles from Bayonne, in repute for its mineral waters, but out of the season now, we thankfully find. The country is exceedingly beautiful, the mountains just like the Tuscan ranges, with plenty of oak and chestnut woods, and everywhere the greenest of meadows—the great characteristic of the place. The little fresh river that winds in and out of the hills and vales, the Nive, comes from Spain, which is three hours' walk off. This is the Basque country, moreover, the people talk French with difficulty, and charming girl-faces abound. There is no lack of necessaries, or even something over, and we have some fifty visitors—but after a few yards' striding one is alone to all intents and purposes.

"I went two days ago to see a famous moun-

tain-pass, *le pas de Roland*, so called because
that paladin kicked a hole in a rock, which
blocked the way, to allow Charlemagne's army
to pass. Very striking and picturesque it was,
while the meadows by the riverside were delightful. But it is strangely hot, in spite of the
greenness, though this morning there is scirocco
and approaching rain; the wind being so many
puffs from a blast-furnace. Well, our plan is to
stay here three weeks longer, till the 13th, and
then spend the rest of our holiday at St-Jean—
say three weeks, bathing assiduously to make up
for lost time. There will be room and to spare,
and we may recover our position; for the last
two years in the dear rough old Ste. Marie,
stark-naked as she was of all comfort to the
British mind, put this smug little village in unpleasant relief. I don't see the sea all day long.
On the other hand my sister, who never was so
far south, is delighted with everything, for we
have *cicale* and other unusualities. Moreover,
there is a certain temptation which we *may* be
unable to withstand—and if so, farewell to St-
Jean. We are within an easy day's journey of
Madrid, and P.'s ears prick up like unto one of
these Spanish mule's at his mates on a hilltop.
After all, one would sacrifice something for a
sight of the Titians and Velasquez. Still, I hold

for my original scheme till forced to strike my flag. Be where we may we return to Paris in the first week of October, and if you are really to be found there how good it will be you know well enough. I shall content myself with saying that nobody used to the quantities of you which I can boast to have been could bear the miserable London allowance with such a superhuman equanimity as I think you appreciate in myself, in spite of a mock reproach or two. Now in earnest I am grieved to hear that Story has been ill; I suppose that the quiet days and perfect friendliness at Mount Felix would set all wrong right. You see you need to keep trimming the family boat, which doesn't make way unless every member of the crew is in his exact place, well and merry. Why should Story work and worry and spoil everything?"

Meanwhile, during the War, Story had heard at moments, characteristically and in spite of the stress of public affairs, from the friend at home most engaged in them.

Charles Sumner to W. W. Story.

"WASHINGTON, *May 1st*, 1863.

. . . "I heard of your brilliant success through public report and various articles. It was great—just what my instinct always told me would be yours. Those two statues were victories, beautiful and noble. What next? I hear of 'Judith.' But what then? Do make in marble the record of our national regeneration, which is now at hand. Let that be your contribution.

"Already we feel most hopeful and confident. Perhaps there will be other reverses. I am not sure that Providence has given us all the chastisement needed for our case. Had we prevailed earlier we should have escaped from our sin too easily. More of expiation was required. But we shall throw it all off. Of this be sure. The Rebellion will be crushed, and Slavery too. If at any moment the way has seemed uncertain, it is so no longer. Our army is in admirable condition. But better than [an] army, at last we have a *policy*. . . . I wish I could talk with you while we sipped the white wine of Rome. It would be refreshing to have a day of art. But I am at work always. At home I look upon my few marbles and bronzes, and wish I had more; but here in Washington there is nothing; . . . But you are angry. Perhaps you will not write. Then let Emelyn. She cannot be angry. But I must hear from you. The temporal power seems to hold like Slavery. Prince Napoleon told me when he was here that he gave it six months longer. That was all. His prophecy was like some of those to which we are accustomed."

And the following is not less expressive of the man, the time, all the feelings of the hour.

Charles Sumner to W. W. Story.

"WASHINGTON, *Jan. 1st,* 1864.

. . . "Of course I watch your ascending glory. Nobody followed with intenser interest your English success; and now I am preparing for something grander; for George Russell tells me that your 'Saul' is 'the finest statue he ever saw.' Good! It made me happy and proud to hear this. When will it be in marble? And where will it go? But don't become impatient with us here. The time will come when all that you have done will be recognised. I wish it were at once. But I know something of hope deferred. . . . You will be happy to know that the fate of Slavery is settled. This will be a free country. Be its sculptor. Give us, give mankind, a work which will typify or commemorate a redeemed nation. You are the artist for this immortal achievement. . . . England will yet regret every act or word of her *semi*-alliance with Slavery. The Rebellion, you know, is nothing but *Slavery in arms.* That concession of Belligerency to *Slavery in arms* was insufferably wicked. Pardon me; I cannot help it. Longfellow's son had a ball enter under one shoulder, traverse the body and come out under the other. It was from an English rifle—typical!'"

To which this, again, may serve as a sequel.

Charles Sumner to W. W. Story.

"BOSTON, *Aug. 9th,* 1864.

"I have just returned from a week with Longfellow in your Nahant home, where I was installed in your room. The air, the breeze, the sea, were kindly. I sat on the piazza much of the time when I was not asleep. There I read, or rather *we* read, the new volume of Tennyson and enjoyed it more than air or breeze or sun. Is it not exquisite? But answer me this question. How can a country which produces such fruit, send forth such doctrines and sympathies as it shows now with regard to belligerent Slavery? Tell me. You are there and can ascertain. I have never felt the supremacy of Tennyson more than now when I feel how low down our England—dear old England—has gone. . . . Pray, try to fashion and carve the English mind into its old beauty; awaken its earlier sympathies with freedom and justice; tell Englishmen that their country has fallen into a moral insensibility different and yet kindred to that when Charles II. ruled. I cannot see it otherwise. Sad enough, but so it is. I imagine you anxious at the tidings of each packet. Have faith. This republic is a lifeboat which cannot be sunk. Grant assures the President that he shall take Richmond. He delays now to avoid effusion of blood. Sherman is a consummate commander, whose march has shown the greatest military faculties. Have faith."

This was clearly a delightful correspondent to hear from. Sumner remained to the end the same generous friend who, years before, in a letter I have not cited, had written to Story: "I marvel at your work on the law, and I wish I could go to Europe with you." His friendship embraced and comprehended, as friendship in every case should.

Charles Sumner to W. W. Story.

"BOSTON, *Oct. 8th,* 1864.

"I know not which I enjoyed most, the poem of Leonardo in 'Blackwood' or the criticism on English neutrality in the 'Daily News.' I doubt if anybody has ever lived before who could have produced those *two* things, which testify to equal eminence in jurisprudence, art and poetry. I took 'Blackwood' to the 'Transcript,' and Whipple was so inspired by the poem that he printed it, although war and politics exclude everything else now. I have asked Denis to see that the article is printed in a pamphlet here. It ought to be in England and a copy sent to M.P.'s generally. Will not Americans, and Englishmen who love peace and justice, see that this is done? You have done a patriotic service, and I am anxious that its influence should be extended. I cannot think of England without a pang. Her true course was as plain as a turnpike. Indeed she had marked it out by her previous policy for more than a generation. She should have had nothing to do with the support of belligerent Slavery. It was her *Concordat* with this monster that disturbed me. I felt that all who loved her best ought to protest and to cry out. Private relations were nothing by the side of public duty. . . . I

should not be surprised if the next Christmas
saw us very near peace and with gold at par.
The opening of the cotton-trade will tell everywhere, but nowhere more than in London.
Don't draw from America if you can help it.
Live on Europe as long as you can. But does
not Europe rejoice to support you ? I am disgusted with the delays about the statue of
Quincy. . . . Among visitors here are the
Auguste Laugels — much liked. He has held
the pen for us bravely. I wish you were minister at Rome. I have always said you ought
to be, but Seward keeps that place as a sort of
'preserve' for himself and friends. But General
King is a most amiable gentleman."

And of *this* interesting docket there are a few
final words which, though of two years later
date, I give here for their appreciative ring.
The memorial referred to in the second place
was not to become a reality till, after Story's
death, Augustus Saint-Gaudens brought to its
slow completion the monument now erected, on
the edge of Boston Common, opposite the State
House, to Colonel Robert Gould Shaw, who,
commanding the first regiment of coloured troops
raised in the North, fell in the assault on Fort
Wagner, in South Carolina. "I wish," Sumner

writes, "you might make a statue of Lincoln. He is an historic character worthy of bronze and marble. I do not give up the Shaw Statue. In my absence there was an indescribable torpor of the committee. But [illegible] says it shall be done; and I say so too. . . . I sorrow for Seward, who seems to be more than usually perverse. But he lost his head when he lost the nomination at Chicago, and has done nothing but blunder since. He never understood our war, and now does not understand how peace is to be secured."

IX.

ENGLAND AND SOCIETY.

It was, as I have mentioned, during the years immediatedly following Story's first artistic "success" in London that his English visits, friendships, familiarities of every cordial kind, most increased and multiplied, nourished as they moreover were by frequent Roman opportunities, points of contact with the English colony abroad, comings and goings of old acquaintances and "introduced" travellers. Both his reputation and his activity continued to grow, and the twelve or fifteen years from 1862 were doubtless in all sorts of ways the happiest of his life. He liked the "world," and the world also thoroughly liked him; he was not the artist to whom solitary brooding is a need or a luxury; concentration he arrived at (with the artist's usual struggle) during the fresh, the early hours of the insidious Roman day; but on the basis of that common and consecrated triumph there

were doubtless few things of more relish for him
than his easy hospitality and, as may be frankly
said, his personal success. Talk was his joy
and pleasantry his habit—to all of which the
human, the social panorama constantly, richly
ministered. Living in a large circle—for during
all the brightest years it grew and grew—he
carried about with him, in every direction, his
handsome, charming face, his high animation,
his gaiety, jocosity, mimicry, and, even more
than these things, his interest in ideas, in people,
in everything—his vivacity of question, answer,
demonstration, disputation. In England at least
he was still in time for the "good" years, the
period during which, in society, it was possible
to be yet a while longer unconscious of the emphasised rule of the mob. He may have heard
the growl of the rising tide, the roar of the
flooding waters, but it is our fancy — though
perhaps but the fond fancy *any* later generation
is apt to cherish—that if the menace was then
near enough for vigilance (which indeed, within
the circle, would have added a zest) it was not
quite near enough for alarm. We make our
landmarks, we find support in our dates, so far
at least as we are musingly retrospective, or as
we try to be finely observant ; and we thus settle
upon the dread year of the Franco-German War

as—for the chronicler with a sense of shades—
the hitherward limit of the *liveable* era, the age
that had not wholly thrown up the sponge of
Selection.   In some such pleasant world as must
have been formed by some such principle as
that, I like, in imagination, at all events, to see
our friends launched, and I only regret that in
respect to these liveliest middle years I find few
letters or journals at hand.

This is a proof, no doubt, that life itself was
more exacting; but in the absence of documentary detail Story's English summers and
autumns, which became, for some years, customary and regular, are in danger of showing mainly
as a list of persons and "places," an array of
celebrated names, country visits and other social
occasions.   He had other things to do, in these
years, than keep records; his artistic production
was constant and profuse, and there were complications enough connected with an existence
carried on partly in Rome and partly, as his
children grew older, beyond the Alps and the
Channel, in the land of preferred schools and
universities, preferred sport, preferred interest
as to many of the deeper connections.   He was
to send his two sons, in due course, to Eton
and to Oxford; he was to introduce his daughter,
with every auspicious omen, to English society;

he was to feel, for himself, the attraction of English sport and to take for several seasons a Cumberland shooting-haunt, Crosby Lodge, near Carlisle—which I come, amid the contents of my box, upon faded photographs of, yellowing mementoes that have their share of that particular sweetness, particular sadness, defying notation, that attaches to grouped families, happy clustered house-parties, seen in their *other* years, other aspects, fashions, combinations, so often seemingly impossible, against a background of ivied friendly walls, old gardens or woods. It is to this period and the immediately following that his numerous invitations to commemorate eminent Americans belong—the monuments, in especial, of Edward Everett in the public garden at Boston, the Chief-Justice Marshall for the United States Supreme Court, the Joseph Henry for the American Institute of Science, the President Quincy for Harvard University, the Colonel Prescott, to stand in the shadow of the great bleak obelisk at Bunker's Hill, the George Peabody, to sit in bronze, as we have noted, in that of the London Royal Exchange. Some of these things I have not seen in position; but of those of which this is the case the impression, I find, has fixed itself; notably that of the Boston bronze of Everett the orator, so happily conceived both as a portrait of the man and as a presentment of the speaker. Complete indeed, in this statue, is the fusion of the speaker and the man, so that it is, quite characteristically, the latter who stands there for ever, in presence of a benched and hushed posterity, throwing back his fine, cold head, raising high his practised arm, maintaining his lofty level and rounding his admirable period. No monumental portrait, as I remember this one, could characterise more closely while remaining conscious of the need to generalise nobly.

Hand in hand with this work for public uses— fertile, always, for artists, from Michael Angelo down, in frustrations of idea, in the inexorable element of compromise, in worries of every sort— went the frequent production of portrait-busts, now valued private possessions, and went also, above all, the multiplication of those studies of legendary, poetic, symbolic character, to the imposing array of which each year, for a long time, added a figure, so that they were to become, as ingenious personifications and embodied ideas, the leading note of the sculptor's talent and the supplementary affirmation of the poet's. They are dispersed to-day over many cities—the Saul and the Sardanapalus, the

Semiramis and the Judith, the Alcestis, the
Medea, the Delilah, the panting, resting
daughter of Herodias, the tenderly - brooding
Electra, the grandly tragic Jerusalem Desolate,
the so simple and striking Nemesis, watching,
under her hood, with hidden and as if fumbling
hands; London and Paris, Washington, New
York, Boston, Philadelphia have them to show
either as ornaments of ample habitations or as
gifts and bequests to open collections.   Deep
and living, in Story, was the sense of the grace
of women, at its finest; which never took on,
with him, moreover, the least hint of affectation
or of "manner," in spite of its inclining, inevitably, given his romanticism, to modern types
—in spite especially of his being so haunted with
the American, in its delicacy, that we feel how
quickly, in his studio, without other light, we
should guess the land of his birth.   I have
already mentioned how this spacious reliquary,
where everything that came from his hands
exists in repeated form, offers to-day, quite in
the image of the silent workshops of the Canovas,
Teneranis, Thorwaldsens, places of elder pilgrimage, the close record of his persistent unfolding.
It is pre-eminently the history of a worker,
of a man who, whether in felicity or in frustration, required of himself all he had to give.

He was never, meanwhile, at any time, free from the literary obsession. Restless, as I have more than once noted, was his literary, in especial his poetic, curiosity; subject to easiest provocation in fact his love of knowledge in any direction, various illustrations of which we shall presently meet. Story's passion, however, was predominantly for the poetic mystery, which he kept constantly sounding and exploring for his personal satisfaction, as might be said—while offering to the public, that is, a comparatively small quantity of the verse that he, almost uncontrollably, distilled. It was drawn from him, the total quantity, by every emotion and impression, by almost any occasion or any accident; there can have been no free hour, no aspect presented or renewed, under suggestion of which he was not thus all unpretentiously improvising. Fairly curious the case, in presence of the gathered evidence, and fairly enviable, above all, the easy play of the gift. In few poets not of the first felicity can the love of the lyric, and scarce less of the dramatic, idea so have worked, and we remain rather puzzled by the failure of the love to cover the whole precarious ground. Story's poetry is prompt and sincere, and has often the happiest moments; yet we feel it not to

move *passibus æquis* with his lively interest
in his medium. Of any such treachery, at
the same time, he would doubtless himself never
have complained. He treated his muse as a
consoler, cheerer, beguiler, and would honestly
have said, beyond question, that she had done
enough for him in letting him live with her.
To have had such a connection to cultivate had
assuredly been for him, from the first, a partial
provision for happiness.

But in making these points I brush by my
dates perhaps too fast, and I retrace the way
a moment to pick up a letter that I may not
omit.

W. W. Story to T. G. Appleton.

"MOUNT FELIX, *Oct. 1st*, 1862.

. . . "I thank you most sincerely for all the
very kind words you say about my statues.
They have had a success here far above their
merits, but it none the less has been most
grateful to me. Yes, I am really glad not to
be called an amateur any longer, and patted on
the head and patronised (in words, not in commissions) by my countrymen. . . . We have
been greatly enjoying our summer in England,
and though I find the sympathies of all Englishmen completely in favour of the South, yet I

am personally treated with the greatest kindness and courtesy, and all my arguments are listened to with consideration. I flatter myself that I have made some little impression sometimes, but it is impossible to clear up the English mind on the subject of the War. There is the greatest ignorance and the greatest prejudice. The Englishman knows no logic but that of facts, has little perception of principles, no notion of what a written constitution is, and gets into such an inextricable muddle between the Declaration of Independence and the Constitution of the United States that I at last am always obliged to give up the task of enlightening him as hopeless. But nothing can exceed their personal kindness to me, and I can never forget it. . . . I hear sometimes from Motley at Vienna. He is terribly excited about American affairs—too much so, as everybody reports. H. writes that he is more violent than a diplomatist 'doit être ou au moins paraître.' Adams I see sometimes—he is doing admirably; cool to coldness, never losing his temper, and giving back as hard blows as he gets when necessity demands. Montalembert expressed himself to me the other night as deeply sympathising with the North, and said it was amazing to him to hear the opinions expressed in England in favour of the South. Do you know Montalembert? He is most agreeable. You see I keep getting back into this question. . . . We have just returned from a series of visits in the north which were delightful. Next week we pass at Lord Lansdowne's, and afterwards go to the Ashburtons, Cranworths and Wensleydales—if we can make time. But we are anxious to get back to Rome. The Roman question is in a state of ferment, but I do not see any strong indication that Louis Napoleon means to withdraw his troops. Nothing will force him to this but a shot on the Boulevard. Russell and Julia Sturgis are the same as ever—both as handsome and as kind as they can be."

On the close of the war, during the summer of 1865, Story returned to America, with his wife, for a few weeks—for light on which brief visit I avail myself of the latter's frank and interesting communications. Our friends looked at things, on this occasion, inevitably, with a fresh eye—that is, with an eye now accustomed, in many respects, to other conditions and appearances; they became aware, as repatriated Americans of the earlier time seldom escaped doing, of a change in the value, proportion, dignity, decency, interest, whatever it might be called, of objects and aspects once agreeably, once innocently enough familiar to them. These perceived differences furnished, precisely, in general, some of its liveliest passages to the drama of repatriation. The drama, it must be added, was well advised, for the most part, not to be too publicly played, and the liveliness I speak of was perhaps the greater for finding itself not a little compressed and curtained. The echo of it here was, be it remembered, altogether confidential. The need for precautions, in the case, has, however, long since vanished, if only because of the difference, to - day, in many of the facts themselves. Any such present impression of them would, doubtless, at a hundred points, utter itself in a different voice; the fresh eye would in fact probably need, quite urgently, all its freshness.

Mrs Story to her Daughter.

"Boston, *July 24th,* 1865.

. . . "I have never yet taken a step out of doors, though I often drive with friends in the lovely environs of Boston. We went to the Commencement exercises at Cambridge, where great was our disappointment over the general shabbiness and seediness of the procession. Tell

[Mrs Russell Sturgis] that in memory of the glorified past she should never lift this veil and behold the actual fact. It is too dreary. Fancy the musty old professors dressed not in the academic robe of former days, but according to the caprice of individual New England taste, than which nothing is more eccentric. Consider the motley group upon the stage, some dressed in light tweeds, others in linen sacks, with straw hats and boots uncleaned. . . . All this in a whitewashed church, to the sound of Latin verse and classical quotations. We met many an old friend there, and it went straight to my heart to see papa walking arm-in-arm with James Lowell. But the day of days at Harvard was that of 'Commemoration,' two days later, when all the world of mutual admiration, with many an outsider, were convened to talk over the War, its heroes and victories, deciding, as it seemed to me, that the State of Massachusetts had fought all the battles and raised all the money and troops. I never heard such a crowing as there was, and though I quite agree that Massa-chusetts *has* distinguished herself beyond the rest and come out of the struggle with the fairest record, yet I can admit some virtue in the sister States, some laurels for other sons than those of Harvard. It was a charming

scene and full of interest to us. I wish you had
been with us, and as Emerson's well-remembered
tones fell upon my ear I found it hard to be
comforted for your absence. I should so much
have liked you to hear my old favourite. There
too James Lowell read a very fine poem, full of
spirit and pathos. I met so many old friends
and acquaintances that I was entirely beleaguered
by the cloud of old associations that they recalled.
My long-dead past seemed actually to live again.
Papa has not yet decided as to whether he
will make the Everett statue. If they agree to
his views about position, material, &c., I think
it probable that he will undertake it. Miss
Stebbins's statue of Horace Mann has been received by the populace very unfavourably and
is everywhere denounced. In fact, it is the very
worst thing I ever saw. We dined with the
Wilds and met there S. C. and John Field—it
savoured of the Siena days. I enclose a list of
papa's wine left from his father's cellar. If
[Russell Sturgis] would like any, let him say so
and it shall be freely his."

To all of which I may add that a single name,
in these last lines, touches the train of association and causes the shades again to hover.
John Field, of Philadelphia, of Newport, of

Washington, of London, of Paris, of twenty
places beside, John Field, the personally valued
friend of our friends and, again, of numbers of
their friends, of more people elsewhere, everywhere, than I can pretend to indicate, has already
hovered for us to the extent of a glimpse afforded
by one of Lowell's letters. He had ridden with
the latter (to whom he remained long devoted,
even through anxious Madrid days,) with Black
and Charles Eliot Norton up and down the still
primitive Sicily, and the small mild memory of
a brief hour of which he was the centre obtrudes
itself on me, here, too irresistibly either to suffer
contradiction or to need apology. The Storys
were to go, shortly after the despatch of the
above, to Newport—the Newport of the ancient
days and of more of those sweet old impressions,
long since bedimmed by change, than can, at
this time of day, be reproduced or reckoned, and
my innocent anecdote refers itself, visibly, to the
short interval before they had come. It refers
itself to a hot summer night, of that (again)
irreproducible quality of the Newport evenings
of other years,—evenings when, after closely-
peopled hours of talk, of movement, of idleness,
through which the light of blue seas, yellow
sands, pearl - grey lichened rocks, lily - sheeted
inland ponds and daily intensities and lustres of

sunset seemed breezily to play, the air was filled
with something soft and multitudinous that
might have been all at once the murmur of
stirred shrubberies, the waft, from wide, glowing
windows, of dance-music and song, the latter in
especial, the high, brilliant notes of women's art—
the general presence, above all, of clustered gossiping groups on vague verandahs, where laughter
was clear and the "note" of white dresses,
waistcoats, trousers, cool.   Of the company on the
vague verandah of *my* reminiscence no other
member remains, not one of the kindly intimates
who listened to John Field's recital of the scene
described, less indulgently, in Mrs Story's letter
—listened with interest enough, yet interest
doubtless in no case greater than that of the
youngest of the party, who sat on the steps of
the porch where the shade of evening · was
thickest, and who wanted to ask more questions
than his modesty, his juniority, allowed.   Not
yet perhaps had the sense been so sharp in him
that his seniors never asked enough, or not at
least the right ones, the particular ones *he*
desired.

The day — it must have been the previous
day, or even the one before that—had been,
in Boston and at its Cambridge suburb, of
maximum heat, and the talker, coming back

from it, acknowledged the refreshment, the benediction of Newport—all of which conveyed something of the high historic pitch, the patriotic and poetic temperature of the other scene. A wealth of eloquence and cheer had attended the Harvard celebration of the return of Peace, at which our friend had gone up to be present, but the climax had been Lowell's delivery of his noble Commemoration Ode, as to which one now sees—as to which one even then perhaps mutely, mystically made out — that a great thing that was to live had been but half-notedly born. The occasion, I daresay, might actually figure, had we time to extract the moral, as a convenient measure of the way in which great things with a future *are*, for the most part, born. The future of this one (which was heard of, naturally, with all interest) sat there unseen and unfelt with us, or very nearly ; and yet it is now the one member of the party particularly alive. That, however, is not the moral of my reminiscence — and all the less that a moral was what, in the course of the talk, especially disengaged itself. *This* element, for our reporter, had been that he had spent his day with William and Emelyn Story, whom it had been a joy to see again, and who were still wonderful (even to putting every one else present to shame) for youth and good looks. The lesson was none other, accordingly, than the dear old lesson, once more, that "Europe," bless its dear old name, was the real *fontaine de Jouvence*, the true and sovereign preserver. Such was the appearance presented by those who had been happily able to keep drinking at the spring. We had all drunk as we could, and the taste was still on our lips; only we had had, unlike the Storys, to snatch our lips away. I remember, after long years, how, in the charitable gloom, which veiled, from each of us to each, the fierce American ravage, we sighingly acknowledged our loss. I hear again the good John Field—I am conscious again of the response. "I told them how Europe had kept them—" and then the resigned unanimity of the "So *we* might have been kept—!" But there was only one of us for whom it was not perhaps already too late.

W. W. Story to his Daughter.

"NEWPORT, *Summer of* 1865.

. . . "Mrs Robert Sturgis had a little dance, and we stood round on the edges and were probably a lot in the way. I didn't see a handsome face there — all wan and worn and haggard. There was a famous Miss ——, Jewish in style, hollow-cheeked, with two drumsticks for arms, broken and sharpened off at the elbows. To her immense attention was paid, because she is very rich. All the talk here is about dollars, how much money this and that one has got, and a dreary and monotonous thing is it to hear it so constantly. The girls are excited in their style, and do not articulate half their words. . . . Mrs —— —— was by far the prettiest woman in the room, but pert as usual, and not successful in imitating J. S. I am writing while everybody is talking, and Wild has just immensely amused us by a story about Edward Everett, which I will tell you. He was going 'down east,' a short time before his death, and as usual the train was crowded and there were more people than seats. Mr Everett then kindly took on his knee a little girl and carried her thus for a considerable distance. When the child came to a station where she was to stop she rose, and her benefactor said as she was leaving him : 'Perhaps you would like to know, my little girl, who has been holding you on his knee all this time. It is the Hon. Edward Everett.' To which the little girl answered ingenuously and interrogatively : 'Salem man, sir ?'

. . . "Newport is all shingle and clapboard,

with a lot of pretentious wooden houses each
on its little acre, or half-acre, of land, and subject each to the supervision of at least one
neighbour. There is no such thing as privacy,
and nobody seems to desire it. The great thing
is to drive every day up and down the Avenue,
as it is called, which is a loose line of wooden
cottages with board ornamentation, or to bathe
from the beach or to go on Saturday evening
to the 'Ocean House' to dance. The air is
scirocco cooled off by the sea. Yesterday we
went out on a yachting party — Commodore
Stevens's yacht, *The Maria*—and had a charming sail in the bay. . . . There were two
young — girls, one-inch-one in the waist and
half-an-inch in the arms, and rather attractive
notwithstanding! In the evening, at the Ocean
House, we were greatly amused. There was a
great crowd, coming from everywhere, and
among them some very pretty persons. The
band played, and the great hall was crowded
with dancers. People came in from the cottages
—girls, old men, servants and shopkeepers mixed
together, and yet there was nothing disagreeable in the manners of any of them—all were
decorous and pleasant. I have scarcely seen a
mutilated man—there was not one last night;

and another thing that has surprised me is the entire absence of soldiers in the streets. Here and there you see an officer, but no soldiers. It is scarcely possible to believe that we have just finished a long and terrible war. Nobody thinks about it, nobody talks about it. In fact, one hears it more spoken of in one day in Europe than in a month here. Everything looks prosperous, nobody is depressed in spirits or in hope. Shoddy and petroleum have raised their heads very high, but money is not an aristocracy and cannot make one in a day. People begin to affect being poor as dividing them at once from such sources of wealth."

The above, as descriptive of Newport architecture and Newport roads, becomes, in the light of social and material revolutions, a bit of very ancient history. The first allusion in the following, it may be added, is to a "cottage" that had belonged, on the cool Massachusetts promontory,[1] to Story's parents and his childhood and youth. "Aunt Julia" is Mrs Russell Sturgis, younger than Story, and affectionately invoked in that beneficent character by his children.

[1] Nahant.

W. W. Story to his Daughter.

"BEVERLY, MASS., *July 30th*, 1865.

. . . . "Very pleasant indeed it was to see the old places and the old faces and to hear the old voices. Some of the beards—shall I say all? —were greyer; but there was the old ring of the voice. Longfellow is aged very much and wears a grey beard and long hair. He and Tom Appleton are in *our* old cottage, which is entirely unaltered in every respect; the same old papers on the walls, the same plates on the table, the same chairs and furniture, and one old tea-caddy with all our names on it, beginning with Russell Sturgis and Julia Boit, and now ending with Edith Longfellow. It was the flowery-pekoe tea-caddy, which is now, I am sorry to say, quite empty. We had Chowder at dinner, tell Aunt Julia, and it was stupendous. . . . They were all as kind as could be, and old Mrs Cary was as peaceful and full of repose as if she had never lived in America. The old hotel is but a mass of ruins, and it was mournful to see them. It was in those old walls that I first saw Aunt Julia—and I didn't call her aunt then. . . . We go driving about in a sort of toy carriages, which are so slight that I expect each moment to be smashed. The roads are outrageous and everywhere cut up with the rails of the horse-cars. These horse-cars are the pest of the country, but you must take them or walk, unless you choose to pay a fortune away in carriages. There are no such conveniences as cabs. The first day I arrived in Boston I saw framed in the inside of a horse-car an advertisement of 'Reversible Food' and one of 'Overstrung Pianos.' I had seen enough reversible food on shipboard to derive any pleasure from the idea of it; but the Over-strung Piano struck me as thoroughly American. Isn't everything here overstrung?"

If I find myself, amid the play of allusion, in the presence of names delicately spectral, divided between the desire not to pass without some grace of recognition, and the desire, on the other hand, to spare even spectral sensi-bility, in what case could I more justly hesitate than in the connection indicated (all for acknow-ledgment of kindness shown) by the second sentence of the following? Yet a word of greeting is, for us, at any moment but the lay-ing of a flower on a grave. Even had she not come a little too late for the pioneer-time Miss Weston would have been, for a precursor, already too formed, too initiated and, as it were, too decorative. She was a person to arrive, in her gentleness, when the road was made and the service organised. She was a person also to remind us that one of the main effects of such a retrospect as this is to illustrate, for our perception, on the part of the general company, some of the finest, even if strangest, possibilities of union and fusion. There positively existed, among our vanished cosmopolites, combinations of elements, practical mixtures and harmonies, that were not to have been expected. That the tone of New England "at its best" should melt into the tradition of France at *its* best and that the result should be something consistent and exquisite, was, for example, a charming surprise—the simple recall of which may serve as our salutation. And shall I offer another to Alleyne Otis, a figure, almost *the* figure, for supreme sophistication— a rudimentary shade of it—of the old Newport days? If I should hesitate here it would be for fear of going too far. Yet we owe something, always, to those who, at the time of our freshness, were revelations, for us, of type, who rendered to our development the service of fitting images to names that were otherwise but as loose labels. Newport, somehow, even for young observation, was not Thackerayan, but the figure and face, the attitude and approach

and address of Alleyne Otis unmistakably were.
He "did" nothing—he only *was:* which, in the
antediluvian America, was always a note of
character, always argued some intensity. He
persisted in survival, in idleness, in courtesy, in
gallantry, and yet, even though gallant, persisted
also, it seemed, in mystery, in independence of
apparel, above all in an imputed economy that
was his finishing mark and that indicated real
resources. Given his "social position" he was
the more Thackerayan for this eccentric thrift,
which was a touch, for the *personage*, almost
recalling Balzac or Saint-Simon, some master of
literary portraiture. Was he not, *au besoin*,
nobly impertinent, latently insolent?—which is
what *they* would infallibly have made him. I
cannot make him as well as they, but I do, as I
cast about me, what I can. The particular resources I allude to were wanting, if he lacked
them, to his perfection. But I have already gone
too far.

Mrs Story to her Daughter.

"Newport, *Aug.* 8*th*, 1865.

. . . "My heart aches for the poor Van de
Weyers—what a terrible thing! Emma Weston
has written to ask us to stay with her; they
are full of anxious sympathy for the Van de

Weyers. We arrived here last night, meeting John Field at the train. We were behind our time by one train, and so missed a bevy of friends who had gone to the terminus to meet us. The Turner Sargeants were there among others to take us home in their carriage. We find it most pleasant and charming here. James Lowell, here for the day, came to breakfast with us. He is just as loveable and cordial as ever, and as I write he sits joking and chatting with papa after the old fashion so delightful to me to hear. I feel as if I were in a dream; the past is so vividly brought before me. Tell [Mrs Russell Sturgis] that Alleyne Otis still disports himself and does the old beau."

The American visit, however, was a brief parenthesis, and the rich-coloured Roman life, interrupted only for the summer and the autumn, continued, with its happy activities and relations, to account, almost monotonously, for Story's maturer years. The general serenity of his career would give indeed small advantage to the biographer. Misfortune may be detailed or analysed, but happiness eludes us more, and Story was as happy as a man could be who was doing, on the whole, what he liked, what he loved, and of whom the gods had

shown jealousy but on the one cruel occasion
of the death of his eldest boy. As the world was
interesting to him, so likewise the world was
kind; he rejoiced in his near relationships,
which cost him no second pang. The difficulty
is, in any case, that our privilege of evocation
rather shrinks as the years float us on. The
procession of friends and guests thickens, but
there are fewer we can take by the sleeve. One
of the most valued, fortunately, is commemorated
for me, on the occasion of her death, by Mrs
Story's hand—in addition to which I find in
an old heterogeneous scrap-book the interesting
article contributed to "The Morning Post," at
the same moment, by Mrs Grote. I can well
remember that in the early years of a long
residence (that was to be) in London, a good
deal of light was thrown for me — as it has
always had to be thrown for the stranger
acquainted with other capitals—on the habit,
rooted in English society and less exceptional
now than then, of receiving in the evening
only by invitation. It was explained that in
the annals of comparatively modern London
but a single person had proved it possible to
be successfully "at home" on other than designated and published occasions. Lady William
Russell had achieved this feat, which had re-

mained, for all the world, a monument to her powers. During the later years of her life, which had begun in a distant and magnificent era, she had never, summer or winter, quitted her house, and yet had never found herself alone. The aspect thus presented was impressive to the inquirer—especially in the pleasant light of nearer approach to the circle of the wondrous lady. There are no such figures in the world (so far as it is a world of conversation) as those of the interesting women who have only to sit still to find themselves a centre of life; and the very places in which they sit, the constituted scene of the spell, seldom fail to make for the student of manners an attaching, an inspiring picture. In this case the scene, with many of its features, is still more or less to be identified. It had a dim but a rich historic background, that of a youth spent almost amid the clash of Napoleonic arms — quite, at all events, amid the glitter of ancient allied Courts, to the tune of what was to become Lady William's legend, the glory of her having, in Paris, at the Restoration, among the gathered sovereigns, been able to flirt with each potentate in his own language. The Storys had entertained, from early Roman days, a lively sympathy for her second son.

"As we had a great friend in Lord Odo, he made us acquainted with his mother as soon as she arrived in Rome, and from that moment grew up one of the most intimate and interesting friendships of our life. Lady William was full of all good things, heart and head. I learnt from her much of the philosophy of life, and her lessons are never forgotten. Full of gifts, accomplishments and knowledge, she was yet wholly without pedantry, and was extraordinarily wise about the world without being at all *of* it. Her ideas and feelings were all noble. After her carriage-accident in Rome, by which her leg was broken, I sat by her bedside during long visits, for she could even then talk and carry me back to old and wonderful days. She had been for years, abroad and in England, at Court and at home, the centre of everything that was distinguished and wise and witty. The devotion of her sons, especially of her best-beloved Odo, was perfect; Odo ministered to her wants with the tenderness of a woman, watched her and took care of her as if she had been his child. Her own care of the three, and of their education, had been beyond praise; they had been her sole companions during her widowhood; she had studied with them and for them, taught them Latin and Greek and everything she had learned or *could* learn. She was a linguist of the first order, so that when one listened to her different facilities one scarcely knew which to think the greatest. An old-fashioned disciplinarian as to manners and customs, she (while their intimate and best friend) exacted from her boys the utmost consideration and deference; often, when they were young, keeping them standing in her presence and sometimes obliging them to have their hats off even when driving with her. By whatever means employed, she had absolutely gained their confidence and devotion; it was a relation unlike any I have seen in other sons. Often, at this time, when I left her bedside, I walked back to Palazzo B. with the Duke of Sermoneta, who was then at the height of his cleverness and brilliancy, a particularly witty talker. We were thus brought so much together and so associated with Lady William that, long after, when he married again, he brought me all the letters she had ever written him (a large collection) and formally gave them to me to be kept with mine, suggesting for them a motto from Virgil.

"When at last she was well enough to make the journey we left Rome together for England, and she was carried all the long way in her

own carriage, which, with her devoted maid and
Odo in constant attendance, was placed on the
railway - trains and the deck of the steamer.
Lord Loughborough joined us on the way, and
our party became a large one (the latter reading us his verses when, at night, we couldn't
sleep!), but we all saw her from time to time.
She bore the journey extraordinarily, and we
were together in Paris for some days; then
we preceded her to London and saw her again,
a little later, in Audley Square. We found,
at this time, that, thinking, as she had already
often done, of what she could do for us, she
had written to various friends asking them to be
good to us. Thus, without delivering a single
letter of introduction, we found ourselves warmly
welcomed by her family and hosts of her friends.
It was to her original kindness that we owed
what was most pleasant, from the first, in our
London periods, and I remember how, late every
evening, when the full day was over, I went
to open the budget of our impressions to her,
and found her always amused and interested
and sympathetic. Her own comments and
judgments, her remarks on people and things
she knew so much better than I, were immensely
to the point and often the most trenchant imaginable. When I made a new and apparently

agreeable acquaintance I went to her for light
and information as to character and antecedents,
and never found her the least at a loss. She
knew about everything and every one, circumstances, history, family, root and branch. Her
faithful German maid, Mati, librarian, companion
almost, and housekeeper in one, was a feature of
much interest in the household and was treated
with great affection. To her Lady William
would apply for a book, old or new, and no
matter in what tongue, and it always appeared
without delay. A certain, a very considerable,
number of cats of low degree were given harbour
as the pets of Mati, and, though they were by no
means pets of her mistress, it would never have
done for even the dearest friend to speak of
them to Lady William as objectionable. If,
however, she could bear the cats to please
her maid, she couldn't bear bores to please any
one, and, constantly repeating that life was too
short for them, declined to receive them on any
terms. Her doorkeepers had been taught very
carefully to sift for her, and mistakes in this
respect were very seldom made.

"She had more than once spoken to me of her
having lately embraced the Catholic faith. Her
earliest religious impressions had come to her
at Vienna, where her father was English Am-

bassador. She was left almost entirely to the guidance of a French governess, who, as a strong Catholic, carried her at the most impressionable age to the ceremonies of that Church, which produced a deep effect on her young mind. The impressions then received revived in after years and sustained and consoled her under the stress of sorrow and illness. She was at the same time never narrow or violent in her faith, and when once Mrs H., in her presence, began to use arguments to convert *me*, Lady William reproved her and said 'Don't meddle with her beliefs; they are what she needs — probably better than any you can supply.' Again, at a time when she was really ill, and I was with her, and a Monsignore was announced, she wrote on a slip of her queer paper and handed it to me: 'Tell them not to let him come in. I will *not* see him.' No such 'good' Catholic could have been, in short, more easy — which converts so rarely are; and she was buried not in Catholic ground, but at Chenies with her husband's folk."

We wander here still among shades — not the less, I feel, at a moment when the late Louisa Lady Ashburton, one of the most eminent of the friends from early years, joins the company. This so striking and interesting personage, a rich, generous presence that, wherever encountered, seemed always to fill the foreground with colour, with picture, with fine mellow sound and, on the part of every one else, with a kind of traditional charmed, amused patience — this brilliant and fitful apparition was a familiar *figure* for our friends, as, throughout, for the society of her time, and I come, in my blurred record, frequently upon her name. The difficulty is really that she is one of those vivid, represented characters, one of those stamped and finished appearances that tempt the historian (especially if he have memory and imagination always at his heels) only too much and challenge him too far. There are figures we may pass with a look and touch with a finger, feeling any recognition kind and almost any adequate. But there are others whom to pass at all is, as it were, to pass *before* them—on the stairs or out of the room ; so that we wait on them a little and hover, and while we thus wait find ourselves again in relation with them ; than which any more summary process would be, we seem aware, both a breach of manners and a loss of opportunity. It easily happens, however, that the "relation," the old impression, the cluster of reminiscence, would take too much explaining, or require perhaps even too much

profaning; so that we find ourselves wishing we
only had, so to speak, a free hand and a clean
slate altogether, the really right conditions for
transposing and reproducing. All of which
simply means, I think, that the prose-painter
of life, character, manners, licensed to render
his experience in his own terms, might do
more justice to such a subject than the mere
enumerator, to whom liberties, as they are
called, are forbidden. What matters indeed,
what results from faded notes, I hasten to add,
is that Lady Ashburton *was*, admirably, delightfully, a subject—for irresistible consideration, for,
positively, a sort of glow of remembrance, the
glow from which artistic projection sometimes
eventually springs. This friendly light rests
on occasions, incidents, accidents, in which a
liberal oddity, a genial incoherence, an *expected*
half funny, half happy turn of the affair, for
the most part, appears to declare itself as the
leading note. I come across too brief a mention,
in particular, of a baffled visit to Loch Luichart
in August, 1869—baffled, for the little party
consisting of our friends, their daughter and
Browning, because the lady of the Lake was
far from home at the date of the appointment,
and her guests made merry, for the time, instead,
at a little inn, then described as " squalid," on

Loch Achnault, near Garve, with assistance from picnics (of the four) in the neighbouring heather, where, the rough meal not unsuccessfully enjoyed, Browning loudly read out "Rob Roy." Many persons will remember how freely it belonged to what I have called the fine presence (if presence be here the word) of the absent hostess of such occasions that the occasions themselves always somehow, before it was too late, recovered their feet, their breath, or whatever it might best be, and wound up in felicity. The episode of August, 1869, was, at any rate, it appeared, no exception to the rule; the delayed visit took place, with compensations abounding, with, in fact, for the consciousness of the present chronicler, more interesting passages of personal history than may here be touched upon.

I move here, indeed, between discretions and disappearances, in a somewhat dim backward labyrinth, where names and places are mainly the clue, though where, also, vague, small, pleasant lights, as in some old-time pleached walk, break in through the dusk. At the Grange, with the same incalculable friend, the Storys seem to have been, more or less repeatedly, from the first, in interesting company, and if names without faces—that is, without the provided peg to hang them to—were not, at the

best, but a meagre array, I might be content
simply to enumerate. It is something of a peg
possibly that in the autumn of 1862, which must
have been the first occasion at the Grange, our
friends listened to an interchange between Carlyle, the then Bishop of Oxford (Wilberforce)
and (odder collocation still) General Sir William
Gomme; an echo of which has remained with
the youngest of the party. She remembers
Carlyle's discussing with the Bishop, after dinner,
the merits of a good conscience, a discussion interrupted by the return of the party to the
dining-room, where, amid the still-lingering fumes
of the rich repast, the Bishop read the evening
prayers and then addressed the party, including
the clustered domestics, an army, who had been
busy clearing the board, on the virtue of self-
sacrifice. It appears to have been at some hour
of this sojourn that Carlyle, in an image that
was to reverberate, described the American Civil
War, then raging, as the burning-out of the
smokiest chimney of the century. It was at all
events perhaps after their restoration to the
drawing-room that he took up again the other
matter. "Good conscience, my Lord Bishop—
what was ever the use of such a thing to any
man? Take two of the best men that ever lived
—what good did his good conscience ever do to

Oliver Cromwell or to St Paul?" And then on the Bishop's protesting against his speaking of these celebrities in the same breath : "Well then, confine it, if ye will, to St Paul. With *his* good conscience he was the most meeserable of men." Which is doubtless indeed a sufficiently pale gleam, even when I find it noted that a visit to Bowood had more or less immediately preceded this occasion. Visits to Naworth and to Ashridge were also, I gather, not a little in order in these years — the friendliest relation having, in one of those connections (and to name only the dead), established itself with Lady Marian Alford. "At Naworth"—I find the note in reference to a sequel to the episode, just related, of Loch Luichart—"Browning read aloud to us parts of 'The Ring and the Book.'" Taking scraps, further, as they come, in reference to this general period, I light upon a memorandum of Mrs Story's on her husband's acquaintance, and her own, with the first Lord Houghton, which, though that so distinguished and so amiable man has not wanted for commemoration, I reproduce, in part, from an equal impulse of sympathy. To what commemoration of him may not another friendly, another grateful, another highly vivid memory feel prompted to allow all its advantage?

"We first knew R. M. Milnes in London," Mrs Story writes, "before his marriage, and I remember our breakfasting with him, the first time, in company with Mrs Norton and Stirling of Keir. He was wonderfully kind to us, and we owed him many of our pleasantest acquaintances. After his marriage we continued to breakfast, for these occasions, thanks to his gentle and amiable wife, were still more attractive. Later on they became, I think, a little less 'select,' and even had sometimes, with the incongruous people, rather a Bohemian cast. Sir William Stirling used to call him the Bird of Paradox. I often met him at Lady William Russell's—who didn't, however, perhaps, do him full justice; and I recall one memorable night when he discussed with Abraham Hayward, with great warmth and far into the small hours, the question of the birth and extraction of Mary Fox, Lady Holland's adopted daughter. We never went to Fryston till 1884, though we had promised it ten years earlier. Then, at last, he was out of health and out of spirits, and, though full of kindness, it was not as of old. He came to Rome in 1885, and he at this time asked to sit to W. for his bust. At the sittings in the studio I made a point of being present that he might be diverted and content not to go to sleep while W. worked — as sitters not always are. At times he was in excellent 'form,' most amusing, and very anecdotic; but he had also his silences, and then his slumber was deep. He reminded us of Landor by his going back with such vividness, as people of his age almost always do, to his far past life, his caring to talk almost only of what he had seen and done in youth.   Landor he had known and talked of frankly and freely; and, like Landor himself, of Lord Byron, Lady Blessington, Louis Napoleon and others.   The bust seemed a surprising success, considering his deficiencies as a sitter, and he said of it, with a laugh, when it was finished, 'It looks, I think, the Poet and the Peer.'   He came to breakfast one morning, with Lady Galway, to meet Bishop Whipple of Minnesota, and he afterwards amiably said that this had been the thing in Rome that had given him the greatest pleasure—which we thought a great tribute to the excellent company of the Bishop. Lord Houghton would go anywhere, to the last, in spite of infirmity and fatigue, to see any one or anything that might amuse him, no matter who or what or where they were. He was truly brave in this pursuit."

It is perhaps early to take up some of these later of the old names, yet memory protests a

little against letting them quite go. And moreover if the London of Abraham Hayward is
divided by but twenty years from the London
of our new century, it seems really to look
on at us from a greater antiquity. It was considerably more than twenty years ago that,
dining out during the phase, as it now appears
to me, of initiation and wonder, I received a
hint of the stamp that the time and place
were indeed assumed to have taken from the
distinguished talker just named. I had begun
by addressing myself to the lady on my left,
who, however, gently enough, though with a
certain anxiety, checked me. "Don't you think
we ought to listen, rather, to what Mr Hayward
is saying?"—she evidently had her opportunity
on her conscience. My own was, accordingly,
at that moment revealed to me, and I never
failed, afterwards, with the renewal of my
privilege, to listen. There links itself with this
recollection—they may make a pair—that of
an ancient gentleman—an ancient gentleman
full of type, full of a tone that was dying out—
who lived in a street, out of Piccadilly, in which
the houses overlooked an amplitude of preserved
space, and who entertained at a round table of
noble dimensions. At this table, I learned from
my host, one might precisely not hope *ever* to

"listen to Mr Hayward"—and for reasons that were, in the warning, sufficiently emphasised. I may not emphasise them here—and all the less, doubtless, as they appear to have been somewhat special to my friend, who was decidedly "quaint" and who afterwards suffered some cerebral disturbance. I was still able for a year or two to listen often enough for the lesson that practically resulted—the lesson that the talk easily recognised in London as the best is the delivery and establishment of the greatest possible number of *facts*, or in other words the unwinding, with or without comment or qualification, of the longest possible chain of "stories." One associated Mr Hayward and his recurrent, supereminent laugh thus with the story, and virtually, I noted, with the story alone—taking that product no doubt also, when needful, in the larger sense of the remarkable recorded or disputed contemporary or recent event, cases as to which the speaker was in possession of the "rights." What at all events remained with one was a contribution, of a kind, to the general sense that facts, facts, and again facts, were still the thing dearest to the English mind even in its hours of ease. I indeed remember wondering if there were not to be revealed to me, as for the promotion of these hours, some other school of talk, in which some breath of the mind itself, some play of paradox, irony, thought, imagination, some wandering wind of fancy, some draught, in short, of the *idea*, might not be felt as circulating between the seated solidities, for the general lightening of the mass. This would have been a school handling the fact rather as the point of departure than as the point of arrival, the horse-block for mounting the winged steed of talk rather than as the stable for constantly riding him back to. The "story," in fine, in this other order—and surely so more worthy of the name—would have been the intellectual reaction from the circumstance presented, an exhibition interesting, amusing, vivid, dramatic, in proportion to the agility, or to the sincerity, of the intellect engaged. But this alternative inquiry, I may conclude, I am still conducting.

Aids of the causal sort I have just gathered from Mrs Story project, at all events, but faint shadows over the field of the pleasant Roman years, the happiest time of production, the fullest also of surrender (in hospitality, in curiosity, in free response) to the sovereign spirit of the place. The spirit of the place is what most comes back, in respect to any occasion, for the fond invoker of memories still denounceable as

at their best too meagre; since it is only as
holding fast *that* key to all impressions, heterogeneous or other, that one may keep them
either together or apart. Was it not, in old
days, the special solvent of *all* appearances, *all*
encounters, the element into which they simply
melted, so that it mattered comparatively little
who or what they individually were—mattering,
as it did, so very much more, for the mind,
that they were part of the general experience
of Rome? This experience was in itself so
constant and penetrating that almost nobody
one might meet, almost nothing one might see,
could aspire to any higher dignity than that
of a note struck, just sensibly sounded, but
made quite humble and relative, for the effect of
the symphony. The symphony was a majestic
whole, with which the individual would have
been ill-advised to take a liberty, so that the
greatest celebrities became thus nothing more
than placed and waiting fiddles in the mighty
orchestra, receiving their cue, as one took one's
own explicit order, the sharp rap or recall, from
the controlling influence that kept us all in
tune. The spirit of the place figured, in fact,
the master-conductor of a great harmonious
band in which differences were disallowed, so
near did one performer come to being as im-

portant—in other words as insignificant—as
any other. That certainly was the great charm
and the great ease—that no one, really, could
be a bore about Rome, or even, to any purpose,
under its cover, about anything else. For
nothing practically *existed* but that our conditions met every want, and that we were
absolutely in the spirit of them even in trying
to name those they failed to supply. This effect
was wholly peculiar—an action on the mind,
the temper, the life, on speech, manners, intercourse, with which that of no other place could
for a moment compete. People might elsewhere
be stupid, might elsewhere be vulgar or cross
or ugly, for the ways of offence are many;
whereas here you cared so little whether they
were or not that it was virtually as good as
not knowing. They were not, in fact; nobody
was any of these things, for the simple reason
that nobody could afford, for very shame, to
deny the harmonising charm. The truth is
even, no doubt, that nobody could grossly dare
any such profanity and expect still to live.
Something would have happened—something
that never did happen, thanks to our cheerful
humility and exalted equality. I remember that
in days, or rather on evenings, that now seem
to me exquisitely dim, I met Matthew Arnold,

for the first time, at Palazzo Barberini, and
became conscious then and there—more so at
least than I had been before—of the interesting
truth I attempt to utter. He had been, in prose
and verse, the idol of my previous years, and
nothing could have seemed in advance less
doubtful than that to encounter him face to
face, and under an influence so noble, would
have made one fairly stagger with a sense of
privilege. What actually happened, however,
was that the sense of privilege found itself
positively postponed; when I met him again,
later on, in London, *then* it had free play. It
was, on the Roman evening, as if, for all the
world, we were *equally* great and happy, or
still more, perhaps, equally nothing and nobody;
we were related only to the enclosing fact of
Rome, before which every one, it was easy to
feel, bore himself with the same good manners.

They then, as it were, the good manners, became the form in which the noble influence was
best recognised, so that you could fairly trace
it from occasion to occasion, from one consenting
victim to another. The victims may very well
not have been themselves always conscious, but
the conscious individual had them all, atten-
tively, imaginatively, at his mercy — drawing
precisely from that fact a support in his own

submission. He had the rare chance of seeing people kept in order, kept in position before the spectacle, so as to be themselves peculiarly accessible to observation. This faculty had, of course, in the nature of the case, to feed more on their essence and their type than, as it might have done elsewhere, on their extravagance and their overflow; but at least they couldn't elude, impose or deceive, as is always easy in London, Paris or New York, cities in which the spirit of the place has long since (certainly as an insidious spell) lost any advantage it may ever have practised over the spirit of the person. So, at any rate, fanciful as my plea may appear, I recover the old sense—brave even the imputation of making a mere Rome of words, talking of a Rome of my own which was no Rome of reality. That comes up as exactly the point—that no Rome of reality was concerned in our experience, that the whole thing was a rare state of the imagination, dosed and drugged, as I have already indicated, by the effectual Borgia cup, for the taste of which the simplest as well as the subtlest had a palate. Nothing, verily, used to strike us more than that people of whom, as we said, we wouldn't have expected it, people who had never before shown knowledge, taste or sensibility, had here quite knocked

under.   They haunted Vatican halls and Pala-
tine gardens; they were detached and pensive
on the Pincian; they were silent in strange
places; the habit of St Peter's they clung to
as to a vice; the impression of the Campagna
they stopped short in attempting to utter.   And
just as the lowly were brought up, so the mighty
were brought down, there being no tribute to
the matters in question that was not of the
nature of sensibility.   Such is the pleasant light
with which I see the Barberini drawing-room
suffused.   It was not that there were not during the same years other interiors on which the
benediction also rested; each interior—that was
the secret—had its share of the felicity, very
much as places of reunion to-day have their
share of the electric light.   It was virtually
"turned on," for instance, during the late hours,
that every one *had*, all day, to have been breathing golden air, and that the golden air was ex-
haled again by the simple fact of any presence.
I see, as in a picture, remembered figures sit
content or move about in it; I see, fairly, where
it prevails, a sweetness in any combination of
couples or groups.   I listen to the rich voices
of young women at the piano and find them all
charged with the quality of the day.   For there
had always *been* a day—a day that, moreover,

was never so much of one as when (which was often) there was, for its expectation, to be also an evening. These sequences, these presciences certainly exist by Thames and Seine and Hudson, but quite, as they become familiar, without making us thrill at their touch. Their touch (since we discriminate) is coarse; it was only the Roman touch that was fine—which is the simple moral of my remarks.

LAST ROMAN YEARS

X.

GRAFFITI D'ITALIA.

WE have seen that Charles Sumner wrote to Story in 1864 that he had been reading at once his "Leonardo," in "Blackwood," and his letters on the American Question in the "Daily News," and that he knew no other man who could have shown equal talent in such different styles of composition. The compliment may surely stand, for it was of a sort that, in various ways, Story never ceased to deserve. In turning over his pages and his papers I am even almost prompted, I confess, to commiserate his flexibility of attention. He was of course not so curst as not to have preferences of mind—having in abundance preferences of feeling; yet he almost grazed such a fate, and his success may perhaps be expressed by saying that he had not (either for his own perfect comfort or for that of his reader) enough indifferences. One might have been inclined to wish him the comparative rest of an exclusive passion. Singularity, intensity of genius makes for repose, at its hours, scarcely less than it makes for agitation, and it is a question if we are really happiest when our powers keep such easy pace with our interests. Story was never conscious, when he was interested, of a lack of power—which is a state of mind to make interest a doubtful anodyne. There are eagernesses that genius of the exclusive order drops or recovers from. But he disliked at any time to drop anything, and that was, in a manner, a qualification of his heat. I have already spoken of his poetic spontaneity, the constitution of which might become for us, were we to surrender ourselves to criticism, a riddle worth the guessing. I speak of riddles because we feel in the presence of something that requires an explanation. How could he be, our friend, we sometimes find ourselves wondering, so restlessly, so sincerely æsthetic, and yet, constitutionally, so little insistent? We mean by insistence, in an artist, the act of throwing the whole weight of the mind, and of gathering it at the particular point (when the particular point is worth it) in order to do so. This, on the part of most artists—or at least on the part of those who are single in spirit —is an instinct and a necessity, becomes in fact

the principal sign we know them by. They feel
unsafe, uncertain, exposed, unless the spirit, such
as it is, be, at the point in question, "all there."
Story's rather odd case, if I may call it so, was
that when he wrote, prose or verse, he was
"there" only in part—not, we infer, as completely, as anxiously, as he might have been.
And this in spite of a great and genuine love;
it was not at all as if prose and verse had been
for him perfunctory cares. It was impossible to
be more interested in the things of the mind
and in the forms and combinations into which
they overflow. The question of expression and
style haunted him; the question of representation by words was ever as present to him as
that of representation by marble or by bronze.
Once in a while these ideas move him in the
same direction with equal force; he produced,
for instance, two Cleopatras, and it is difficult
to say that the versified, the best of his shorter
poems, is not as "good" as the so interesting
statue with which it competes. The weight of
the mind, taking the different occasions, threw
itself wholly, we feel, into each; so that the
image is about as living in the one case as in
the other. Here, rather by exception, Story
arrived at literary intensity—making his verses
insist, as I have called it, just as he had, quite

admirably, been able to make the execution of his figure.

"Ah, me! this lifeless nature
    Oppresses my heart and brain!
Oh, for a storm and thunder—
    For lightning and wild fierce rain!
Fling down that lute—I hate it!
    Take rather his buckler and sword,
And crash them and clash them together
    Till this sleeping world is stirred.
Hark to my Indian beauty—
    My cockatoo creamy white,
With roses under his feathers—
    That flashes across the light!
Look, listen, as backward and forward
    To his hoop of gold he clings,
How he trembles with crest uplifted,
    And shrieks as he madly swings!
Oh, cockatoo, shriek for Antony!
    Cry 'Come, my love, come home!'
Shriek 'Antony, Antony, Antony!'
    Till he hears you even in Rome.

.   .   .   .

I will lie and dream of the past time,
    Aeons of thought away,
And through the jungle of memory
    Loosen my fancy to play;
When, a smooth and velvety tiger,
    Ribbed with yellow and black,
Supple and cushion-footed,

.   .   .   .

I wandered my mate to greet.
    Come to my arms, my hero,
The shadows of twilight grow,
    And the tiger's ancient fierceness
In my veins begins to flow.

> Come not cringing to sue me!
> Take me with triumph and power,
> As a warrior storms a fortress!
> I will not shrink or cower.
> Come, as you came in the desert,
> Ere we were women and men,
> When the tiger passions were in us,
> And love as you loved me then!"

"Giannone," in "Graffiti d'Italia," is another
charming thing that has *come*, by its own force,
or that has, in other words, held the author
hard enough to make him, in turn, squeeze out
of his subject all it had to give, at the same
time that the hand displayed is certainly a light
hand, not concerned sternly to press. What
happens here is that the poet really gives himself to the charm of his vision, so that there
is no reserve: the pleasant image of the idle
and hapless young Roman of the Pio Nono, of
the Antonelli time stands before us with intensity, catching the light at every inch of
his surface. The subject indeed really is the
modern Roman temperament itself—as exhibited
in youth; a little excised square of the Roman
social picture. Nothing of Story's has more of
the felicity (as also of the moral reaction) of
his earlier experience.

> " 'Tis years, as you know, that I've lived in Rome,
> Till now it's familiar to me as home;

And 'tis years ago I knew Giannone,
A capital fellow, with great black eyes,
And a pleasant smile of frank surprise,
And as gentle a pace as a lady's pony,
Ready to follow wherever you bid;
His oaths were 'Per Bacco!' and 'Dio Mio!'
And 'Guardi!' he cried to whatever you said;
But though not overfreighted with esprit or *brio*,
His heart was better by far than his head.
His education was rather scanty;
But what on earth could he have done
With an education, having one,
Unless he chose for the scarlet to run,
And study the Fathers and lives of the Santi?
Nevertheless I know he had read,
Because he quoted them, Tasso and Dante;
And so often he recommended the prosy
'Promessi Sposi,' I must suppose he
Had also achieved that tale of Manzoni.
And besides Monte Cristo and Uncle Tom,
And the history of Italy and Rome
(For he thoroughly knew how liberty's foot
Had been pinched and maimed and lamed in her boot),
He had studied with zeal the book of the mass
And *libretti* of all the operas.

.   .   .   .

A 'guardia nobile' was Giannone,
By which he earned sufficient money
For his gloves, shirt-buttons, boots and hat,
Though it was scarcely enough for that.
And splendid he was on a gala day,
With his jingling sword and scarlet coat,
And his long jack-boots and helmet gay,
When along the streets he used to trot;
And great good luck it was to meet
Giannone when you wanted a seat

To hear the chant of the Miserere,
Or to get on the balcony high and airy,
To see the papal procession go
Over St Peter's pavement below,
Streaming along in its gorgeous show.
And then at Carnival such bouquets,
Such beautiful bonbons and princely ways,
Such elegant wavings of hat and hand,
Such smiles as no one could withstand,
Such compliments as made ours seem
Like pale skim-milk to his rich cream."

The end of this sketch of Roman manners in
the unreformed day—a picture half humorous,
half tender and all vivid—is that the ingenuous
young man suffers himself to be entrapped by a
governmental spy, who is not less neatly presented, and who extracts from him, in his cups,
the secret of that little locked-up spark of
liberalism which could glow even in the heart of
a feather-headed dandy : whereby fate abruptly
invests poor Giannone with a quite mismatched
tragic dignity, and the shadow of the Inquisition,
or of some other salutary discipline, like a wheel
breaking a butterfly, passes over him so straight
that he is reduced to the unknowable. He becomes interesting by being missed. These, at
any rate, are a couple of the many-coloured
flowers of "Graffiti d'Italia," which volume contains Story's most substantial poetic work. The
sixty pieces or so of which it consists, and of

which the fine "Ginevra da Siena" is the most
sustained and most important, had appeared
from time to time, during some ten years, in
"Blackwood," and this collection was in 1875
in its second edition. I have before me the
whole of the author's copious correspondence
with Mr John and Mr William Blackwood,
than which nothing could more sufficiently show
that Story abounded, whether for verse or for
prose, in literary ideas. Not all of these, indeed
but a small portion of them, did he find occasion
to carry out; living, as he did, in the pleasantest
place in the world, it was his fate, inevitably, to
be interrupted and scattered, to expend himself
for results of which, when time had sifted them,
little remained but the appearance of his having
been happy. But there was at the same time
almost nothing he did not like to think of himself as doing, not dream of being able to do if
this or that condition had been present. The
conditions, the present and the absent, come
back, no doubt, as we look at his life—which is
called, we are well aware, being wise after the
fact. It becomes interesting, in the light of so
distinct an example, to extract from the case—
the case of the permanent absentee or exile—
the general lesson that may seem to us latent
in it. This moral seems to be that somehow,

in the long-run, Story *paid*—paid for having
sought his development even among the circumstances that at the time of his choice appeared
not alone the only propitious, but the only
possible.   It was as if the circumstances on
which, to do this, he had turned his back, had
found an indirect way to be avenged for the
discrimination.   Inevitably, indeed, we are not
able to say what a lifetime of Boston would
have made, in him, or would have marred; we
can only be sure we should in that case have
had to deal with quite a different group of results.   The form in which the other possibility
perhaps presents itself is that of our feeling that,
though he might have been less of a sculptor
"at home," he might have been more of a poet.

Speculations as to what might have been are
ever, I know, almost as futile as they are fascinating; but as alternative visions in respect
to the American absentee in general I confess
to finding that even at the worst their fascination justifies them.   When I say "at the
worst" I allude to those existences, numerous
enough, that, in alien air, far from their native
soil, have found themselves (sometimes quite
unconsciously, but sometimes sorely suspecting)
the prey of mere beguilement.   That really rises
before us as the formula of Story's Roman years,

making us—unless we yield, in the view, too
much to wanton fancy—figure his career as a
sort of beautiful sacrifice to a noble mistake. I
cannot, in truth, otherwise describe the mistake
than as that of the frank consent to be beguiled.
It is for all the world as if there were always,
for however earnest a man, some seed of danger
in consciously planning for happiness, and a seed
quite capable of sprouting even when the plan
has succeeded. To have said "No—I give up
everything else for a lifetime of the golden air;
the golden air is *the* thing, no matter what
others may be, and to have had it, all there
is of it, that alone, for me, won't have been
failure": to have expressed one's self in that
sense, which was practically what Story did,
was to make one's bid for felicity about as
straight as possible. For, simply enough, it is
of the old-time victim of Italy, and not of any
more colourless fugitive from the Philistines, that
I am thinking. His conception of the agreeable
as of something constant, crude, immediate was
doubtless the conception most involving an ultimate penalty. And so, accordingly, does our
critical imagination play. The experience he had
invoked, the experience he achieved, suggested
to our friend a variety of subjects that might
not otherwise have come in his way. That is

much, for any poet—so much that it may be
asked what more there need have been. Only
one thing more, in truth; to which I attach
myself as to a tangible thread in this possibly
too vague speculation. If the verse and the
prose might, in other conditions, as I have
hinted, have more completely filled out their
scheme, the reason would seem to be not in any
question of the encounter of other subjects, but
in something deeper still—say, taking subjects
for granted, in the *relation* of the writer to any
of these and to all. The golden air, we tend
to infer, did not make that relation quite intense, quite responsible; partly, no doubt, by
taking it too much as a matter of course. Subjects float by, in Italy, as the fish in the sea
may be supposed to float by a merman, who
doubtless puts out a hand from time to time to
grasp, for curiosity, some particularly iridescent
specimen. But he has conceivably not the
proper detachment for full appreciation. And
I come round by the aid of this analogy to the
truth I have been feeling my way to.

This truth—to make the matter comfortably
clear—is that the " picturesque " subject, for
literary art, has by no means all its advantage
in the picturesque country; yields its full taste,
gives out *all* its inspiration, in other words, in

some air unfriendly to the element at large. I
seem, for instance, to see Story gouge out
"Ginevra da Siena" from the block of his idea
with a finer rage in — let me tell the whole
truth—Boston by the Charles, or even in London
by the Thames, than in Rome, in Florence, or,
most of all, in the shuttered noon of the Sienese
day itself. In London, in Boston, he would have
had to live with his conception, there being
nothing else about him of the same colour or
quality. In Rome, Florence, Siena, there was
too much—too much, that is, for a man for
whom, otherwise dedicated, it had not been in
question to become a second Gregorovius. Was
it not this "too much" therefore that, given the
nature of Story's mind and that disposition in
it to flit rather than to rest for which I have
almost commiserated it — was it not this too
much that constituted precisely, and most characteristically and gracefully, the amusement of
the wanton Italy at the expense of her victim?
It may easily be said of course that such penalties should be smoothly faced, and my contention, I know,—for all it is worth,—is apparently
refuted on the spot by the history of Robert
Browning and *his* inspiration, suggestive as
they both are of a quite opposed moral. Italy,
obviously, was never too much for the author

of "Men and Women." He wrote "The Ring and the Book" indeed after he had come away, just as he had written most of his finest earlier things before he had migrated. As to "Men and Women," however, produced on the spot and face to face with the sources of his inspiration, his ten years of Florence and Rome may claim a full participation. There is nothing therefore to say in that connection but that the writer's "relation to his subject," which I have so freely made the golden air responsible for undermining, was, in Browning, constitutionally stout and single. That weight of the whole mind which we have also speculatively invoked was a pressure that he easily enough, at any point, that he in fact almost extravagantly, brought to bear. And then he was neither divided nor dispersed. He was devoted to no other art. This quite irrespectively of the question of his inherent power.

Story had been introduced to the Blackwoods by Colonel Hamley—in later years General Sir Edward Bruce Hamley — an intimate friend of his hosts of Mount Felix, where they must have met at an early date. The author of "Lady Lee's Widowhood" was, in respect of Maga, an excellent introducer, whose good office was, later on, to renew itself, happily for all concerned,

on behalf of another, one of the youngest, of
his Mount Felix associates. I may add that
his name meets me, as it comes up, with that
imputed recognition to which we have responded
for every figure in our dim procession, he too
being, in his degree, one of the friendly, the less
ghostly, shades. It was given me to know him
in years subsequent to the dates just indicated,
and I recognise to-day a small passage of history
—the history of a sentiment and its accepted
catastrophe, or at least conversion — in those
pleasant relations with him that I like here to
note. I remember his having been at the beginning of the Civil War one of the English
names of warning to ears reached by social
echoes—echoes wafted across the sea even from
the lawn of kind Mount Felix. We had all
read, in the North, "Lady Lee's Widowhood,"
and had admired the author even if we had not
paid him; and it was, to express the thing
mildly, a chill to our admiration to hear of his
neither wishing nor prophesying success to our
arms, but, on the contrary, quite luridly (as we
gathered) calling down on them the last humiliation. Had we not, even during the War itself,
flocked in our thousands to the romantic drama
that Lester Wallack, the scenic idol of the
period, had extracted from the charming book

and was causing everywhere to be played—
whether or no to the advantage of the author's
"rights"? I can scarce say to-day by what
accident the legend of Hamley's ironic voice in
particular acquired consistency — ironic voices
having, in every quarter, sufficiently abounded;
it is enough that I suffer myself to call back,
across the gulf of forty years, and amid so many
ghostly things, the shy, faint ghost of an impression. The impression is that of youth and
a Newport summer night, that of three charming young women (two of them now no more)
in a lamp-lit room the long windows of which
stood open to a verandah and to the heavy September air. A young man, happy then in his
kinship with the two, had sociably "looked in,"
and vividly remembers still how he was held by
the charm of the third presence, that of the
beautiful visitor who was staying for a week and
who had just come back from England and from
Mount Felix, where she had been entertained as
a niece and a cousin. She was anecdotic, the so
handsome girl, and I seem to have in my eyes
again the light of happy experience and high
social adventure with which, as well as with
that of her noble beauty, she struck me as
shining. One of her reminiscences bore upon
a passage in which she had found herself patri-

otically engaged with the "chaffing" Artillery
officer encountered at her uncle's house, whom
(thanks to his association with that light literature of which I fear I consumed quantities)
I was able to place, and whom I yet liked to
think of as perhaps retreating before his brisk
adversary in no too good order. Such were
to remain the consequences of the imaginative
habit—that trifles light as air (I leave my impression for that) only had to offer an appearance of interest to become absurdly concrete,
in which form they constituted figures, pictures,
stories. There was, I daresay, no other origin,
or at least no better one, for my subsequent
sense of a prepossession than this sweetly-
uttered Newport echo, which, the other impressions mixed with it helping it to last, had
not even after more than a dozen years died out.
Which precisely was fortunate, as the history
of our impressions goes; inasmuch as *if* it had
faded away I should have missed the pleasure,
the amusement, the interest (I scarce, again,
know what to call it) of feeling the new association displace and supersede the old. I
prolong more than I had meant my very small
story—the second chapter of which was to be
simply my coming to know, in London, at a
later stage of my development and of his own,

the false prophet, or whatever he might be named, of Mount Felix, the not wholly unchivalrous figure of the Newport anecdote. I think he must have accepted by that time the true revelation ; or perhaps rather it then scarce mattered if he had not. We had lived on into the modern world and there was plenty of fresh ground. I seem to remember him as justifying one's conception of one of the finest of types, that of the "cultivated" soldier, of the lover of letters who was also apt for action. If he had written on the art of war he had also written on Voltaire. He was firm enough, obviously, for anything, but his firmness was also itself a fineness, of which his talk gave the measure. So one had lived on to be amused at the other connotation, as the philosophers say, of his name— just as one was, less fortunately, to live on to see the whole strong personality avail him little when his hour had come, to see once more the grim play of the high London tide that reaches up and, with a single silent lap of its monstrous tongue, engulfs and washes away. I have liked, with that sad final vision, to rewrite his name.

"Ginevra da Siena," which appeared in "Blackwood" in 1872, is the most important of that group of poems as to which it was inevitable that Story should incur the charge of trying to fit his tread to the deep footprints of Browning. These things — the "Padre Bandelli Proses," the "Leonardo da Vinci Poetises," the "Contemporary Criticism on Raffaelle," the "Primitive Christian in Rome" —affect us indeed as marked with two different degrees of the inevitable. The author's *ambiente* was for years the same as Browning's; his impressions, contacts, ideals were the same, producing for him—given indeed his difference of mind — very much the same intellectual experience. Italian history, the *cinquecento*, its figures, passions, interests, imagery, appealed to him, beset him, while at the same time he saw his friend, his master (as he would have liked to hold him) still more largely exposed to the influence and strongly moved by it to produce. His disposition, moreover, as his sculpture sufficiently shows, was to project characters, individuals, states of mind and of feeling; which was what Browning had again done with splendid success. The only way in which Browning could have warned him off would have been, perhaps, by the splendour; he had certainly done nothing to discredit the attempt—had only made the challenge of the general field more effective and inspiring. He had placed the challenge, in a word, in its light, for Story, or for any one, to take up, and Story took it up as being, so to speak, the person nearest. He is surely not to be accused of having Browningised without being Browning; in the first place, because the effort *not* to write about an importunate Italy is an unfair strain to impose on any responsive mind; and in the second because, as the experiment shows, the tone achieved is as little Browningesque as possible. Story is limpid, so far as he goes—is crystalline; he is simple, in fine, where Browning bristles with complexity. He arrives, naturally, at a very much lower degree of intensity, but there is at any rate nothing either presumptuous or ridiculous in his handling of the bow. He bends it, and the arrow goes straight enough.

> " At last, however, as you see, 'tis done—
> All but our Lord's head, and the Judas there.
> A month ago he finished the St John
> And has not touched it since that I'm aware.
> And now he neither seems to think or care
> About the rest, but wanders up and down
> The cloistered gallery in his long dark gown,
> Picking the black stones out to step upon;
> Or through the garden paces listlessly
> With eyes fixed on the ground, hour after hour,
> While now and then he stoops and picks a flower,
> And smells it, as it were, abstractedly.
> What he is doing is a plague to me!
> Sometimes he stands before yon orange-pot,

His hands behind him, just as if he saw
Some curious thing upon its leaves,
And then with a quick glance as if a sudden thought
Had struck his mind there standing on the spot,
He takes a little tablet out to draw;
Then, muttering to himself, walks on agen.
He is the very oddest man of men!
Brother Anselmo tells me that the book
('Twas left by chance upon a bench one day,
And in its leaves our brother got a look)
Is scribbled over with all sorts of things—
Notes about colours, how to mix and lay,
With plans of flying figures, frames for wings,
Caricatures and forts and scaffoldings,
The skeletons of men and beasts and birds,
Engines and cabalistic signs and words,
Some written backwards, notes of music, lyres,
And wheels with boilers under them and fires,
A sort of lute made of a horse's skull,
Sonnets and other idle scraps of rhyme—
Of things like this the book was scribbled full.
I pray your Highness now, is this the way,
Instead of painting every day all day,
For him to trifle with our precious time?"

—which, as may easily be gathered, is the
contemporary view of Leonardo during his
troubled work on his Last Supper. We feel
the contemporary view, I think, quite pleasantly
enough caught to refresh our conviction of
the puerility of any pretended estimate of
property in *subject*. A subject is never anything but his who can make something of it,

and it is the thing made that becomes the property. But as between the thing made and the making the distinction is not to be seized, it is to the treatment alone that the fact of possession attaches—from which it is superfluous to warn us off. The treatment—it was long ago said in another way—is the man himself, whom we may be left free to plagiarise if we are able. Such, in other words, is the looseness with which we speak of another's doing the thing "like" him. Its being the fruit of another's identity may ever be trusted to make it different enough.

In "Ginevra," at all events, Story's subject is fine, as he had almost inveterately, and in a degree that his success in production scarce matched, the sense of the fine subject. Ginevra is a young, unhappy wife—as to whom we feel a little that, though the place about her gives out a colour, her period is ambiguously expressed —practically shut up for life, through long, blank years, in punishment for the *appearance* of infidelity to her husband. Childless, neglected, forlorn, she has conceived a passion for a young man who offers her the happiness her husband denies her—a passion under stress of which she has stood with him, for an hour, on the edge of their common abyss. What has

happened, however, is that, the abyss somehow
yawning too ominously, they have receded in
a sort of accepted terror and have separated
while still innocent in fact. "Ideal" beauty,
rather perhaps than familiar, or at least than
historic, truth, is the mark, at this moment, of
their conduct—the presentation of which does
for them, none the less, all it artfully can. The
case as given us is moreover the interesting
one, since the subject springs straight out of it.
This consists, in three words, of the fact that
the husband, cognisant, and willing to be, only
of their secret passion, with its offence to himself alone vivid to him, charges the young
woman, formidably, with the guilt from which
she has really, at the crisis, recoiled, and,
whether wholly convinced or but coldly vindictive (since she is, after all, but too tangibly
in love), will receive no denial and grant no
mercy. The pair, for him, naturally perjured,
cannot *not* have done the deed and stained his
honour, and of the mystic influence under which
we are to understand that they recovered themselves in time he is incapable of taking account.
He vows vengeance upon the lover, whose life,
he declares to his wife, is now forfeit, so that
she, seeing her friend doomed, and doomed for
nothing, has a wonderful, and not unnatural,

revulsion and outbreak. She too is doomed, and doomed, like the young man, for a completeness of union she has never known; so that not to have known it is what becomes for her, of a sudden, horribly intolerable, and, as if to falsify the barren fact even to her own sense, she frantically proclaims and publishes what she has at first denied. Her confession *then*, for her husband, has not the truth of her original protest; the character of the passion of her second attitude contrasts with that of the passion of her first. By a revulsion of his own thereupon, he is obliged to embrace something even more detestable than the idea of his wrong, some notion of the refinement of devotion, on the part of each of the others, that had, at any rate for the time, operated; and this vision it is—practically a deeper defiance of him than any other—that most inflames and determines him. He challenges, fights and slays the lover; after which he has with his wife an encounter that marks the dramatic climax of the situation, bringing out as it does, for each, the tragic vanity of all that has happened. For this humiliation, however, *he* has at least the remedy of the old-time marital power; Ginevra can but drink to the dregs the cup he compels her to drain. Banished and rigidly confined, she be-

comes another blighted Mariana, with the lone
Sienese villa for her moated grange, where she
is visited at last by a friend of her younger
years, to whom she counts over the links that
chain her to the past. She sits, she roams, in
the maddening stillness with her "fault"—that
worst of faults (now a mere mocking mistake)
of which the bitterness is that she has not even
the memory of possession. So at least, to my
eyes, the subject presents itself, though I will
not engage that this is the closest possible
report of Story's treatment of it. He has none
the less, through the whole thing, felicities of
tone, happy notes and shades that are like
memories of the Tuscan midsummer on terraces
where the lizard darts and in rooms where the
fixed frescoes, in long siestas, give upon nerves
strained by exile.

The poems contained in "Graffiti d'Italia"
were in 1885 republished by the author in a
general collection of his verse. These two
volumes, designated respectively as "Parchments
and Portraits" and as "Monologues and Lyrics,"
contain a number of pieces—notably "A Roman
Lawyer in Jerusalem: the Case of Judas"—not
included in the Graffiti. Dear to Story's imagination, he repeatedly showed, was the rank
Rome of the earlier or later Empire; witness,

for instance, in the "Introduction" to the poem
just named, his mention of what he covets more
than any of the so numerous lost literary
treasures of antiquity—

> "Stern Agrippina's diary and life,
>   Writ by herself, recording all her thoughts,
>   Deeds, passions—all the doings of old Rome,
>   Swarming around her, rife with scandals, crimes."

He speaks of these things always with force
and felicity—

> "He pants to stand
>   In its vast circus all alive with heads
>   And quivering arms and floating robes, the air
>   Thrilled by the roaring *fremitus* of men,
>   The sun-lit awning heaving overhead,
>   Swollen and strained against its corded veins,
>   And flapping out its hem with loud report;
>   The wild beasts roaring from the pit below,
>   The wilder crowd responding from above."

"A Roman Lawyer," the most sustained and on
the whole the most successful of his attempts to
reconstitute, as an individual case, some outlived
view of some historic event, joins to the merit
of a great deal of ingenuity and of point the
misfortune of a want of the poetic quality. This
deficiency, of a truth, it shares with Browning's
"Mr Sludge" or "Bishop Blougram," yet with
the elements of irony and philosophy less potent
than in those examples. What most strikes us,

on Story's behalf, in the particular instance, is
the play of a mind that had enjoyed a legal as
well as a poetic training. Had the author ad-
hered to his original profession it would doubtless
have come in his way to do his best for no small
number of Judases not known to fame, or condemned at least to a more limited execration;
in which direction, also, he would probably have
obtained his due proportion of acquittals. He
works brilliantly, at all events, in "A Roman
Lawyer" for that of his supposititious client, for
whose good faith he pressingly pleads, for whom
he in fact claims the distinction, among the
other followers of Christ, of supreme loyalty.
Judas's apparent lapse from this attitude was a
mistake of judgment and an excess of zeal. He
was but too passionately impatient to act in the
sense of his Lord's sublimest pretension and to
help him to the opportunity to be deified. The
changes are richly rung on all the possibilities
of the paradox, and what the author enjoys, we
feel, is his finding it intellectually, professionally,
so workable. He becomes thereby himself the
Roman lawyer, circulating in memory amid the
scenes and objects to which his fondest fancy
was attached.

Visibly, during all his Roman years, he lived
a double, or perhaps rather a triple inner life.

I count his personal and social existence as his outer. Then came, in the first place, his communion with the forms that the art of the studio was to translate. After that came the constant appeal of the actual and present Roman world, always nudging him with suggestions for satires, for portraits, for pictures grave and gay. Most deeply within, to all appearance, sat the vision of the *other* time, the alternative, the incomparable, real Rome; in the light of which I am mistaken if the past was not still more peopled and furnished for him than the present. *There* was the crowd in which, in excursions of the spirit, he lost himself. Let me add, however, that the echoes of the contemporary scene, in the two volumes of 1885, testify to the colour, to the innumerable sharp accents, of surrounding life in a way to excite, at a distance, our bitter envy of so much precious opportunity. I have mentioned "Giannone," and should like, with more margin, to advert to such things as "The Antechamber of Monsignore," as "Il Curato," as "Baron Fisco at Home," as, above all, "Zia Nica," this last-named (the portrait of an old tavern-crone in whom the memory of adventures and the fires of passion still smoulder) being a small cabinet-picture brilliantly brushed. To one of the poems in particular contained in "Parchments and Portraits" attaches, I think, the interest of a high degree of sincerity. "Girolamo, detto il Fiorentino, Desponds and Abuses the World"—this heading is borne by a composition of some eight pages which is further ushered in by an extract, in the original Italian, from a *lettera inedita di Girolamo* really proceeding, we feel, from the same pen. The whole thing expresses finely and pathetically the weariness of the artist who, with whatever native distinction, has had, at maturity, his full share of disappointment and frustration.

> "Success! Yes, while you stinted me in praise
> My pride upheld me; to myself I said
> 'Some time they'll praise me, after I am dead.
> The work is good, although the world delays;
> I for the prize can wait.' But now you blow
> The trumpet in my honour I bend low,
> And from my eyes my work's best charm has fled.
> Once I compared it with the world's neglect,
> And proudly said ''Tis better than they see.'
> Now I behold it tainted with defect
> In the broad light of what it ought to be."

Such passages in an artist's projection of another artist may mostly be taken as the revelation of the former's own emotion. Not less autobiographic, and touching precisely by reason of their slenderness of artifice, are, among the lyrics, the

few verses entitled "The Sad Country," evidently
the persistent echo, after years, of the least endurable of the writer's bereavements.

> " There is a sad, sad country,
>   Where often I go to see
> A little child that for all my love
>   Will never come back to me.
>
> There smiles he serenely on me
>   With a look that makes me cry ;
> And he prattling runs beside me
>   Till I wish that I could die.
>
> That country is dim and dreary,
>   Yet I cannot keep away,
> Though the shadows are heavy and dark,
>   And the sunlight sadder than they.
>
> And there, in a ruined garden,
>   Which once was gay with flowers,
> I sit by a broken fountain,
>   And weep and pray for hours."

The lyrics in this collection are the least numerous pieces, and, though Story was, as I have
noted, familiar with his lyre, are not perhaps the
most successful. Among them nevertheless is
the fine "Io Victis !" which was apparently to
excite a very general admiration. It will be
found, if I mistake not, in many an American
anthology.

" I sing the hymn of the conquered, who fell in the Battle of
    Life,
The hymn of the wounded, the beaten, who died overwhelmed
    in the strife.
Not the jubilant song of the victors, for whom the resounding
    acclaim
Of nations was lifted in chorus, whose brows wore the chaplet
    of fame,
But the hymn of the low and the humble, the weary, the
    broken in heart,
Who strove and who failed, acting bravely a silent and
    desperate part;
Whose youth bore no flower on its branches, whose hopes
    burned in ashes away,
From whose hands slipped the prize they had grasped at, who
    stood at the dying of day
With the wreck of their life all around them, unpitied, un-
    heeded, alone,
With Death swooping down o'er their failure, and all but their
    faith overthrown."

The two small volumes entitled respectively
" He and She: A Poet's Portfolio" and " A
Poet's Portfolio: Later Readings," and published
in 1884 and 1894, strikingly commemorate Story's
lyric overflow, really illustrating, on this account,
a case of some oddity. The Poet meets the Lady
in a woodland place, and, spending summer hours
together, they talk of many things, more or less
of everything; during the intervals of which—
and the intervals diminish as the book proceeds

—he reads out to her the loose verses, "fugitive" pieces, as such things are called, that he happens to have on hand. He is well provided, for his portfolio produces them as freely as if they had long been, from twenty quarters, regularly returned with thanks. The friends discuss them a little, but not overmuch, for it is the sign of the colloquial form, as Story liked to use it, that the talk is off on the instant, in any direction, whenever the scent is crossed. And so the "inedited" poems succeed each other, untitled and unclassified, almost like improvisations of the moment, till they beget at last that perplexity as to the author's poetic *consciousness* which I have already noted. It becomes, in a manner, an irresponsible outpouring; so that, to repeat, we wonder at the mixture of so much eloquence with so much indifference. The lyric voice is all there, but it seems detached and automatic, sounding—even when most charmingly—as from some pleasant but unregulated habit. Story therefore affects us as concurring, curiously, almost perversely, in some fine extravagant waste or leakage, the consequence of his living with a certain poetic magnificence. He has the air, through the two volumes in question, of caring inordinately little to *present* his compositions, to prepare them for company or otherwise insist on their individual dignity. Such are the eccentricities of free and abundant dreamers. Touching, in a high degree, at the same time, on a possible supposition, is the particular device of form that I have described. The supposition is that some of the many lyrics so gathered in may have returned to the fold, disconcerted, out of countenance, after a rough experience of the periodical press. Had some of them really wandered far without encountering sympathy? Their fate would have differed in this case markedly from that of many members of the same general flock, who, going forth to seek their fortune, had also promptly enough found it. Yet one catches one's self, critically, fairly liking to think, for the beautiful pathos of it, that we have here an almost unique case of free ventures practically shipwrecked, bruised and scared creatures welcomed back, in all the silence of their misadventure, without a complaint or a sigh. It is as if the author had really said, with proud good-humour, "Well then, poor dears, *I*'ll do what I can for you"; and then, having detached from each the little tinkling bell of its original appeal, had mustered them all afresh and dropped them into the promiscuous pot, so that lent, as it were, to the tragi-comic joke, they should at least flavour the broth. So, at any rate, on their behalf, a restless critic may embroider.

I gather, meanwhile, however, that our friend's fondest dream in a poetic way would have been to write some play susceptible of presentation— a possibility round which his imagination, it must be added, all too sceptically hovered. It was the effort in the world that most required confidence, and not only confidence in general, but an adequate dose of the particular theatric intimacy. He published "Nero" in 1875, and, more reservedly, he caused "Stephania" to be privately printed a few years later. I do not speak of the two or three small comedies offered during bright Roman winters to Barberini audiences—or at least speak of them, and of Shakespearean evenings equally offered, and of his personal love of the actor's art, and of the handsome young costumed figures, the Portia, the Nerissa, the Antonio, the Bassanio, that I seem to see clustered as in a Veronese picture round his vivid Shylock, only for their recall, which I find in its way touching, of that discouraged scenic curiosity which would yet not consent to become a sound indifference. Having printed "Stephania," of which the subject (given the kind of thing) is, again, full of possibilities, he sent the piece to his old friend Lord Lytton, whose acknowledgment is before me. Their correspondence had, with the lapse of time and the multiplication of the other occupations of each, inevitably shrunken, and Lytton was at this time British Ambassador to France. Story, I may premise, had heard from him a short time previously, in a note of February 21st, 1888. "A thousand affectionate thanks," he then wrote from Paris, "for your letter of the 18th, just received. I have already had the pleasure of making your son Julian's acquaintance here at the Embassy, and have long been impatient for an opportunity to make acquaintance with his studio. But human language cannot describe the incessant rush of my life at Paris up to the present moment. Niagara is nothing to it. I have scarce time to breathe, and as for literary work——! Good heavens, how I envy you the life of calm creation, and how I wish I had never set my foot on this treadmill! You will have a charming Ambassador [to Italy] in Dufferin, and I envy him, and congratulate you, on his appointment." At the time of his later writing Story was at St Moritz, in the Engadine, where, as we shall see, he had built himself a final refuge from the stress of the Italian summer.

Lord Lytton to W. W. Story.

"HÔTEL BERNINA, SAMADEN, *Aug. 22nd*, 1888.

. . . "I can't tell you how delightful to
me was my little glimpse of you the other day,
nor what old and sweet associations it revived.
I have often thought of your Engadine home
and wondered what it was like, for I fancied
you had built your tabernacle among these
mountains many years ago, knowing that you
had long been a Swiss proprietor. And, though
I have not fallen in love either with the
scenery or the climate of this lofty land, I
must say that the loveliest spot I have seen
here is your domain, and that I think your
house, 'both in conception and execution,' a
real creation of genius. I missed however, or
perhaps I ought to say neglected, the opportunity of a word with you about your 'Stephania,'
which I read at Paris with great interest. The
fact is, I felt shy of talking about it before a
family audience; and the more so as my impressions of the play are mixed and not easily
describable without tedious reference to certain
notions of my own about dramatic construction.
I read it under the great disadvantage of having
read not long previously an acting play on the
same subject by Karl Edler, which had powerfully
affected me, and parts of which, indeed, I had

read with very wet eyes. I came therefore to
the perusal of your play with a mind prepos-
sessed by the emotional effects of a different
conception and treatment of its subject. I have
never read any imaginative writing of yours
that has not seemed special to yourself, and
your 'Stephania' is no exception. What little
I know of the story of Crescentius and his
wife inclines me to think, moreover, that your
treatment of it is probably more true to history
than Edler's; but his, at least in its effect
upon myself, is more pathetic; and, rightly or
wrongly, I have accustomed myself to regard
drama as the most emotional of all arts. Conflict of motives, producing in circumstance situations from which there is apparently no issue,
and in feeling or action problems that on the
face of them strike the audience or the reader
as insoluble, seems to me to lie at the foundation of all its effects; and it deals in such
rapid and vehement contrast that of all arts it
is perhaps the most opposed in every one of its
conditions to the art in which your genius has
found its fullest and freest, as well as highest,
development."

The situation depicted in "Stephania" had
already been presented by Story in that com-

pressed volume on Castle St Angelo which may
be taken as a sequel or appendix to "Roba di
Roma." The record of mediæval turbulence finds
itself in those pages rather too foreshortened
for lucidity, but the anecdote of the perjury
of the Emperor Otho III. and of Stephania's
vengence emerges sufficiently distinct. Crescentius, Consul of Rome in 1002, holding the castle
against the Emperor at some customary crisis,
surrenders at last on Otho's taking a solemn
engagement to spare his life. In possession of
the stronghold, and with Crescentius in his
power, Otho then, in defiance of his sacred
pledge, causes his victim to be hanged from
the ramparts, after which he departs from Rome.
Stephania, meanwhile, the Consul's beautiful and
brooding widow, takes refuge in a convent,
nursing her wrong and her grief till, in the
fulness of time, Otho reappears. Her opportunity, with this, dawns upon her; she comes
back to the world and obtains access to the
Emperor, on whom she exerts such fascination
that, though aware of her identity, he offers
her the apparent possibility of becoming his
wife. He, more substantially, does make her
his mistress, which she consents to become in
order to carry out the more effectively her
prime intention—that of making him pay with

his own false life for her husband's. This, in
the end, is what she accomplishes : Otho dies
by her hand when most completely in her
power. The subject, for a writer getting into
close quarters with it, had much to give, the
general measure of which is all to Story's
honour. His difficulty, however, has been that
he marches through it with too straight a
step and reaches his catastrophe by too simple
a process. He had evidently, after his "Nero,"
felt, for the dream of representation, the importance of being simple ; but endless are the
possible vicissitudes of that perilous pursuit.
The writer who holds his situation tight squeezes
too much out of it—more than managers, actors,
more even than the round-mouthed public itself
can swallow, or at any rate digest. The writer
who holds it loosely, on the other hand, lets
it slip through his fingers. So, possibly, would
Story's correspondent have described the misadventure that, dramatically speaking, had lain
in wait for "Stephania." The drama was to
turn inevitably to the play of inward things,
of mixed and discordant feelings, and of this
progression the heroine's mind and attitude were
to become the open field. This, I take it, represents the "emotion" for which the situation
would have been valuable to Lord Lytton.

Story cuts the emotion short—considers it too little, flattering himself, no doubt, that he has in hand a vivid picture of action. This is too questionably the case; the theme, all round, requires amplification; its interest is in its possible details and in the amount of illustration the heroine's ambiguous behaviour demands. Story has faced indeed the ambiguity, shown her as apparently tempted—that is pacified, or, as we say, "squared"—so long as she can believe in her chance of becoming Empress. It is when this chance fails that her purely vindictive passion revives; she would otherwise, we seem to gather, have been precariously bribable. The complication is interesting, though making the story materially less the illustration of a mere vindictive *plan*. The author may very well have thought the mere vindictive plan too stale a theatrical property. Only in that case he should have insisted more on his alternative.

"Nero," published in 1875, is not open to the charge of a want of amplification, inasmuch as its five acts deal, in successive scenes and jumps of space, with every incident of the engaging protagonist's career. The author speaks of it as a play, and as if it might have been placed on the stage; yet it is in fact but a scenic chronicle, of a sort for which he had, in the Elizabethan drama, or even in Goethe's "Götz von Berlichingen," plenty of precedent. More than anything, indeed, this production exemplifies that fondest habit of the writer's fancy at which we have already glanced, the curiosity, the artistic sympathy, that he held at the disposal of the more "lurid" Roman past. The thing becomes thus a piece of not particularly pondered intellectual sport, an imaginative romp, for exercise, through Tacitus and Suetonius. I find its most attaching page, I confess, its dedication. In this epistle, addressed to the late Frances Anne Kemble, he recalls the occasion of his having, during the winter of 1873-74, read his composition aloud to three or four friends, of whom Mrs Kemble had been one. The author of these reminiscences happened to be another, and he well remembers how the shock of earthquake to which the letter alludes contributed to our general impression of evoked horror. For Story read so richly and forcibly that he did vividly evoke, and that the interpretation for which he enviously sighs might well have rested in his own hands. To know Mrs Kemble was to know, certainly, the one, the supreme reader—a range of tone, an expression, a variety that nothing could equal; but it was to know

at the same time, wonderfully enough, a listener
almost as articulate, whose admirable face was
then scarce less at play than when it accompanied her admirable voice.   I seem to recall
that, though my ears, on the far-away evening
in question, were all for Story, my eyes were
for our distinguished companion, in whom the
whole matter was mirrored, commented, silently
*re*presented.

By nothing that Story published is he perhaps so completely characterised as by the two
volumes of " Conversations in a Studio " which
appeared in 1890, after having run their course
in " Blackwood."   Their particular weakness
may be mentioned at once, to get it out of the
way : they suffer, that is, as prolonged colloquies
between a pair of talkers, by the absence, in any
case, of a thesis or argument, and above all by
that of any exemplified opposition of view between the interlocutors.   A talk, a " real " talk,
when of interest, is in its degree, at the least,
a drama, with some question or conclusion in the
balance and in suspense ; and that the author
should, in these things, not have been mindful
of that truth illustrates markedly enough that
friendly and confident attitude in him toward
his subject which ever lightened his sense of
difficulty.   A letter from his publisher, while

the Conversations were coming out in Maga, expresses regret that the two discursive friends should not have been more differentiated; to which Story's reply was, precisely *with* his confidence, that he had not intended in any degree an action or a scene, or that anything should depend on Belton's or on Mallett's character. What he *had*, none the less, we take it, meant, was that something should depend on their differences—nothing less in fact than the full squeeze to be administered, at every turn, to the idea in hand. Yielding or not, at any rate, to the highest pressure, the idea, in these pages, does spring up and abound, testifying to the variety of the author's preoccupations and curiosities. These are historic, æsthetic, scientific, theologic, and to each of his lively hares, as he starts it, he gives the most animated chase. Wit and fancy, as well as a multifarious reading, accompany the pursuit, with the single drawback, as I say, that our friends hunt too much together. It had been the author's notion, we can scarce doubt, that one of them should have represented his own mind, own sympathies and convictions, and that the other should have offered a surface to react or rebound from; but this purpose, if entertained, soon fails of effect. The speakers abound mainly in each other's sense, and with the consequence, really, that this sense becomes *all* the author's. They project together on one occasion a "night of revel," in which certain of the great figures of history may meet round a table splendidly spread ; whereupon Story inevitably strikes his leading note. " My first man then shall be Antony, with his bull-neck, his rich curling hair, his robust figure, his deep-set sparkling eyes and his brave open look." It is impossible to do more for Antony — with what the " Graffiti " had already done for him in the verses, of such breadth and ease, that show him as panting to rejoin Cleopatra and as yielding blindly to his impulse.

I should add that the " first man " of the second speaker is, no less characteristically, Shakespeare, for Story is a signal case of the obsession of that name, which seldom fails to shine out for him, at the end of a few steps, in whatever direction he moves. His vision of Goethe, in truth, is scarce less importunate, but quite to the opposite end, his tolerance of the great German being probably the shortest ever placed on record and his antipathy expressed with amusing frankness. Shakespeare, on the great occasion, will be " the handsomest man at the table, whoever comes "—which gives as

nothing could do the scale and tone of our
friend's loyalty. It was certainly for his peace
of mind that he was not to live to be present
at the so marked multiplication of our late-
coming wonderments, questions, doubts. We
feel that he could scarce decently have endured
them; we feel assuredly that they would have
darkened his close of life; while nothing indeed
is, further, more apparent than the dramatic
value, as it may be called in the connection
here suggested, of so typical a case of Shake-
speareolatry. So much of Story's attitude can
be gathered from his various prose pages that
we feel him to present uncritical adoration in
its most ingenuous, though truly not in its
least militant, form; and we get thereby an
interesting measure of the positively personal
ravage that might become the consequence, far
and wide, of any effective movement for the
revision of the most attaching of literary mysteries. We fairly see it, the question of the
title of the Stratford player, loom before us,
in this lurid light, as a sort of huger Dreyfus
Case of the future, splitting the Anglo-Saxon
race into monstrous hostile camps, dividing and
desolating families and friendships as nothing
has ever done, arraying in short mighty armies

face to face. The vision is apocalyptic, and
may give us all pause; and I meanwhile feel
it, without joking, a point made for peace that
our irrepressible friend is out of the fray.

When Belton, in the "Conversations," suggests
Sir Philip Sidney for their symposium, his
companion, though admitting the claim, hopes
the author of the "Arcadia" will not wish to
read that work to them. "No fear of that,"
Belton wittily answers; "he is a gentleman
every inch of him"—than which nothing could
better cover all the delicacies of the case.
Whereupon the current suddenly floats us, as
is its wont, a million miles away, to the question
of the wines of antiquity, and of the queer composition of several, in which the writer shows
himself intimately versed. This carries us,
through other matters, to an amusing echo of
the most popular manner of Longfellow, boldly
but not viciously thrown off by Mallett, on
whom, as so far from the first to see how his
illustrious friend, as the phrase is, lent himself,
the guilt of parody may doubtless sit lightly.

> "Spake full well in ages olden
>   One of the Teutonic race:
>   Speech is silvern—silence golden;
>   Everything should have its place.

Least said is the soonest mended;
　We must give as we would take;
And the bow too rudely bended,
　In the end is sure to break."

But I may not attempt an enumeration of the constant heterogeneous haul, in these pages, of Story's large loose net. He darts from the Roman Code to the Decay of Enthusiasm, and from a long and extraordinarily enumerative disquisition on recorded longevities to the pronunciation of Latin, taking Byron, Michael Angelo, Lope da Vega, Dryden, Goethe and a hundred other matters by the way, and looking in on Shakespeare with or without an occasion. Gallantly frank is his impatience of "Faust," which he regards as a strangely overesteemed performance; making dauntlessly the point— obviously makeable—of the curiously inadequate nature of the bribe offered by Mephistopheles, the meagre bait (the mere taste of youth and of a simple girl) with which so seasoned a sage is caught. The question is interesting and may be, has been, argued; the critic's idea being that the *quality* of the miracle was worthy neither of the tempter nor of the tempted; but to follow here at all is to follow too far. I follow, for the moment, but into the volume of "Excursions in Art and Letters," published

in 1891 and consisting of five papers, on technical
subjects, that had already appeared.   They are
animated studies, and when Story went into
things he went in well, astride, for the most
part, of some active hobby of his own, and rode
hard to a conclusion.   He concludes, for instance,
almost with passion, against the presumed connection of Phidias and the Elgin marbles.   He
concludes, as to the history of the art of casting in plaster, against the views of his old friend
of Boston and of Rome, Charles C. Perkins—
author of "Du Moulage en Plâtre chez les
Anciens" — controverts with a success I may
not estimate the assumption of the early birth
of the process, placing it, to his own satisfaction,
at the dawn of the Renaissance.   And when
I speak of his inclination to find subjects it is
with a sense of the bravery that makes it
possible for him to call down into colloquy the
shade of Marcus Aurelius, with whom he dis-
cusses, and on no poor level, the respective
merits of Paganism and Christianity.   He was
as attached to the great philosophic emperor
as he was indifferent to the great German poet.
"There he stood before me as I knew him from
his busts and statues, with his full brow and
eyes, his sweet mouth, his curling hair, now
a little grizzled with age, and a deep meditat-

ive look of tender earnestness on his face. I
know not why I was not startled to see him
there, but I was not. Nothing seemed more fitting. . . ." The case being, admirably, that
on the stormy winter night, in the old Roman
palace, when the bells of the Capucin convent
had struck two, the student of the Meditations
sat so under their noble spell that communion
of spirit with spirit rose to its highest possibility. The student's reverence indeed is not
paralysing, else we should have had none of
the beauty of the conversation, which comes
out admirably, for instance, in the emperor's
retort upon his guest's challenge in respect to
the puerility of so much of the ancient annals
of Olympus. What had the Christians to show,
was inquired on this occasion, if they compared
their weak Madonna and her emaciated Son
with the splendour of the Greek types? "Who
could look at that magnificent impersonation
of Zeus at Olympia, by Phidias, so grand, so
simple, so serene, with its golden robes and
hair, its divine expression of power and sweetness, its immense proportions, its perfection of
workmanship, and not feel that they were in
the presence of an august, tremendous and im-
passionate power?" Which is a question that,
letting the answer drop, we may like to leave

our accomplished friend contentedly, gratefully submissive to; in the attitude of charmed response to the sovereign suggestion of Rome, housed, alike for study and for society, by the brave Barberini walls, and with the familiar, the year-long sound from the neighbouring convent just figuring the voice of the siren.

XI.

AMERICAN COMMISSIONS.

STORY paid, with his wife, in 1882, a visit of some length to his own country, where his time was mainly spent in New York, Boston and Washington. His daughter had married in 1876 a distinguished Florentine and retired soldier, the Commendatore Simone Peruzzi, attached to the service and high in the confidence of the late King Humbert, and, separated in consequence from her parents, she was from this time the correspondent to whom their letters were mainly addressed. I find one of these, from the neighbourhood of Boston, but undated, and I refer it, from presumption, though not with entire confidence, to this summer of 1882.

Mrs Story to her Daughter.

"ELM HILL, ROXBURY, *Aug. 6th.*

. . . "I can get no time for retiring to my own occupations; life is all *en évidence*, and

pretty nearly all of it passed in full conclave
somewhere or other. But this is the necessary
consequence of a short visit at the end of a
long absence. We had a most charming and refreshing visit at the Dexters'—refreshing in more
senses than one, for the heat of Boston is beyond
anything you have ever dreamed of. We returned there to Grandmama's house, but were
forced to flight again by the heat of the nights
and the army of mosquitoes. Here at Elm Hill
it is most charming; a beautiful house in a
lovely spot, handsome and agreeable people and
lovely children, horses and carriages to any
extent, and sweet corn and tomatoes to the
same. I have a thousand things to tell you,
but am so pressed for time that I have only one
thought—which is how to carry out the day's
programme without getting into positive disgrace
with somebody. Papa enjoys himself, but is so
utterly unable to get a moment for work of any
sort that he does not even write a letter. He
is distracted with engagements and longs for
the peace of shipboard—think of that. We have
a dozen large boxes to pack, and no end of belongings scattered about in all directions. If I
could get all this *roba* out to Rome it would
help to fill up the dear old barrack-palazzo.
What do you think of Nice for a fortnight *en*

route? I long to hear about Miss Thesiger. Milnes Gaskell, how is he? . . ."

To which the following, of a few days later, may serve as postscript.

Mrs Story to her Daughter.

"BOSTON, *Aug. 17th.*

. . . "I thought that my visit to America would be the means of uniting more firmly the family circle, but, alas! I fear we but sow the seeds of bitterness, for they are all jealous of the duration of our visits and fearful that we shall unfairly distribute our time and attentions. Often it is not where we *would* go, but where we must, imperiously dictated by the powers that be. I do not see how we can possibly squeeze into our remaining days one-half of the visits we have accepted, and these are not a tenth part of our invitations, the greater number having been on the instant declined. As we were sitting on the lawn yesterday afternoon at Elm Hill, watching the game of croquet, Mr Sumner drove up with Laurence Oliphant, who had ar- rived that very morning in the steamer. They stayed some time and then we drove into town with them. Mr Oliphant leaves to-day for Newport, and Papa has given him some letters to friends there."

This next more definitely places itself.

Mrs Story to her Daughter.

"NEW YORK, *Nov. 17th*, 1882.

. . . "We have had the committee here,
and they have discussed the monument to Judge
Marshall, leaving it all to Papa's taste and
genius.   He is to go to Washington to select
the site, but they wish him to be there during
the session of Congress, so that his selection
may be at once confirmed by the House.   You
remember well enough the whirl of a London
season; this is like it for us, and I can never
find time to write at ease.   Some stray tired
moment is all I can find, and the card-leaving,
which must all be done in *person*, and the notes
to be answered, and the lists, very complicated,
to be kept without mistake of time and place,
give me more than enough to do.   At the
weddings and afternoon tea-parties the fine
clothes surprise me.   I have never seen such
gorgeousness on such small occasions.   We saw
at Mrs Paran Stevens's on Sunday night the
jeunesse dorée, and it reeked—one half of it—of
Worth.   Young ladies, 'buds' they call them,
in sleeveless gowns!   Mrs —— is not a success
either as an actress or as a beauty.   Of the
latter they have scores of a superior brand.   The

climate is at this time very trying—one day
Siberian, the next tropical, and the rest the
worst kind of heavy scirocco. We die over the
heat of the houses, and the hotels are suffocating."

One of Story's professional concerns during
this sojourn was the question of the site, at
Washington, for the monument to Chief-Justice
Marshall, for which he had accepted the commission a year or two earlier. This work, placed
in position in 1884 and, as the pedestal records,
"Erected by the Bar and the Congress of the
United States," has, in a high degree, the mass
and dignity prescribed by its subject, and the
great legal worthy, seated aloft, in the mild
Washington air, before the scene of his enacted
wisdom, bends his high brow and extends his
benevolently demonstrative hand in the exemplary manner of the recognised sage and with
all the serenity of the grand style. I find a
letter from the Librarian of Congress informing
the author that the work was on May 10th
"unveiled with appropriate ceremonies"; and
with this communication connects itself that of
an eminent Washington friend who writes to
him immediately after the proceedings. "You
have a right to be proud of the admirable work,
as I am for you. The image is fully up to the

greatness of the original, and that is enough to say, for he was one of the really great Americans of his time." The spring of the previous year had meanwhile seen due honour rendered to the bronze image of Joseph Henry, revered in American science and long the animating genius of the Smithsonian Institute — the Professor Henry whose name, I cannot here forbear to record, thanks to a former family connection with the bearer of it (the connection, remembered, cherished, anecdotic, on the paternal part, of grateful pupil with benignant tutor), had had for my early years such a suggestion of mysterious greatness as inevitably determines now, to my fancy, the character of the memorial. "This is the week of the annual meeting of the American Academy of Science," writes another Washington friend in April, 1883—a friend whose name would figure again one of our "shades," a shade of old Newport days, could our shades still be pursued. "Its members and magnates were all present," Mr Alexander Bliss continues, "as well as the officials of State, all the Judges, the Senators, and all the Members in town. The President only was absent—he being, as the papers will have told you, fishing in Florida. The day was bright and joyous, and the bronze eyes of the good old *savant* first saw the light amid the budding trees of his own Smithsonian, in its fresh spring garb. The Misses Henry are thoroughly satisfied, as they will doubtless report to you. Chief-Justice Waite was rather the presiding genius of the occasion, making the address at the actual dropping of the veil." I turn over light mementoes, of pleasant suggestion, of this Washington winter, invitations to dine at the White House, "to meet H. E. the Govr.-Genl. of Canada," lady's dinner-cards, relics of such banquets, with the names and the order of each of the thirty-six guests, courteous requests from high officials—a list of eminent signatures—for a hearing of the lecture on Michael Angelo already elsewhere delivered and eventually published in the "Excursions." The particular pleasantness of Washington still abides in these reminders, giving out, for any initiated sense, a faint fragrance as of old dried rose-leaves; so fast, as we feel in the American air the pulse of change, does even a comparatively recent antiquity take on, with faded flowers and ribbons, with superseded performers, "the tender grace of a day that is dead." I should call up ghosts indeed were I here to be beguiled into any reference to my own handful of impressions of the American federal capital more than twenty years ago.

I find myself doubtless better employed in noting two or three occasions, belonging to the previous period, that had still served, for Story, as opportunities of intercourse with his own country. His bronze statue of Colonel William Prescott, who survived, heroically, the battle of Bunker Hill, was set up, on the anniversary of that day in 1881, in the immediate presence of the existing monument. I find it noted that, modelled in the Roman studio, the features of the young colonial general, as to which documents were not abundant, had been visibly inspired by those of the artist's friend Arthur Dexter, Prescott's great-grandson. Mr Robert C. Winthrop, who delivered the elegant address that accompanied the unveiling of the image, alludes to Story's presentation of the hero " in the light banyan coat and broad-brimmed hat which he is known to have thrown on in the intense heat of the day and the battle, in exchange for the more stately and cumbrous uniform in which he had marched from Cambridge the night before and which may be seen dropped beneath his feet. His eagle gaze," this speaker continued, " is riveted with intense energy on the close-approaching foe. With his left hand he hushes and holds back the impetuous followers who are to await his word ; with his right he

is about to lift the sword that is to be their
signal for action"—the sword still preserved,
for us, at a distance, in that literary commemoration given it by Thackeray, who relates
in the opening passage of "The Virginians"
that he had seen it crossed with another, the
weapon carried by an ancestor on the Tory side,
over the chimney-piece of the soldier's grandson,
the historian of Mexico and Peru. The lecture
on Michael Angelo, just mentioned, brings back
to me the remembrance of one of Story's later
and more interspaced visits to London—an impression with which the presence of Lowell is
much mingled—and the somewhat blurred vision
in particular of the beautiful great room of a
generous house facing the Marble Arch, in which,
one summer afternoon, a host of distinguished
people gathered to listen to the lecturer. The
latter's compendious tribute to the supreme
sculptor-painter, which may now so conveniently
be read, had all the interest and eloquence that
his special authority could give it, but I seem
to have preserved from the scene much less the
sense of the address itself, and of the points
made in it, than that of a fine, a delightful
illustration of one of the great London fashions.
This fashion, at the height of the "season," with
so wonderful a rush, was to slip in a slice of

Michael Angelo, or of any other cold joint from
the sideboard of the higher life, between three
and four o'clock, between the copious lunch and
the drive to Hurlingham, the impending private
view, the garden-party out of town, the tea-
party at home, between the jaws in fine, powerfully made to gape, of the gorged afternoon, and
to have available for each of these sequences the
same unperturbed blandness. The occasion was
thus surrounded, amid the courtesies and splendours of the house, with the rustle and fragrance
and shimmer that were the mark of great enter-
tainments, so that one could freely admire, in
the rich and artful light, that triumph of good
manners which consists in the mastery of such
signs of attention as will serve for any one social
object as well as for any other, such attestations
of presence as will almost represent a felt relation.
Not one of these had been wanting for one of the
auditors who afterwards walked westward, south-
ward, over the green stretches of the Park, to
Kensington ; and yet what was mainly striking
to him, as I say, was not the stuff of the lecture,
to which he was to do justice in the future, but
the brilliant, graceful, successful comedy of all
the rest of the matter. Which view of the case
may be noted, moreover, without prejudice to
any one concerned. The act of homage, all

round, was an act of aspiration, of noble yearning amid dire distractions, and the sculptor's—
that is Story's—florid Sardanapalus throned in
one of the rooms.

A demonstration of a simpler strain had
meanwhile doubtless been the delivery at Salem,
Massachusetts, in 1878, of the Ode addressed by
Story to the memory of the founder and first
Governor of the province, John Endicott, the
anniversary of whose landing on the site of the
present city, September 18th, is kept from half-
century to half-century.

> " I send my voice from far beyond the sea ;
>   Only a voice—and therefore fit to be
>   Among the dim and ghostly company
>   That, from historic realms of shadowy gloom,
>   And from the silent world beyond the tomb,
>   This day shall come, their living sons to greet
>   With voiceless presence, and with noiseless feet,
>   To join the long procession in the street,
>   And listen to the praise
>   Of the old deeds and days
>   That in our memories evermore are sweet."

Incorrigibly absent and, from the native point of
view perhaps, sadly Romanised, the poet invokes
with evident sincerity, and with all due lyric
dignity, the traditions and the personal memories
of his younger time—rejoicing in his task more-

over if only for the occasion given him poetically
to greet his father.

"Dearest to me, and first of all the throng
  That slowly moves along,
    Is one belovèd form, with face benign,
    Whose birthday fell on the same day as thine,
    Oh pleasant town of mine!
  'Tis the great Jurist, all his features bright
  With an irradiating inner light."

He warms again, as he fixes it, in his alien air,
to the picture of his New England boyhood and
the renewed voice of its attendant spirits.

"They peer from every window-pane,
  From every alley, street and lane
    They whisper on the air.
  They haunt the meadows green and wide,
  The garden-walk, the riverside,
  The beating mill adust with meal,
  The rope-walk with its whirring wheel,
  The elm grove on the sunny ridge,
  The rattling draw, the echoing bridge;
  The lake on which we used to float
  What time the blue jay screamed his note,
  The voiceful pines that ceaselessly
  Breathe back their answer to the sea."

And then, with this note, he recalls, as the richest treasure of the time, that breath of outlandish
ports that was borne home, for watchful young

senses, by the tokens, so early to shrink, of great sea-traffic.

> "Ah me, how many an autumn day
>   We watched with palpitating breast
> Some stately ship, from India or Cathay,
>   Laden with spicy odours from the East,
>   Come sailing up the bay!
>   Unto our youthful hearts elate
>   What wealth beside their real freight
>   Of rich material things they bore!
>   Ours were Arabian cargoes, fair,
>   Mysterious, exquisite and rare;
>   From far romantic lands built out of air
>   On an ideal shore;
>   Sent by Aladdin, Camaralzaman,
>   Morgiana or Badoura or the Khan;
> Treasures of Sinbad, vague and wondrous things,
> Beyond the reach of aught but youth's imaginings."

With Browning, in these later years, his correspondence ceased to be frequent, not from any diminution of friendship, but because of their opportunities for meeting, eventually more repeated, in particular through Story's multiplied excursions to England. Other chances than these latter, moreover, came up; autumn weeks in Venice—the rigid limit, for so long, of any movement of Browning's toward Florence, and the August and September days in which Switzerland, year after year, made them more or less neighbours. The high places, for the annual absences from Italy and from England, called them both, and the Storys, from early in the eighties, had become, as I have mentioned, "braced" proprietors in the Engadine. My shrunken collection of documents yields, however, a remnant or two, at contact with one of which I find association promptly waking up.

Robert Browning to W. W. Story.

"29 DE VERE GARDENS, W., *July* 19*th*, 1888.

"MY DEAR STORY,—I had just telegraphed to Dulwich that I should be unable, to my great regret, to go there this morning, when your message comes—still more adding to my regret. I have a vile cough, and a general sense of indisposition which quite prevent my attendance on an occasion which I think will interest you— as it used to do in my case. Ever affectionately yours, ROBERT BROWNING."

"As it used to do in *my* case," too, the author of these notes is almost emboldened to subjoin, remembering old summer afternoons when the *consigne*, among the children of light—which was a fair description of the favoured friends of the then Governors, Mr Charles Roundell and the Rev. William Rogers, Rector of St Botolph's, Bishopsgate—was the annual reception at Dulwich College. Even though, as I hope, these hospitalities still take place for new generations, I view them, afar off, in a mellow social light which is one with the sweet-coloured glow of the long picture-gallery of that fortunate institution, a vista of Dutch and other of the minor masters, looking down upon tables of tea and of heaped strawberries and ices, upon smiling pilgrims from town, amiable women and eminent men, upon hosts as genial as their background of treasures, upon individuals and couples detached and absorbed, preferring eagerly the precious pictures even to the strawberries, nowhere else so big, upon high doors opened, to the ripe afternoon, for adjournment to beautiful grounds. With which, but for the fear, under the touch of Browning's note, of waking up to excess, I should trace my association, as I have called it, further still, suffer it to pursue my second-named of the Dulwich dispensers, much-doing, much-enduring and all-beneficent and delightful man, to the sober shade (as I reconstitute it) of the Bishopsgate parsonage, to the small and intimate dinner, exactly, that, both for company and for cheer, one felt as of the sound City tradition—the City familiar and at home; with the high political world, with even the Bank, made human, made charming, fairly seated opposite and speaking in a voice as pleasant as the ring of new-minted money.

I turn over still another of Browning's letters —not addressed, this one, to either of our friends, but to their daughter, whom he had known from childhood and who had sent him, in the summer of 1884, the translation she had lately made of the Autobiography of Giovanni Dupré, the so interesting Tuscan sculptor. " It is not so very ' little ' an affair; and, in the fear that, when my sister has finished it, I may have to begin my own reading, and end it so late as to lead you to suppose that either book or letter has gone wrong; on *this* account I write at once to thank you most heartily. My sister says the Autobiography is *fascinating* : I can well believe it, for I never knew such a work to be without interest, and this of Dupré must abound in precisely the matters that interest me most. . . . When I have thoroughly gone through the book I will write again, if you permit me — as I know your old memories will be indulgent in the case. There is not much likelihood of our going to Italy this autumn; the silly quarantine regulations [against cholera] effectually hinder our attempting that : and in no case should I—probably—trust myself again in Florence. Yet such an event *might* be; and

if you are within reach you will be certain to
see the old friend who always rejoices when
he hears of your wellbeing and trusts it may
continue." And I go on—not for the special
weight of the words, or for any close relevancy
in their reference; rather merely to feel this
last link in my hand as long as possible. "Pen
is very well; at Dinant, just now, painting
landscape in the open air. I have told him
already of the book, which I know he will
delight in reading. I am occupied this very
day in sending his statue of Dryope to Brussels,
where the Exhibition will give it a chance of
being judged by better knowledge than is found
here. Your own brothers' works are capital—
Julian's picture at the Grosvenor admirable in
many respects and above the works on each
side of it. Waldo's statuette is exceedingly
good also; they have, each of them, enjoyed
a better education than is easily obtainable here.
My sister sends her kindest love to you. We
are ordered to find mountain air for her and
must somehow manage it; but our Gressoney
in the Val d'Aosta is a barred paradise at
present; Switzerland is our resource, I suppose.
What do you think? We get this moment a
word from your mother to say she—or 'we'—
may be seen in town this day only, as she

leaves early to-morrow. I shall contrive to call this evening, and will keep my letter open to make it worth your reading by my news. Their plan is to go somewhere for a week or two's refuge from the heat, and thence, returning to London, get to Rome as soon as the difficulties on the frontier are removed."

There were other meetings after this, but my only other records are half a dozen notes, of the autumn of 1889, from Mrs Story in Rome to her daughter in Florence. "We have had a week of such emotions that I have been much upset, and, having had to write so much, have not had a moment for you. Browning is lying dangerously ill at Palazzo Rezzonico. Write at once to Pen—it will help him to hear from you. I have letters and telegrams every day, but they are very disheartening, and I fear the worst. His heart is very weak and he is seventy-five. His admirable constitution and temperate life are greatly in his favour. Still, I despair. I cannot tell you how we rejoice to have seen him so lately at Asolo, when he was so well and in such force, brilliant and delightful as ever. Mrs Bruce's death was a terrible shock to us all, and Uncle James's state, though not worse, gives me profound anxiety." Mrs Bruce, gentlest of ladies, who had retired, in ill-health,

from the service of her Queen, and whom I
remember as presented, in alternation, against
the background of the old Barberini drawing-
room and her own, of the homelier note, in
grey St James's Palace, was a friend of many
years and a regular participant in the Roman
winter. "Uncle James" was the title conferred
by long intimacy upon J. R. Lowell, at this time
under the shadow of the illness which was to
lead, somewhat more than a year later, to his
death. The happy days at Asolo had been spent
by the Storys under the roof of their supremely
amiable countrywoman, Mrs Arthur Bronson, long
resident at Venice, but devoted to the little hill-
town immortalised (as we must verily say) in
"Pippa Passes," which, from under its ruin-
crested *rocca*, looks out across the purple plain
to Bassano, Padua, Vicenza, other places, other
names, charged with memories. Here, beside
the "gate" where our friends had seen their
last of Browning, also a visitor tenderly protected
by her, she had established one of the quaintest
possible little places of *villeggiatura*—the gate
being the empty arch of one of the old town
entrances, a barrier long since humbly removed,
to match with all the other final humilities,
and the house itself resting half upon the dis-
mantled, dissimulated town-wall. No sweeter

spot, in all the sweetness of Italy, could have offered itself to old Italianised friends for confident renewals and unwitting farewells.

The note I have just quoted from Mrs Story had its inevitable sequel. "Our dearest Browning died last night at ten o'clock in Venice. I think you can help poor Pen, who wants to have his father buried at Florence beside his mother. Get Simone to intercede with the authorities and telegraph yourself to Pen at the Rezzonico." And again on the morrow : "We are utterly prostrated by our loss and grief. His last words to us, as he stood at the gate at Asolo, having bade us a most tender farewell, were 'We have been friends for over forty years without a break.' I knew not how to break the news, when it came, to dear Papa, but I waited, in the evening, till he had eaten some dinner, and then, in a quiet moment, I told him. He spent the evening in tears and in talking about him and the old time. What can we say or do? How golden seem the memories of those rich days and hours with him at Asolo! How grateful are we for this comfort, and how nearly I had missed it! I feel sure that if he expressed any wish it must have been to be buried beside his ever-beloved wife at Florence. No Westminster Abbey could in his loyal heart have had an allurement to be named beside that dear Florentine grave. I hope you and Simone may be able to help to this end. . . . His new book of Lyrics was to have been published yesterday! But how dreary cold looks life to-day! The loss of him is beyond words a blow to us." After which a final line expresses, as the sense of our friends, a preference coloured by their attachment to Italy. "I now hear from Venice that Browning is to be buried in London, in the Abbey. I am sorry; one feels it so much more suitable that he should lie in Florence and beside *her*. But I suppose the stupid authorities would not, after what they have done, permit the intramural burial. What a mistake to have forfeited such an honour and glory to Florence! There is to be a service to-day at the Rezzonico." All visitors to Venice remember the imposing palace of that name, one of the creations of a late and no longer super-stitiously "sincere" period, which, with its wide florid front, all staged and pillared and embossed, commands a bend of the Grand Canal and, like certain others of its company, reminds one, from the low level of the gondola, of some broad-breasted mythological sea-horse rearing up from the flood with the toss of a sculptured crest and with emergent knees figured by the water-steps.

To this stately temple of the rococo, admirable in its order and which had become the property of his son, the author of " Men and Women" was to bequeath the association most interesting for ourselves. Only, the association remains, through the years, as may be said, scarce assimilated, slightly discordant—an impression (the impression of the strange short ways life and death are apt to take with us) not dispelled by the beautiful, cold, pompous interior, partly peopled though the latter be, in its polished immensity, by every piously-kept relic of Casa Guidi and of London years. For all his "difficulty" Browning was, with his lovers, the familiar and intimate, almost the confidential poet, fairly buttonholing the reader with the intensity of his communication and the emphasis of his point. The Italy of the Rezzonico was not, in spite of "A Toccata of Galuppi," the Italy we felt and cherished in him—not a place consonant with the charged messages I speak of, but the suggestive scene, much rather, of emptier forms and salutations, conventions and compliments. After which it may doubtless be added that we are ever ill-advised to challenge, on behalf of a mortal memory, any benefit whatever of chance, any object with a power to preserve, to mark a passage through the sands of time. Let us put it that the Rezzonico, even though all mirrored in the Adriatic channel, rises above these sands very much as the Sphinx or the great Pyramid rises above those of the desert. The travellers of the future will not trouble about shades of affinity when the gondolier of their day, coming on from the Rialto and the Mocenigo toward the palace of the Venetian Pope, pronounces, mispronounces, with his hoarse, loud cry, the name of the English poet he has learned to add to those of Shakespeare and Byron.

Browning's death, for our friends, was to make that of Lowell, which took place a year and a half later, the more of a loss. They had found Lowell in London from time to time, while he occupied the post of American Minister, and then again during the years, signally interesting to a near observer of them, as I am impelled to say, that saw him regularly reappear as a visitor, indifferent to the rigour of custom in such cases, on the scene to which his official period had so deeply attached him. It was the situation made for him by this lasting attachment that was interesting in the degree I mention—interesting to a fellow-countryman who often found occasion to rejoice that his own predicament, in the same air, was comparatively simple; though indeed

it may be added that the personage in question
sometimes felt a kind of cruelty in his comparative independence.   London, when she takes the
trouble to bite at all, bites deep, and one who
had himself been bitten inevitably watched with
attention such other marks of the teeth as met
his view.   They had entered Lowell's life sharply
enough, but he had the inconvenience, I think, of
not being quite free to confess to the wound.   As
he was representative, and his representative
character stuck to him, so he was responsible—
which created elements of situation that rather
failed to hang together.   Speaking of it, I mean,
as his last period made it, he was, while un-
official, too distinguished a stranger to be private, and yet was too private to have been "sent";
which latter fact in turn spoiled a little the
harmony between his theory and his practice.
His theory was that of the American for whom
his Americanism filled up the measure of the
needful; his practice was that of freely finding
room for any useful contribution to the quantity
from without.   The best account of his incon-
sistencies would doubtless be that they were
for no one more "funny" than for himself, who
could always moreover, for occasion, make the
funny funnier still.   To which recollections,
however, I can do no justice in a glance by

the way. I am afraid that what is easiest to express in them is the observer's near "subjective" and perhaps too imaginative sympathy; something like a resentful vision of the way in which those who sacrifice to great democracies and sovereign peoples, occupying in their service what are called " high posts," are apt all too soon to become the sport of fate, the victims of a fleeting hour. With limited philosophy perhaps, but with lively sensibility, one deplored, on behalf of one's admirable friend's distinction, all his high quality, the rudeness of the political game that could so take and leave, so want and yet so waste him. It was a question of " treatment," of his having been, as it were, almost more abused than used. And the fact that it was the System but made the case worse; it would have shown as less ugly had it been a rare accident. So, at any rate, before the spectacle, in London, of other ordered ways, and doubtless fantastically enough, one contrasted the luxury of the European " career " with the mere snatched dignity of the American—indulging really in wanton wishes that ever so many things might have been different, and profiting by the licence of friendship to dream extravagant dreams. These were but the melancholy air-castles of fond, disinterested fancy. Neither participant

in the relation I thus recall could possibly have
so discriminated for himself.

But I must not multiply words over the too
few remaining lines in my boxful of letters that
have a connection here. I find scarce more
than a note or two, the earliest of which in
date belongs to March 5th, 1885. It is from
the house in Lowndes Square that he occupied
during his diplomatic term, and refers to the
death of his second wife, three weeks before.
"I had had a letter to you on my conscience
for a good while but never found a time when
moods and leisure made it possible. I little
dreamed that when I wrote it would be within
these black boundaries. I cannot yet say,"
he presently adds, "what my own plans will
be. I suppose that there is little doubt that
some one will be sent to take my place here
But I cannot now go back to live at Elmwood
as I hoped. Probably I shall stay here for the
present, as I took on my house till the end of
the year. . . . I cannot say enough of the
kindness and sympathy I have received here.
Lady Lyttelton especially has been as a sister.
It has done me all the good that can be done
—and that *is* something. I thank you and
Emelyn, dear old friend, as you know, but find
it hard to say what I would *as* I would. God

bless you both, and keep you together!" After which comes another scrap, of June 2nd, 1887, again from London, but during a friendly visit. Story was about to go to Oxford to receive the honour of a D.C.L. degree. "I am delighted to hear that Oxford is to do for you what she ought to have done sooner. It will be no addition to you, but a very sensible one to me, since it will give me the chance to see you again. I won't say we are getting old, but we are getting *on*, and every milestone is nearer to the inevitable twilight. . . . Let me know also the date of Commemoration, that I may go down with you to say *Placet*. I will keep the day open. London is unhappy just now with the eternal Irish indigestion, but I still find it pleasanter than any other place in the world. I who lived a hermit so long and found my burrow delightful, find the sense of enormous human neighbourhood here comfortable in my old age. It shelters me from the wind. . . ." Which makes the right place for the following.

W. W. Story to his Daughter.

"16 HALF MOON STREET, *July 8th*, 1887.

. . . "The heat here has been most exhausting—I never knew it hotter in Rome; and we long to get out of the turmoil of life into some quiet. By the end of next week we shall in all probability leave for St Moritz. Mama is trying to arrange here about furniture, but the heat is so great that she can do very little. Our Oxford experience was very pleasant; we stayed at the Deanery (Christ Church), and the Dean and Mrs Liddell were extremely kind and did everything for us. I appeared in my red gown and college cap, and was warmly received and cheered by the undergraduates in the college theatre. In the afternoon we had a charming garden-party, where all the Oxford world was, with bands and glees and part-songs and a collation under a great tent; and we wandered about by the water and under the trees till twilight, when I went to a great banquet in C. Ch. Hall, and sat on the dais, in my red gown, with the Dons and Doctors. There were speeches, of course, and toasts, and though I had been assured that I should not be called upon, another Dr having been appointed to answer for the new Drs, yet when he sat down there was such a shout and call for me that I was obliged to get up. I hope it was not disgraceful. We also attended an open-air representation of 'As You Like It' in Worcester College grounds, which was most interesting and delightful. The actors were from London and the whole effect charm-

ing. . . . The Jubilee procession (in London)
was remarkable and effective, though the intervals between the different bodies were altogether too long. The conduct of the crowd was
what surprised me most. They patiently waited
for hours under the burning sun—some of them
from 2 o'clock in the morning till 12 noon—without riot or confusion. And when the royal
cortége passed there were universal cheers that
split the air, a great spontaneous outburst of
enthusiasm and loyalty. After that it is no use
for Gladstone to talk of masses as opposed to
classes. We saw the procession from Lord
Rothschild's as it went down and from the
Becketts' as it returned."

This was a period of interesting University
episodes, for Story was in the following year
invited to represent his own Alma Mater at
the great commemorative celebration of Bologna,
in respect to which he writes to his wife on June
12th. Lowell, it may be mentioned, was another
of the Harvard deputies, but, on the scene of
action, had been taken inopportunely ill and
was most of the time confined to his hotel.
"We had a *fiaccolata* of the military last night,
which we saw admirably from our balcony, with
various friends of the Covaglia family. It was

really splendid : each man carried a tall frame-
work of coloured lamps, red, green, yellow,
representing stars, flowers, towers, and producing
an uncommonly splendid effect. They all filed
down Piazza Galvani on which this house fronts,
and turned our corner, so that far away on both
sides we saw them coming and going. Immediately afterward I dressed for the Royal reception
at the Prefettura, and went at 10. The Queen
most gracious, and asked particularly for you;
shook hands with the King." All of which
brilliancy appears to have been, in some degree,
a medal with a reverse—as I gather at least
from a very concise diary kept by Story at the
time. On June 10th, the day after his arrival
from Rome, "Went to the University to get
programme and orders. Such a confusion in all
the arrangements I never saw; more of the
names on the list wrong than right, and the
printed list full of the most ridiculous mistakes
—South America coming under the head of
Canada, and New Jersey appearing as an independent republic with the designation 'Neo-
Cesarensis.' My own name was on no list and
I was obliged to write it down myself. . . .
Lowell in wretched quarters and very unwell,
and all the American deputation irritated at the
want of recognition and the confusion of every-

thing." It was Story's fate, in the various processions, to be consigned, insistently, to the South American section; after which, on his finally protesting that the United States were on the northern continent, the error was rectified. "Ah, then, you must go under Australia!" And the last words are that Carducci, alas! was dull, and that the heat was suffocating.

I give in this connection the last words I find from Lowell.

J. R. Lowell to W. W. Story.

"ELMWOOD, CAMBRIDGE, MASS., *October 2nd*, 1890.

"MY DEAR WILLIAM,—It was very pleasant to see your well-remembered handwriting again, and to see it without any hint of that quaver in it into which the hand as well as the voice is betrayed by the accumulating years. I say this not in malicious sympathy, but as a respectful tribute to your seniority—it isn't great, to be sure, but at our time of life even ten days have a value of which youth could not conceive.

"But why do I talk of old age, I in whom autumn (of all seasons of the year) has renewed my youth? I was seriously ill last winter and spring, even dangerously so, I believe, for a day or two, and all summer have been helplessly languid and inert. Not that I didn't feel much

as usual in body, but my mind had no grip,
'couldn't seem to catch hold,' as our vivid
American phrase puts it.   And my memory
fumbled in vain when it tried to pick up anything smaller than a meeting-house.   But all of
a sudden ten days ago I got up in the morning
a new man.   My memory still boggles a little
about dates, but, as well as I can make out, I
am about fifty. . . . I am here in my birth-
place and I find it very gracious to me.   I look
upon the trees and fields I first saw and find
them as good as then. . . . I still have elbow-
room, but I am more and more persuaded that
the new generation shouldn't be allowed to start
till the old be off the stage.   It would save much
unseemly hustling and many heartburnings.   It
is very good of you to tempt me with Rome and
the Barberini, but, setting aside any scruples I
might have as an American about living in a
palace, I am anchored here for the winter. . . .
Then too, if I am well enough, I am to read over
again some old lectures in Philadelphia, for it
pleases me to earn a little money in this way
and convince myself that my hand can still keep
my head.   I shall send you one of these days a
little book to which I have written a preface,
and which will have the value of being at once
pretty and scarce—250 copies printed for a club.

It isn't much of a preface, but a good deal of a book, being Milton's 'Areopagitica.' . . . Though I cannot come now, I am not without hope of seeing you in Italy again before I vanish. A longing has been growing in me for several years now, chiefly, I confess, for Venice, but with subsidiary hankerings after Rome and Florence. Neither of them is the old one, of course, but they are better than anything else. But it grows harder and harder for me to get away. For reasons into which I need not enter, but which are imperative, I am not my own man so much as I should like to be, and as I expected to be, in my old age. For better or for worse one is married to duty, and one mustn't dally with other baggages."

The history of our friends' closing years is not, it will be perceived, a chronicle of events. Life continued largely serene for them, inflicting no deep wounds and making no cruel demands ; the golden air, as we have called it, was never really darkened for them, nor the spell of old Rome broken. Story worked bravely on, from year to year, meeting as he could the conditions, often, inevitably, the reverse of inspiring, involved in the appeals reaching him for monuments to American worthies—making, that is, the best of the dire ordeal of the sculptor fighting for his idea, fighting for his life, or for that of his work, with an insensible, an impenetrable, a fatal committee. To 1869 belongs his London statue, that of George Peabody, massive, yet human, seated, by the Royal Exchange, where the sound of quick feet, on sharp City errands, most abounds; but much of the later time was occupied with the most elaborate of his productions in the public order, the large memorial to Francis Scott Key, author of " The Star-Spangled Banner," presented to the city of San Francisco by her so largely munificent son Mr James Lick. Looking out to the Golden Gate of the Pacific, uplifted on a pedestal embossed with a frieze of reliefs, and surmounted with a canopy which itself carries further aloft a colossal statue of America partly enshrouded in the folds of the flag, this image, probably precious beyond any other in the world as an example, on the part of the originating body, of the sense of proportion defied, must have represented, on the side of the artist, the sharpest of inward, the queerest of æsthetic, struggles. There is always, fortunately, for the strained consistency of the sculptor so confronted and so divided, an efficient salve in the consciousness that though his work may not do, or undo, what he would like, it is

still at least preventive in respect to worse mis-
deeds. A colossal statue to Mr Key demands
a particular perspective, but what perspective
would have been possible with, for instance, an
uncompromising obelisk? Who can deny that
the obelisk was possible, a landmark from afar
for Pacific voyagers? We may dream at any
rate that Story averted the obelisk. Echoes of
these productive years, as well as of projects
and possibilities that failed of effect, sound for
me, here and there, in stray letters and other
scraps of reminder. His impressive statue of
"Jerusalem Desolate" paused, in London, in
1873, on its journey to America, and, being
offered for a short time on view there, elicited
the following.

A. W. Kinglake to W. W. Story.

"I went on Monday to see the Jerusalem, and
was so fortunate as to find in the room a lady
who knew me, who understood the glories of
sculpture, and was in a state of enthusiasm about
your great work. My appreciation of high Art
has been so poorly cultivated that I was exceedingly glad to have her guidance. Her delight in the general conception alternated with
admiration of the separate beauties. Pointing
out for instance the arms, she taught me to

appreciate the power with which you have forced
the cold marble to express glowing flesh. You
must be very happy. The aspect I preferred to
all was the one towards the left of the statue."

Story writes in 1886 to Mr Wurts Dundas in
response to a proposal that he should enter the
field as a competitor for the design of a monument to General Grant. " I had never supposed
I should be thought of in relation to it, knowing
as I do the strong pressure which would be made
in many directions to obtain it, and having in
this as in all other cases no intention to offer
my services or to put forward any claim. As
for competition, I have always steadily refused
to enter into it. It requires a great deal of
knowledge and experience to be able to decide
upon models for a great monument, and the
judging committees are generally incompetent."
After which he enumerates, lucidly enough, the
drawbacks and disasters involved in the process
in question. " It is very easy," he adds, " to
make a mistake in judging of a great monument
from a small sketch. Effects are quite different
in small from what they are in colossal proportions, and my own experience is that I have
invariably found it necessary in the large to
modify much that is fairly satisfactory in the

small." And more of the letter is worth quoting. "Various schemes have occurred to me; a triumphal arch, a portico, a tabernacle, or a far more grandiose and effective combination of all, with a great frieze in high relief representing all the distinguished coadjutors and generals of the War, or, round the portico, a triumphal, or even a funereal, procession of the same (in relief), with a colossal statue of Grant in the centre. Otherwise a mausoleum surrounded on the outside by such a procession, surmounted by America Victrix and with a colossal figure of Grant on a platform in front. I have in my mind such a combination, which it is impossible to explain in words—in addition to which my ideas are of course as yet but first impressions, and require much further consideration. . . . The monuments at Edinburgh and at Berlin to Scott and to Fritz are, as you mention, admirable in themselves, but I think that with unlimited money something more imposing than these ought to be produced. I am now making a monument to Francis Key, in which I have embodied some such general scheme as that to Scott at Edinburgh, though it is different enough. It consists of an open loggia or tabernacle on four Corinthian columns, standing on a base and surmounted by a statue of America with the

Flag. In the centre of the tabernacle is the statue of Key, and on the base a bas-relief of singers and players performing the song. I am very tired of the stale idea, so often repeated, of a monument with a portrait-statue on top and four figures at the corners of the base; it is the resource of all commonplace sculptors. What we want in this case is grand character, real interest, poetic conception. But I thoroughly agree with you that all violent action is to be avoided. It is always unhappy, in the end, however striking, often, at first sight. The idea of victory should be indicated not by any violence or energy in the figure, but in some big symbolic way, making the man the director and inspirer, not the physical actor. Grant never went about gesticulating wildly and crowing, but was remarkably quiet and sternly calm, the soul, not the body, of the War." Returning to the subject in another letter to the same correspondent, he gives his reasons for disapproving of an elaborate scheme of which some detailed account had been published, criticising it mainly as a feeble and confused attempt to arrive at mere size and quantity. What becomes, he asks, in such a mere material jumble, of beauty or of lucidity? "Such ideas did not animate the Florentines when Giotto built that exquisite campanile that gives a grace and beauty to the whole city and is the delight of the world. The Washington monument in our national capital is double its size, and we may brag of it as the tallest obelisk in the world. But we must in honesty also add that it is the ugliest, unable to compete, for anything like beauty, even with many a factory chimney. As a monument to Washington it means absolutely nothing whatever. Think of the grand Mausoleum at Halicarnassus and of that to Hadrian at Rome, and then look at our *biggest* of all chimneys to the father of his country!"

In the "finds" of antiquity he would have been, by the mere habit of an old Roman, always interested; but they moved him, beyond this, so far as he could take cognisance of them when occurring elsewhere than at Rome, to special and individual emphasis of attention and judgment. A long letter to Mr Richard Greenough, of the spring of 1882, expresses the opinions he had promptly formed on the authorship of the beautiful Hermes then lately brought to light at Olympia. He is against the attribution of the work to Praxiteles, and thinks the evidence adduced for it "very lame on certain points. Of course it stands in the first place simply upon the curt statement of Pausanias,

and the immediate question is of the value of
his testimony, even if this could be shown
directly to apply. It seems always to be forgotten that he wrote his book towards the end
of the second century of our era, that is at
least 500 years after Praxiteles—in itself a very
damaging fact." And he goes into the matter,
for some eight pages, much further than we may
follow him. "I am much disturbed, again, by
the account of the execution of the hair, evidently merely blocked out and left unfinished
or carelessly treated"—which launches him into
much archæological learning and reasoning; interesting to us now mainly as evidence of his
disposition, on all such questions, immediately
to "rise." The rise, as we say, on behalf of
his own opinion, could always promptly be obtained from him, with plenty of information and
acuteness to support it. Nor may I follow him,
further, through a correspondence maintained for
many years with the late Sir Charles Newton,
of the British Museum, interesting as the letters
before me (Newton's own) may be held as communications of the results of the writer's archæological work, and as a series of answers. Yet
I like not simply to brush by this valuable
relation, which, beginning apparently in 1862,
was to continue for years. "I read out your

'Leonardo' poem," he writes in 1864, "to my wife, who enjoyed it as a true artist should. If you will write a small volume of poems equal to this and the others you read me in Rome, I venture to prophesy that you will take rank among English poets when many now extolled are forgotten. I am vexed to think that I missed you at the Museum, and that we saw so little of each other here. I wanted particularly to have shown you the cast of Mausolus. And I have just received a wonderful collection of antiquities from Rhodes, among which is a cup with a figure of Aphrodite, on a swan of extraordinary beauty." With which, further, "Panizzi desires to be kindly remembered to you, and will you ask Tilton to relieve me of the custody of his pictures?" This last inquiry causes again a sad, faint wraith to walk a little; that is by the dim light of a further allusion, made the same year. "I find that Mrs Newton wrote to Lady Eastlake about Tilton's pictures, but Sir Charles has not yet been to see them. Lord Overstone saw the Claude and thought that £200 would be a fair price for it. Colnaghi thought that Tilton has greatly over-estimated both pictures. Lord Somers saw the Claude yesterday and thought it was by a pupil of Claude's, of whom he also has a picture. But

he admired it." All of which brings back to
my own recollection the little cherished Claude,
thrown up to the surface in some small untraceable Roman convulsion, and the subject of high
hopes, deferred, renewed, blighted, yet blooming again, on the part of Story's neighbour and
countryman in the other wing of the Barberini.
One had been present at revelations of the
treasure—truly, in memory's eye, a delightful
possession; one was sympathetically interested
in its fortune, having the impression of all that
was involved, and one at the same time embraced the case as almost romantically, quite
"picturesquely" typical, by its general analogy
with all the other cases (a class by themselves)
of Italian *decaduti* looking for redemption from
the surrender of an heirloom inordinately valued.
The "Claude" was not an heirloom—was only
a mysterious and charming acquisition, which,
it is to be hoped, has since ceased its anxious
wanderings and is comfortably placed; but the
reminiscence is, as I say, quickened for me by
the sense of this cold whiff of the irony of fate
directed upon it from the faded note. The old
London millionaires and connoisseurs round off
the little drama.

Our friend's correspondent, at any rate, writes
in the autumn of 1875 about another matter. "I

have consulted my colleagues. Mr Pincher, who
is our new Assyriologue, and Dr Birch, and they
tell me there is no portrait of Sardanapallos in
Assyrian art, but that there are portraits of
the king who was so designated by the Greeks.
I send you by to-day's post a batch of photographs from our Assyrian sculptures. At the
back of each is written the name of the king
as Pincher reads it. I cannot tell you how
the dress of these worthies was put on, but I
hope to see you in Rome next month, when
we will go into these matters with the photos.
I leave for Berlin on the 10th (November) to
see the cast of the Olympian statue (the
Hermes)." Story was working at his great
seated figure of the personage in question, for
the "putting-on" of whose dress, as well as
for the art of his reconstituted "swagger," this
suggestion of research and of the invocation of
learned aid establishes an interesting history.
Let me add that I cannot drop the question
of our friend's ever-lively disposition to fumble
in odd corners of the past without mention of
his so characteristic plunge, undertaken during
a few idle weeks of summer, into the history
of the town of Dieppe. It has been noted that
he made a stay there in 1856, shortly after
the death of his eldest boy, which led to his

betaking himself promptly, after his wont, to an exploration of the local archives. The knowledge acquired, the speculations provoked by these studies, bore fruit long afterwards in a copious monograph—" A Sketch of Dieppe and its Early Navigators, with their Discoveries in Africa, the Indies and America"—which was by a perverse fortune not in his lifetime to see the light. The perversity lies in its being before me in the proof-sheets of a conspicuous London periodical, under the care of the editor of which it was so far prepared for publication. It was then found too long, extending to more than even two numbers, so that, sacrificed at the eleventh hour, it exists for the present mainly as a striking illustration of the almost whimsically inquisitive side of Story's mind and of that element in him that his friends mostly greeted (with an affectionate enjoyment of it shared by himself) as the courage of his convictions. It had substantially become his conviction, in a word, during his Normandy summer, that the Dieppe mariners had discovered the New World, and that, by the great sailor Jean Cousin in especial, the laurel of Columbus was gravely menaced. The paper is full of curious facts, of a detailed investigation of evidence, of a computation of the probabilities, into which

I may not, at this point, enter. He builds up
the vision that had come to him, at the end
of September, with the dispersal of the crowd
of bathers and idlers; he strolls along the
shore while the history of the place takes hold
of his imagination. " There is nothing between
us and America but the wide expanse of sea ;
and, sitting on the pebbles and gazing out
over the sea-horizon, the mind naturally goes
back to the time when, perhaps on the very spot
where we pause, once wandered Descaliers and
Cousin, Braquemont and Parmentier, Ribaut
and Dominique de Gourgues, Villegagnon, Cartier
and Duquesne,"—the brave captains, in short,
who first tried the unknown seas of the east
and west. "As we sit here in quiet the long
scroll of history unrolls before us its sorrows
and adventures, its triumphs and defeats. Full
of interest as these incidents are to all the
world, they are, as we shall see, especially interesting to America, the discovery and colonisa-
tion of which is so closely linked with this port
of Dieppe." If certain claims made for Cousin
in the last century " can be substantiated, there
is no doubt that he was not only the original
discoverer of the new continent, but was also
the first to double the Cape of Good Hope,
and show the way on to the East Indian seas."

It is to this substantiation that Story, through
a long and minute discussion, addresses himself,
not indeed absolutely concluding but marshalling
the presumptions in his hero's favour, and preparing the ground for a return, if possible, to
his subject. He has perhaps left it a little suspended in the air. But I must quote, for the
pleasure of it, his final paragraph—the pleasure,
I say, in particular, because we catch him here
in a generous inconsequence of feeling. It was
not in all manifestations, it was rather in too
few, that the genius of France, in general,
appealed to him.

"One fact seems to me clear, and that is that
the French were the pioneers of discovery in
the south and east as well as in the west. The
vaunted voyages of Spain and Portugal, which
so vividly illuminate the pages of history, were
in fact quite secondary to those of France. It
was she who led the way by her energy, her
enterprise and her daring, and of her early
navigators none are entitled to take precedence
of those who issued from the port of Dieppe.
If, besides those whom we have named, and
some whose deeds we have attempted to sketch,
we pass along the coast beyond the limits of
their little town, how large and brave an assem-
blage should we find—too large indeed for the

limits of so slight an essay as this. Their very names alone would testify to the constant connection of America and France, and strengthen the bonds which unite these two great nations. Scarce more closely connected with the later history of America are the names of Lafayette and Rochambeau, than with its earlier history those of Champlain, the father of New France, Cartier, De la Rocque, La Roche, Du Monts, Lescarbot, Poutrencourt, Saussaye, and Argall, and the already-named hardy captains of Dieppe and Rouen."

The little desultory diaries meanwhile, whether Story's or his wife's, are the record, through the revolving years, of the extremely peopled Roman life, and of ease and industry exempt, happily, from sharp interruptions. The anxieties and complications inevitable in all full lives take quite the minor place for the reader of the pleasant scroll, and the golden roof of Rome spreads with its noble span, and with an almost equal benignity, over the pleasures and the pains. The Roman names, as they recur, themselves brighten the page, which creates a wistfulness even when repeatedly beginning with "Scirocco, always scirocco!" Mrs Story is the more copious, but too concise and too intimate for quotation; with only here and there the detached Roman note, as for instance " Our poor Cardinal Pecci lies dying in the room below, and I cannot receive "—a frustration made up for, visibly, on many another occasion when the names of visitors abound. " A dinner of forty-three persons in the studio above," Story notes on the Shrove Tuesday of 1892, "arranged by Marion Crawford and Waldo to celebrate the death of King Carnival. Great gaiety and many costumes—Marion as Mephistopheles and I as Cimabue. Dufferin and Lady D. and their daughters came in, and he made a very happy and graceful speech. It was really a jollification in the manner of old days. We had the whole English Legation and several of the French, besides Vitelleschi, Simone P. Lübke and more." After which, on April 30th : " The Queen (of Italy) with the Marchesa Villa-Marina came to the studio and stayed some three - quarters of an hour, mainly to see ' Nemesis,' which I have still kept in the clay. She was most kind and amiable, looking also at everything else, and surprising me by her re-membrance of what she had seen previously. I went with Edith in the evening to a small musical reception at the Quirinal—some twenty to thirty persons, and a trio, sonata and quartet, the music all Beethoven's—where she was again most gracious." He had taken some time before

this date, largely for the use of his sons, a small
rough shooting-lodge, the "capanna" of many
entries, at Castel Fusano, and the note of Whit-
sunday in the same year records the day as
exquisite and as spent there with several friends.
" To bridge in carriage and then took boat and
was punted along an hour, with the shore all
alive with birds, who kept up a tremendous
chatter.   The sea enchanting and the coolness
of the breeze quite life-giving.   Found at the
capanna Louise Broadwood and Maud, Reschid
Bey and Waldo ; after which presently took gun
and roamed along the shore—to shoot but a
solitary quail.   Luncheon very gay, and when
it was half over a sudden party of friends, the
Marion Crawfords and (others).   M. C. went
off to walk alone with Mrs M., and they were
gone all the afternoon.   We punted again
through the *stagni*, and the sunset was beautiful.   The whole day delightful."   This impression appears to have been renewed the following
year (May, 1893).   " The quails were abundant,
but I was out of practice and shot but four.
Waldo slept on the floor of the dining *capanna*,
and the rest of us in the other.   Dinner was
jolly, and the evening not less, so that we were
not in our beds till midnight.   But we were up
the next morning at five, and every one went

for quail. I got a few, but only shot for an
hour. The others were out till luncheon, while
I wandered, in the delicious air and the perfect
day, along the beach. After luncheon we shot
again, and Waldo admirably; so that we got
in all some 100 birds. That night, it appeared,
I for some reason talked Greek in my sleep,
better, I hope, than I should have done awake.
I didn't shoot next day—Wednesday, 10th—
but walked and wandered again, and liked that
better. Chigi came over on horseback, stayed
to lunch and was very pleasant; after which
we fired rifles at a tin target, but with success
only for him and Waldo. I came back on
Wednesday P.M., feeling as if I had laughed
all the while, and also as if I had consumed
(with the aid of the others) much wine and
even much whisky."

In the midst of which gentle journalising turns
up, with slight inconsequence, another page, still
gentle, but referring to a date—January, 1886—
considerably previous. "At work at Key's statue,
which is well on. Alma Tadema called to see
me, and was warm in praise of Salome and the
second Cleopatra. How sincerely, however, who
can tell?" On February 4th he was still engaged with Key. "But he is now all together
and only needs superficial finish. Guthrie, Ren-

nell Rodd and Ralph Curtis to dinner. Shakespeare Wood died yesterday." A letter of Mrs Story's, of August 23rd, 1886, from St Moritz in the Engadine, mentions that, "As the weather promises to be fine, though we are under a fearful moon, we are to-morrow to lay the corner-stone of our Villa of the Future in honour of your birthday." And she adds on the morrow: "It all went off so well—the afternoon charming. We had asked every one, and Italians, English and Americans crowded alike about us with warmest wishes and felicitations. Every one admires the position. Papa had written a verse of dedication, which he read aloud, and a parchment was enclosed in a strong box in which, after the motto, were inscribed the names of all present. This was placed by me in the hollow of the corner - stone, and then by me plastered over. Then rose the singing voices of those who *could* sing (and even of some who couldn't !), and the glorious old Anthem 'Praise God,' &c., was re-echoed by the hills. Your health was drunk with three loud cheers; and then we had tea; after which Papa and I sat alone together on the logs. We believe more than ever in the place, and shall not be able to tear ourselves away before the middle of

September or even later." The house was in
course of time built, solidly and spaciously, of
rugged stone and on a perfect site, and, as a
cool Alpine refuge after so many years of the
Italian climate, was precious to them for the
too few remaining years.

XII.

VALLOMBROSA.

A RESORT of briefer moments, meanwhile, had
been the admirably placed summer home of
their daughter, the high - perched Lago di
Vallombrosa, in Tuscany, more than two thousand feet up from Pontassieve, in which, on
October 31st 1893, they had celebrated their
golden wedding (an occasion still present to
me in the form of a goodly pile of notes and
telegrams of congratulation), and in which, after
his wife's death, Story's last days were to be
spent. This immitigable loss overtook him in
the spring of 1894 and, it may frankly be said,
was practically his own deathblow. Mrs Story
had been, in his existence, too animating and
sustaining a presence to leave it, when withdrawn
from it, unshattered—to leave it in fact, for its
lonely nominal master, at all workable, or even
tolerable. "She was my life, my joy, my stay
and help in all things." So he writes to an

old friend in the summer of the sad year, and
he expresses his case without reserve. "What
is left seems to be but a blank of silence, a
dead wall which, when I cry out—and I *do*
cry out—only echoes back my own voice.   I
cry out Where is she? and no answer comes."
To which the compiler of these notes, under
the impression of the whole record, may be
permitted to add his own sense of the admirable
efficacity, as it were, of Mrs Story's presence in
her husband's career—a presence indefatigably
active and pervasive, productive in a large
measure of what was best and happiest in it.

In sight here of the term of his own years
I find myself aware of not having given him
the benefit of two or three minor biographic
facts — of the earliest in date of which, for
instance, I meet this record.

Lord Arthur Russell to W. W. Story.

"ATHENÆUM CLUB, *March* 10*th*, 1874.

"MY DEAR STORY,—I write in haste to inform you that you have been elected a member
of this Club by the Committee, one of the 9
illustrious men who are annually chosen.   The
honour is very great, because the Committee
must be unanimous and is composed of the first
intellectual authorities in England — of whom

I am one! A single objection is fatal. Accept therefore my sincere congratulations. The first effect you will experience will be a demand for 37 guineas from the Secretary, 30 as entrance-fee and 7 for your annual subscription. But now you can scold the waiters and complain of the dinner, which you could not do properly when you were an invited guest. And you will have other privileges. I had an opportunity of seeing while I worked in your cause how many friends you have here. It was a great pleasure to me; and I am, with kind remembrances to Mrs Story—Yours sincerely,

"ARTHUR RUSSELL."

It was a less lasting advantage (besides being of a different order) that he was appointed in 1878 one of the United States Commissioners on the Fine Arts to the Paris Universal "Exposition" of 1878, after which he received the ribbon of the Legion of Honour—an opportunity for interest signally attenuated by the circumstance, expressed in his excellent and copious Report, that the American Government not only had failed to appropriate a fund "to enrich our country," in his words, "with treasures of art," but had doomed itself by its parsimony to make, in the case, a sadly insignificant figure.

" The small sum of 150,000 dols. actually appropriated to cover all expenses of every kind, was not only insufficient in itself, but was so tardily given as to render it impossible for America to make an exhibition worthy of a great country, not only in the department in the fine arts, but even in those of industry, commerce, machinery, manufactures, natural products and mechanical arts." What more nearly touched Story moreover was that, thanks to this meagreness of provision, American sculpture had no place and no representative. It was completely absent. " The expenses and risks incident to an exhibition of sculpture are of course far greater than those which are required for an exhibition of paintings, and had such an exhibition been determined upon, these would have fallen solely upon the sculptors themselves, some of whom were unable and some unwilling to bear them. Those whose reputations were already established had little desire to assume such burdens, with nothing to gain and everything to risk, while others who properly had a right to be represented had not the means." And he recalls the fact that " with most nations the department of the fine arts has ever been looked upon as the flower of their exhibition," the department repaying most, for effect and honour,

the expenditure of pains and money. He recalls
in particular the grand style of the Roman Court
in the London Exhibition of 1862, and may
well be imagined to have inwardly contrasted
his own so fruitful opportunity there with his
excluded and eclipsed situation in Paris. The
Report, however, is concerned with European
work ; with the effect, read over at this day
(which is the effect, for that matter, of all Reports), of making the pensive contemporary live
back into old sympathies and antipathies, old
curiosities, admirations, mistakes. Such a document, as we turn it over, seems to consist half
of the record of old, or even of young actualities
that have since faded, and half of young, or
even of old, obscurities that have since bloomed.
Strange and sad the vision renewed for us of
all the freshness that has now turned stale, all
the earnest speculations that have lost their
point. It is astonishing, in short, how soon such
pages begin to strike us, on their critical side, as
the mirror of an age less complicated, less initiated.
Story himself had indeed — which is precisely
what I am remembering here—other initiations
and extensions, other activities of curiosity, on
subjects to all appearance rather casually determined, that profit still for us by their concern
with questions rather of science than of taste.

His inedited relics are numerous, and I find among them, for instance, a poem in blank verse, of many pages, bearing the title of "An Agnostic's Foolish Confession to his Friend the Priest"; which I should, I admit, more confidently refer to the class of meditations inspired by "science," were it not for the adjective that qualifies the supposed overflow. This is followed, however, it is further to be discerned, by a critical monologue, still in verse, from the priest himself, which shows us the abyss that, in spite of friendship, separates the pair, and from which we gather that the "foolishness" of the Agnostic is in having dreamed a bondman of the Church could understand him. Current criticism, had it had an opportunity to occupy itself with the pages in question, would certainly not have spared the author the irritation of the sage discovery that they offered an echo of the manner of Browning. And that imputation would probably have extended even to another composition, "An Author's View of Copyright" — a view of which, whimsically, blank verse is again the medium. If instead of "Author" Story had written "Poet and Sculptor," the whimsicality would rather more have hung together, making possible perhaps a reply, the other side, also

in verse, on the thesis that sculptors and poets
have nothing to do with anything so sordid.
But into the province of the unpublished, on
our friend's part, I must not propose to penetrate.
I leave aside, from that necessity, the Lecture
on Art delivered by him repeatedly in the
United States during the winter of 1877-78;
just as, in the absence from my material of any
correspondence or diary relating to it, I left
the sojourn itself (made in company with his
elder son) unmentioned in its order. The character of the performance in question, I take it,
had been that of the talked *conférence*, animated,
expressive, and in which the personality of the
speaker counted for much in the success enjoyed,
counted for more than half; so that mere verbal
publication would have been a comparatively
colourless record. My discrimination attaches
better to his Study of "The Proportions of the
Human Figure," to his "Mystery or Passion
Plays," published in the "Blackwood" of December 1869, and best of all perhaps to a paper
on "The Origin of the Italian Language" in
"The North American Review" of January-
February 1878 and two others on "The Pronunciation of the Latin Language" in the issues
of the same periodical for March and April 1879.
These disquisitions are, to the mere unlearned

sense, quite delightfully coloured by irresistible
Italian sympathies—a remark which especially
applies to the second and third. He inclines
to the opinion, of which Cesare Cantù was at
the time he wrote the most authoritative ex-
ponent, that—thrilling thought!—the Italian
tongue is a survival and development of a
language actually spoken, the *lingua rustica*
of the Latin populations, as distinguished from
their urban, and still more from their literary
speech ; and not a resultant of Transalpine influences wrought by invasions and migrations.
In the articles on pronounced Latin he naturally
therefore concludes in favour of the hypothesis
based on analogy with this same far-descended
Italian, and treats himself, as any human sense
that has been Romanised through long years
of the golden air infallibly must, to a luxury of
reaction from the hapless subjection of the
uttered phrase to the thin English scheme of
sound. Story felt that an irresistible conviction
on this matter was almost the result of any
good talk—for how delightful and suggestive
such talks might be no one knew better—with
one of those brave, sane Romans of the people,
deep-voiced sons of the soil, or of the City,
whose words come out, one by one, with the
distinction of classed coins in a museum-case.

and whose sentences stand up for the ear very much as an inscription on a triumphal arch stands up for the eye.

Old Italy, at all events, was never to have closed so beneficently round him as when the end approached. The end was already almost there by the time he had finished the only work that occupied him after the death of his wife. "I am making a monument to place in the Protestant Cemetery," he wrote to a relative in the spring of 1894 ; "and I am always asking myself if she knows it and if she can see it. It represents the angel of Grief, in utter abandonment, throwing herself with drooping wings and hidden face over a funeral altar. It represents what I feel. It represents Prostration. Yet to do it helps me." The figure thus produced, unsurpassed, in all his work, for intensity of expression, mingles the sincerity of its message now, for all time, as we may say, with that exquisite, soundless collective voice that nowhere hangs in the golden air with such a weight— resting here, so sensibly, straight upon the heart —as in that flower - smothered corner, beneath the time - silvered Pyramid, where Shelley's ashes supremely ennoble the interest and the passion of his verse, hauntingly, returns upon the beauty ; the spot, in a word, at which the mind never glances without some fine enjoyment of the fact, even some harmless triumph in it, that the place of sweetest sanctity in all Rome should so oddly chance to be dedicated to the great other, the great opposed faith. His studio closed, our friend spent the summer of 1895 with his daughter, in the Tuscan hills, as he had in the previous years paid her other visits. Relevantly to which — that is, to one of the interesting connections made present to him by her marriage—I may quote here the greater part of a letter that he had addressed to Madame Peruzzi, from the Baths of Ragatz, in October 1891.

. . . "I have thought of something which I hope may result in some benefit to you. It is a *grand peut-être,* but still it is a *peut-être* and I thought it worth trying. Mrs McClellan sent me an excerpt from some Italian paper containing a statement of the Bardi and Peruzzi claim for the loan made to Edward III., by means of which the battles of Crécy and Poictiers were fought, and on reading over this I wrote a long letter to Lord Hartington, setting forth the facts and saying that I could not but think that if the English Government were made aware of the state of things, and that this

Loan, large as it was, was never repaid, even
in the smallest part, it would, or might, be induced to take some steps to recognise the debt,
and if not wholly repay it (for *that* would be
impossible), at least do something toward re-
munerating the Peruzzi for a loss which had
been ruin to them. I endeavoured to urge him
to bring the matter before the House of Lords,
telling him that (as I had been told) such was
the determination of the late Duke of Welling-
ton, who was prevented from doing so by death.
Perhaps, *chi lo sa?* he may do something, and
then again he may not. But I thought that
for your sakes I would at least make the
attempt."

It is perhaps scarcely needful to add that the
attempt has not, up to the present writing,
been crowned with success. I meet, at all
events, in an old scrap - book a reminder of
Story's presence at Vallombrosa, on I know not
which of many occasions, in the form of a little
photograph of a pair of very animated interlocutors seated together, in light summer attire,
under a spreading tree. One of the vivid talkers
is, quite inevitably, Story; the other is, not *more*
dramatically, Tommaso Salvini. The rare actor
was a friend of the house and, whether in the

country or in Florence, a frequent visitor. Given Story's interest in the tricks of the great trade professed by the latter, it is visible that the pair of guests are, in the picture, discussing some question of interpretation, of scenic effect, from which the name of Shakespeare, constantly supreme with both, is not absent. How sharply present all such questions could be for Story is shown by his careful paper on some "Distortions of the English Stage," originally published in "Blackwood" and reprinted in his "Excursions." He there deals with the perversion of the characters of Macbeth and his wife as our theatre traditionally presents them, and uses much ingenuity—some of it I think misapplied—to show that, as the heroine of the play in which they figure, she is much more sentimentally interesting than we are accustomed to allow, and that, as the hero, the Thane of Cawdor is much less so. For the fashion of representing Lady Macbeth as bold and bad the magnificent personality of Mrs Siddons was, early in our age, responsible; she imposed upon us, by her great authority, a conception of the part quite at variance with a careful study of the text: which careful study places also in its true light the nature of her husband, whose assumedly rich mystic side, that of a man struggling, amid dire temptations, with his soul and his conscience, it effectually dispels. One of the parties to the monstrous chain of crime is, in a word, all nerves and sensibility, all disinterested passion and exquisite anguish, while the other is all ruthless ambition, monstrous, mad, delirious, and thereby dishumanised. The paradox is pleasant enough, and is artfully supported, but the difficulty is that we scarce see how the interest of the play, and still more how the interest of any performance of it, gains by the contention. In proportion as the protagonist is fatuous, rhetorical and brutal (as Story insists), in that proportion do tragedy, poetry, sincerity, all his *general* significance, fall away from him, cutting off his moral connections and leaving him a mere ugly, bloody, abnormal case.

Be this, however, as it may, the collocation puts before me again another hour—an hour of the noble house in Via Maggio that was for the Storys the Florentine alternative to Lago— from which high ingenuity was as little absent. Meeting there the potent old actor who gratified graciously some of my curiosities, I was impressed by nothing so much as by *his* original view of a great Shakespearean passage. He held, his rich voice and grave face explained, that Lady Macbeth's walk in her haunted sleep

had been an incident originally attributed by the
poet to Macbeth himself, and transferred from
the latter's to the former's part either because
the poet had yielded to the cajolery of a charming actress, or because some actress, vain and
rapacious, had, early in the career of the play,
laid such successful hands on the morsel that
the abuse had become established. When it
was suggested in response to this argument
that the poor woman's mention of her "little"
hand offered a difficulty, Macbeth's own bloody
fist having been probably of normal size, the
answer was, pertinently enough, that the word
had of course been speciously put in (anything
was possible in those times) by the performer
herself. I remember well how little it could
seem proper on this occasion to plead any such
clumsy fact as that Mrs Siddons's remote predecessors had been, at the worst, but beardless
boys. It is not, moreover, in any memory of
contention that I invoke these charming or
these mighty shades. My particular reminiscence was to remain with me as an interesting
example of the sincerity of the artistic temperament. The admirable actor, conscious of the
splendid use he would have made of the opportunity, had always so hungered and thirsted
for it as to come finally to think of it as of a

right of which he had been deprived. One can surely but regret that he had not on some occasion supremely affirmed his sincerity by restoring the scene, at least experimentally, to his own part.

It is with the shades of Vallombrosa itself, those of the great Miltonic line, that we are directly concerned—the green density of which, and the soft murmur through all the summer months, make an undertone for our friend's short idyllic novel entitled "Fiammetta," composed in the course of an early visit paid to his daughter and published in 1886. This single piece of prose fiction produced by him with the exception of "A Modern Magician," which appeared in "Blackwood" in May 1867, contains an inscription to his wife and his hostess, recording that he had read it aloud to them "on three beautiful mornings as we sat under the shadows of the whispering pines. You thought well of it—too well, I fear—and encouraged me to print it. To you therefore I dedicate it, with my truest love and in memory of those happy summer days in the 'Etrurian shades.'" The tale, simple and sincere, lightly and easily told, is that of a maid of the mountains, the hills and woods there present, who, for a few weeks of inward ecstasy to herself, sits, by a pool in the forest, as model

to a young painter engaged on the picture of
a naiad, and dies of her apparently unrequited
love when the artist has, as the phrase is, no
further use for her. Her mother, to the young
man's knowledge, has had a misadventure, been
seduced and forsaken, so that Fiammetta herself
is a child of passion and despair; and this, with
him, the fear of setting in motion a like doom,
has been a reason for mounting guard on his
conduct. He does so to such purpose that the
wrong he has wished to avoid—or something
practically as bad—springs directly from his desire for the right, and the ironic note, in the
catastrophe, mingles with the tragic if we pause
long enough to listen for it. Such pausing indeed perhaps is scarcely fair—it was clearly not,
for us, the author's intention. Romantic, in
imagination, to the end, Story saw his theme
all sentimentally, and was content to leave it
for the lightest of woodland elegies. The other
light that plays in but plays for us as the gaps
open and the patches mockingly flicker under
the idle breath of analysis. Transpose the situation into a different tone, the tone of the real,
we thus for convenience say, and we get a
different meaning: the scruples of the youth,
the yearning of the maiden, the rupture of the
contact, the loss of the possibility, all so logically

produce it. He would have died, or almost, rather than not respect her, and what is fatal to her, at the end, is that she *has* been consistently respected. Which is the honest fashion, as I say, of turning it all about.

But the full voice of Vallombrosa is meanwhile in the author's charming monograph bearing the name of the enchanted place, originally published in "Blackwood," and reissued, as a volume of scarce more than a hundred pages, in 1881. Preceding "Fiammetta" by several years, it gave the first freshness of Story's impression. I am too conscious of the difficulty, I fear, however, of giving the first freshness of mine. That spur of the Apennines on which the convent visited by Milton stands in its shrunken but still impressive forest only welcomes the occasion to plant in the mind of a tourist submissive to Italy and addicted to long walks and long lounges one of the most romantic of Italian memories. Comparatively cockneyfied doubtless now, scarred and dishonoured by the various new contrivances for access without contact and acquaintance without knowledge, it was still, a few years since, a solitude tempered by hospitalities convenient enough and enlivened, as the Italian scene when sufficiently left to itself almost always is, by a natural elegance, the light stamp, everywhere,

of the grand style, the touch of the true Arcadian
picture. Story describes better than I can do
the charm alike of the " dense Etrurian coverts "
and of the open, vertiginous views, as well as
the aspect of the habitation to which he finally
retired. " I had been invited by a friend to pass
a few days with her and her family in one of
the most lonely regions of the large tract which
bears the name of Vallombrosa. The once famous
convent lies at a distance of about three miles
from this spot; and here, in one of the hollows,
they had hired an old deserted house, built
centuries ago by the Medici as a stronghold and
hunting-box, which they had fitted up and put
into habitable condition as a summer retreat from
the heats of Florence. Originally the house was
flanked by two tall towers, and was castel-
lated in form; but within the last few years
the present Government, caring little for the
picturesque, and apparently seeking rather to
obliterate than to preserve the traces of the past,
had ruthlessly and for no sufficient reason levelled
the two towers and raised the upper storey : so
that the house is now a square unpicturesque
but solidly-built construction two storeys high,
and with walls massive enough to resist the
assault of anything but modern cannon. Here
my friends had made their summer home, far

from all society and neighbours, to enjoy freedom,
solitude, and the silence and charm of nature.
There is no highway to lead the wandering
tourist to their doors, . . . but the foot-
passenger, with stout boots and country dress,
is amply repaid for his walk, whether he come
by the way of Podere Nuovo on the north, along
a winding path through the woods, or by the
monastery on the south, over a road commanding
the loveliest and largest views of an exquisite
and varied valley strown with far - gleaming
villages and towns, bounded by swelling outlines
of hills or mountains, one rising after another
against the delicate sky."

My own most intimate recollection, from the
greater part of a summer spent some years ago
at this admirable altitude, is of the small settlement that at that time clustered about the old
forest monastery, and the extent of the recent
growth of which has been, I believe, much more
marked than its felicity. The convent, grey and
massive amid the murmurous green, and perched
on its broad mountain-ledge, still squared itself
like a fortress, but the good brothers had been
expropriated and all but completely dispersed,
with their foundation transformed into a State
School of Forestry. About on the level of the
convent was a small, decent hotel, the happiest

feature of which was a subsidiary guest-house
or minor annexe, standing considerably higher
up the mountain and having of old served as
the *foresteria* of the convent, its place of reception for visitors. This interesting structure,
which has of late become private property, formed
of itself, in those days, an ideal mountain-inn,
lifted above the small bustle of the little community, niched against its high background of
wooded slopes and summits, with its ancient
thick-walled cells making cool, clean rooms, and
the small stone-paved terrace before it, propped
upon the steep and guarded by a parapet, pro-
truding into space like the prow of a ship. Here
everything had poetry, but the fresh evenings,
under the stars, had most. The outlook, by
day, divine as the afternoon deepened, was
the prospect Story perfectly describes. " There,
far away in the misty distance, can be seen
the vague towers and domes of Florence ; and
through the valley the Arno and the Sieve
wind like silver bands of light, through olive-
covered slopes and vineyards that lie silent in
the blue haze of distance, spotted by wandering
cloud-shades and taking every hue of changeful
light from the pearly gleams of early morning
to the golden transmutations of twilight and
the deep intensity of moonlit midnight. Nearer,

magnificent chestnuts throng the autumnal slopes, their yellow leaves glowing in the autumn sun. Sombre groves of firs, marshalled along the hillsides for miles, stand solemn and dark. Beech-trees rear at intervals their smooth trunks, or gather together in close and murmurous conclave. The lower growth of gorse and broom and brush and feathered fern roughen the hills where the axe has bereft them of their forest-growth; and in every direction are wild and enchanting walks through light and shadow, alluring us on and on for miles. Here and there columns of wavering blue smoke tower and melt away into the blue sky, where the charcoal-burners are at work. Little brooks come trickling down at intervals, finding their devious way among the rocks and leaves and singing to themselves a slow and silvery song. Now and then a partridge whirs up beneath your feet, or a whistling woodcock suddenly takes flight, or a startled hare with up-cocked tail may be seen tilting through the underbrush, or a sly fox steals cautiously away."

Our friend gives the romantic history of the convent, founded in 1008 by the Florentine San Giovanni Gualberto, on his secession from the house of San Miniato with a view to a more rigorous life. But what more closely concerns us, and meets my own reminiscence, is the road

connecting Vallombrosa with Lago, the one road
of approach, in his time, and commanding those
"loveliest and largest views" his mention of
which I have quoted. He vividly sketches it
again, though inadvertently exaggerating its
number of miles. This I used to find the
direction to take, since I was so privileged,
when the afternoon ramble was not preferably
higher and higher, up through the shade, so
clear as to be almost faintly blue, of the straight
fir-woods, which left the belts of generous chestnut and mighty beech far below, and out upon
the uncovered tops of the hills, where the cloudless air was cool, the great grassy hollows more
violet than green, the far horizon, with its tinted
lights, a warm shimmer of history, and the crown
of the impression, when it was possible, a plunge
of the eye and the imagination, from over some
final buttress, down into the rich Casentino. The
passage to Lago, level, after a short descent,
along the sides of the heights, had more of the
social motive, being both lonely and gay, like
a woodman's song, and with no company by the
way but that of the great friendly chestnuts and
an occasional vast princely beech. Sociability
was the end, was in the greeting and all the
persuasion of the green cleared circle in the
woods, where the rather dark-faced lodge kept

guard and the tea-hour, the hour of talk in the open, made for all gossip and gaiety one scarcely knew what murmurous undertone of tree-tops, of history again, of poetry, almost of melancholy. It was all so beautiful that it was sad—with a distinction the sense of which weighed like an anxiety. Something of that sort, something supreme in the solemn sweetness with which the whole place surrounded him, I can imagine our friend to have felt as he sat, with the last patience, in the September days, listening to its voices. They might have been saying to him how far he had come from the primary scene, and how much he had left by the way, as well as, indeed, how much he had found and laboured and achieved. They might, above all, have seemed to breathe upon him the very essence of the benediction of the old Italy he had chosen and loved and who thus closed soft arms about him. Death came to him, as with a single sound-less step, early on the October morning, and, two days later (October 7th, 1895), he was laid to rest near his wife.

INDEX.

to, 234—visit paid to the Storys by, at Palazzo Barberini, ii. 29 *et seq.*—death of, 46—letters from : see Letters.

Taglioni, Marie, notice of, i. 198.
"Tannhauser," by Lord Lytton and Julian Fane, reference to, ii. 92.
Tennyson, Lord, references to, ii. 100, 141, 159.
Thackeray, Annie (Mrs Richmond Ritchie), taken to her first ball by Mrs Story, i. 367.
Thackeray, W. M., a touching recollection of, i. 286—lectures of, in Boston, 301—references to, 321, 367 ; ii. 116—death of, 147.
Tocqueville, Alexis de, reference to, i. 366.
"Tolla," by Edmond About, reference to, i. 359 *et seq.*
"Treatise on Sales of Personal Property," publication of, i. 19, 30.
"Treatise on the Law of Contracts," publication of, i. 19, 30, 31—new editions of, 240, 299, 311.
Trent, affair of the, in the American war, Browning on, ii. 104 *et seq.*, 108, 110.
Trollope, Mrs, references to, i. 112, 116.

Ursuline nuns, destruction of a convent of, near Boston, i. 54.

Vallombrosa, Story's monograph on, ii. 332—the convent of, 333 *et seq.*
Venice, a visit to, i. 188—impressions of, 189 *et seq.*
Vienna, a visit to, i. 187.

Walton-on-Thames, residence of the Storys in, at Mount Felix, i. 322; ii. 73—references to, 150, 156, 228, 229, 231.
Webster, Daniel, record of a journey made with, i. 36.
Weston, Emma, notices of, ii. 37, 185, 187.
Wordsworth, Wm., anecdote of, ii. 22.

THE END.